# Learning from the Past

# Learning from the Past

## Historical Voices in Early Childhood Education

JENNIFER WOLFE

Piney Branch Press
Mayerthorpe, Alberta

**Canadian Cataloguing in Publication Data**

Wolfe, Jennifer, 1945 –
Learning from the past

Includes bibliographical references and index.
ISBN 0-9685849-1-8

1. Early childhood education. 2. Early childhood education — History.
I. Title
LB1139.23.W64 2002 372.21 C2002-911009-2

1st edition 0-9685849-0-X published 2000.

**Cover Design:** Bob Robertson
**Interior Design and Text Layout:** Paragraphics Incorporated
**Editor:** Shelagh Kubish
**Printing and Binding:** Priority Printing

Printed and bound in Canada.

Piney Branch Press
Box 1022
Mayerthorpe, Alberta
T0E 1N0
Canada
Phone 780-786-4459
Fax 780-786-4113
www.telusplanet.net/public/jwolfe

*To George and Bee Wolfe, who nurtured my research skills and my love of inquiry and books.*

# Contents

# Preface

*"The past just as past is no longer our affair. If it were wholly gone and done with, there would be only one reasonable attitude toward it. Let the dead bury their dead. But knowledge of the past is the key to the understanding of the present. History deals with the past, but this past is the history of the present."*

**—John Dewey, *Democracy and Education***

The history of early childhood education spans thousands of years. For this book, I have selected 11 historical figures — from Plato to Lucy Sprague Mitchell — to illustrate some pivotal ideas of early childhood education as well as some issues facing the field today. Many others could have been chosen, but each of these 11 people has some unique lessons to teach.

There is much to learn from understanding the historical foundations of this field as a profession. Vitorino Magalhaes Godinho, a Portuguese historian, reflected on an additional value of studying the past:

> *"It's by knowing the past that we better understand the present and we can better plan the future."*

In any profession, an understanding of history helps current practitioners build their work on the ideas of those who have preceded them. The ideas we follow today are not necessarily new; some key ideas have endured over many years. Moreover, understanding the ideas of past educators helps us to more effectively implement current methods and theory. In working with young children, it is important to analyze the past to make certain we are progressing and not eliminating valuable and essential features of theory and practice. It is also important to realize that many of the ideas of the historical figures are still unrealized dreams, despite the progress that we think has occurred in the field. Modern issues can gain new perspectives from other times, voices and places.

We learn from the past and integrate it with our practice with children and families. Theories about how children grow and learn influence both education and child care. The sources of the methods, materials and equipment we use today reflect the ideas of people about children and their development. We, today's practitioners, can learn from the practitioners of the past.

In a 1973 article entitled "The Free School Movement" in *Today's Education*, Lawrence Cremin, educational historian and former president of Columbia Teachers College, said,

> *"Boundless energy has been spent in countless classrooms reinventing the pedagogical wheel."*

The care and education of young children is a profoundly important field. Studying the past practitioners and theorists in this field provides an inspiration for our work, an understanding of the traditions of our profession, and a sense of pride in our roles as creators of appropriate curriculum, not simply as technicians. We also learn that there is a solid foundation for our practices, and we come to appreciate the broader social, economic and political contexts of educational ideas. We understand, too, that the field continues to need vigilance and advocacy and that we need patience, perseverance and creativity to ensure necessary changes. We are part of a continuum.

In studying the historical figures as individuals, we realize that their own early childhood experiences and life experiences had a profound effect on them. They were a product of their lives and times yet sought to progress beyond the practices of their times as well. We realize in reading their stories that barriers and challenges can be overcome. We come to understand our connections to the past and our place in the history: today's practitioners will be tomorrow's leaders and the future historical figures in the field.

John Dewey had other important things to say about studying and learning from the past:

> *"There is danger of losing a sense of historic perspective and of yielding precipitately to short-time contemporary currents, abandoning in panic things of enduring and priceless value."*
>
> **— *Liberalism and Social Action* [dedicated to Jane Addams]**

> *"History must be presented, not as an accumulation of results or effects, a mere statement of what happened, but as a forceful, acting thing. The motives — that is, the motors — must stand out. To study history is not to amass information, but to use information in constructing a vivid picture of how and why men did thus and so achieved their successes and came to their failures."*
>
> **— John Dewey, *The School and Society***

Jean Piaget once said,

> *"Theories may pass away, but problems endure. They are ceaselessly renewed and diversified and ever retain their initial virtue of guiding and inspiring investigation. In this respect, even inadequate or inaccurate theories have often, in the history of science and technology, been of decisive importance, just because of the new problems they have raised."*
>
> **— introduction to *John Amos Comenius on Education***

History is not only about the past. It teaches us. It is about our lives, our issues, our future and the future of children. History can help us reflect on the kind of ideal society we envision.

There are many themes and threads that weave their way through the annals of early childhood. Issues continue to challenge our beliefs and values about children, change, families and many other topics.

As you study the ideas of these 11 historical figures, you will note some common ideas in their thinking. They understood the value of observation and adapting to the individual child. Their belief in the importance of learning through self-activity and play appropriate to children is proof of a belief in child care as "natural" education.

The people studied in this book understood the uniqueness and importance of early childhood. Some of these thinkers were acutely aware of hardship and poverty around them and saw early childhood education as a potential vehicle in helping children and their families overcome poverty and its effects. The interplay of child-family-community was understood and respected, with an awareness of the need for continuity of home/school experience. Early childhood educators have long believed in a balance between socializing the child to current norms/values and developing a rational, thinking person to question the current reality. Despite all the hardships and challenges some of these historical figures endured, they maintained an optimistic belief that education could create a better world.

Studying the ideas of these 11 historical figures together in one text, you are encouraged to draw connections between them, their times, their theories, and their approaches. Many of the practitioners' ideas emerged from dissatisfaction with existing educational conditions. They understood the need for constant research, reflection and study to keep from repeating the mistakes of the past; colleagues played a key role in helping these forward thinkers develop ideas. They felt that early childhood education could impact on elementary school practice, and they maintained a lofty goal of transforming educational practice to best educate children, believing that the education of young children was of paramount importance. This belief was echoed by American President Roosevelt:

> *"If anywhere in the country any child lacks opportunity for home life, for health protection, for education, for moral or spiritual development, the strength of the Nation and its ability to cherish and advance the principles of democracy are thereby weakened."*
>
> **— Franklin Delano Roosevelt in 1940**
> **White House Conference on Children in a Democracy**

*Learning from the Past* will help put the ideas of the historical figures in the context of their life and times. Their contributions and issues raised will be highlighted to help you reflect on your own practice with children and families, your community and the issues you face in the field of early childhood.

## Note on Historical Dates

The dates of all historical figures have been given in either **B.C.E.** or **C.E.** These refer to **Before the Common Era** and the **Common Era**. They correspond exactly to the dates in **B.C.** and **A.D.** but are a secular, non-religious identification that provides more inclusive language.

## Accuracy of Contact Sites and Historical Facts

Various World Wide Web sites and postal addresses are provided and are correct and current as of the book's publication date.

All dates and historical facts are accurate to the best of my research. At times I encountered conflicting pieces of information. Spelling and quoted text also varied with translators. In such cases, I presented in the text what I considered, based on my reading and research, to be the most accurate information.

# Acknowledgements

This book was created with the support and assistance of Shelagh Kubish, Judi Lord, Sharon Cameron, Nancy Roberts, Marcene Makovec and Michelle Bezenar.

Its development and focus on current issues evolved from students who challenged my thinking, taught me to see ideas in new perspectives and always encouraged me to reflect on the field of early childhood.

TIMEO
ETIC

# Chapter 1 — *Plato*

**427 B.C.E. – 347 B.C.E.**[1]

*". . . the knowledge which is acquired under compulsion obtains no hold on the mind."*

*". . . let early education be a sort of amusement."*

*". . . the beginning is the most important part of any work, especially in the case of a young and tender thing; for that is the time at which the character is being formed."*

**— *Republic***

---

In ancient Greece people had only one name, chosen by the family. For boys, it was typically the name of a grandfather.

---

Early childhood educators know the value of playdough but rarely consider the value of Plato, whose ideas continue to have meaning and relevance for our thinking about children, teaching and society.

**Ancient Greece.**

Plato wrote little about his own life, and information about him is dependent on biographies written centuries later and upon the translation of his works from the Greek. We do know that Plato was born in Athens, one of the city states of ancient Greece. The mountainous terrain of Greece separated many city states that each had unique civilizations and community elan and spirit. The city state of Attica was almost universally known by its capital, Athens, the undisputed centre of Greek culture for four centuries. In Greece, all free citizens could take part in the government and speak in the Assembly, and it was Athens that embodied the highest values of Greek civilization, renowned for supporting both freedom and equality and heralded for its arts, humanities and democracy. At its height, there were about 200,000 people in Attica. Income was generated primarily from silver mines worked by slave labour, while olives, vineyard grapes and pottery provided other income and exports.

Plato's parents, Perictione and Ariston, were both from highly distinguished families. The name Plato means "broad" or "flat," referring perhaps to his shoulders or forehead. His original name was Aristokles ("the best") after his grandfather. Plato had two older brothers, Adeimantus and Glaucon, both of whom appear as characters in his writing the *Republic*. He had an older sister, Potone, who was likely the third child. His father died, apparently when Plato was very young, and his mother married another politically prominent man, Pyrilampes. Plato then had a step-sister, Demus, and later a half-brother, Antiphon. Though he wrote little of himself, his relatives were often part of his writings.

---

[1] There is some debate about the birth and death dates of Plato (428 B.C.E. – 347 B.C.E. or 427 B.C.E. – 348 B.C.E.)

The society of ancient Greece appreciated and valued childhood, and children were understood to be playful. Access to education did depend on social status and family influence and was limited to boys. Priests, elders and philosophers in various fields taught the elite class. Music played a large part with singing and playing of the lyre. Writing was taught on wax tablets with a stylus. Plato showed early poetic gifts and was physically active, wrestling in the Isthmian games.[2]

Plato's aristocratic background allowed him the best available education, and he became both a pupil and friend of Socrates, one of the foremost Greek philosophers of the time. Plato himself wanted to be a playwright or a poet until he met Socrates, and was so enthralled by Socrates he devoted the rest of his life to the pursuit of wisdom. Socrates taught by a conversational Socratic method in which a topic was analyzed and investigated by the use of leading questions and a process of reasoned inquiry. Socrates was often in public places and was well known throughout Athens as a philosopher and teacher.

Socrates had devoted followers, but some people were suspicious of and hostile towards him; in Aristophanes' satiric play *The Clouds*, Socrates is portrayed as an eccentric thinker hanging in a basket in mid-air. Socrates was also portrayed in Aristophanes' comedies the *Birds*, the *Wasps* and the *Frogs*.

## A Childhood and Youth in the Midst of War

Plato's own family was deeply involved with the political life of Athens. During most of Plato's childhood and early adulthood, the Peloponnesian War raged between Athens and Sparta, the more militaristic state. Sparta was an armed camp, controlled by a city state with hereditary kings and founded upon conquest. Spartan education was focused solely on military success. Athens' part in the war was violent as well: the Athenian soldiers put to death the entire male population of Skione and later Melos, selling the women and children as slaves. Euripides wrote the *Trojan Women* as a dramatization of these horrors and a condemnation of war.

In the same year that the Peloponnesian War erupted, a horrendous plague decimated up to a third of the population of Attica.

Defeated by Sparta in 404 B.C.E., Athens was left powerless, shamed and forced to capitulate. Politics were in turmoil, and democracy was abolished. Thirty rulers, some related to Plato, were selected for their allegiance to Spartan beliefs and soon governed Athens. Plato hoped for a return to rational government, but their rule has been described as a bloody, predatory tyranny. The population of Athens was angry, suspicious and eager to look for scapegoats for the situation. A police state developed, and Socrates was arrested and tried. Complicated political issues surrounded the trial and the later execution (in 399 B.C.E.) of Socrates, who was executed by being forced to drink poison hemlock.[3] Socrates' martyrdom created an exalted image of Socrates, and he came to be regarded as a tragic hero.

---

[2] The Isthmian games were athletic events held in Corinth. They were smaller than the Olympic games and held during the years between Olympic games. The Olympics were established about 776 B.C.E and the Isthmians in about 581 B.C.E. Both the Olympics and the Isthmian Games included festivals of the arts and Greek culture.

[3] For a detailed account of the issues, see I.F. Stone's *The Trial of Socrates*.

Plato was a young man when all of this occurred, and it is likely that he did spend some time in military service defending Athens and the surrounding territory. He was deeply affected by the accusations against and trial and death of his mentor and teacher. In earlier times, Plato would likely have been involved with the politics of Athens, but he became bitter and disillusioned with the political process and withdrew from public functions. Some years later, Plato did have one short and unsuccessful interlude in the political life of Sicily. He travelled throughout the Mediterranean world (to Italy, Egypt, Sicily and Cyrene in North Africa), returning to Athens from his self-exile as a middle-aged man in 380 B.C.E.

## Founding of the Academy and Later Life

Aristotle was born 40 years after Plato in 384 B.C.E., and he wrote concrete, useful guidelines for educating young children. Like Plato, he endorsed a balanced education of intellect and feelings and articulated the needs of young children. Most of his views, in contrast to Plato's, came from direct observation of children. Aristotle died in 322 B.C.E.

In about 387 B.C.E., Plato founded the Academy in the Grove of Academe, northwest of Athens. It has been described as the first European university and fixed seat of learning. Plato was responsible for its establishment, administration and ongoing development. The Academy was an intellectual retreat with gardens, temples and walkways. It was dedicated to the Muses, patrons of literature and the arts, and no fees were assessed in Plato's time. People of all ages were free to attend classes in astronomy, biology, mathematics, political theory and philosophy.

This was a college of scholars, teachers and students who worked together. Aristotle came to the Academy as a 19-year-old man and stayed 20 years, until Plato's death. Teaching and research were both part of the Academy's mandate to create a new kind of statesman/philosopher. Plato taught and wrote at the Academy for the rest of his life though there are few records of his actual lectures. Some talks were open to the public; Aristotle told the story of one of Plato's lectures entitled "On the Good." People attended expecting a talk on obtaining happiness. Instead Plato lectured on mathematics and astronomy. Aristotle used this as an example of the importance of fitting the talk to the audience, which Plato had failed to do.

Before Athens had been defeated in humiliation by Sparta, people talked openly about philosophical ideas; in the conquered Athens, this was not possible. Plato and others became spectators and turned to writing down ideas. Socrates had not recorded any of his ideas because philosophy had been "talked" not written. Most of Plato's writings were in dialogue form where ideas were presented in the context of a conversation or discussion among two or more people. Plato's earliest works focused on recording Socrates' ideas. It is primarily through Plato that the world has come to know the ideas of Socrates, as Socrates left no recorded materials.

When Plato was 60 years of age, he went to Syracuse to educate Dionysus II at the request of Dion, the brother-in-law of Dionysius II. This was a chance for Plato to create the educational system he envisioned in the *Republic*. But Dionysius' education had been left too long, and he was not able to benefit from Plato's teachings. Unsuccessful, Plato returned to Athens.

Plato died at the age of 80 and was buried in the grounds of the Academy. He apparently remained unmarried though he had many deep friendships throughout his life. There is no information — only conjecture — about any intimate relationships he may have had.

What was he like as a person? There is nothing definitive known about his physical appearance, but he was described as a man of courage, loyalty, generosity, kindness, and intellectual brilliance. Above all, he loved discourse and was seen as a brilliant conversationalist and a man of unique wisdom.

*Plato started The Academy. What kind of learning or educational institution would you envision creating? What aspects would you include?*

After Plato's death, the Academy flourished in Athens and lasted for almost a millennium, producing leaders for many Greek cities. In 529 C.E. Emperor Justinian closed it along with other "pagan schools"; this coincides with the beginning of the Dark Ages.

## Utopia

Plato's writings, the best source of his ideas and thinking, are almost all in the form of dialogues. There is some confusion about the creator of the ideas as Socrates is often the primary speaker. It seems, however, that in most cases, Socrates is the spokesperson for Plato's ideas.

*The Republic* was originally written on 10 rolls of papyrus, an early writing material made from the sedge plant. This was the common method of writing. Later paper was made from bark, flax and hemp. Papermaking and printmaking were not mechanized until the 19th century.

In the *Republic,*[4] which Plato wrote around 375 B.C.E. and which was one of his key works related to education, Plato described the first Utopia in literature and showed how the perfect state could be created. Living in a city state where greed and privilege superseded the values that Athens had struggled to preserve, Plato felt a need to create an ideal society to improve on the existing situation. Because of his life experiences, he felt it was important to have a class of "guardians" who would live not for themselves but for the general good of society. These guardians had to be above personal gain. Much of the *Republic* describes his ideal state with education at the centre. It is also the first treatise ever written on education. Plato saw the negative effects of leaving education in Athens to private enterprise; he felt a state system of education was required so that education could regain its importance.

Plato wrote the *Republic* in mid-life and the *Laws* in late life. The latter deals with a less utopian and more pragmatic view of life and education.

## Censorship

Plato believed that if guardians were to be wise, ethical adults, their earliest experiences would need to reflect the values that were important to society. Children in Athens received their earliest education by being told stories and hearing poetry. To that end, he forbade the use of ancient myths and legends which told the tales of gods in love and at war:

> *"You know also that the beginning is the most important part of any work, especially in the case of a young and tender thing; for that is the time at which the character is being formed and the desired impression is more readily taken.*

[4] The Greek title would better be translated *On the Just Man* or *On Justice,* and the work does explore the nature of justice and injustice and their impact on people.

**The School of Athens. (1510 – 1511) This painting was created by Raffaello S. Sanzio (known as Raphael) and depicts Plato (on the left), Aristotle (on the right) and other ancient philosophers. Raphael was a major Italian Renaissance painter who lived from 1483 – 1520. Pope Julius II commissioned the painting for the Palace of the Vatican. (Used with permission of Pictures Now.)**

*And shall we just carelessly allow children to hear any casual tales which may be devised by casual persons, and to receive into their minds ideas for the most part the very opposite of those which we shall wish them to have when they are grown up?*

*Then the first thing will be to establish a censorship of the writers of fiction, and let the censors receive any tale of fiction which is good, and reject the bad; and we will persuade mothers and nurses to tell their children the authorized ones only. Let them fashion the mind with such tales, even more fondly than they mold the body with their hands; but most of these which are now in use must be discarded.*

*. . . if we mean our future guardians to regard the habit of lightly quarrelling among themselves as of all things the basest, should any word be said to them of the wars in heaven, and of the plots and fightings of the gods against one another, for they are not true? No, we shall never mention the battles of the giants, or let them be embroidered on garments; and we shall be silent about the innumerable other quarrels of gods and heroes with their friends and relatives. If we intend to persuade them that quarrelling is unholy, and that never up to this time has there been any hatred between citizens, then the stories which old men and old women tell them as children should be in this strain; and when they grow up, the poets also should be obliged to compose for them in a similar spirit. . . .*

*For a young person cannot judge what is allegorical and what is literal; anything that he receives into his mind at that age is likely to become indelible and unalterable; and therefore it is most important that the tales which the young first hear should be models of virtuous thoughts."*

***— Republic***

---

Long after Plato's time, issues related to censorship of materials for children continue. The influence of early experiences on children's lives and their later behaviours and attitudes is central to the issue. Censorship may or may not be the answer, but we continue to wrestle with the problem. In all our work with young children, we make selections about what is appropriate and not appropriate given the beliefs and goals we hold.

Today thoughtful adults must scrutinize videos, television, computer games, the Internet, and books for violence, sexism, racism, ageism, sexual innuendoes, etc. What do we want children exposed to? *The Little Mermaid*? *Little Red Riding Hood*? *Hiawatha*? *Aladdin*? The daily news on television contains discussions and pictures of horrors in places both far away and within our own communities. Should children be "allowed" to view such news? Can they be prevented? What is the adult role in assisting children in processing what they see and hear around them? Plato believed that young people could not separate what is allegorical and what is literal. Is this true?

Plato was concerned with the violence and lewdness of myths and legends, and with their impact on children's values and impressionable minds. The debate over fairy tales and legends continues. Two provocative and dissenting views can be found in Bruno Bettelheim's *The Uses of Enchantment* and Marina Warner's *From the Beast to the Blond.* Herb Kohl wrote *Should We Burn Babar?* which also looks at censorship of children's literature.

---

## Education of Girls and Women

In ancient Greece, girls received an education focused on the domestic arts to enable them to be mothers and wives. Though some upper-class females would receive education from a tutor, their lack of involvement in the political process rendered any other focus superfluous.

Plato had a different vision. Plato's goal of education was to create good citizens for the good state. This very future-directed goal arose from his own life experiences in Athens. He adamantly believed that the health of a society depended on the education that its citizens received. And in this way, education was the key to a society's progress.

*The discussion continues today about the needs of girls and whether these are best met in a co-educational or all-female environment. Do you think boys and girls receive equivalent education today? What about the education of men and women in post-secondary institutions? Is our government equally represented by men and women leaders?*

Men and women in Plato's ideal world would be treated equally. No one would be banned from education based on gender or social class. Males and females, differing only in body functions and strength, would have the same education and same duties in society. Plato saw the current Athenian society as wasting the talents of half its population:

> *"So if we are going to use men and women for the same purposes, we must teach them the same things.*
>
> *You must not suppose that my words apply to the men more than to the women who arise among them endowed with the requisite qualities."*
>
> — ***Republic***

Plato mentioned that women were to be occupied with the process of government, and he felt that both boys and girls should be equally educated if they were to take part actively in governance. He did put this idea — almost unimaginable for the ancient world[5] — into practice, admitting a few "exceptional" women (e.g. Axiothea of Philius and Lasthenia of Mantinea) for study at the Academy. Boys and girls, in Plato's approach, would be in classes together up until the age of six when their education would be separate.

---

[5] Pythagorus had also admitted women to his school of philosophy as he believed that reason was unaffected by gender.

## Play

*Observation of children at play was central to Plato. What are the values of observation for your work with children and their families?*

We now think play is a new innovation in articulating children's ways of learning. However, Plato strongly supported experiential learning through play in several of his writings:

> *"For the free man there should be no element of slavery in learning. Enforced exercise does no harm to the body, but enforced learning will not stay in the mind. So avoid compulsion, and let your children's lessons take the form of play."*
>
> — ***Republic***

> *"He who is to be a good builder, should play at building children's houses: he who is to be a good husbandman, at tilling the ground; and those who have the care of their education should provide them when young with mimic tools . . . The future carpenter should learn to measure or apply the line in play; and the future warrior should learn riding, or some other exercise, for amusement, and the teacher should endeavour to direct the children's inclinations and pleasure, by the help of amusements, to their final aim in life."*
>
> — ***Laws***

The reference to the future builder playing at building houses may be the first reference to the use of building materials (blocks) in an educational manner.

> *"The most important part of education is right training in the nursery. The soul of the child in his play should be guided to the love of that sort of excellence in which when he grows up to manhood he will have to be perfected."*
>
> — ***Laws***

Plato saw mathematics as the foundation for all advanced study and believed that it should be introduced to children through games and puzzles that required calculations.

He recommended the establishment of supervised playgrounds.

## Observation

Observation is at the core of all early childhood programming as a basis for understanding children and their needs. Plato's goal for observation was to see how children were naturally inclined and to plan their education accordingly:

> *"This will . . . help you to see what they are naturally fitted for."*
>
> — ***Republic***

## Activity

Today we know that children must be physically active in programs we provide for them. This stems from our knowledge of child development theory. Plato pre-dated our theoretical base for ensuring activity, not passivity, in programs for young children:

> *"The young of all creatures cannot be quiet in their bodies or in their voices; they are always wanting to move and cry out."*
>
> *"This movement is the origin of rhythm and gymnastics."*
>
> — ***Laws***

*Questioning remains a key skill of an early childhood professional. Bess Gene Holt in* Science for Young Children *gives a full list and explanation of questions that stimulate inquiry and thinking in young children. Most effective dialogue with young children continues to be one-to-one or in very small groups, helping children extend their thinking and dealing individually with their ideas, concerns and feelings. How have you used questioning to encourage a child's thinking and problem solving in a one-to-one situation?*

## Importance of Beginnings

Increasingly the field of early childhood has research to back up the importance of the early years. We see this in relation to individual children and the prevention of later social problems. Plato was the first to articulate the key importance of first beginnings:

> *"The direction in which education starts a man will determine his future life."*
>
> *"The first shoot of any plant, if it makes a good start, has the greatest effect in helping it to attain its mature natural excellence."*
>
> *"The beginning is always the most important part especially when you are dealing with anything young and tender. That is the time when the character is being molded and easily takes any impress one may wish to stamp on it."*
>
> — ***Republic***

*Is education a* ***"secondary or accidental"*** *matter in your community as Plato feared it might become? What about the care of children?*

From Plato's perspective, the minister of education in government should be the most valued and important in leading a society:

> *"It should be the greatest of all the great offices of State . . . the legislator ought not allow the education of children to become a secondary or accidental matter."*
>
> — ***Laws***

## Learning

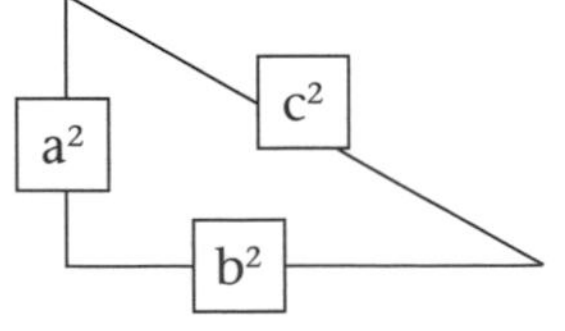


Plato also wrote a dialogue called the *Meno* in which he explored the idea of teaching an illiterate, uneducated slave the Pythagorean Theorem. The mathematician and philosopher Pythagorus had developed the theorem a half century before proving that the sum of the squares of the sides of a right angle triangle equal the square of its hypotenuse ($a^2 + b^2 = c^2$).

The boy had no previous mathematical training. In this dialogue, Plato illustrates the Socratic method of teaching through questions and answers between teacher and student, slowly leading the boy to knowledge. The boy makes reasonable guesses and follows through on the implications of his inferences.

Plato believed that the power of understanding was present in the learner being taught. As opposed to seeing teaching as instruction from without, Plato saw true education as the process of drawing out what is latent in the learner.[6] This kind of education is an active search and possible only if the learner takes it on willingly. The thirst for learning and knowledge was most critical. Teachers were not to transmit knowledge from themselves to the learners. Learners also had to know themselves and realize what they did not know. He called this the science of right choice, allowing wise decision making. Knowing oneself was central to learning anything, and at the core of knowing oneself was the knowledge of what one does not know:

> *"The soul has learned everything, so that when a man has recalled a single piece of knowledge — learned it, in ordinary language — there is no reason why he should not find out all the rest, if he keeps a stout heart and does not grow weary of the search."*
>
> **— *Meno***

*Plato said "**knowledge which is acquired under compulsion obtains no hold on the mind.**" What have been your experiences with being forced to learn material? What learning situations have been more effective?*

Plato's concerns with motivation for learning were reiterated many times in both the *Republic* and the *Laws*. He believed that people could not be compelled to learn and that humiliation would have no part in education. Children would learn respect as their teachers genuinely respected them. Today we have theoretical support for these wise statements but struggle with their implementation these thousands of years later. In Plato's writings there is actually little information about methods of education beyond using conversation and discussion. Plato assumed the "silver" and "gold" citizens would learn without difficulty, and he did not deal with the daily issues of teaching and learning.

## Classes

Plato believed citizens differed in natural capacities and dispositions and described three classes of people aligned with the three metals used in the Olympics.

| | Who | Activities/Purpose | Notable Characteristics | Goal/Virtue |
|---|---|---|---|---|
| **Gold** | Rulers/Philosopher Kings/Guardians | Govern | Intellect | Wisdom |
| **Silver** | Warriors/Auxiliaries Guardians | Assist and support Army/Police/Civil Servants | Courage and Spirit | Courage and Honour |
| **Bronze** | Artisans/Traders/ Manufacturers/Farmers | Provide goods and services for the community | Determination and Desire | Temperance and Productivity |

[6] It is interesting to note that the word "education" comes from the Latin "to lead out" — duc (lead) and ex (out).

The state would function properly and attain justice when all classes acted harmoniously.

Educational theorists today continue to wonder how to educate the diversity of students and debate the value of the separate and enhanced education of those children determined to be "gifted."

Though Plato envisioned these classes, he thought a child could be born into any class and become a "ruler." Aptitude, not family position or influence, would determine the class. Conversely, someone who was cowardly in battle might be repositioned from silver to bronze. It is important to realize that at least two-thirds of Athens' society consisted of slaves who were considered non-persons, as machines to work. They would receive no education even in Plato's ideal state. This was a firmly entrenched tradition in Greece, and there is no evidence that Plato opposed the practice. He did, however, maintain that slaves should be treated humanely and justly.

## Theory of Forms and Knowledge

Plato saw knowledge as fixed, unchanging and infallible as well as real. The opposite of real would be that which was only "appearance." He rejected the belief that knowledge came from the senses because such knowledge can not be certain. Sense impressions are from phenomena in the natural and physical world that are changing and, therefore, are not good examples of true knowledge. Reason, higher level thinking, would bring true knowledge.

Plato used a complex myth of the cave to explain this further. People are chained deep inside a dark cave so they cannot see each other. They can see only shadows on the wall that are reflected as they pass in front of a burning fire. A person breaks free to see the light of day with the sun shining. He returns to the cave to inform the others that the real world is outside and they have been seeing only shadows of the real world, appearances.

Plato conceived of Forms which were the true goal of education. A circle, for example, would only be an object in the physical world. Circularity (a two dimensional figure where all points of the circumference are equally distant from the centre) would be the Form, existing in the changeless world known only through reason. Circularity exists after all physical approximations, outside the world of space and time.

Forms would be real, stable and pure ideas. The ultimate Form would be the Form of Good, illuminating all other ideas. Education would lead people to an understanding of the Forms.

## Balanced Education

Plato believed that education should not focus only on the intellect. The children in the Guardian class would have a curriculum with a balance of the liberal arts (*mousike*), physical training (*gymnastike*) and mathematics.

Plato felt that the arts had a tremendous role in education. Works of art (visual, poetic, musical, literary) were seen as not only aesthetically valuable but also a key way people expressed ideas, emotions and values. To this end, art needed to be central to the process of education:

> *"Rhythm and harmony sink deep into the recesses of the soul and take the strongest hold there, bringing that grace of body and mind."*
>
> — **Republic**

Physical training would be challenging physical education. Simple diet and lifestyle would promote good health.

Mathematics would be the basis for much higher education as it was training in rational thought. Relationships among events, objects and abstractions are at the core of mathematics, and children would see these relationships in their play. This still remains the central focus of meaningful mathematics for young children today.

*Plato affected many students through his teaching. Which teachers positively impacted your growth and development? As a child? As an adult? What did they do to encourage your learning?*

Plato's ideas remained his vision and only a dream. The utopian world he envisioned never came to fruition, and the practical methods were not developed. However, thousands of years later, his ideas continue to challenge and intrigue. They raise issues we struggle with today.

Plato lived and wrote in a remarkable time. Perhaps above all, Plato saw education as the avenue for change in society and for a better tomorrow. Education was central to citizenship in a democracy. Children, both boys and girls, were valued, and early education was pivotal for later development and for the future of a society. Plato stressed that the nature of the learning and the learning process were more important than the subject matter. We would do well to remember and consider his advice today.

Alfred North Whitehead, a 20th century philosopher, clearly stated the place of Plato in the history of philosophy:

> *"Modern philosophy is but a series of footnotes to Plato."*

*Special Collection*
*Plato Microfilm Project*
*[also indexes manuscripts in libraries around the world]*
*Yale University Library*
*New Haven, Connecticut 06520*
*U.S.A.*

*The videos* The Ancient Greeks *and* Plato: The Republic, the Socratic Method, and the Allegory of the Cave *are available from:*
*Insight Media*
*2162 Broadway*
*New York, New York 10024-0621*
*U.S.A.*

## Plato — References for Further Study


Annas, J. (1981). *An introduction to Plato's Republic.* Oxford, England: Clarendon Press.

Bettelheim, B. (1976). *The uses of enchantment.* New York: Knopf.

Brumbaugh, R. (1954). *Plato's mathematical imagination: The mathematical passages in the dialogues and their interpretation.* Bloomington, IN: Indiana University Press.

Brumbaugh, R. (1981). *The philosophers of Greece.* Albany, NY: State University of New York Press.

Brumbaugh, R. S. (1991). *Plato for the modern age.* Lanham, MD: University Press of America.

Cohen, B. (1969). *Educational thought.* London: Macmillan.

Crombie, I. M. (1963). *An examination of Plato's doctrines.* London: Routledge & Kegan Paul.

Egan, K. (1983). *Education and psychology: Plato, Piaget, and scientific psychology.* New York: Teachers College Press.

Field, G. C. (1967). *Plato and his contemporaries.* London: Butler & Tanner.

Field, G. C. (1969). *The philosophy of Plato (2nd ed.).* Oxford, England: Oxford University Press.

Freeman, C. (1996). *Egypt, Greece and Rome.* New York: Oxford University Press, Inc.

Friedlander, P. (1958). *Plato: An introduction.* Princeton, NJ: Princeton University Press.

Grote, G. (1865). *Plato and the other companions of Sokrates (Volume I, II, III).* London: John Murray.

Grube, G. M. A. (1974). *Plato's Republic.* Indianapolis, IN: Hackett.

Grube, G. M. A. (1980). *Plato's thought.* Indianapolis, IN: Hackett.

Guthrie, W. K. C. (1975). *A history of Greek philosophy. Volume IV.* Cambridge, England: Cambridge University Press.

Guthrie, W. K. C. (1978). *A history of Greek philosophy. Volume V.* Cambridge, England: Cambridge University Press.

Hare, R. M. (1982). *Plato.* Oxford, England: Oxford University Press.

Holt, B. G. (1989). *Science with young children.* Washington, DC: National Association for the Education of Young Children.

Jordan, J. (1987). *Western philosophy from Antiquity to the Middle Ages.* New York: Macmillan Publishing Company.

Kohl, H. (1995). *Should we burn Babar? Essays on children's literature and the power of stories.* New York: New Press.

Kraut, R. (1992). *The Cambridge companion to Plato.* Cambridge, England: Cambridge University Press.

Kraut, R. (1997). *Plato's Republic.* Lanham, MD: Rowman & Littlefield.

Lascarides, V.C. & Hinitz, B. (2000). *History of Early Childhood Education.* New York: Falmer Press.

Martin, J. R. (1985). *Reclaiming a conversation: The ideal of educated woman.* New Haven, CT: Yale University Press.

Melling, D. (1987). *Understanding Plato.* New York: Oxford University Press.

Nettleship, R. (1968). *The theory of education in the Republic of Plato.* New York: Teacher's College Press.

Nettleship, R. (1975). *Lectures on the Republic of Plato, VI,* 364. Folcroft, PA: Folcroft Library Editions.

Pappas, N. (1995). *Plato and the Republic.* London: Routledge.

Raven, J. E. (1965). *Plato's thought in the making.* Cambridge, England: Cambridge University Press.

Rowe, C. J. (1984). *Plato: Philosophers in context.* New York: St. Martin's Press.

Stone, I. F. (1988). *The trial of Socrates.* Boston: Little, Brown and Company.

Strathern, P. (1996). *Plato in 90 minutes.* Chicago: Ivan Dee.

Taylor, A. E. (1926). *Plato.* London: Methuen.

Taylor, A. E. (1960). *Plato: The man and his work.* London: Methuen.

The Socratic method by Plato. (1994). *The Physics Teacher, 32* (3), 138-141.

Warner, M. (1994). *From the beast to the blond.* London: Chatto & Windus.

White, N. P. (1976). *Plato on knowledge and reality.* Indianapolis, IN: Hackett.

# Chapter 2 — *John Amos Comenius*

**(Jan Komensky)**
**1592 – 1670**

*"The action of teaching and learning is in its own nature pleasing and agreeable."*

***— The School of Infancy***

*"Everything should, as far as is possible, be placed before the senses. Everything visible should be brought before the organs of sight, everything audible before that of hearing. Odors should be placed before the sense of smell, and things that are tastable and tangible before the sense of taste and touch respectively. If an object can make an impression on several senses at once, it should be brought into contact with several."*

*"A bird learns to fly, a fish to swim, and a beast to run without compulsion."*

***— The Great Didactic***

Imagine a man who never gave up hope for a better world despite personal and professional tragedies. He was a humanist, in a turbulent world, who believed that human beings could give purpose and meaning to life based on reason and responsibility. He was a wandering scholar, pilgrim and citizen of the world and lived in exile 42 of his 78 years. Such is John Amos Comenius, who was born in 1592 in Uhersky Brod,[1] eastern Moravia in what is now the Czech Republic.

**Most researchers believe Comenius was born in Uhersky Brod. (Illustration courtesy of Dorothy Howard.)**

His father, Martin, was a miller, and John was the youngest of five children in a deeply religious family. Hungarian troops invaded his birthplace when John was ten, and both his parents and two sisters died of a pestilence that swept the region. Comenius witnessed unimaginable plundering and killing and the next year saw his town go up in flames. An aunt in a nearby town raised him after these early tragedies.

[1] Some sources mention Nivnice and Komne as other Moravian towns in which Comenius might have been born; documentation varies.

**Comenius grew up in Moravia, which is now in the eastern part of the Czech Republic. It is bordered on the west by Bohemia and on the east by the Carpathian Mountains.**

## Educational Experiences

Early in his schooling, he enjoyed learning despite the harsh teaching methods. He later graphically described his early impression of schools as the "slaughterhouses of minds," "labyrinths of hard labour" and "grinding houses of torment and torture:"

> *"They are a terror of boys, and the slaughterhouses of minds—places where a hatred of literature and books is contracted, where ten or more years are spent in learning what might be acquired in one, where what ought to be poured in gently is violently forced in and beaten in, where what ought to be put clearly and perspicuously is presented in a confused and intricate way, as if it were a collection of puzzles—places where minds are fed on words."*
>
> ***— The Great Didactic***

*Comenius saw his early school experiences as **"slaughterhouses of minds."** What were your school experiences like and how did they affect your learning? How are your current school experiences affecting your learning?*

Teaching methods were poor and based on rote memorization and corporal punishment. He was fortunate to have been befriended by an exceptional headmaster who recognized his intellectual gifts and encouraged him to train for the religious ministry. This teacher gave him his middle name, Amos, which means "loving." Comenius was determined to find ways in which children could learn more easily. These early experiences with poor education and one caring teacher had a lifelong impact on his future directions.

He left for Germany in 1612 to attend the Calvinistic Herbron High School, north of Heidelberg. There he began his studies to become a teacher, and his name was Latinized to Comenius from Komensky.

Attending the University of Heidelberg in 1613, Comenius became a friend with the millennialists who believed that men could obtain salvation on earth. He read widely, studying philosophy, theology, Latin and Greek. He returned home, convinced that earthly salvation was possible with the aid of science.

During the next period of his life, he taught at the town Latin school run by the Unity of Brethren in Prerov in Moravia. While there, he wrote a text for learning grammar which reflected his belief that language was communication with grammar only a tool. He also started work on a Czech dictionary.

## Life In The Midst of War

Even before the Reformation, a 16th-century movement for the reform of the Roman Church, several religious groups had already resisted the power of the Papacy. The Unity of the Bohemian Brethren was one of these sects; they were followers of John Huss who had been burned at the stake 200 years previously. The sect espoused a simple life based on the gospel, and Comenius was ordained a Moravian minister of the Bohemian Brethren in 1618. He also became headmaster of a school in Fulnek, near the border of Moravia and Silesia. Fulnek was the oldest community of the Brethren in Moravia.

*The writings of Comenius were often seen as "dangerous" in his lifetime. How can books or ideas create this kind of situation? Do you know of other examples from history?*

As a young minister, Comenius found life satisfying, but the calm was destroyed by the outbreak of the Thirty Years War in 1618. Catholics were pitted against Protestants in a religious war over territory. Emperor Ferdinand II was determined to re-Catholicize Bohemia. Comenius and other Protestant leaders were compelled to flee. Forced to leave his wife Magdalena and two infant sons, he suffered tremendous personal tragedy when they all died of the plague in 1622. The next year, the school children in his hometown were forced to watch as his entire library was burned in the town square.

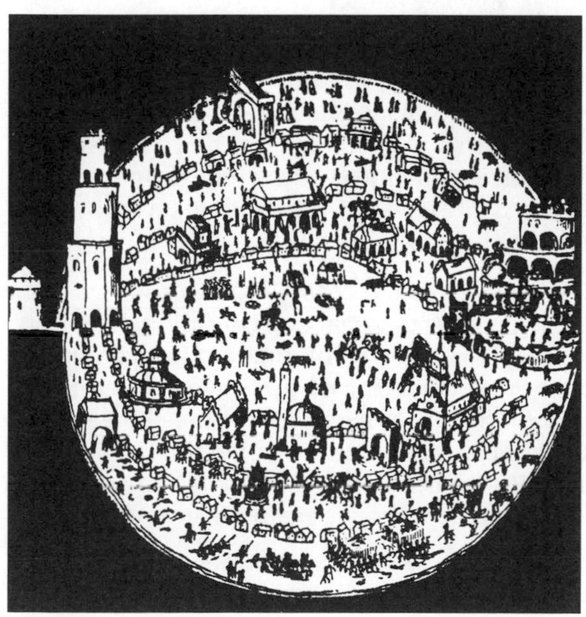

**Comenius wrote and did the illustrations for an allegory called *The Labyrinth of the World and the Paradise of the Heart*. From *Homage to J. A. Comenius* edited by J. Peskova. (Used by permission of Dr. Jaroslav Jirsa of the Karolinium Press, Prague, Czech Republic.)**

While in hiding, Comenius wrote an allegory called *The Labyrinth of the World and the Paradise of the Heart* (1623), a parable of a wandering pilgrim who finds inner peace. In this book, Comenius described his own despair and sources of consolation. A man of many talents, Comenius also created a map of Moravia during this period. It was printed from 12 copper engravings and used for over 150 years.

Further persecution of the Bohemian Brethren caused them to flee to Poland. Comenius and other leaders settled in Leszno, believing that they would someday return to Bohemia. In the relative safety of this area, Comenius wrote extensively of educational reform. Comenius became the director of a school and tried out his emerging ideas. In 1624 he married Maria Dorothea Cyrill, the daughter of the local bishop, and began his second family.

**Comenius was a bishop in the Moravian Church and focused on improving education for all people. (Photo courtesy of Dorothy Howard.)**

During this period of thinking, writing and experimentation in schools, Comenius came up with two key ideas:

**1. A revolution in teaching methods was essential to allow learning to become rapid, pleasant and thorough.** The existing schools focused solely on book, verbal learning with the cane as a supplementary teaching tool. Comenius advocated having teachers follow the footsteps of nature to learn how to make learning positive and fruitful. *The School of Infancy* in 1630 and *The Great Didactic (Didactica Magna)* in 1638 both focused on ways to accomplish this, with the latter intended specifically for mothers.

**2. European culture needed to be made more accessible to all children.** Reacting against the predominance of instruction in Latin memorization, Comenius supported learning in the language of the people. Nature's way would also focus on real life objects and events and not just grammar. *Gate of Languages Unlocked* was written with this approach, with Latin and Czech side by side explaining useful facts about the world. He took 8,000 common words and used them in 1,000 sequenced sentences. The book became popular in many countries, with the Czech replaced by the appropriate regional language of each country.

As the liberation of Bohemia became less certain, Comenius began to work on the liberation of human society through education. Many other Europeans shared his vision. His fame spread, and Cardinal de Richelieu, who had founded the French Academy to promote French literary work and rhetoric, invited him to France. Comenius was even interviewed by the search team for the presidency of Harvard University in Massachusetts, just five years after the University had been established.

Comenius was invited to England by a group of intellectuals and politicians in 1641 to establish a college of social and educational reform based on his book *The Way of Light.* Gathering information from around the world, the college would be devoted to the advancement of learning, educational reform and science. Though Parliament considered the plan to set up the College of Light, all hopes were shattered when the English Civil War broke out in 1642. Comenius seemed to be followed by war and death. Frustrated and disappointed, he was once again forced to move.

Comenius did accept an offer from the Swedish government in 1642 to help reform their schools by writing a series of texts modeled after his *Gate of Languages Unlocked.* While in Sweden between 1641 and 1648, he continued to develop his ideas in pansophy, a philosophical movement that believed in a universal system of human knowledge among all nations. It was seen as a way to gain personal virtue and world-wide peace.

The knowledge gained would allow people to more effectively deal with problems that faced society. He envisioned a Pansophia or Encyclopedia of Knowledge created by one central international body of great thinkers.

Comenius had also expected but did not receive support for the Czech exiles while in Sweden; he felt betrayed by Sweden's leaders because their previous promises of assistance had not been carried through.

The Thirty Years War finally ended in 1648 with the Peace of Westphalia. But the Catholic victory was a blow to Comenius and other Czech exiles as it meant that all hope was lost for ethnic and religious liberty in their homeland. They were unable to return unless they recanted their religious beliefs. In the same year, personal tragedy befell Comenius with the death of his second wife, with whom he had four children and shared 24 years of marriage.

Comenius left for Poland and married Jana Gajusova, who became mother to his children. He also became a bishop in the Moravian Church, the last of the Bohemian Brethren to attain this post.

Moving to the independent state of Transylvania (now part of Romania), he was hired to set up schools but quickly realized that the feudal nature of the area would not allow his ideas to work. His philosophical ideas were far too abstract for such a poor and undeveloped region, and he experienced open hostility from the local people. He was, however, able to reform the teaching of Latin in several schools.

***Orbis Pictus*** **was the first illustrated children's book, published in 1658 and popular for over 200 years. It was translated into languages around the world. (Photo Courtesy of Dorothy Howard.)**

## Orbis Pictus

During this period, Comenius wrote of education, pansophy, universal peace and culture. Through his travels, he had carried his draft of a picture book for children. Handwritten with no woodcuts, it awaited the opportunity to be published. He sent it to Nuremberg, Germany, and the black and white woodcuts were made. Though printing had been developed in the 16th and 17th centuries, little attention had been paid to the use of print for schools and teaching.

Comenius saw a need for a new kind of book:

> *"It may be observed that many of our children grow weary of their books, because they are overfilled with things which have to be explained by the help of words. The pupils, and often the teachers themselves, know next to nothing about the things."*
>
> **— quoted in Monroe, *Comenius and the Beginnings of Educational Reform***

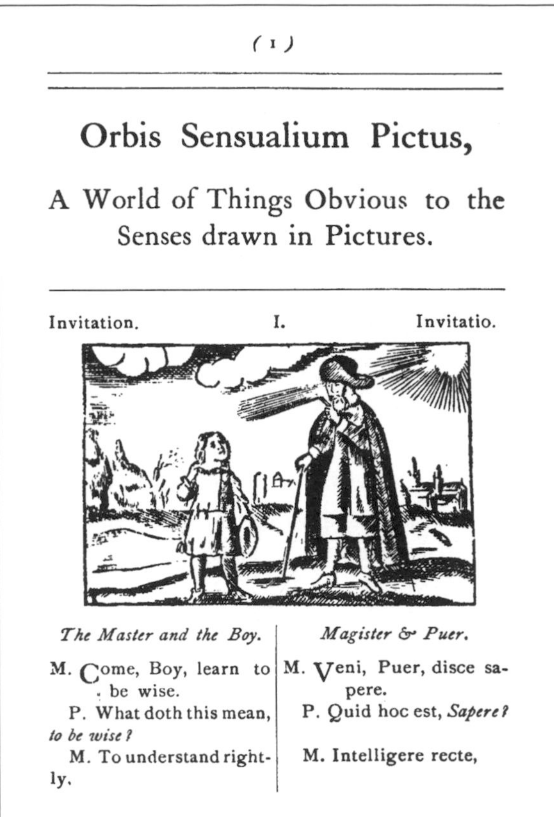

( 1 )

Orbis Sensualium Pictus,

A World of Things Obvious to the Senses drawn in Pictures.

| Invitation. | I. | Invitatio. |
|---|---|---|

| *The Master and the Boy.* | *Magister & Puer.* |
|---|---|
| M. Come, Boy, learn to be wise. | M. Veni, Puer, disce sapere. |
| P. What doth this mean, *to be wise?* | P. Quid hoc est, *Sapere?* |
| M. To understand rightly. | M. Intelligere recte, |

*Orbis Sensualium Pictus.* **The subtitle of the book shows the focus on the use of the senses to learn about the world.**

| Flying Vermin. | XXV. | Insecta volantia. |
|---|---|---|

| | |
|---|---|
| The *Bee*, 1. maketh honey which the *Drone*, 2. devoureth. The *Wasp*, 3. and the *Hornet*, 4. molest with a sting; and the *Gad-Bee* (or Breese), 5. especially *Cattel*; | *Apis*, 1. facit mel quod *Fucus*, 2. depascit *Vespa*, 3. & *Crabro*, 4. infestant oculeo; & *Oestrum* (Asilus), 5. imprimis *pecus*. |

**Flying Vermin. Wasps, hornets, and bees were grouped in one category.**

*Orbis Sensualium Pictus (Visible World in Pictures)* was published in 1658 and became popular in Europe for the next 200 years. This was the first effective and useful children's book and was published in Europe until 1842 and in North America up until 1810. It was unique in content and appearance and was used as both a school text and a picture/information book for home. The first English edition appeared a year after the original, with pictures printed from copper plates instead of woodcuts.

Usually referred to as *Orbis Pictus,* this book was the forerunner of all illustrated schoolbooks and children's picture books. In the book, pictures illuminated Latin sentences and translations into the major language in the country of publication. Comenius felt children would learn to read more easily and enjoyably in their mother tongue.

( 13 )

| | |
|---|---|
| is called a *white Frost.* | dicitur *Pruina.* |
| *Thunder* is made of a brimstone-like *vapour,* which breaking out of a Cloud, with *Lightning,* 11. thundereth and striketh with lightning. | *Tonitru* fit ex *Vapore* sulphureo, quod erumpens è Nube cum *Fulgure,* 11. tonat & fulminat. |

The Earth. IX. Terra.

| | |
|---|---|
| In the *Earth* are | In *Terra* sunt |
| high *Mountains,* 1. | Alti *Montes,* 1. |
| Deep *Vallies,* 2. | Profundæ *valles,* 2. |
| *Hills* rising, 3. | Elevati Colles, 3. |
| Hollow Caves, 4. | cavæ Speluncæ, 4. |
| Plain *Fields,* 5. | Plani *campi,* 5. |
| Shady *Woods,* 6. | Opacæ Sylvæ, 6. |

( 14 )

The Fruits of the Earth. X. Terræ Fœtus.

| | |
|---|---|
| A *meadow,* 1. yieldeth *grass* with *Flowers* and *Herbs,* which being cut down, are made *Hay,* 2. | *Pratum,* 1. fert *Gramina,* cum *Floribus* & *Herbis* quæ defecta fiunt *Fænum,* 2. |
| A *Field,* 3. yieldeth *Corn,* and *Pot herbs,* 4. | *Arvum,* 3. fert *Fruges,* & *Olera,* 4. |
| *Mushrooms,* 5. | *Fungi,* 5. |
| *Straw-berries,* 6. | *Fraga,* 6. |
| *Myrtle-trees,* &c. | *Myrtilli,* &c. |
| *come up* in Woods. | *Proveniunt* in Sylvis. |
| *Metals, Stones,* and *Minerals* grow *under the earth.* | *Metalla, Lapides, Mineralia, nascuntur sub terra.* |

**The Earth and Fruits of the Earth. *Orbis Pictus* had chapters that focused on the world of the child. Illustrations were numbered and labelled in the text, providing valuable information to the reader.**

*Why is it important for children to know about both authors and illustrators of books that they are listening to and reading?*

The book was arranged in short chapters around topics of interest and included words and both labelled and numbered pictures for each lesson.

Topics were grouped into natural categories such as types of birds or insects. The thematic, illustrated groupings assisted students in building from the known to the unknown and functioned as a visual dictionary.

( 61 )

XLVIII.

| The making of Honey. | Mellificium. |
|---|---|
| The *Bees* send out | *Apes* emittunt |
| a *swarm*, 1. and set over | *Examen*, 1. adduntque illi |
| it a *Leader*, 2. | *Ducem* (Regem), 2. |
| That swarm | Examen illud, |
| being ready to fly away is | avolaturum, |
| recalled by the Tinkling | revocatur tinnitu |
| of a *brazen Vessel*, 3. | *Vasis ænei*, 3. |
| and is put up | & includitur |
| into a new *Hive*, 4. | novo *Alveari*, 4. |
| They make little *Cells* | Struunt *Cellulas* |
| with six corners, 5. and | sexangulares, 5. |
| fill them with *Honey-dew*, | et complent eas *Melligine*, |
| and make *Combs*, 6. | & faciunt *Favos*, 6. |
| out of which the *Honey* | è quibus *Mel* |
| runneth, 7. | effluit, 7. |
| The *Partitions* being | *Crates* |
| melted by fire, | liquati igne |
| turn into *Wax*, 8. | abeunt in *Ceram*, 8. |

**The Making of Honey. This illustration shows the process of honey production by bees and humans. Key parts of the illustration are numbered to indicate the section of the text where it is explained.**

Linen Cloths. LXI. Lintea.

| *Linnen-webs* | *Linteamina* |
|---|---|
| are bleached in the *Sun*, 1. | insolantur, 1. |
| with Water poured on | aquâ perfusâ, 2. |
| them, 2. till they be white. | donec candefiant. |
| Of them the *Sempster*, 3. | Ex iis *Sartrix*, 3. |
| soweth *Shirts*, 4. | suit *Indusia*, 4. |
| *Handkirchers*, 5. | *Muccinia*, 5. |
| *Bands*, 6. *Caps*, &c. | *Collaria*, 6. *Capitia*, &c. |
| These if they be fouled, | Hæc, si sordidentur |
| are washed again | lavantur rursum, |
| by the *Laundress*, 7. in | a *Lotrice*, 7. aquâ, |
| water, or *Lye* and *Sope*. | sive *Lixivio* ac *Sapone*. |

**The Potter and Linen Cloths. *Orbis Pictus* showed a unique perspective of the inside and outside of buildings at the same time as well as different steps in the topic explained. This is shown in both the making of pottery and linen.**

Comenius used a creative method to show the processes of making pottery, a mining operation or a stable. He included simultaneous representations of both the inside and outside of a building, thus concurrently illuminating different aspects of the topic in both space and time.

An alphabet illustrated with real objects focused on the sounds of the letters. Animals and other objects from nature were used to illustrate the sounds to help children remember the alphabet and the sounds each letter made. The pictures themselves were relatively small in the original edition (3 1/2 x 2 1/2 inches or 9 x 6 cm). The text was considered a typographical innovation in using a variety of types (e.g. roman, italic, etc.). Unfortunately few copies have been preserved into the 21st century.

*What role do illustrations play in children's books? How do you use illustrations when reading a picture book to children?*

*Who are some of your favourite illustrators? Why?*

The Potter. LXXI. Figulus.

| | |
|---|---|
| The *Potter*, 1. | *Figulas*, 1. |
| sitting over a *Wheel*, 2. | sedens super *Rota*, 2. |
| maketh *Pots*, 4. | format *Ollas*, 4. |
| *Pitchers*, 5. | *Urceos*, 5. |
| *Pipkins*, 6. | *Tripodes*, 6. |
| *Platters*, 7. | *Patinas*, 7. |
| *Pudding-pans*, 8. | *Vasa testacea*, 8. |
| *Juggs*, 9. | *Fidelias*, 9. |
| *Lids*, 10. &c. | *Opercula*, 10. &c. |
| of *Potter's Clay*, 3. | ex *Argillâ*, 3. |
| afterwards he baketh them | postea excoquit |
| in an *Oven*, 11. | in *Furno*, 11. |
| and glazeth them | & incrustat |
| with *White Lead*. | *Lithargyro*. |
| A broken Pot affordeth | Fracta Olla dat |
| *Pot-sheards*, 12. | *Testas*, 12. |

Illustrations all from *Orbis Pictus* (1887 edition) published by C.W. Bardeen, Syracuse, New York.

( 3 )

| | | |
|---|---|---|
| *Cornix* cornicatur, The *Crow* crieth. | à à | A a |
| *Agnus* balat, The *Lamb* blaiteth. | b è è è | B b |
| *Cicàda* stridet, The *Grasshopper* chirpeth. | cì cì | C c |
| *Upupa* dicit, The *Whooppoo* saith. | du du | D d |
| *Infans* ejulat, The *Infant* crieth. | è è è | E e |
| *Ventus* flat, The *Wind* bloweth. | fi fi | F f |
| *Anser* gingrit, The *Goose* gagleth. | ga ga | G g |
| *Os* halat, The *Mouth* breatheth out. | hà'h hà'h | H h |
| *Mus* mintrit, The *Mouse* chirpeth. | ì ì ì | I i |
| *Anas* tetrinnit, The *Duck* quaketh. | kha, kha | K k |
| *Lupus* ululat, The *Wolf* howleth. | lu ulu | L |
| *Ursus* murmurat, The *Bear* grumbleth. | mum-[mum | M m |

The illustrated alphabet was written in both Latin and the vernacular (language of people of a specific country or region) and included in *Orbis Pictus*.

*Orbis Pictus provided the perspective of multiple images in time and place, for example, in the illustration of linen or pottery making. How does such a perspective aid children's understanding? What is the advantage of such a multiple images perspective?*

Johann Goethe (1749 – 1832), German poet, novelist, dramatist and scientist, wrote in his autobiography that *Orbis Pictus* was the only children's book of his youth. G. Stanley Hall, leader of the child study movement in the U.S. in the late 1800's, said that it "sheds a broad light over the whole field of education" (quoted in Monroe's *Comenius and the Beginnings of Educational Reform).*

## Life's End

In 1655 the King of Sweden ordered an attack on Poland, and in the following year most of the country was occupied. Leszno was burned, and once again Comenius had to flee for his life with only the clothes on his back. He lost his library, his savings and most of the manuscripts he had been working on since his youth. In 1665 his third wife died.

Almost penniless, he moved his family from place to place and then found sanctuary with the De Geer family in Amsterdam, where he lived for the remaining 14 years of his life. Comenius wrote and worked to provide Moravian relief assistance for the war-torn region. At the time of his death in 1670, he had written more than 200 works, and his textbooks were in half the schools in Europe, translated into 17 languages.

Comenius was a man who remained positive, optimistic and energetic throughout his life despite the violence and tragedies around him.

**Statue of Comenius in Uhersky Brod. Comenius remained optimistic and hopeful despite a life surrounded by war and often filled with persecution. (Photo courtesy of Dorothy Howard.)**

## The Importance and Nature of Early Education

Comenius believed the early years were the key period for learning since so much depended on education:

*"It is the nature of everything that comes into being, that while tender it is easily bent and formed, but that, when it has grown hard, it is not easy to alter. Wax, when soft, can be easily fashioned and shaped; when hard it cracks readily. A young plant can be planted, transplanted, pruned and bent this way or that. When it becomes a tree these processes are impossible."*

— ***The Great Didactic***

After his own experiences with education in schools that he referred to as the "slaughterhouses of minds," Comenius knew such schools needed to be replaced by positive experiences full of joy and pleasure. He felt that the intellect would be violated if children were forced to carry out tasks beyond their ages and capabilities.

Following the order of nature, teachers needed to be aware of the order of development and not rush or force learning before children were ready. "Developmentally appropriate" is a phrase that came into use much later but was at the core of what Comenius believed. He knew that children developed at different rates and could not be forced by standardized teaching:

> *"All children do not develop at the same time, some beginning to speak in the first year, some in the second, and some in the third."*
>
> **— *The School of Infancy***

*What does current research say in relation to healthy starts for children? What is being done in your community?*

Comenius also suggested that pre-natal medical care for mothers was the real beginning of education for children, providing a healthy start for children's development.

## Sense Education

Sense learning would be at the core of learning and needed to be developed while the children were very young. It formed the basis of all other learning. *The School of Infancy,* written for both mothers and teachers, articulated methods for this approach. Senses would be exercised to help children distinguish objects around them.

Seeds of knowledge would be planted and would provide a strong foundation for further learning.

Most early childhood theorists see sensory learning and exploration at the centre of early learning. The senses also provide the child with observation and information gathering skills and central cognitive skills in all "academic areas" such as social studies, math and science.

> *"Those things, therefore, that are placed before the intelligence of the young, must be real things and not the shadows of things. I repeat, they must be things; and by the term I mean determinate, real and useful things that can make an impression on the senses and on the imagination.*
>
> *Everything should, as far as is possible, be placed before the senses. Everything visible should be brought before the organs of sight, everything audible before that of hearing. Odors should be placed before the sense of smell, and things that are tastable and tangible before the sense of taste and touch respectively. If an object can make an impression on several senses at once, it should be brought into contact with several."*
>
> **— *The Great Didactic***

Children learned about animals, plants and the names and uses for their own body parts. They learned to distinguish colours and to appreciate beautiful things. Geography would begin with knowledge of the room, the streets, the farm and the fields. By counting, they would begin arithmetic. History would develop from an understanding of what happened to them yesterday and the day before. A sense of chronological order would emerge from the experiencing of the passage of day and night, hours, weeks and celebrations and festivals.

Memory and understanding would develop naturally from the use of the senses.

Comenius' ideas on sense education would later be developed into object lessons by Pestalozzi (see chapter 4).

## Active Learning

*The School of Infancy* described activities, play, games, rhymes, fairy tales, music and manual tasks to help children learn in active ways. The book focused on children from birth through six years of age.

Children needed to be allowed to play freely:

> *"They are delighted to construct little houses, and to erect walls of clay, chips, wood, or stone, thus displaying an architectural genius."*
>
> ***— The School of Infancy***

Block play? Though he does not develop the idea, the roots of block construction are in his words.

Comenius was convinced that the nature of childhood was to be active, and both parents and educators needed to be aware of this:

> *"In a word, whatever children delight to play with, provided that it be not hurtful, they ought rather to be gratified than restrained from it; for inactivity is more injurious to both mind and body than anything in which they can be occupied.*
>
> *Too much sitting still ... is not a good sign."*
>
> ***— The School of Infancy***

*Comenius and Plato before him emphasized that* ***"too much sitting still ... is not a good sign."*** *How do you incorporate movement and dance into your program with children?*

Children's programs today could be reviewed for "inactivity" and "too much sitting still." These are still not good signs.

Comenius supported the use of objects familiar to the child and what we would now call educational materials/toys:

> *"When it is not convenient to give them real instruments, let them have toys like leaden knives, wooden swords, ploughs, little carriages, sledges, mills, buildings."*
>
> ***— The School of Infancy***

## Interests and First-Hand Experience

From senses comes memory, and from memory come understanding and judgment. Children's interests must be aroused to create the desire to learn:

> *"Every study should be commenced in such a manner as to awaken a real liking for it on the part of the scholars."*
>
> ***— The Great Didactic***

**Czechoslovakian money honouring Comenius.**

***"Things are the kernel, words the shells and husks,"*** *stated Comenius. How would you explain this with current child development theory?*

Premature use of language or writing would harm the understanding and the learning:

> *"Things are the kernel, words the shells and husks."*
>
> — ***The Great Didactic***

In the 20th century, the progressive educators (John Dewey, Patty Hill Smith, Caroline Pratt and Lucy Sprague Mitchell) would focus on real life experiences in schools, but the roots of this focus lay long before in the words of Comenius:

> *"In schools, therefore, let the students learn to write by writing, to talk by talking, to sing by singing, and to reason by reasoning. In this way schools will become workshops humming with work."*
>
> — ***The Great Didactic***

Intrinsic motivation rather than external rewards would encourage children's learning. The child would gain the knowledge after seeing the need for it.

## Principles of Teaching

Preceding later psychological studies of the child, Comenius set forth principles of teaching that reflected his understanding of the ways of nature. Nature was truly his guide:

> *"Following in the footsteps of nature we find that the process of education will be easy*
>
> i if it begins early, before the mind is corrupted
>
> ii if the mind be duly prepared to receive it
>
> iii if it proceeds from the general to the particular
>
> iv and from what is easy to what is more difficult
>
> v if the pupil be not overburdened by too many subjects
>
> vi and if progress be slow in every case
>
> vii if the intellect be forced to nothing to which its natural bent does not incline it, in accordance with its age and with the right method
>
> viii if everything be taught through the medium of the senses
>
> ix and if the use of everything taught be continually kept in view
>
> x if everything be taught according to one and the same method.
>
> *These, I say, are the principles to be adopted if education is to be easy and pleasant."*
>
> — ***The Great Didactic***

In Comenius' mind, the teacher's role was to assist the natural development of the child:

> *"Man is not a block of wood from which you carve a statue which is completely subject to your will; he is a living image, shaping, misshaping and reshaping itself."*
>
> — ***The Great Didactic***

> *"The duty of the teachers of the young, therefore, is none other than to skillfully scatter the seeds of instruction in their minds, and to carefully water God's plants. Increase and growth will come from above."*
>
> — ***The Great Didactic***

This gardening image would reappear many times in the history of early childhood.

## Child Guidance

Comenius was vehemently opposed to corporal punishment and was convinced that punishment would create an aversion to and hatred of school work. The teacher needed to create the love of learning. Comenius used many natural images to make his point:

> *"The sun itself offers us an excellent example of such prudence: it does not, in early spring, blaze suddenly upon new, tender plants to overwhelm them with the fire of its rays.... The gardener shows the same foresight, handling new plants skillfully and delicate shrubs with greater care. A musician, if his guitar is sharp or his violin be out of tune, does not strike the strings with his fist or with a stick. In the same way, a harmonious love of study must be developed in the pupils, if we do not want their indifference to change into hostility and their apathy into stupidity."*
>
> — ***The Great Didactic***

In *The Great Didactic,* Comenius devotes a whole chapter to school discipline and looks at positive sanctions such as encouragement and emulation rather than negative methods:

> *"I am therefore of opinion that rods and blows, those weapons of slavery, are quite unsuitable to freemen, and should never be used in schools."*
>
> *"The desire to learn can be excited by teachers, if they are gentle and persuasive and do not alienate their pupils from them by roughness, but attract them by fatherly sentiments and words."*
>
> — ***The Great Didactic***

## Equality of Access/Universal Education

Comenius believed that humans were born in the image of God and therefore people should have education to help them aspire to godliness. Equal in God's eye, girls and boys should receive equal education.

Struggles to attain equal education for children, whether rich or poor, have continued throughout history. Today inner-city schools and rural schools still battle for resources equal to those available in more affluent areas or in areas where parents can raise additional funds.

Comenius' belief in equal education for girls and boys was an extension of his belief that children from all classes and social status should receive education:

> *"No mind can be so ill-endowed that it cannot be gradually improved by education.*
>
> *All young children of both sexes should be sent to public schools.*
>
> *Why should we merely let them learn their ABC and then lock them away from the study of books?"*
>
> — ***The Great Didactic***

Girls and boys could learn equally, even though he did feel that they ultimately had different roles in life.

He proposed a system of universal education that would be open, accessible and free to all from early childhood through university. He saw four stages of formal education:

| | | |
|---|---|---|
| **Infant School** | up to age 6 | Character training, vernacular competence, sense training |
| **Vernacular School** | 7 – 12 years of age | Basic curriculum of reading, writing, arithmetic, singing, Latin, and another language |
| **Latin School** | 13 – 18 years of age | Classical education of Latin, Greek, Hebrew, mathematics, sciences, fine arts and useful arts |
| **University** | 18 – 24 years of age | World of professional training |

Comenius also saw learning as lifelong and formulated eight developmental stages of growth: birth, infancy, boyhood, adolescence, early manhood, full manhood, old age and death.

## Teachers as Professionals

Who are professionals?

Today's professions, as distinct from occupations, jobs or amateur practice, typically have six characteristics:

- professional organization
- commensurate compensation
- autonomy in practice
- high level of expertise and skill
- mastery of specialized knowledge
- ethical behavior

*Does the general public see people working with young children as **professionals**? Why or why not? Do you see yourself as a professional? What makes a professional in your view?*

Comenius pre-dated this current definition of a professional. He believed that teachers needed to be paid well, respected by the public, of high character, skilled in the tools of the trade and well educated outside their discipline.

*Comenius maintained a positive view and persevered with his vision of a better society through education. Who do you see with this commitment and positive approach today? Despite the low pay and low regard for day care workers, what keeps people committed to this field?*

Like Plato's, Comenius' vision included harmony among all people. Lifelong learning with a strong early childhood foundation would facilitate this goal. Jean Piaget's tribute to Comenius in 1957 reflects his enduring contribution:

> *"Comenius is thus among the authors who do not need to be corrected or, in reality, contradicted in order to bring them up to date, but merely to be translated and elaborated."*
>
> *"But the supreme merit of the great Czech educationist lies in the fact that he raised a series of new problems."*
>
> ***— John Amos Comenius on Education***

**Comenius wrote many books such as *The School of Infancy, The Great Didactic,* and *The Gate of Languages Unlocked* to help make learning more accessible to all children. From *Homage to J. A. Comenius* edited by J. Peskova. (Used by permission of Dr. Jaroslav Jirsa of the Karolinium Press, Prague, Czech Republic.)**

*Comenius Museum*
*Kloosterstraat 33*
*1411 RS Naarden*
*Netherlands*

*This is an educational museum honouring Comenius who lived the latter part of his life in Amsterdam. He was buried in Naarden, and the Comenius Museum is next to the Comenius Mausoleum. The museum has a library and exhibits related to the ideas and life of Comenius.*

*Special Library Collection —*
*Comenius Widener Library*
*Harvard University*
*Cambridge, Massachusetts 01238*
*U.S.A.*

*A film on his life is entitled "Jon Amos Comenius" and can be obtained from:*

*Gateway Films/Vision Video*
*P.O. Box 540*
*Worcester, Pennsylvania 19490 – 0540*
*U.S.A.*

## John Amos Comenius — References for Further Study

Butler, N. (1892). *The place of Comenius in the history of education.* Syracuse, NY: C.W. Bardeen.

Calkins, N. A. (1863). The history of object teaching. *Barnard's American Journal of Education, 12,* 633 – 645.

*Christian history.* (Volume VI, No. I). (1987).

Comenius, J. A. (1650). *The gate of languages unlocked or a seed plot of all arts and tongues.* (J. Robotham, Trans). London: William Du-gard. [microfiche].

Comenius, J. (1779, 1887, reissued in 1968). *The orbis pictus of John Amos Comenius.* Detroit, MI: Singing Tree Press.

Comenius, J. (1956). *The school of infancy.* (E. M. Eller, Trans.). Chapel Hill N. C.: University of North Carolina Press.

Comenius, J. A. (1957). *John Amos Comenius on education.* (Introduction by J. Piaget). New York: Teachers College Press.

Comenius, J. (1967). *The great didactic of John Amos Comenius.* (M. W. Keatinge, Trans.). New York: Russell & Russell.

Comenius, J. (1967). *Orbis sensualium pictus.* (Introduction by J. Bowen). Sydney, Australia: Sydney University Press.

Comenius, J. (1995). *Panorthosia.* (A.M.O. Dobbie, Trans.). Sheffield, England: Sheffield Academic Press.

Comenius, J. (1998). *The labyrinth of the world and the paradise of the heart.* (H. Louthan & A. Sterk, Trans.). New York: Paulist Press.

Hendrich, J., & Prochazka, M. (Eds). (1998). *J. A. Comenius' heritage and education of man for the 21st century. Section 5, Selected paper. Comenius and the significance of languages and literary education.* Prague, Czech Republic: Karolinum.

Hradecna, M. (Ed). (1998). *Comenius heritage and education of man for the 21st century. Papers of section 2. The development of the child's personality and the rights of the child.* Prague, Czech Republic: Karolinum.

Keatinge, M. W. (1931). *Comenius.* New York: McGraw-Hill.

Komensky, J. (1991). *Orbis sensualium pictus.* Prague, Czech Republic: Trizonia.

Kozik, F. (1958). *Johan Amos Comenius.* Prague, Czech Republic: SNTL.

Lascarides, V.C. & Hinitz, B. (2000). *History of Early Childhood Education.* New York: Falmer Press.

Laurie, S. S. (1892). *John Amos Comenius.* Syracuse, NY: C.W. Bardeen.

Lenk, K., & Kahn, P. (1992). To show and explain: The information graphics of Stevin and Comenius. *Visible Language, 26,* 3 – 4, 273 – 281.

Monroe, W. (1900, reprinted 1971). *Comenius and the beginnings of educational reform.* New York: Arno Press & The New York Times.

Murphy, D. (1995). *Comenius: A critical reassessment of his life and work.* Dublin, Ireland: Irish Academic Press.

Osgood, J. (1963). The contribution of Comenius and Pestalozzi to the theory of teacher training. In *The Yearbook of Education* (pp. 59 – 69). London: Evans Bros.

Osgood, J. (1963). The contributions of Comenius and Pestalozzi to the theory of teacher training. In Bereday, G. & Lauwerys, J. (Eds.), *The education and training of teachers.* London: Evans Brothers Limited.

Panek, J. (1991). *Comenius: Teacher of Nations.* Prague, Czech Republic: Vychodoslovenke vydavatelstvo.

Peltzman, B. R. (1998). *Pioneers of early childhood education. A bio-bibliogaphical guide.* Westport, CT: Greenwood Press.

Peskova, J. (Ed.). (1991). *Homage to J.A. Comenius.* Prague, Czech Republic: Charles University in Publishing House Karolinum.

Rood, W. (1970). *Comenius and the low countries: Some aspects of life and work of a Czech exile in the seventeenth century.* Amsterdam: Van Gendt & Co.

Spinka, M. (1943). *John Amos Comenius: That incomparable Moravian.* New York: Russell & Russell.

Steiner, M. (Ed). (1998). *Comenius' heritage and education of man for the 21st century. Papers of section 6. Comenius's general consultation.* Prague, Czech Republic: Karolinum.

# Chapter 3 — *Jean-Jacques Rousseau*

**1712 – 1778**

*"I wish some trustworthy person would give us a treatise on the art of child-study. This art is well worth studying, but neither parents nor teachers have mastered its elements."*

*"Childhood has its own ways of seeing, thinking and feeling; nothing is more foolish than to try and substitute our ways."*

*"Hold childhood in reverence."*

*"Leave childhood to ripen in your children."*

— ***Emile***

**The 1700's** — What comes to mind? Mozart? The French Revolution? The Enlightenment with its emphasis on science? Ben Franklin flying his kite and discovering that lightening is a form of electricity? James Watt's improvements on the steam engine?

Jean-Jacques Rousseau lived in this time of incredible change and ferment. In France the nobility and the clergy still ruled, and this Ancient Regime was being attacked by critics such as Voltaire, Turgot, Montesquieu, Diderot, and Rousseau. The social and economic problems of the times precipitated the French Revolution in 1789, just after Rousseau's death. The king ruled with little regard for others, imprisoning people without charges or trial. He governed without legislature or cabinet. The nobility of France, only one per cent of the population, owned one-fifth of the land. Absentee landlords extracted exorbitant rents from poor tenants and still paid no taxes. The French clergy was a wealthy hierarchy, controlling one-third of the lands in France; it too was not taxed. Existing institutions needed reform, and the French Revolution culminated in the emergence of the bourgeois and landowning classes as dominant powers.

## Early Life

Rousseau was born in 1712 in Geneva, Switzerland, of French parents, Isaac and Suzanne Bernard. The population of Geneva at this time was about 20,000; it was a walled and independent state. After his first son, Francois, was born, Isaac went to Constantinople to work as a watchmaker for six years to support the family. Jean Jacques was born ten months after his father returned to Geneva, but nine days after his birth, Rousseau's mother died of puerperal fever. Isaac was left in charge of Jean-Jacques and Francois.

**Rousseau was born in Geneva, Switzerland but lived primarily in France.**

Isaac Rousseau lacked parenting skills, but despite a haphazard life, Jean-Jacques learned to read by six years of age and by seven was reading the Greek (including works by Plato) and Roman classics. He remembered reading at his father's knee the novels that had belonged to his mother and the impact that early reading had on his love of books and learning. He and his father would sometimes stay up the entire night reading. Isaac was also a dancing master and fiddle player. His aunt's love of singing affected Rousseau, creating in him a lifelong passion for music. She used to play the theorbo[1] while Isaac played his fiddle.

[1] 17th century lute with two sets of pegs on one neck.

Jean-Jacques was a sickly child, and ill health would plague him the rest of his life. Francois was apprenticed to a watchmaker but ran away soon afterward, and nothing is known of his later life. Rousseau later described his father as unstable and physically abusive to both him and his brother.

When Rousseau was ten, his father had a dispute with a captain in the French army and struck him with a sword. Isaac fled before the trial but was convicted in absentia. He remained an exile, and Jean-Jacques was sent to live with some of his mother's relations in Lyon, France. At 12 he was apprenticed to a notary public who sent him back, describing him as a totally incapable student. Another apprenticeship, with an engraver in Geneva, also failed as Rousseau resented the cruel and brutal treatment he was subjected to. His love of books remained with him even in this difficult time, and he sold his shirts to borrow library books. He worked with the engraver three years until just before turning 16.

## The Vagabond Life

After leaving the engraver, Rousseau embarked on a vagabond life, dabbling in many types of work to support himself. He had little formal school but was a multi-talented young man. He taught music and developed a new form of musical notation. He worked as a secretary to several ambassadors, including the French Ambassador to Venice, and to Louise-Marie Dupin, who was writing a book on the oppression of women by men. He did the research and scribe work for her. His interest in education may have been sparked by a tutoring position with two young boys, although he later recalled this experience as being totally unsuccessful. A womanizer, he was also the companion of several wealthy, older women. In his travels, often on foot, he saw the subjugation and poverty of the peasant class in France.

Attracted to Paris, the capital of free thought and expression, Rousseau began composing opera. He became a close friend of the French philosopher and writer Denis Diderot, who had been commissioned by The French Encyclopedia (*Encyclopedie*) to write articles and edit the compilation of existing knowledge. Rousseau himself wrote over 400 articles, primarily on music, for the *Encyclopedie*. These were later revised and included in the *Dictionnaire de Musique*. Through this association, Rousseau came into contact with most of the leading intellectuals of the day. These thinkers immediately recognized Rousseau's genius but also had grave concerns about his erratic, unpredictable behaviour and his cruel sarcasm.

At the age of 33, Rousseau met Therese Levasseur, a waitress[2] in an inn. He fell in love with the 24-year-old woman despite their different interests and educational levels. They had five children and a stormy, unstable relationship[3] for the next 35 years. Rousseau's own early years without nurturing parenting may have been a factor in his inability to maintain a

---

[2] Some references refer to her as a "servant."

[3] Rousseau and Levasseur both continued to have associations with other partners throughout their relationship.

healthy relationship or to parent. All his children were given up to a Vincent de Paul's Foundling Home where the odds of surviving were small. There is no record of what happened to any of them, but only one in four children survived in these foundling homes. Rousseau later wrote that poverty and ill health thwarted his ability to be a parent.

## A Revelation and New Focus

In 1749, at the age of 37, Rousseau was on his way to visit Diderot, who was imprisoned in the Bastille for a "scandalous" letter. France had entered a period of severe censorship by the government, and the Bastille was a prison fortress for political prisoners in Paris. He saw an announcement of a contest held by the Academy of Dijon, challenging people to write essays addressing the question, "Has the progress of science and the arts tended to the purification or the corruption of morals?"

> *"The moment I read this I saw a new world and became a new man . . . All at once I felt my senses dazzled. In a thousand lights . . . Not being able to breathe and to walk at the same time, I dropped beneath one of the trees of the avenue and there I passed half an hour in such agitation that when I arose the whole front of my coat was wet with my tears though I was not conscious of shedding them. Oh, sir, if only I could have written even a fourth part of what I saw and felt under that tree, with what clearness would I have set forth the contradictions of our institutions, with what simplicity would I have shown that man is naturally good and that it is these institutions alone which make him bad."*
>
> — ***Confessions***

Rousseau went directly home, wrote the essay (Discours sur les Arts et les Sciences or Discourse on the Sciences and Arts), and won the prize. He became instantly famous. The essay attracted immediate public attention as in it Rousseau denounced society, the sciences and the arts and challenged men to break from their bondage and live freely and well. He argued that human beings had been corrupted by society and progress, creating "wants" that tied people down. His ideas were appealing, contrasting to the stilted and artificial life of the upper class, the absolute monarchy and the control of the Church. People listened. Rousseau himself began to live according to the maxims in the essay, adopting a simple life, even selling his watch, saying he would have no further need to know the time.

**Jean-Jacques Rousseau about 1750. (Used with permission of Bibliotheque Nationale Suisse-Bern.)**

After the publication of this essay, Rousseau returned briefly to Geneva and then spent the next several years moving from place to place. His personal relationships suffered as he exhibited bizarre behaviours, alienating friends and colleagues when he accused Diderot, Voltaire and others of conspiring against him.

He also continued to write and settled in the Hermitage at Montmorency. *Julie, ou La Nouvelle Heloise* (1761) was a novel in letter form, describing the love of a low-born man and a girl of rank. The man is rejected as the woman marries a free thinker of her own class. The book was semi-autobiographical, relating one of his love affairs. Its sections on child rearing foreshadow *Emile*:

> *"Nature . . . wants children to be children before they are men. If we deliberately pervert this order, we shall get premature fruits which are neither ripe nor well flavoured, and which soon decay. We shall have youthful sages and grown-up children. Childhood has ways of seeing, thinking and feeling, peculiar to itself; nothing can be more foolish than to seek to substitute our ways for them."*
>
> ***— Julie***

*Emile*, completed in 1760 and published in 1762, articulated Rousseau's ideas on child rearing and education. Education would produce the free, autonomous individual, a citizen of a society.

Rousseau's *The Social Contract* (1762) was a political treatise developing the case of civil liberty. He spoke eloquently of a government based on the consent of those governed. This stood out in sharp contrast to the rule of absolute monarchy, in which the ruler had unlimited power. *The Social Contract* was one of the key documents that helped prepare the ideological background of the French Revolution by defending the popular will against divine right to rule. It attempted to harmonize freedom and order — individual rights — with the rights of the State. Rousseau saw that individual freedom could be balanced with the general will, which looked to a greater, common good.

## A Swift Reaction from the Establishment

*Rousseau seemed to have an unstable and stormy life with both family and friends. He did not live many ideas he wrote about in his books. Does this undermine the credibility of his ideas for you? In what ways? Should philosophers and theorists be able to live their ideas as well as articulate them?*

Rousseau's books antagonized French and Swiss authorities and were burned in Paris, Bern and Geneva. Dutch authorities condemned them. The chief judicial body in Paris, the Paris Parlement, issued a warrant for his arrest and declared him an outlaw. Even nobles who had protected him feared for their own safety and urged him to flee. Overwhelmed by the reaction and the hate that emerged against him, Rousseau became a fugitive.

He escaped to the Swiss region of Neuchatel in Yverdon. The furor was about to die down when he again wrote an essay that attacked his enemies, the Church, and Geneva. Night-time attacks on his house forced him to flee again. He found refuge on the Ile de St. Pierre, in the lake of Bienne, but was forced to leave by order of the government of Switzerland.

In 1766 Rousseau fled to England. David Hume, a philosopher who rejected rationalism, provided Rousseau protection, and during this period Rousseau began to write his autobiography, *Confessions*. The relationship with Hume ended as Rousseau accused him of conspiring with Diderot in the imagined plot against him.

**Rousseau. (Used with Permission of the Library of Congress, Washington, DC. LC-USZ62-10747.)**

## Later Life

Rousseau returned to France in 1767 under the assumed name of Renou, still officially liable for arrest. Each of his letters ended with "I am innocent," as he felt his friends and the world had turned against him. He married Therese in 1768. Deeply suspicious and paranoid, he spent his last years reflecting on his life, completing his autobiography and copying music. After a period of extreme poverty and ill health, depressed and estranged from others, he died in 1778 of a cerebral edema at the age of 66, in Ermenonville in North Central France. Rousseau was not to know the tremendous impact his ideas had on politics, literature and education.

## Emile — Education and Child Rearing

In *Emile*, half novel, half treatise, Rousseau outlined his main ideas on education according to nature. Harold Bloom in "The Education of Democratic Man: Emile" described the book as a "*Phenomenology of the Mind Posing as Dr. Spock*" and compared its depth to that of Plato's *Republic*. In spite of the publication ban of *Emile*, the book was an instant success and widely read. It was an attempt to outline a system of education according to nature where children's natural attributes would be preserved by carefully controlling the environment.

Dr. Benjamin Spock (1903-1998) was an American pediatrician and professor at Case Western University. In 1946, he wrote *The Common Sense Book of Baby and Child Care* and later *A Baby's First Year, Feeding Your Baby and Child* and other books that provided information and guidelines about raising children with accurate medical information and with respect. He encouraged parents to trust themselves.

Previously, education and learning had been seen as filling the child with knowledge. Childhood was not even seen as a stage of human development. Children were seen as miniature and imperfect adults. John Locke's notion of the child's mind as a blank slate or tablet (known as *tabula rasa*) was the prevailing view. Rousseau believed the opposite: that knowledge was there to be drawn out of the child. Emile would be separated from corrupt society, in contact only with his tutor, to protect his natural goodness.

Emile's model of learning was Daniel Defoe's Robinson Crusoe, who lived on an island in harmony with nature, his survival dependent upon his resourcefulness. For Emile, knowledge would be organized around utility and would focus on learning that had immediate relevance. Emile, for example, would find his way home using knowledge about astronomy. Although Rousseau condemned the early use of books ("I hate books. They only teach us to talk about what we do not know") for Emile, he did use a book's character to illustrate his ideal model of teaching and learning.

Rousseau saw the child as the centre of the educative process. The child's potential was unrealized, and the child needed education to foster growth and learning. Education would therefore be the environment that would allow the child to reach his potential, developing his talents and supporting his individual nature. Education would protect the child from the outside world. Rousseau did not imagine people would take his imaginary situation as a literal model or guide for practical life. He primarily intended the novel to draw attention to his ideas.

## The Uniqueness of Childhood — Origins of Child Study

Rousseau believed that children were not fully understood by the adults who taught them. He pleaded for children to be seen as children. Children were, by nature, different from adults:

*"Nature requires children to be children before they are men."*

*Rousseau valued childhood and emphasized the need for adults to learn more about this unique period of life. How will you continue your study of children after you have finished your formal education?*

*"Nothing is known about childhood. With our false ideas of it the more we do the more we blunder. The wisest people are so much concerned with what grown ups should know that they never consider what children are capable of learning. They keep looking for the man in the child and not thinking of what he is before he becomes a man. It is to this study I have given special thought in the hope that even if my method should prove false, there will always be profit in my observations. I may have gone off wrong in my view of what is needed, but I believe I am right in my view of the person on whom we have to work. Begin then by studying your pupils better; for assuredly you do not know them."*

*"Hold childhood in reverence . . . .Give nature time to work before you take over her business."*

*"Before developing character, we must study it."*

*"A prudent tutor will observe his pupil well before he speaks his first word."*

*"I wish some trustworthy person would give us a treatise on the art of child-study. This art is well worth studying, but neither parents nor teachers have mastered its elements."*

***— Emile***

*In Rousseau's ideology, the teacher's responsibility was clear — to know the nature of each stage. How much instruction in child development do teachers of young children receive? Is programming based on child development or what society wants children to know and do?*

There could be no more eloquent set of statements on the value of observing children and appreciating childhood. Childhood needs to be lived and not rushed. Children need to be children first. Rousseau thus initiated the child study movement.

Rousseau may have been wrong in his method, and even he thought so, as he wrote, *"I may have gone off wrong in my view of what is needed"*; nevertheless, he was sure the CHILD needed to be the centre of the process.

## Stages of Development

*How has your understanding of the stages of child development helped you in your work with children?*

In *Emile*, Rousseau proposed stages children would pass through. Each stage would have distinct characteristics and patterns:

- infancy (Book I) — first five years of life,
- childhood (Book II) — 5 – 12 years of age,
- pre-adolescence (Book III) — 12 – 15 years of age, and
- later adolescence (Book IV).

Rousseau's views of nonrestrictive child rearing in the early years contrasted the prevalent practices in France at the time.[4] Well-to-do families gave up their children to wet nurses, had them dressed in constrictive clothing and allowed little movement.

Today early childhood specialists see the potential problems in young children learning numerals and doing computations long before they understand the logical mathematical nature of "number." Constance Kamii's *Number in Preschool and Kindergarten* is an enlightening book on how children acquire this concept and what teachers can do to support the process.

His stages may not fit our current theoretical conception, but his focus was on knowing that there were stages. Beyond this, Rousseau adamantly felt that a stage should not be seen as preparation for the next stage. This would miss the whole point! In each stage the child was encouraged to live as fully as possible within that period. The best preparation for the next stage was the complete development within the current stage.

## "Negative" Education

Rousseau believed that children were born "good" and "free":

> *". . . everything is good as it comes from the hands of the maker but degenerates when it gets into the hands of man."*
>
> — ***Emile***

---

The Romantic poets shared Rousseau's belief in the purity of childhood. In his poem "Intimations of Immortality from Recollections of Early Childhood," William Wordsworth explored the significance of the intensity of childhood. Wordsworth wrote that in childhood one was closest to the glory of God: "But trailing clouds of glory do we come/From God, who is our home/Heaven lies about us in our infancy!" As we mature, we "fade into the light of common day," and retain only "shadowy recollections" of our former glory.

The Romantics saw and felt things intensely. They loved nature, the wild landscape, and youth. The Romantic movement in literature took place in Europe roughly between 1770 and 1850. Other Romantic poets in Britain included Samuel Taylor Coleridge, John Keats, and Percy Bysshe Shelley. The writings of Jean-Jacques Rousseau are considered to be Romantic in tone, with their assertion of the need to return to nature and primitive innocence.

---

Rousseau believed the aim of education was to preserve this natural goodness of children and develop the child's potential.

[4] A view of the practices can be seen in the novel *Madame Bovary* by Gustave Flaubert.

*Today we have walled communities, shopping malls with many security guards, police and video surveillance in schools. Have we too begun to remove children from what we believe to be a corrupt society?*

Like Plato, Rousseau felt the child needed a good political state in order to develop. But if the state was corrupt, then the child needed to be isolated from the environment.

Rousseau's solution to a corrupt state was "negative education." The child was to be shielded from corruption until he or she developed independence, judgment and understanding, qualities which would enable the child to cope with the distorting environment.

Though called "negative education," Rousseau actually meant it in a positive framework:

> *"I call a negative education one that tends to perfect the organs that are the instruments of knowledge before giving this knowledge directly; and that endeavours to prepare the way for reason by the proper exercise of the senses."*
>
> — ***Emile***

*All early childhood programs still hope to develop qualities, skills and attitudes that will "last" and help children cope with other situations. How can we apply what we know about "resiliency" to the development of programs for children? At what age should children confront "corruption"? Can we protect the self-image of children if they are subjected to "corruption"?*

Since society was constantly changing, Rousseau strongly believed that adults could not predict what children would need to know in the future. Present needs were to be the guide for teaching.

## Education of Girls

Rousseau's views on the education of girls, traditional to the extreme, were explored through the character of Sophie in *Emile*. Book V in *Emile* deals with Sophie's education as she was to become Emile's wife. Her education would revolve around her dual wife and mother role:

> *"The whole education of women ought to be relative to men."*
>
> *"Woman is made to please and to be dominated."*

All the educational principles for Emile were reversed for Sophie — her play would be restricted and interrupted, use of judgment was de-emphasized and extrinsic rewards were used in her education. Unlike Plato's vision, in Rousseau's view, a person's sex did determine the nature of education and his or her place in society:

*Why do you think Rousseau had such a negative and derogatory view of female education?*

> *"Sophie ought to be a woman as Emile is a man. That is to say, she ought to have everything which suits the constitution of her species and her sex in order to fill her place in the physical and moral order. "*
>
> — ***Emile***

Rousseau saw Emile's role as the reverse and complement of Sophie's role. Emile would be the authority in the family, the decision maker, and the patriarch. Rousseau selected very different roles and traits for men and women though he also wanted to make sure Sophie had a childhood full of play, song, dance and the pleasures of being young.

Perhaps Rousseau's lack of positive early experiences and later turbulent relationships with women influenced these ideas; the tenor of the times would also have reflected these views on women. However they were developed, Rousseau's attitudes about educating women do make us contemplate our own views on the roles of women in society and in a family relationship. Rousseau was aware of more egalitarian views of women, but he chose to mirror the existing views around him.

## Freedom

Some people have seen Summerhill School in England as a 20th century example of Rousseau's no interference, "laissez-faire" approach to child rearing and education. A.S. Neill, the founder of Summerhill, was concerned that the school fit the child rather than the child having to adapt to the school. Neill established a school in England based on children's freedom. His ideas may have been based on Rousseau's, but Neill developed his ideas from many other sources as well:

> *"My view is that a child is innately wise and realistic."*
>
> *"We set out to make a school in which we should allow children freedom to be themselves."*
>
> *"Self-regulation implies a belief in the goodness of human nature."*
>
> — **A.S. Neill, *Summerhill***

---

Summerhill School continues its goals and can be contacted:
Summerhill School
Leiston
Suffolk, England
IP16 4HY
World Wide Website http://www.s-hill.demon.co.uk/

A video of the past and present of Summerhill called *The Children of Summerhill* is a 60-minute documentary showing this unique experiment. It is available from
Les Films De L'Interstice
51, Rue Georges Clemenceau
94100 St. Maur des Posses,
France

Another video about Summerhill was made in 1966 by the National Film Board for Canada
VHS # 113C0166072
Sales and Customer Services, D-10
P.O. Box 6100, Station Centre-ville,
Montreal, Quebec
H3C 3H5 Canada
Website: http://www.nfb.ca/e/

There are several books by A.S. Neill on his ideas and the school as well as other descriptive books on Summerhill by such authors as Croall, Snitzer and Hemmings, all listed in the reference section.

Summerhill is still controversial today as shown in two 1999 articles in *The New York Times Magazine-Education Life Supplement,* one by A. Neustatter ("Diary of a Mad Progressive") and the other by A. Riding ("Summerhill Revisited").

---

Rousseau also looked at quality of life and what it meant to live and to enjoy and feel life's experiences:

*"Each generation uses its children for its own purposes, and the purpose of the present generation seems to be to rush and to acquire."*

— Millie Almy, in P. Greenberg, "What wisdom should we take with us as we enter the new century."

> *"The important thing is not to ward off death, but to make sure they really 'live'. Life is not just breathing; it is action, the functioning of organs, senses, faculties, every part of us that gives the consciousness of existence. The man who gets the most out of life is not the one who has lived longest, but one who has felt life most deeply."*
>
> ***— Emile***

## Rousseau's Hurried Child

Rousseau addressed what is now called "the hurried child," one who is forced to grow up too quickly in an ever-changing and stressful society. Early childhood professionals learn to value and appreciate the special nature of childhood and to plan experiences that meet the stages of development instead of hurrying children into academic work or responsibilities earlier than appropriate:

*Rousseau addressed the premature loss of childhood and promoted an appreciation for this stage. How do you see children today being forced to grow up too quickly?*

> *"Your first duty is to be humane. Love childhood. Look with friendly eyes on its games, its pleasures, its amiable dispositions. Which of you does not sometimes look back regretfully on the age when laughter was ever on the lips and the heart free of care? Why steal from the little innocents the enjoyment of a time that passes all too quickly?"*
>
> ***— Emile***

Rousseau warned against premature instruction and stated the need to focus upon children's interests:

> *"Nature wants children to be children before they are men."*
>
> ***— Emile***

## Manners

In another section of *Emile*, Rousseau discusses what we would call manners.

*What are your views of teaching "manners"? How do manners become meaningful and not "empty formulae" or "magic words"?*

Rousseau was concerned with the meaning behind the words children used. He eloquently decried meaningless words used by children to gain power over those around them and get what they want. Rousseau used the phrase "magic word" over two centuries ago, and we still hear adults asking children for the "magic words" of *please* and *thank you.* Rousseau also raised questions about empty politeness, questions that are still relevant today:

> *"Be specially careful not to give the child empty formulae of politeness, to serve as magic words for subjecting surroundings to his will and getting him what he wants at once. For my part I am less afraid of rudeness than of arrogance in Emile, and would rather have him say 'Do this' as a request, than 'Please' as a command. I am not concerned with the words he uses, but with what they imply."*
>
> ***— Emile***

*The concept of empty formulae of politeness can be extended to include I Love You Valentine cards for every child in the class or adult-generated thank you words after a field trip. What are we really trying to teach children about manners and how is this best accomplished? What is courtesy? What is genuine acknowledgment and appreciation? What are developmental perspectives on these expectations? Are there cultural variations? This, like many early childhood issues, helps adults re-evaluate their own views and many aspects of their own lives. It is a vibrant and engaging field in theory and in practice.*

## Methods

Rousseau did not articulate many actual teaching strategies that we might employ today, but he seemed to capture the essence of meaningful childhood experiences. Rousseau knew that children needed to want to learn first:

> *"'What is the good of that?' Henceforth this is the sacred question, the decisive question between him and me, in all situations of our life."*
>
> — ***Emile***

Rousseau pre-dated the progressive educators (see Chapters 7, 8, 10 and 11) in advocating a "here and now" curriculum relevant to children's life experiences. John Dewey was later to talk about giving children something to "do," not something to "learn," and programs today reflect both approaches:

> *"If you proceed on the plan which I have begun to sketch . . . if you no longer carry your pupil's thoughts to a distance and make him ceaselessly wander in strange countries, climates, and ages; if, instead of transferring him to the extremities of the earth and even to the skies, you keep his attention fixed on himself and his immediate surroundings; you will then find him capable of perception, of memory, and even of reason."*
>
> — ***Emile***

Rousseau believed education had to have a purpose that the child could understand. Why learn to measure if there is nothing that a child needs or wants to measure? Children need to see "the good of that" in what would otherwise be too abstract an idea. To learn effectively, at any age and stage of our lives, we need to be able to apply the learning.

Rousseau espoused the need for first-hand, real experiences:

> *"As a general rule — never substitute the symbol for the thing signified, unless it is impossible to show the thing itself; for the child's attention is so taken up with the symbol that he will forget what it signifies."*
>
> — ***Emile***

Children need to learn through discovery:

> *"Let him not be taught science, let him discover it . . . why not begin by showing him the real thing, that he may at least know what you are talking about."*
>
> — ***Emile***

Today's practices that would be considered naturalist would include a focus on interpersonal problem solving skills as well as reading programs based on events and things from the environment.

Emile would learn about plants by exploring them in the garden and geometry by drawing figures and seeing their relationships in space. To develop reading skills, children would learn the use of the skills before learning the mechanics. For example, Emile would receive a note inviting him to a trip on the river, and he would then see the value in learning to read.

*Though Rousseau wrote relatively little about specific methods, he did support first-hand experiences, discovery learning, and physical activity. How are these incorporated into programs for young children that you have seen?*

In geography, children would learn local and immediate knowledge first. Rousseau decried the prevalent approach to geography that created children who could not find their way from Paris to Saint Denis with the rules they learned.

Children were also seen as active beings, needing movement and activity:

> *"Children are always in motion; quiet and meditation are their aversion . . . neither their minds nor their bodies can bear constraint."*
>
> — ***Julie***

## Play

The recurring theme of children learning through play is reflected in Rousseau's writing. He wrote of the child:

*In what ways did Rousseau support child-centred education? What meaning does that phrase have for you now?*

> *"Work and play are all one to him, his games are his work; he knows no difference. He brings to everything the cheerfulness of his interest, the charm of freedom, and he shows the bent of his own mind and the extent of his knowledge."*
>
> — ***Emile***

Rousseau saw no dichotomy between work and play; both would evolve naturally from daily living:

> *"they will only learn what they feel to be of actual and present advantage, either because they like it or because it is of use to them."*
>
> — ***Emile***

The general public continues to question the value of play as a learning mode. Children frequently are not only rushed to learn more and learn earlier but to do what some people consider to be "real work" in a watered-down elementary curriculum during their preschool years. We push for children to acquire skills and knowledge earlier and earlier without heeding Rousseau's advice about allowing children to be children and holding childhood in reverence.

Self-chosen tasks, education without compulsion, ensured learning. Interest and desire would motivate children toward inquiry.

## Teaching Aids

*In Rousseau's time there were cards and dice. Today we have packaged phonics kits or computer programs "guaranteed" to cure all reading problems. In fact they are sometimes even seen as cures for society's general educational problems. What kinds of universal educational remedies have you seen?*

Rousseau discussed the misuse of artificial teaching aids that can occur without the underlying motivation and desire to learn. He spoke of this specifically in the teaching of reading:

> *"People make a great fuss about discovering the best way to teach children to read. They invent bureaux and cards, they turn the nursery into a printer's shop. Locke would have them taught to read by means of dice . . . There is a better way than any of those and one which is generally overlooked — it consists in the desire to learn. Arouse this desire in your scholar and have done with your bureaux and your dice — any method will serve."*
>
> ***— Emile***

## The Natural Child

The philosopher Immanuel Kant called *Emile* "the teacher's gospel," and Schiller, the poet, called Rousseau the "new Socrates." Rousseau inspired the whole future of education.

**Rousseau advocated a return to nature and a naturalistic approach to raising and educating children. (Used with permission of Bibliotheque Nationale Suisse-Bern.)**

Rousseau was an ardent proponent of "naturalism," which to him meant abandoning society's artificiality and pretense. A naturalistic education would permit growth without undue restrictions.

Rousseau focused on what the child was able to learn. He was the forerunner of all child-centred education, believing that the child was naturally good and at the centre of the curriculum. He addressed individual differences, motivation, stages, learning styles — all of which are equally important to our current understanding of children.

Years later, the American physicist Albert Einstein echoed Rousseau's call for freedom in children's learning:

*"It is in fact nothing short of a miracle that the modern methods of instruction have not yet entirely strangled the holy curiosity of inquiry, for this delicate little plant, aside from stimulation, stands mostly in need of freedom: without this it goes to rack and ruin without fail."*

In 1967 Marshall McLuhan, a Canadian communication theorist who focused on the effects of mass media on thought and behaviour, issued a similar appeal for natural education:

> *"Education in the formal sense will go. Classrooms are already obsolete.*
>
> *The planet itself is now a little school. It's like being back to primitive times again. Then nature was education. You learned from nature around you. In this audio-tactile world it's happening again — only this time it won't be haphazard."*
>
> — ***The London Sunday Times Weekly Review,* August 13, 1967**

Rousseau re-focused education from what children should know to what children were capable of learning. He was central in developing the concept of "childhood" as a specific period.

---

A school run by Marietta Johnson in Fairhope, Alabama followed "organic education" methods, and John Dewey saw it as a living embodiment of Rousseau's educational principles. In John and Evelyn Dewey's book, *Schools of Tomorrow*, John Dewey states: "Her main underlying principle is Rousseau's central idea; namely: The child is best prepared for life as an adult by experiencing in childhood what has meaning to him as a child: and, further, the child has a right to enjoy his childhood." The Marietta Johnson School of Organic Education was featured more recently in Semel and Sadovnik's *"Schools of Tomorrow," Schools of Today.*

More information and photos of the Marietta Johnson School of Organic Education can be seen in chapter 7 on John Dewey.

---

*Special Library Collection*
*University of Wisconsin-Madison*
*Memorial Library*
*728 State Street*
*Madison, Wisconsin 53706*
*U.S.A.*

The New Educators *looks at the lives and ideas of Rousseau, Locke, Wollstonecraft and Froebel. It is available from:*
*Insight Media*
*2162 Broadway*
*New York, New York 10024-0621*
*U.S.A.*

## Jean-Jacques Rousseau — References for Further Study


Archer, R. L. (Ed.). (1964). *Jean Jacques Rousseau: His educational theories selected from Emile, Julie and other writings*. Woodbury, NY: Barron's Educational Series.

Babbitt, I. (1979). *Rousseau and romanticism*. Boston, MA: Houghton Mifflin.

Bloom, H. (1988). The education of democratic man: Emile. In H. Bloom (Ed.), *Jean-Jacques Rousseau*. New York: Chelsea House Publishers.

Boyd, W. (Selected and translated). (1962). *The minor educational writings of Jean-Jacques Rousseau*. New York: Teachers College, Columbia University.

Boyd, W. (Selected, translated and interpreted). (1964). *Emile for today*. London: Heinemann.

Clayton, L. (Ed.). (1969). *Rousseau*. London: Collier-MacMillan.

Cohen, B. (1969). *Educational thought*. London: Macmillan.

Cranston, M. (1983). *Jean-Jacques: The early life and work of Jean-Jacques Rousseau. 1712-1754*. London: Allen Lane.

Cranston, M. (1991). *The noble savage: Jean-Jacques Rousseau 1754-1762*. Chicago: The University of Chicago Press.

Croall, J. (1983). *Neill of Summerhill: The permanent rebel*. London: Routledge & Kegan Paul.

Dewey, J., & Dewey, E. (1915). *Schools of tomorrow*. New York: E. P. Dutton.

Green, F. C. (1955). *Jean-Jacques Rousseau: A critical study of his life and writings*. New York: Barnes & Noble.

Greenberg, P. (2000). What wisdom should we take with us as we enter the new century: An interview with Millie Almy. *Young Children, 55* (1), 6 – 10.

Grimsley, R. (1983). *Jean-Jacques Rousseau*. Brighton, England: Harvester Press.

Hemmings, R. (1972). *Children's freedom: A.S. Neill and the evolution of the Summerhill idea*. New York: Schocken Books.

Hemmings, R. (1972). *Fifty years of freedom: A study of the development of the ideas of A.S. Neill*. London: Allen and Unwin.

Hendel, C. W. (1937). *Citizen of Geneva: Selections from the letters of Jean-Jacques Rousseau*. New York: Oxford University Press.

Jimack, P. D. (Ed). (1993). *Jean-Jacques Rousseau: Emile* (B. Foxley, Trans.). London: J.M. Dent.

Joker or genius — or both. (1967, August 13). *Sunday Times Weekly Review*.

Kafker, F. (1988). *The encyclopedists as individuals: A biographical dictionary of the authors of the encyclopedia*. Oxford, England: The Voltaire Foundation.

Kamii, C. (1982). *Number in preschool and kindergarten: Educational implication of Piaget's theory*. Washington, DC: National Association for the Education of Young Children.

Keehane, M. (1970, May). A.S. Neill: Latter day Dewey? *Elementary School Journal*, 70, 401-410.

Kessen, W. (1978). Rousseau's children. *Daedalus, 107* (3), 13 – 26.

Lascarides, V.C. & Hinitz, B. (2000). *History of Early Childhood Education*. New York: Falmer Press.

Leigh, R. A. (arranged, with introduction and notes). (1978). *Jean-Jacques Rousseau 1712-1778*. Catalogue of an exhibition at Cambridge University Library, 1978. Cambridge, England: Cambridge University Library.

Martin, J. R. (1985). *Reclaiming a conversation: The ideal of educated woman*. New Haven, CT: Yale University Press.

Neill, A. S. (1960). *Summerhill: A radical approach to child rearing*. New York: Hart Publishing.

Neill, A. S. (1970). *Summerhill: For and against*. New York: Hart Publishing.

Neill, A. S. (1972). *Neill! Neill! Orange peel!: An autobiography*. New York: Hart Publishing.

Neill, A. S. (1983). (Foreword by Z. Neill). (J. Croall, Ed). *All the best, Neill: Letters from Summerhill*. London: A. Deutsch.

Neustatter, A. (1999, November 7). *Diary of a mad progressive*. New York Times. Education Life Supplement.

Peltzman, B. R. (1998). *Pioneers of early childhood education: A bio-bibliographical guide*. Westport, CT: Greenwood Press.

Riding, A. (1999, November 7). Summerhill revisited. *New York Times. Education Life Supplement.*

Rolland, R. (1946). *The living thoughts of Rousseau*. London: Cassell and Company.

Roosevelt, G. G. (1990). *Reading Rousseau in the nuclear age*. Philadelphia, PA: Temple University Press.

Rousseau, J. J., & Blair, L. (Trans.). (1974). *The essential Rousseau: The social contract, Discourse on the origin of inequality, Discourse on the arts and sciences, The creed of a Savoyard priest*. New York: New American Library.

Rousseau, J. J. (1945). *The confessions of Jean-Jacques Rousseau*. New York: Modern Library.

Rousseau, J. J. (1988). *The social contract*. Buffalo, NY: Prometheus Books.

Rousseau, J. J. (1967). *Discourse on the origin of inequality*. New York: Washington Square Books.

Scruton, R. (1998). Rousseau & the origins of liberalism. *The New Criterion*, 17 (2), 5 – 17.

Semel, S., & Sadovnik, A. (Eds.). (1999). *"Schools of tomorrow," Schools of today: What happened to progressive education*. New York: Peter Lang.

Snitzer, H. (1964). *Living at Summerhill*. New York: Collier Books.

Walmsley, J. (1969). *Neill & Summerhill: A man and his work*. Baltimore, MD: Penguin Books.

Walter, S. (1996). The 'flawed parent': A reconsideration of Rousseau's Emile and its significance for radical education in the United States. *British Journal of Educational Studies, 44* (3), 260-274.

# Chapter 4 — *Johann Heinrich Pestalozzi*

**1746 – 1827**

*"Learning is not worth a penny when courage and joy are lost along the way."*

***— The Education of Man: Aphorisms***

*"This interest in study is the first thing which a teacher . . . should endeavour to excite and keep alive . . . I would go so far as to lay it down for a rule, that whenever children are inattentive, and apparently take no interest in a lesson, the teacher should always first look to himself for the reason."*

***— Letters to Greaves***

Johann Heinrich Pestalozzi was born in Zurich, Switzerland in 1746 of middle-class Protestant parents of Italian origin. They had fled Italy because of religious persecution and found sanctuary in Zurich. His father was a well-respected physician and surgeon. Zurich, on the shore of Lake Zurich with the Alps in the background, was the cultural centre of northern Switzerland. His parents had five children, two dying early in life.

**Zurich, birthplace of Pestalozzi. Engraving by F. Hegi of Zurich, Switzerland about 1810. (Used with permission of Zentralbibliothek, Zurich.)**

When Heinrich was only five, his father, Johann Baptist Pestalozzi, died at age 33. He left his family in dire financial circumstances. His mother, Susanna Hotz, devastated by her multiple losses, relied on a family servant, Barbara Schmid (known as Babeli) to help her raise her three remaining children (Johann Baptiste, Anna Barbara and Johann Heinrich). Babeli prevented the children from having much peer contact, and this isolation affected young Pestalozzi tremendously. He had a childhood full of dreams and fantasies and was physically frail and weak. Teased by other children, he was called a name which can be translated as "Henry Oddity from Foolville." In the midst of these problems, the two women did provide a loving and secure childhood for Pestalozzi.

Heinrich's only source of masculine influence was his grandfather, Andreas Pestalozzi, who was a pastor in a rural church in the village Hoengg, an hour's walk from Zurich. As a child during summer holidays, Pestalozzi went with his grandfather on his pastoral rounds and saw the plight of poor farmers who were victimized by absentee landlords. He questioned the discrepancy between the lives of the rich and the lives of the poor. Feeling immense sympathy for the situation of the poor, he vowed to become a minister like his grandfather.

## The Impact of Early Experiences

Pestalozzi received a conventional school education, but three experiences in schools affected his future career aspirations:

1) In the college preparatory Latin school, he was an excellent pupil although he was often distracted if his interest was not excited. He became a favourite of the teachers and was flattered to be chosen to conduct a religious service in Latin. In the middle of the service, he began laughing when he considered the gap between the solemn Latin words of the sermon and the everyday words of youth in the streets. The comical disparity of these two sets of words ended both the somber religious service and his ambition to enter the ministry.

*Several childhood/school experiences affected Pestalozzi's choice of profession. How did you choose early childhood as a field of study?*

2) At another time in school, a small earthquake caused everyone to rush out of the building. The teachers preceded the students. Once again Pestalozzi saw the ludicrous contrast between the classroom study of the heroic deeds of the Greeks and Romans and the very unheroic actions of his teachers. For Pestalozzi, valid teaching needed "truth in its presentation." Actions spoke more strongly than words.
3) The third incident related to his lifelong passion for fighting oppression. From an upper story window at school, he saw a child of a local farmer cornered by a group of rowdy city youths. He leaped from the window to help the other child. As it was a long fall, he would have broken his legs, but he landed on one of the attackers. Later in his life, his own ideas and actions were publicly attacked by many, and others came to support him. He reflected then on this childhood experience: "What can a man do more for a friend than leave a quiet, secure and comfortable life and leap into an insecure, pressing and dangerous situation for him?"

## Helvetic Society

After high school, Pestalozzi entered the Collegium Humanitatis, a two-year humanities program for students going into professions such as law, theology or medicine. At 17 he went on to the Collegium Carolinum in Zurich, a school started in the 8th century by Charlemagne. Here Pestalozzi studied philosophy and philology (language) and became associated with Johann Jakob Bodmer, a critic and thinker who combined intellectualism and plain living. Bodmer, a professor of history, had founded the Helvetic Society, which Pestalozzi joined. It was a youth movement of liberal political ideas intended to elevate Swiss morality through discussions instead of revolution. Urging social reform, the Helvetic Society published a weekly journal called *The Monitor,* which attacked some of the political abuses and corruption in Zurich. The journal was suppressed, and Pestalozzi and other contributors were briefly jailed.

After rejecting the ministry as a career, Pestalozzi had decided to enter law to pursue his championing of the poor, but because of his affiliation with the Helvetic Society, he was seen as a dangerous radical and was denied admission to the faculty of law. Pestalozzi left formal studies at this point.

## Agricultural Endeavours

Pestalozzi's literary and intellectual mentor was Jean-Jacques Rousseau. Pestalozzi had obtained Rousseau's banned book *Emile* and called it his "dream book":

> *"The principle of liberty revived by Rousseau and presented under an ideal form, fortified the desire in my heart to find a larger field of action in which I would be able to be of use to the people."*
>
> — ***Swan Song***

In a somewhat similar way, people today still try to find the answer to social problems by advocating a return to a simpler life or to the revitalization of the traditional family structure.

Impressed by Rousseau's writings about returning to nature, Pestalozzi then turned to agriculture. He went to an experimental farm near Berne to train in scientific farming. He lived with Johann Tschiffeli, an agronomist who introduced madder, a dye plant, into Switzerland. Rousseau believed that working the soil would restore the ideal of the family farm, and morals would then be returned to society.

## Fatherhood and Education

Pestalozzi borrowed money to buy 60 acres of farm land near the village of Birr to grow madder and cotton. In 1769 he married Anna Schulthess, a childhood friend who came from a wealthy Zurich family that opposed her marriage to a farmer, perceived to be someone of a lower class. Anna was well educated, capable and eight years older than Pestalozzi. They had only one child, whom they named Jean-Jacques, after Rousseau, though they called him Jacobli.

**Aschmann engraving of Neuhof – 1780. Pestalozzi began his first experiment in education and agriculture in Neuhof. (Used with permission of Zentralbibliothek, Zurich.)**

In 1771, Pestalozzi settled with his wife and newborn son in Neuhof ("new farm") near Zurich and tried again to farm. Unfortunately, Pestalozzi had little business sense and even less knowledge of the challenging hill farming.

In 1774, Pestalozzi added a spinning mill and a school for poor children to Neuhof. The school, called the Neuhof Institute, combined work, manual training and learning. The children also received clothing and food. The school drained Pestalozzi's financial resources, and Pestalozzi's goal of teaching was thwarted when the school was forced to close in 1779. Only financial help from friends and Anna's family prevented Pestalozzi from becoming homeless. Despite the "failure," he had learned a great deal about education and poverty and began to record his ideas.

During this period Pestalozzi also focused his attention on educating his son, Jacobli. He was a weak child who suffered illnesses throughout his life. Despite the difficulties, Pestalozzi had high hopes for him and attempted to apply the natural educational ideas from Rousseau's *Emile* to his upbringing. When Jacobli was three, Pestalozzi kept a diary of his educational progress:

In Pestalozzi's words and beliefs, you can see the strong effect of Rousseau. Jean Piaget later used the observations of his own children to develop his theories of development.

> January 27, 1774
> *"I showed him the water which ran rapidly down the slope of the hill. He was delighted with this. As we went down the hill he said, 'Look papa, the water comes too, it comes from above, and it always goes lower.' We followed the course of the water and I repeated to him several times 'the water flows from the top to the bottom of the mountain.'"*
>
> February 19, 1774
> *"Whatever you can teach him from the nature of things themselves, do not teach him by words. Leave him to himself to see, hear, find, stumble, rise again and be mistaken. Give no words when action or deed is possible. What he can do for himself let him do. Let him be always occupied, ever active, and let the time when you do not worry him be by far the greatest part of his childhood. You will come to learn that nature teaches him better than men."*
>
> **— How Father Pestalozzi Instructed His Three and a Half Year Old Son quoted in De Guimps, *Pestalozzi: His Life and Work***

*Pestalozzi learned from observing the growth of his own son. What have you learned through observation of a child that has aided your program or knowledge of that child?*

Though Pestalozzi still espoused "natural education," this experience with his son raised some serious questions about the methods Rousseau had articulated. According to some sources, Jacobli was unable to read or write at age 11. Though this inability may have been affected by Jacobli's illnesses,[1] Pestalozzi sought better ways to address teaching principles. Pestalozzi's son eventually was apprenticed to a merchant, married and had several children. His lifelong physical ailments caused his death at the age of 30.

Another ongoing problem Pestalozzi had with running a school was his inexperience with poverty. His only direct contact with poverty had been as a child when he visited the poor with his grandfather. Parents and children of the school were suspicious of Pestalozzi and felt he was using them for his own benefit. But the experience with the school prompted him to clarify his educational ideas.

*If you have not grown up in poverty, what are ways you can begin to understand it and help low-income families?*

Poverty is a complex social condition and cannot be changed with simple solutions by people who know little of its causes or solutions. Many people today help by serving Christmas dinner in inner-city agencies or giving to the food bank. Though helpful in the immediate moment, these kinds of assistance do not create long-term change or address causes of poverty. Creating fundamental change means understanding the factors that create situations of poverty and changing the conditions that cause it.

[1] He likely had epilepsy.

## Writings of a Literary Period

In the next period of his life, Pestalozzi began to write rather than work directly with children, and he published a number of works on educational practice, including the following essays:

- "How Father Pestalozzi Instructed His Three and a Half Year Old Son"(1774)
- "Essays on the Education of the Children of the Poor" (1775 – 1778)
- "The Evening Hour of a Hermit" (1775 – 1778) (shows strong influence of Rousseau).

B.F. Skinner is a 20th century example of a theorist who wrote his behaviourist ideas in novel form with *Walden Two.*

None of these writings attracted attention to his ideas. Remembering the impact of *Emile* as a novel, Pestalozzi wrote *Leonard and Gertrude* in 1781. Short of money to buy paper, Pestalozzi wrote the book on the blank pages of an old accounting book. Although Pestalozzi had not intended his book to be popular entertainment, people read it as a romantic story and were exposed to Pestalozzi's idea that social regeneration is possible through education. The book won a gold medal from the Berne Economic Society.

*Leonard and Gertrude* tells of a fictional village of Bonnel, modeled after the one Pestalozzi's grandfather lived in. The bailiff Hummel, a local administrator who also owns the village tavern and controls the life of Bonnel through lies, deceit, fear and bribery, exploits the villagers. A cotton-spinning mill brings the villagers new money, but they are naïve in terms of their roles as workers and consumers.

In *Leonard and Gertrude*, Pestalozzi revealed in a more naïve but no less impassioned way the power imbalances that Paulo Freire addressed in the *Pedagogy of the Oppressed* (1970). Freire was a Brazilian educator who focused on literacy and power in a community context. He also wrote *The Politics of Education: Culture, Power and Liberation* (1985).

Gertrude is the mother figure who initiates the regeneration of the village. She enlists the help of Arner, who is the absentee landlord, and the pastor and the schoolmaster support Gertrude in her appeals to the aristocrat. It is clear that Pestalozzi retained faith in the enlightened paternalism of the landed aristocracy. The book's model of social reform and education is in the home of Gertrude, who is the perfect working-class mother and housewife. She is the first teacher of the children and guides them through use of their senses and observation of nature. She also helps them with work activities to assist the family's economic well-being. The school, in the story, functions as the moral, educational and vocational heart of the village.

The novel outlines the fundamental doctrines of Pestalozzi's beliefs about education:

- The distorted environment creates sources of evil.
- Humans may be poor and uneducated but they are capable of regeneration.
- The peaceful process of education is the true path to social reform.
- Human development begins in the home circle with the mother.
- Natural education fosters the development of a person's natural moral, intellectual, and physical powers.
- Genuine education will create economically independent individuals.

**Pestalozzi in Stanz. Pestalozzi worked at an orphanage and school in Stanz, improving and developing his methods. (Used with permission of Bibliotheque Nationale Suisse-Bern.)**

A former student described in vivid terms the kindly image he saw in Pestalozzi:

"Imagine my children, a very ugly man, with rough bristling hair, his face scarred with small pox and covered with freckles, a pointed, untidy beard, no neck-tie, ill-fitting trousers, stockings down, and enormous shoes; add to this a breathless, shuffling gait, eyes either large and flashing or half-closed as though turned within, features expressing either a profound sadness or the most peaceful happiness, speech slow and musical, now thundering and hurried, and you will have some ideas of the man we called 'Father Pestalozzi'"

**— quoted in J.A. Green, *The Educational Ideas of Pestalozzi***

*Leonard and Gertrude* is the most readable of Pestalozzi's books, but others focused on education as well. *Christopher and Elizabeth* (1782) is a series of dialogues in which Christopher's family discusses the ideas in *Leonard and Gertrude.* In 1787 Pestalozzi wrote *Illustrations For My ABC Book* (later called *Fables For My ABC*), which were short epilogues to *Leonard and Gertrude. Researches into the Course of Nature in the Development of the Human Race* (1797) was a treatise that was probably the first sociology of education ever written. *How Gertrude Teaches Her Children* (1801), a sequel to *Leonard and Gertrude,* is a series of letters to his editor about natural education. *Swan Song* (1826) was his last book, and in it he continued to refine and present his educational ideas.

From 1782 – 1783 he published his own newspaper, *Swiss News,* writing articles about education, cures for poverty and home life. The readership for the newspaper was too small, so Pestalozzi discontinued its publication. Later he became editor of *The Popular Swiss Gazette,* published by the Helvetian Republic. It lasted only 19 issues, largely because it did not support the new government.

Pestalozzi's involvement with writing for news publications ended soon after because he did not want to remain, as he described it, a "mere writer."

## Stanz — A Return to Educational Practice

In 1799 Pestalozzi returned to teaching, pleased to work directly with children again. Remaining in Switzerland, he was appointed headmaster of an orphanage and school of 80 children in Stanz, at the tip of Lake Lucerne. All the children were poor and devastated by the effects of war. The French Revolution had spread to Switzerland, and the country was embroiled in clashes between revolutionaries and the French and the Swiss governments. French soldiers had burned Stanz, killing all the adults.

Pestalozzi's goals remained the same as in his Neuhof experiment, but he set out to improve his methods. Funds were limited, and the local people were hostile to Pestalozzi's work in educating the poor. However, he had the freedom to plan the entire program. Seeing himself as a "father figure," Pestalozzi wanted to establish an atmosphere of calm and emotional security for the children in his care. He felt that once the children felt secure, he could effectively employ his educational strategies.

Pestalozzi expressed his excitement in seeing children enjoy learning and sense their own power:

> *"They felt their own power, and the tediousness of the ordinary school tone vanished like a ghost. They wished, — tried, — persevered, — succeeded, and they laughed. Their tone was not that of learners, it was the tone of unknown powers roused from sleep."*
>
> **— *How Gertrude Teaches Her Children***

A video, *Johann Heinrich Pestalozzi*, is available in English from:

Centre de Documentation et de Recherche Pestalozzi
Case postale 138
CH 1400
Yverdon-Les-Bains
Switzerland

*Or from:*

Pestalozzianum Verlag
Zurich
Beckenhofstr.35
8035 Zurich
Switzerland

Unfortunately the school closed abruptly when the French were defeated by the Austrians and the school building was secured for military hospital uses. The local officials were uneasy about the kind of education that was emerging. Pestalozzi soon began to realize the immensity of the task he had proposed in educating children of poverty. There was no magic formula.

## Burgdorf

Later in 1799, the Helvetian government approached Pestalozzi to work at a vernacular school at Burgdorf, a town about 70 kilometres south-west of Zurich. This was another school for poor children of agricultural and industrial workers. Pestalozzi was to be the teaching assistant to a headmaster, Samuel Dysli, who was also the town cobbler. The two disagreed on teaching methods, and Pestalozzi disapproved of the focus on memorization and recitation without understanding. He was dismissed after Dysli turned the parents against him.

Friends obtained another position for him in a school for children from five to eight years of age. Pestalozzi had the freedom to utilize his teaching ideas and found the younger age group much more appropriate for his methods. The School Commission of Burgdorf examined the children and wrote a favourable report that encouraged Pestalozzi to continue.

During this period, his supporters (The Society of Friends of Education) raised funds to set up a school based solely on his ideas, and it was set up in the castle Burgdorf. Intended as a centre for educational research, teacher training and materials preparation, the school opened in 1801. Pestalozzi focused on education which would guide children toward the best realization of themselves and of aspects of the world. It ran for the next three-and-a-half years until the demise of the Helvetian government. He had several young men as teaching assistants including Joseph Neef (see chapter 6 for a description of his work with Owen), Anton Gruner (who worked with Froebel; see chapter 5), and Hermann Krusi.

## Yverdon

Forced to move on, Pestalozzi tried several other schools including one at Munchenbuchsee and finally opened one in the castle Yverdon on Lake Neuchatel in 1804. Yverdon is midway between Bern and Geneva. The local municipality supported his initiative, and the area allowed for much diversity of thinking and beliefs. It was here at Yverdon that Pestalozzi achieved his greatest successes. He became well-known throughout Europe and North America. People from around the world came to see his ideas in action and to study with him. Friederich Froebel (see Chapter 5) came as a visitor in 1805 and a teaching assistant in 1808. The social reformer Robert Owen (see chapter 6) and Andrew Bell, educator with the monitorial system (older children educating younger ones), also came to observe.

**Yverdon Castle. Pestalozzi set up his most successful schools at The Castle Yverdon on Lake Neuchatel in Switzerland. (Used with permission of Centre de Documentation et de Recherche Pestalozzi in Yverdon-les-Bains.)**

**Yverdon in 1810. Hegi engraving. (Used with permission of Zentralbibliothek, Zurich.)**

Roger de Guimps, a student for nine years at the Institute, gave a full account in *Pestalozzi: His Life and Work.* He described the curriculum and schedule in this account:

| | |
|---|---|
| *"6:00 a.m.* | *First Lesson of the Day* |
| *7:00* | *Morning Bath and Breakfast of Soup* |
| *8:00* | *Lessons Resumed* |
| *10:00* | *Rest Period with a Light Snack of Fruit or Bread* |
| *12 noon* | *Recreation and Games* |
| *1:00 p.m.* | *Dinner of Soup, Meat, Vegetables* |
| *1:30 – 4:30* | *Lessons Resumed* |
| *4:30 – 6:00* | *Collation, an informal meal, followed by Recreation* |
| *6:00 – 7:00* | *Lessons* |
| *7:00 – 8:00* | *Free Time* |
| *8:00* | *Supper"* |

The castle at Yverdon still stands as it did in Pestalozzi's time.

**The Castle Yverdon today. (Used with permission of Centre de Documentation et de Recherche Pestalozzi in Yverdon-les-Bains.)**

Teachers trained by Pestalozzi and his followers established schools that used his methods throughout Europe.

Bâtiment qui abrita l'Institut des jeunes filles créé à Yverdon en 1806 par H. Pestalozzi.
(Dessin de A. Bioley, Yverdon, 1986)

**Institute for Girls. Pestalozzi set up four schools for children in Yverdon. This illustration shows the Institute for Girls in nearby Clindy. (Courtesy of Centre de Documentation et de Recherche Pestalozzi in Yverdon-les-Bains.)**

**Pestalozzi with Grandson. By Schoner in 1805. (Used with permission of Zentralbibliothek, Zurich.)**

Eventually there were four schools at Yverdon: the main one for boys from 7 – 15 years, a Girls' Institute, the first Swiss school for children who were deaf, and a co-educational school for poor children in Clindy.

School was seen as a chapter in real life; the following describes from a student's point of view a chapter (lesson) in geography taught in the open air:

> *"They began by turning our steps to an out-of-the way valley near Yverdon, through which the Buron flows. This valley we had to look at as a whole, and in its different parts, until we had a correct and complete impression of it. Then we were told, each one, to dig out a certain quantity of the clay, which was embedded in layers on one side of the valley, and with this we filled large sheets of paper, brought with us for the purpose . . . . When we got back to school . . . each child had to build with the clay . . . a model of the valley where we had just made our observations. . . . Then, and only then, did we turn to the map, which we had only now gained the power of correctly interpreting."*
>
> **— Green, *The Educational Ideas of Pestalozzi***

Pestalozzi remained at Yverdon for 20 years.

The school eventually closed in 1825 due to Pestalozzi's disagreements with teaching assistants, philosophical differences even among the assistants, lack of funds and his poor administrative skills.

## Return to Neuhof

Returning to Neuhof in 1825 at 80 years of age, Pestalozzi continued to write and remain involved in many activities. One of his former students visited him in 1825 and described him:

> *"I had not seen him for thirteen years, and found him . . . on the whole very little changed. He was still active and strong, simple and open; his face still wore the same kindly, plaintive expression; his zeal for human happiness, and especially for the education of poor and little children, was as keen as thirteen years before."*
>
> — **quoted in Holman, *Pestalozzi***

He lived to see the birth of his great grandson, Karl Pestalozzi, who was his last direct descendent.

Pestalozzi died in February 1827. *Swan Song*, his final statement on education, maintained that education must conform to the order of nature to cultivate human capacities. His tomb read:

***Here lies Heinrich Pestalozzi***
***Born in Zurich on the 12th day of January, 1746,***
***Died at Brugg on 17th February, 1827.***
***Saviour of the poor at Neuhof,***
***Preacher to the people in Leonard and Gertrude,***
***Father of the Fatherless in Stanz,***
***Founder of the new elementary school at Burgdorf***
***And Munchenbuchsee,***
***Educator of humanity in Yverdon.***
***Man, Christian, Citizen.***
***Everything for others, nothing for himself.***
***Blessings be on his name.***

**This statue of Pestalozzi was erected in 1890 in Yverdon by Roger de Guimps, a pupil of Pestalozzi. The statue was created by Charles Alfred Lanz, a sculptor from Paris, France. (Used with permission of Bibliotheque Nationale Suisse-Bern.)**

A monument of Pestalozzi with two children, created by Charles Alfred Lanz in 1890, stands in Yverdon. It is inscribed

**Tout pour les autres, pour lui rien**
*(All for others, for himself, nothing).*

## Educational Laws

Pestalozzi articulated the Laws of Human Unfolding which stated that individuals developed according to certain definite laws. These would not be considered theories but more principles or guidelines. They arose from a study of both the child and the environment.

The teacher must know the laws of development to shape the educational system to fit the laws. We continually raise the question of schools reflecting the current state of child development knowledge or research in the field of early childhood.

The laws or principles that Pestalozzi established guided his educational practice. Pestalozzi believed the following:

*Pestalozzi supported the development of the* hand, head and heart *in an integrated fashion. How is this approach supported by current psychological theory?*

1. Children were made up of the **hand, heart and head**. The hand represented the body; the heart was a combination of feelings, morals and interpersonal relations; the head was the mind or intellect. These three had to remain integrated and united, with the heart as the unifying element. Pestalozzi introduced the concept of the "whole child" long before contemporary textbooks or 20th-century theorists:

   *"Only that which affects man as an indissoluble unit is educative . . . it must reach his hand and his heart as well as his head."*

   ***— Swan Song***

*Today post-secondary education (and even secondary education) often looks at jobs as the end product. Training for a job or going to university for a job is stressed rather than the general education of thinking people to become citizens in society. What do you think of this focus?*

2. Vocational skills were important, but education of fundamental capacities of children had to have priority.
3. Pestalozzi believed one may know and not do. Children could not simply be fed the truths that others discovered or constructed. They needed to discover the ideas and truths themselves through self-activity:

   *"It is good to make a child read, and write, and learn, and repeat — but it is still better to make a child think. The mode of doing this is not by any means to talk much to a child, but to enter into conversation with a child . . . to question the child about it, and to let him find out, and correct the answers."*

   ***— Letters to Greaves***

---

Current constructivist theory supports this third law (principle) of Pestalozzi in its emphasis on the goal of children learning to construct their thinking and understanding of concepts in interaction with experiences in the world. The child organizes, reorganizes and structures experiences in accordance with current schemes of thinking. These schemes change as the person interacts with both the social and physical world. The child's activity is critical in constructing knowledge.

---

Punishment, rewards and rivalry certainly still remain embedded in many of our current educational programs, and student discipline is not always seen in a contextual basis looking at causes and situational factors.

4. Pestalozzi maintained that nature strives to grow, to develop and to unfold. The innate impulses of the child developed best when they were ready to unfold, and therefore education had to wait until the child was ready. How would a teacher know when the child was ready? By understanding the child! This addresses the current issue of what entails readiness and what readiness programs look like in practice.
5. Learning had to be stimulated by the interest and motivation of the child. **Punishment, fear, rewards and/or rivalry** were external and therefore dangerous to real learning. Teachers needed to look first at the system if they saw behavioural problems with children. Positive student behaviour would be a natural outgrowth when children were involved in engaging activities that suited their needs.
6. Since education was to follow the order of nature, the teacher would be like a gardener. Education was the art of helping a child to unfold. The teacher (gardener) would contribute nothing of the power of growth, which was inside the child, but the teacher had to know the laws of development to foster growth:

   *"But what is the true type of education? It is like the art of the gardener under whose care a thousand trees blossom and grow. He contributes nothing to their actual growth; the principle of growth lies in the trees themselves."*

   ***— Address to My House***

7. Pestalozzi maintained that since true education made no sudden leaps, all instruction had to be suited to the gradual and consistent route to learning.
8. Learning at each stage had to be completed before moving on to the next stage. The next stage depended on the child accomplishing the developmental tasks of the current stage. Pestalozzi saw tremendous need for children to master skills and knowledge before going on to the next stage.

**Pestalozzi in 1818. (Courtesy of Centre de Documentation et de Recherche Pestalozzi in Yverdon-les-Bains.)**

Later in the 20th century, Jean Piaget would reveal the psychological basis for this guideline, and the National Association for the Education of Young Children would publish its *Developmentally Appropriate Practice*. Pestalozzi foreshadowed the psychological research base for this.

## Object Lessons

Pestalozzi was one of the first theorists to develop instructional methods that could be used directly in the classroom. Pestalozzi believed the basis of knowledge was *Anschauung.* A difficult word to translate, it roughly means "first impressions of objects" or "intuition." He believed that knowledge came through the senses, and he began to study ways sense impressions could be organized to facilitate learning. This thinking led to his work with **object lessons**, which became a central part of his contribution to education. He believed that the best way to learn many concepts was through manipulative experiences, such as counting, measuring, and touching. Children needed to be exposed to objects that had the essential characteristics of the class to which the objects belonged. The method had a three-step process for teaching:

1. Expose the child to the object.
2. The child will recognize the appearance, form, structure and outline of the object.
3. The name of the object will be learned.

*Do you use modifications of Pestalozzi's object lessons in your work with children? In what ways?*

> *"The infant mind should be acted upon by illustrations taken from reality . . . we ought to teach by things more than by words."*
>
> — ***Letters to Greaves,*** **quoted in Green,** ***The Educational Ideas of Pestalozzi***

While Comenius added pictures and illustrations to children's learning, Pestalozzi added direct contact with real objects, manipulatives, as the central focus.

---

The method is somewhat different but also similar to how we would now look at teaching the nature of an apple, for example. Children would need to see an apple in many forms. Different types, colours, and uses would all be explored first-hand. The understanding of what really makes an apple would depend on exposure to and touching of many apples in many forms and varieties from dried apples to applesauce, from Yellow Delicious to Gala. What makes an apple an apple? What defines it? It must be seen in many forms to understand the essence of its characteristics. The word "apple" is merely a label and learned by rote learning, not through experience with the object. The same principle of learning, the nature of an apple or other object is used in mathematics and is called the multi-embodiment principle. It is used to learn the nature of shapes for example. It is not the size or colour of a triangle but the three straight sides forming an enclosed figure that define it. Children must see many triangles of many types to understand the essence of triangle.

---

Pestalozzi saw that knowledge inherent in the natural world would be gained through direct observation with the senses:

> *"Any child who has learned to look carefully at water at rest and in motion, or its various forms — dew, rain, mist, steam, hail, snow, etc. — and then again has learned to observe its various effects on other bodies, can express himself with clearness concerning them, has already got the foundations of the physicist's way of looking at things."*
>
> — ***Swan Song***

## Mathematics Teaching

Pestalozzi believed that the teaching of mathematics must start with real objects, moving to substitute objects (fingers, pebbles, dots) and finally to abstract numbers.

Pestalozzi insisted that children learn arithmetic by counting concrete objects, such as steps, threads in weaving, or panes in a window, to understand what number really meant. He devised mathematical boards that had squares where dots or lines could be added to represent units up to 100. Using them, children would gain a better understanding of digits and addition.

**Mathematics and Art Teaching. Pestalozzi is shown at Stanz helping children to learn both mathematics and drawing geometric forms. Note the charts on the wall. (Used with permission of the Library of Congress, Washington, D.C. LC-USZ62-41995.)**

Pestalozzi knew then that children needed to understand arithmetic, not merely learn it by memorizing a rule:

> *"How would you make the child understand that two and two make four unless you show it to him first in reality? To begin by abstract notions is absurd and detrimental."*
>
> **— *Letters to Greaves***

The method would prove itself in children who came to understand why they performed certain calculations and to comprehend the underlying principles:

> *"First, they were perfectly aware, not only what they were doing, but also of the reason why. They were acquainted with the principle on which the solution depended; they were not merely following a formula by rote; the state of the question changed, they were not puzzled, as those are who only see as far as their mechanical rule goes, and not farther."*
>
> **— *Letters to Greaves***

*Pestalozzi did not want children to learn a "formula by rote." What have been your experiences about learning by rote?*

*"The science of numbers must be so taught that their real properties shall not be obscured in the mind by arithmetical abbreviations. If this be neglected, the study of number will be degraded into a mere plaything of the child's memory and imagination and its object, of course, entirely defeated. If, for instance, we learn by rote that three and four make seven, and we build upon this seven as if we actually comprehended it, we deceive ourselves; we have no real apprehension of seven, because we are not conscious of the real fact, the actual sight of which can alone give truth and reality to the hollow sound. The first impressions of numerical proportions should be given to the child by illustrating the variations of more and less with real objects placed in view."*

***— How Gertrude Teaches Her Children***

---

**Cookbook Math vs. Understanding the Logic of Math**

How many of us memorized the "rule" for division of fractions? *Invert and multiply!!*

But why does this rule work? What is the underlying principle or action that will allow us to do other kinds of problems with the same principle?

Any number can be multiplied by 1 without changing its value!

The goal then becomes getting a common denominator in the original problem so you can divide.

Understanding this underlying principle allows you to solve many problems with fractions and other areas of mathematics, not relying on the "formula" or "mechanical rule" that Pestalozzi condemns. The underlying logic, not the memorized rule, is the essential understanding.

---

Pestalozzi's object lessons were intended not just for young children but for older children as well. For example, children from 10 to 12 might be exposed to a chart that had a square divided into halves, thirds, fourths, fifths, and so on, all the way through to tenths. Children would then be given a real problem of mental arithmetic like this to solve:

> A man paid $^{3}/_{8}$ of his debt and later $^{1}/_{4}$ of the remainder. Then, he paid $^{2}/_{7}$ of the second remainder. He still owed \$40.00. How much did he originally owe?

*Pestalozzi developed illustrative charts to help children learn fractions and other mathematical relationships. What have been your experiences learning mathematics? What was most helpful? How do you utilize math in your life?*

Pestalozzi also had charts for teaching counting, multiplication, division and fractions.

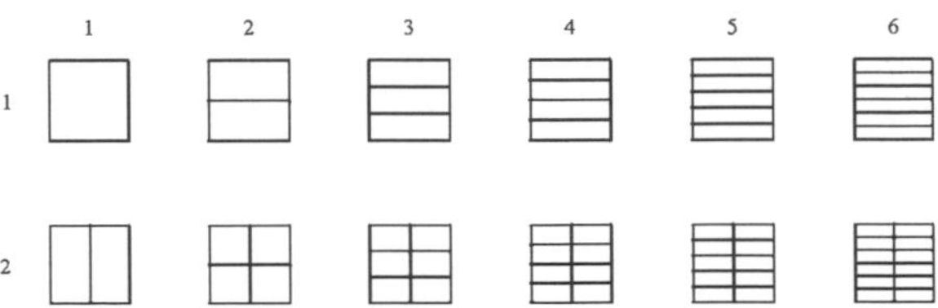


The charts provided visual images of the concepts intended, but we now know that young children need the concrete objects as well. The charts remain only symbolic.

## Other Educational Elements

Pestalozzi believed strongly that learning depended on the teacher's role. The child's initiative was a starting point but could not be solely relied upon. He felt that the best teachers were those who taught children, not subjects.

The values of mixed-aged grouping, children with varying age spans learning together, are still being articulated today while Pestalozzi saw the importance in the 1700's.

Parents were seen as capable and critical in the education of their own children:

> *"the time is drawing near when methods of teaching will be so simplified that each mother will be able not only to teach her children without help, but continue her own education at the same time."*
>
> ***— How Gertrude Teaches Her Children***

Pestalozzi felt progress in society would depend on parents' feeling competent in their educational roles with children in the home. Confidence in their abilities as well as a deep interest in education were essential. Once children reached school age, formal education should resemble home education as much as possible. He saw the home as the child's first and foremost teacher.

## Learning

Pestalozzi's own early school experiences taught him that theory and practice should not be separated. The deeds of the teachers must be consistent with the tales they told. Developing this further, he felt that knowledge must be based on real-life actions. Verbal knowledge alone was inadequate and unacceptable. Knowledge without meaning and action was empty knowledge:

> *"Depend upon it, there is a wide difference between knowing and doing. He who is carrying on his business by knowledge alone, lest he forget how to act."*
>
> ***— Leonard and Gertrude***

> *"To arrive at knowledge slowly, by one's own experience, is better than to learn by rote, in a hurry, facts that other people know."*
>
> ***— The Education of Man: Aphorisms***

Children's interests must be the motivation. He had great faith in children's ability to learn if a teacher was sensitive to their development. Children wanted to learn:

*What wise words! Do you reflect on your own practice when challenges arise with children? What other aspects do you consider?*

> *"I would go so far as to lay it down for a rule, that whenever children are inattentive, and apparently take no interest in a lesson, the teacher should always first look to himself for the reason."*
>
> ***— Letters to Greaves***

## Art and Music through Patterning

*How does change occur? This question lies at the crux of current social dilemmas, and still we have no clear answers. Do individuals need to change to effectively impact the systems around them? Or do the systems and environments around them need to change first? Pestalozzi felt it was the individual who should be the beginning point of change. Robert Owen (see chapter 6) would follow with the opposite approach.*

Pestalozzi saw art and music as integral parts of the curriculum, not extra or subsidiary areas of study. Pestalozzi saw that both art and music reflected the sequence from simple to complex, based on the senses. Prior teaching of art focused on copying drawings and on drawing human figures. Pestalozzi articulated a different drawing method that was based on lines, curves and angles. Through sense impressions, children were systematically led through a series of exercises. Skills learned from drawing geometric shapes were the basis needed for drawing simple objects. Later the children invented designs and illustrations. Children learned music from exercises in rhythm, melodic elements, dynamic elements and later notation.

## Education and Change in Society

Pestalozzi's overriding aim of education was to restore human dignity and a sense of individual worth to people, particularly children in poverty. He felt that lasting reform must start with the individual to give him the strength and virtue to change the environment. How? Each person would gain the power to help himself by developing self-respect and self-confidence.

Pestalozzi condemned the use of

- paternalism
- philanthropy
- ready-made social reforms.

He felt all three would weaken the individual and make him or her dependent on others or institutions. Instead, children needed to acquire the power to help themselves, and this power was to be cultivated in the educational system.

*What examples of paternalism, philanthropy and ready made, packaged social reforms do you see used in your community to deal with social problems (e.g. Food Bank)?*

*What approaches are used in your community to address the issues of poverty? Which are short term and which focus on fundamental change?*

*Pestalozzi deeply valued teacher education and thought it was undervalued by most people. What were the reactions of your family and friends when you chose a career in early childhood education?*

*How do we help teachers working with children who are poor or children of immigrant families or any children who might have different life experiences than our own? This remains an issue for teacher education programs.*

## Teacher Education

Pestalozzi also strongly supported teacher education and a state-supported school system. He decried the general public's lack of interest in education and in well-educated teachers. He believed education should be raised to the level of a science based on sound knowledge of human nature:

> *"No profession on earth calls for a deeper understanding of human nature nor for greater skill in guiding it properly."*
>
> ***— Aphorisms***

Pestalozzi's concern for teachers of the poor led him, in 1818, to establish a special teacher training school in Clindy, near Yverdon. In this school he tried to attract people who had come from poverty themselves to more effectively teach children. The school lasted only ten months before being assimilated into the main program at Yverdon. It did attract widespread attention, especially in England where there was growing concern for the education of lower classes.

## Pestalozzi's Impact in Canada

In Canada, proponents of Pestalozzi's ideas had a strong influence on some schools and some textbooks for children in the mid and late 1800's. Adolphus Egerton Ryerson (1803-1882), instrumental in establishing the Ontario educational system, traveled to Europe to collect Pestalozzi teaching materials for an exhibit in an educational museum in Toronto.

Alexander Forrester of Nova Scotia gave the following description of an object lesson intended for Canadian teachers in 1867:

> *"You all know what this is. A piece of coal. Who can tell me some of its properties or qualities? It is pure black. Anything else? It is glistening bright. Can you see through it? No. Then it is not transparent, and if so, it must be . . . opaque. John, bring a hammer, apply it and it breaks into a thousand pieces. You call this property . . . brittle. I am going to throw one of these pieces into the fire, watch what becomes of it. It burns with a bright flame, and gradually becomes . . . red hot, and then . . . a cinder, or ashes. This shows it to be . . . You don't know the term . . . combustible . . . like wood, or peat, or turf. It is then one . . . of the inflammables. Do you know any other quality this coal possesses? Yes — some kinds of coal have a great deal of gas. This is extracted and lights . . . cities and dwelling-houses."*
>
> ***— The Teacher's Text Book***

Other writings highlighted Pestalozzi's beliefs about learning from "simple to complex" and developing abilities of the mind. A Pestalozzi-based geography text published in 1835, Zadock Thompson's *Geography and History of Lower Canada*, had children study their own homes and townships and afterward make maps of important places and facts.

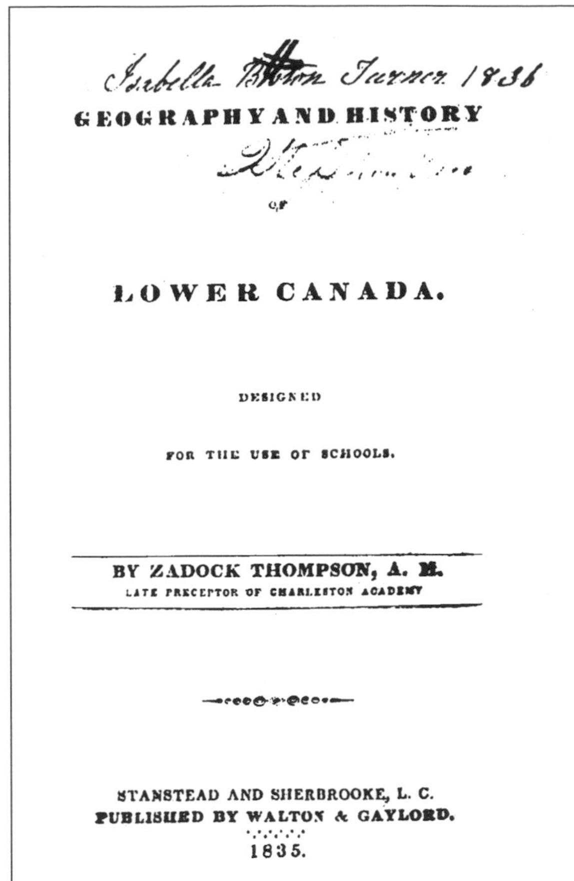

Isabella Turner 1836

GEOGRAPHY AND HISTORY

OF

LOWER CANADA.

DESIGNED

FOR THE USE OF SCHOOLS.

BY ZADOCK THOMPSON, A. M.

LATE PRECEPTOR OF CHARLESTON ACADEMY

STANSTEAD AND SHERBROOKE, L. C.

PUBLISHED BY WALTON & GAYLORD.

1835.

*"The pupil should begin at home, with his own neighborhood, and with those objects which are open to his personal observation. The knowledge which he has at the outset, and that which is successively gained, then becomes continually, a stepping-stone to still greater advancement, and a standard by which his subsequent attainments are measured and arranged in their relative order. Without a standard of this kind, what the pupil commits to memory from his book and recites to his teacher, leaves no definite or durable impression upon his mind. It is really believed that children have sometimes studied geography for months and perhaps years, whose thoughts have hardly extended beyond the paper and ink of which their geographies are composed.*

*In using this book, before the pupil passes beyond the second lesson, he should be made familiar with his own township . . . and be required to draw a map of it, on a large scale, with all the important objects in it."*

***— Geography and History of Lower Canada***

***Geography and History of Lower Canada*** **was based on Pestalozzi's teaching methods and focused on students learning their immediate environments. (From Zadock Thompson's *Geography and History of Lower Canada* published in 1835 by Walton & Gaylord, Stanstead, Lower Canada.)**

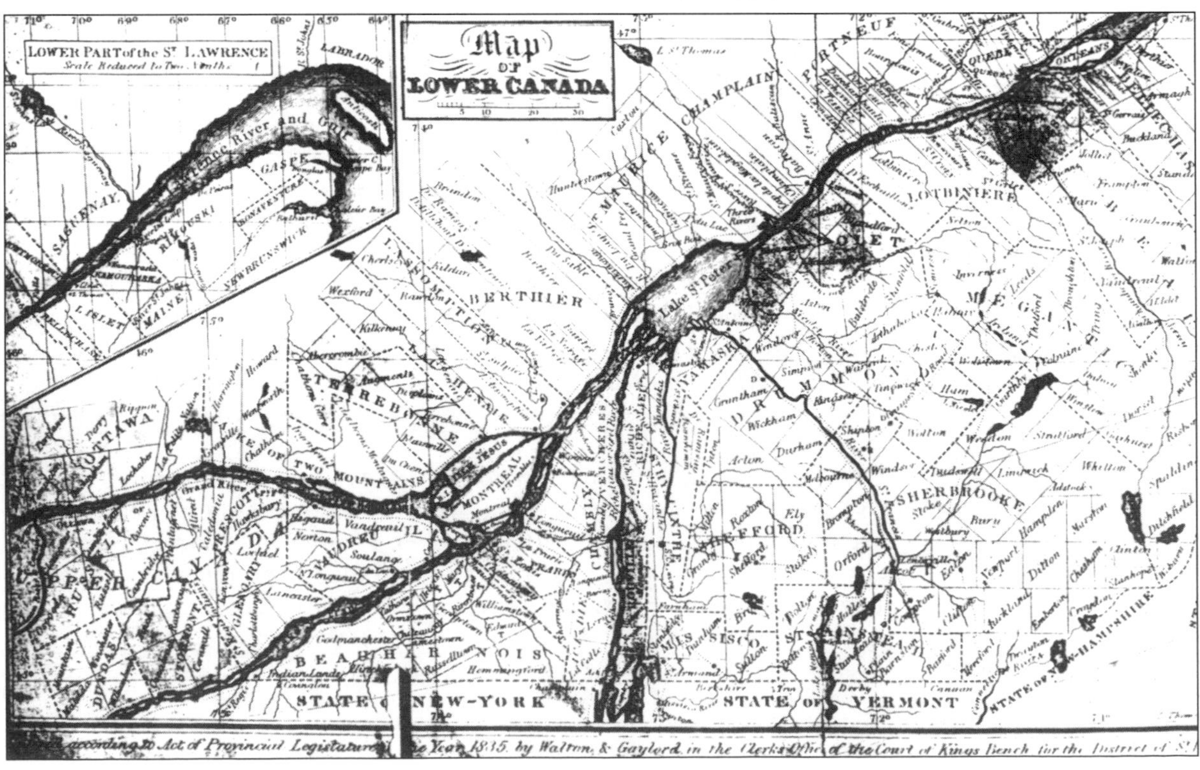

## Object Lessons in the United States

Followers of Pestalozzi introduced his ideas in the United States early in the 1800's. Teachers were beginning to see that children could not learn what they did not understand and wanted to help children see applications of knowledge. Pestalozzi's insistence that schools should be pleasant places of learning was also making some headway in the schools.

Object lessons became the focus in the Oswego Normal School[2] in 1861, and this marked a turning point in the influence of Pestalozzi's ideas across the United States. Edward Sheldon, founder of the Oswego Normal School, had visited Toronto where Egerton Ryerson had collected the full set of Pestalozzi teachers' guidebooks and lesson materials and displayed them in the National [Educational] Museum. Oswego students learned how to select lessons, organize them and conduct the object lessons with children.

Though the ideas of Pestalozzi had been used in isolated areas in the United States, they now became the primary focus in most normal schools. As schools proliferated after the Civil War, teachers turned to the object lesson as a key method of instruction.

**Student teachers at the Oswego Normal School hold various items used for object lessons. One woman in the front row is holding a cube, sphere and cylinder (Froebel gift #1). (Used with permission of Special Collections of Penfield Library, SUNY at Oswego, New York.)**

---

[2] One of the professors at Oswego was Hermann Krusi, Jr., the son of one of Pestalozzi's first assistants. Krusi also wrote a biography of Pestalozzi, *Pestalozzi: His life, work, and influence*. Krusi, Jr. was born in Yverdon, Switzerland in 1817, and his father had assisted Pestalozzi at Burgdorf and Yverdon.

Object Lessons in Oswego New York, 1863

"Worsted [yarn and cloth] and cards of various colors, were placed upon the table. The teacher called upon one child to select all the reds, and place them together; another, to select all the yellows, and place them together; another, the blues; another, the greens, etc. The children were then requested to name all the red objects that they could see in the room; then those of the other colors successively. Next, one child was called upon to name a color, and another to name an object of the same color. Then one child would name an object, and another name its color."

"First objects were placed on a table, and the children requested to observe the position of each, after which the teacher would remove them, and call upon individuals to put them in the same position again. Then the position of these objects on the table were represented by drawing on a slate held in a horizontal position. Then the same positions were represented by drawings on the blackboard. Children were called upon to point with their fingers; also to walk in different directions; also to tell in what direction they must walk to go from their seat to some given part of the room. The teacher would name a point of compass, and request the children to point toward it, while she would point in some other direction. This made each pupil think and act for himself."

**— from Phelps et al, "Primary Instruction by Object Lessons"**

Followers of Pestalozzi such as William Maclure, Joseph Neef, William Russell, Bronson Alcott, Henry Barnard, Edward Sheldon, Hermann Krusi, Jr., William Harris, James Carter, Charles Brooks and Mary Sheldon Barnes (wife of Earl Barnes) each had a strong influence on the incorporation of Pestalozzi's ideas into the United States.

Details of the work of the Pestalozzi leadership in the United States are contained in W. Monroe's 1907 book *History of the Pestalozzian Movement in the United States*. In addition, the following articles, most from the 1800's, give a detailed account of the people who spread Pestalozzi's ideas:

"Pestalozzi in America" by Gardette (1867)
"William Torrey Harris and St. Louis Public Schools" by Barnard (1880)
"Object System of Instruction as Pursued in the Schools of Oswego" by Wilbur (1865)
"Object Teaching" by Sheldon (1864)
"Primary Instruction by Object Lessons" by Phelps (1863)
"The History of Object Teaching" by Calkins (1863)
"A. Bronson Alcott" by Sanborn (1877)
"James G. Carter" by Barnard (1858)
"William Channing Woodbridge" by Alcott (1858)
"Pestalozzianism in the United States" by Barnard (1880)
"A Memoir of William Maclure" by Morton (1844)
"An Epitome of the Improved Pestalozzian System of Education as Practiced by William Phiquepal and Madam Fretageot" by Maclure (1826)
"Primary Education" by Alcott (1827)
"The Oswego State Normal School" by Aber (1893)
"The Pestalozzian System" by Boutwell (1893)
"Death of Professor Mary Sheldon Barnes" by Monroe (1898)
"Pestalozzian Literature in America" by Monroe (1894)
"Herman Krosi [sic], An American Pestalozzian" by Monroe (1903)
"Joseph Neef and Pestalozzianism in America" by Monroe (1884)

## Enduring Influences

Attracted first by Rousseau's back-to-nature ideas, Pestalozzi went far beyond these to look at sense education and the nature of manipulative experiences for children. He focused on what we would call (and many textbooks use as a title) *the whole child.* Concerned with poverty and the effects it had on people, he worked a lifetime to educate children with new methods. Any education should be directly connected to life:

This approach would be inspirational today for any family day home provider.

> *"The instruction she gave them in the rudiments of arithmetic was intimately connected with the realities of life. She taught them to count the number of steps from one end of the room to the other, and two of the rows of five panes each, in one of the windows, gave her an opportunity to unfold the decimal relations of numbers. She also made them count their threads while spinning, and the number of turns on the reel, when they wound the yarn into skeins. Above all, in every occupation of life she taught them an accurate and intelligent observation of common objects and the forces of nature."*
>
> — ***Leonard and Gertrude***

**A Reflective Pestalozzi. (Illustration courtesy of Centre de Documentation et de Recherche Pestalozzi in Yverdon-les-Bains.)**

Pestalozzi's work also stimulated others to improve instructional methods based on inquiry and investigation, excursions with children and the extensive use of natural objects.

William Heard Kilpatrick (American educational philosopher) gave this tribute to Pestalozzi in 1946:

> *"As the years come and go, however, it will be the great loving heart of Pestalozzi that stands out. He loved his children and they responded to his love. Men saw this and heeded. School children have been happier ever since; and besides that, they have learned better. This is the debt we owe Pestalozzi."*
>
> — **"American Education's Debt to Pestalozzi"**

Kindergarten and primary aged children today doing worksheet after worksheet or drills on the computer do not reflect the ideas and dreams of Pestalozzi in the late 1700's.

 *Pestalozzianism in the U.S. — Hermann Krusi Papers*
*Special Library Collection*
*Penfield Library Special Collections*
*SUNY at Oswego*
*Oswego, New York 13126*
*U.S.A.*

## Johann Pestalozzi — References for Further Study


Aber, W. (1893, May). The Oswego State Normal School. *Popular Science Monthly,* 51-76.

Alcott, A. B. (1827, January). Primary education. *American Journal of Education, 3,* 26-31.

Alcott, A. B. (1827, February). Primary education. *American Journal of Education, 3,* 86-94.

Alcott, W. A. (1858). William Channing Woodbridge. *Barnard's American Journal of Education, 5,* 51-64.

Barnard, H. (1858). James G. Carter. *Barnard's American Journal of Education, 5,* 407-416.

Barnard, H. (1880). William Torrey Harris and St. Louis public schools. *Barnard's American Journal of Education, 30,* 625-640.

Bigler, R. (1972). *Pestalozzi in Burgdorf.* Logan, UT: Utah State University Press.

Black, H. (1969). Pestalozzi and the education of the disadvantaged. *The Educational Forum, 33* (4), 511-521.

Boutwell, G. (1893, November). The Pestalozzian system. *Popular Science Monthly,* 55-56.

Bredekamp, S., & Copple, C. (Eds). (1997, revised edition). Developmentally appropriate practice in early childhood programs. Washington, DC: National Association for the Education of Young Children.

Calkins, N. A. (1863). The history of object teaching. *Barnard's American Journal of Education, 12,* 633-645.

Channing, E. (Trans.). (1889). *Pestalozzi's Leonard and Gertrude.* Boston: D.C. Heath & Co.

Culver, S. (1986). Pestalozzi's influence on manual training. *Journal of Vocational and Technical Education, 2* (2), 37-43.

De Guimps, R. (1890). *Pestalozzi: His life and work.* New York: D. Appleton and Company.

Efland, A. (1983). Art and music in the Pestalozzian tradition. *Journal of Research in Music Education, 31* (3), 165-178.

Fales, W. (1946). New light on Pestalozzi. *Harvard Educational Review, 16* (1), 1-9.

Forrester, A. (1867). *The teacher's text book.* Halifax, Canada: A. & W. Mackinlay.

Freire, P. (1985). *The politics of education: Culture, power, and liberation.* South Hadley, MA: Bergin & Garvey.

Freire, P. (M. Ramos, Trans.). (1993). *Pedagogy of the oppressed.* New York: Continuum.

Gardette, C. D. (1867, August). Pestalozzi in America. *Galaxy, 4,* 432-439.

Green, J. A. (1969). *The educational ideas of Pestalozzi.* New York: Greenwood Press. (Original work published 1914)

Gundersen, A. (1960). A survey of the influences of Pestalozzianism on American education. *Educational Administration and Supervision, 46* (1), 27-33.

Gutek, G. L. (1968). *Pestalozzi and education.* New York: Random House.

Hackensmith, C. (1973). *Biography of Joseph Neef, educator in the Ohio Valley, 1809-1854.* New York: Carlto Press, Inc.

Harris, W. (1893, May). Herbart and Pestalozzi compared. *Educational Review, 5,* 417-423.

Hayward, F. A. (1979). *The educational ideas of Pestalozzi and Frobel [sic].* Westport, CT: Greenwood Press, Publishers. (Original work published 1904)

Heafford, M. (1967). *Pestalozzi: His thought and its relevance today.* London: Methuen.

Hodgins, J. S. (Ed.). (1883). *The story of my life by the late Rev. Egerton Ryerson, D.D., LLD.* Toronto, Canada: William Briggs.

Holman, H. (1908). *Pestalozzi: An account of his life and work.* London: Longmans, Green & Co.

Kilpatrick, W. (1946). American education's debt to Pestalozzi. *Education Digest, IX* (6), 41-43.

Krusi, H. (1875). *Pestalozzi: His life, work, and influence.* Cincinnati, OH: Van Antwerp, Bragg & Co.

Lascarides, V.C. & Hinitz, B. (2000). *History of Early Childhood Education.* New York: Falmer Press.

Maclure, W. (1826, February). An epitome of the improved Pestalozzian system of education as practiced by William Phiquepal and Madam Fretageot. *American Journal of Science and Arts, 10,* 145-156.

Maclure, W. (1880, March). Pestalozzianism in the United States. *Barnard's Journal of Education,* 561-572.

McDonald, N., & Chaiton, A. (Eds.). (1978). *Egerton Ryerson and his times.* Toronto, Canada: Macmillan of Canada.

Monroe, W. (1894). Joseph Neef and Pestalozzianism in America. *Education, XIV* (8), 449-461.

Monroe, W. (1894, May). Pestalozzian literature in America. *Kindergarten Magazine, VI* (9), 673-676.

Monroe, W. (1898, September 15). Death of Professor Mary Sheldon Barnes. *Journal of Education, 48,* 75.

Monroe, W. (1903, November 5). Herman Krosi [sic], an American Pestalozzian. *Journal of Education, 53,* 304-305.

Monroe, W. (1969). *History of the Pestalozzian movement in the United States.* New York: Arno Press & The New York Times. (Original work published 1907)

Morton, S. G. (1844, October). A memoir of William Maclure, Esq. late president of the Academy of Natural Sciences of Philadelphia. *American Journal of Science and Arts, XLVII* (1), 1-17.

Mueller, G. (1946). Heinrich Pestalozzi: His life and work. *Harvard Educational Review, 16* (3), 141-159.

Osgood, J. (1963). The contribution of Comenius and Pestalozzi to the theory of teacher training. In *The Yearbook of Education* (pp. 59-69). London: Evans Bros.

Osgood, J. (1963). The contributions of Comenius and Pestalozzi to the theory of teacher training. In Bereday, G. & Lauwerys, J. (Eds.), *The education and training of teachers.* London: Evans Brothers Limited.

Pestalozzi, J. H. (E. Channing, Trans.). (1906). *Leonard and Gertrude.* Boston: D.C. Heath.

Pestalozzi, J. H. (1951). *The education of man: Aphorisms.* Introduction by W. H. Kilpatrick. New York: Philosophical Library.

Pestalozzi, J. H. (1969). *The education of man: Aphorisms.* New York: Greenwood Press.

Pestalozzi, J. H. (1977). *How Gertrude teaches her children.* Washington, DC: University Publications of America.

Phelps, W. F., Cochran, D.H., Camp, D., Harrison, T. Wilbur, H.P., Farnham, G. L., & Nicoll, W. (1863). Primary instruction by object lessons. *Barnard's American Journal of Education, 12,* 605-628.

Phillips, C. (1957). *The development of education in Canada.* Toronto, Canada: W. J. Gage & Co.

Pollard, H. M. (1956). *Pioneers of popular education 1760-1850.* London: Murray Publishing.

Robinson, D. (1977). *Series B psychometrics and educational psychology Vol. II. J. H. Pestalozzi.* Washington, DC: University Publications of America, Inc. [includes *How Gertrude teaches her children, Letters to Greaves, The swan song* and other writings].

Sanborn, F. A. (1877). A. Bronson Alcott. *Barnard's American Journal of Education, 27,* 225-236.

Sheldon, E. A. (1864). Object teaching. *Barnard's American Journal of Education, 14,* 93-102.

Silber, K. (1965). *Pestalozzi: The man and his work.* London: Routledge & Kegan Paul.

Skinner, B. F. (1948). *Walden Two.* London: MacMillan

Thompson, Z. (1835). *Geography and history of Lower Canada.* Stanztead, Lower Canada: Walton & Gaylord.

Walch, M. R. (1952). *Pestalozzi and the Pestalozzian theory of education: A critical study.* Washington, DC: The Catholic University of America Press.

Wilbur, H. B. (1865). Object system of instruction. *Barnard's American Journal of Education, 15,* 189-208.

Wiskemann, E. (1953, April 17). Children of eight nations – The Pestalozzi Kinderdorf. *The Times Educational Supplement,* 337.

# Chapter 5 — *Friedrich Wilhelm August Froebel*

**1782 – 1852**

*"The plays of childhood are the germinal leaves of all later life."*

*"To lead children early to think, this I consider the first and foremost object of child training."*

*"Knowledge acquired in our own active experience is more living and fruitful than that conveyed only by words."*

**— *The Education of Man***

*". . . the present and future living conditions of men of all social classes rest on the careful consideration and rounded mental and physical care of early childhood."*

**— written by Froebel in 1839 and quoted in Liebschner, *A Child's Work***

## Early Life

Friedrich Wilhelm Froebel was born in 1782, in the small mountainous village of Oberweissbach, now in eastern Germany near the town of Weimar. Oberweissbach was known throughout Germany for the herbal remedies found in its surrounding woods. Froebel's mother died when he was a baby, and his father, Johann, a hard working Lutheran minister trying to serve 5,000 rural parishioners scattered among many villages, had little time for his family of six boys (August, Christoph, Christian, Juliane, Traugott, and Friedrich). His father remarried when Froebel was four years old, but Froebel remembered his childhood as filled with frustration, loneliness and neglect. He saw his father as a stranger, too preoccupied with his church work. His step-mother also had no time for Friedrich as she was involved with a new baby while Friedrich was young.

Plagued by reading problems and assumed stupid by his teachers and parents, Froebel dropped to the bottom of his class and was sent to the village girls' school where he became both introspective and rebellious. He later recalled school learning as parrot-like tasks that had no connection to the real world. He remembered finding solace in the natural world:

> *"Nature, with the world of plants and flowers, so far as I was able to see and understand her, early became an object of observation and reflection to me."*
>
> **— *Autobiography***

This affinity with nature and connection to its elements permeated his later educational and philosophical ideas.

When he was ten years old, Friedrich's step-mother and father sent him to his mother's brother, Johann Christoph Hoffman, in Stadtilm on the river Ilm where he gained confidence, got along with other children his age, and learned well in school. He felt he "gained freedom of soul and strength of body." Returning home at 15, he was apprenticed to a forester, surveyor and assessor in the Thuringian forest but left the trade at 17, interested more in learning botany and mathematics. His father and step-mother accused him of being a failure when the forester sent a letter complaining of Froebel's conduct. Froebel, in his defense, felt that the man had given him no teaching about the trade, but his father would not listen. Gloom and disillusionment returned, and Froebel saw no escape from his problems.

Soon after his return home, Froebel was sent to deliver money to his older brother Traugott, who was studying medicine at the University of Jena. Froebel found university life stimulating, and he obtained permission to stay as a visiting student until the end of the term. Soon afterwards, when he turned 18, he inherited a small amount of money from his birth mother's estate and returned to Jena to enroll as a full-time student.

Jena was the intellectual centre of Germany with some of the major thinkers and writers of the time including Friedrich Schiller, Johann Goethe and George Hegel. Excited by the academic climate, Froebel learned, studied and grew in his thinking. He was drawn to the intellectual life, searching for meaning and answers to questions that he had. He studied a wide variety of subjects including mathematics, surveying and architecture. Botany and natural history retained their earlier fascination, and he continued to see nature as an interconnected whole.[1]

This university experience ended in sadness and defeat for Froebel. His brother refused to repay some money that Froebel had lent him, and Froebel's own debts grew. His father would not assist him, and Froebel was thrown into the university prison for nine weeks. He spent the time studying Latin, geometry and literature. Finally his father agreed to bail him out by paying off his debts, but Froebel returned home at the age of 18, humiliated with an increased sense of failure ("a heavy heart, a troubled mind and an oppressed spirit"). Froebel even contemplated emigrating to Russia or America.

## Wanderings

In 1802 Froebel left home, drifting and working at many jobs to support himself.

He found work as a farmer, private secretary, clerk, accountant, surveyor, architect and map maker. Though he found none of these satisfying as a career, Froebel benefitted from each and continued his path of study and learning to attain "inner perfection."

Froebel next accepted a position as a teacher in the Frankfurt Model School, which had recently opened and was run by Anton Gruner, one of Pestalozzi's proteges. He had a class of 40 boys and was exceedingly happy in his vocation. In the summer of 1805 Froebel visited Pestalozzi for two weeks in Yverdon, returning from the school refreshed with new ideas and understanding. He focused his teaching on knowledge gained from life experiences and proceeding from the known and familiar to the unknown and remote. For example, he had children explore the area around them and create maps from their trips.

[1] William Wordsworth, John Keats and Percy Shelley were poets in England expressing similar ideas about unity.

After two years in Frankfurt, Froebel became a full-time tutor for three brothers, children of Caroline von Hozhausen. The children lived with Froebel in a small cottage on the grounds of the estate. Froebel tried educating them according to Rousseau's model of natural learning in *Emile*. He involved the boys in nature study, gardening and indoor modeling with wood and paper. It was totally unsuccessful, and Froebel found that the boys' education lacked any guiding principle.

**Friedrich Froebel. (Used with permission of Bibliotheque Nationale Suisse-Bern.)**

In desperation, Froebel took the boys to Yverdon in 1808 and enrolled them in formal classes. At the same time, he became a student of Pestalozzi at the Pestalozzi Institute. Froebel remained there for two years as both teacher and pupil. Though impressed with Pestalozzi's work, he was concerned about the lack of focus on unity and interdependence and felt the various elements of Pestalozzi's curriculum were unrelated:

> *"What I saw was to me at once elevating and depressing, arousing and bewildering. . . . [Pestalozzi] could never give any definite account of his idea, his plan, his intention. He always said, 'Go and see for yourself' (very good for him who knew how to look, how to hear, how to perceive)."*
>
> ***— Autobiography***

Throughout this period Froebel maintained an intimate relationship with Caroline von Hozhausen who was openly neglected and ignored by her aristocratic husband. Caroline severed her relationship with Froebel in 1816. She, however, remained his idealized vision of mother and woman.

*Froebel studied many academic subjects in his quest for knowledge. How is your work with children enhanced by a knowledge of other fields of study?*

Leaving once again after two years, he enrolled at the University of Gottingen in 1811 and at the University of Berlin a year later. At this point in his intellectual journey, he was searching for a theoretical basis for and an understanding of the concept of **unity**, which he had heard about earlier at the University of Jena. He pursued studies in crystals, physics, natural history, chemistry, Arabic and Hebrew to further his philosophical goal. The idea of the organic unity in life (in crystals, language, trees, or in the developing child) would affect and underlie Froebel's educational theories, materials and methods:

> *"The most pregnant thought which arose in me at this period was this: All is unity, all rests in unity, all springs from unity, strives for and leads up to unity, and returns to unity at last. This striving in unity and after unity is the cause of the several aspects of human life."*
>
> ***— Autobiography***

Froebel was not particularly interested in the politics of the day, but he could not ignore the increasing nationalism in the sovereign states of Germany and was caught up in the patriotic furor that was sweeping the country. The Napoleonic Wars catapulted the youth to fight as Napoleon marched across Europe causing devastation in his path. At 31 in 1813, Froebel became an infantry soldier, taking up arms in the Prussian army to fight Napoleon with the corps of "Black Riflemen." After the Peace of Paris and Napoleon's defeat, Froebel was discharged after only a few years of service. He saw little action as a soldier and continued his natural history studies. Though the military was not to become a career for him, he did make two close friends in the army, Wilhelm Middendorf and Heinrich Langerthal, who would later play prominent roles in Froebel's educational career.

## First Schools

After leaving the army in 1814, Froebel went to Berlin and became a curator at the Mineralogical Museum at the University of Berlin, using his skills and knowledge of the natural and physical world. In this job, he continued his own academic studies of crystals and minerals; recent scientific discoveries had allowed classification based on molecular structure. Froebel enjoyed his job but missed his social contacts as he worked in a locked and silent room cataloguing specimens. He left the museum in 1816 when the widow of his recently deceased brother Christoph[2] wrote asking for advice on educating her three boys. Froebel moved to their town, Griesheim, and began a small school in her home. The two sons of another brother, Christian, were also in this initial class. The first lesson, held along the local stream, involved damming up the water to test the effects of erosion.

With his sister-in-law's financial support, Froebel set up a Pestalozzian school called the Universal German Educational Institute at nearby Keilhau in 1817. His brother's widow was in love with Froebel, assumed he would marry her and sold her property and silverware to help support the school. She enrolled her two sons, and other nephews also enrolled. In many senses, this was the Pestalozzian dream with the teacher being the uncle and the pupils being his nephews.

This was Pestalozzi's image of a school as a family. The school's philosophy was actually a combination of Rousseau's and Pestalozzi's ideas. The children wore simple clothes, spent large amounts of time outdoors and studied as their needs arose. Children designed their own building blocks, which were then made by a local carpenter. The children were not asked to do any tasks that the adults were not also prepared to do, from harvesting crops to building a new roof. Rules were the same for teachers and pupils. It was home-like and informal. In the second year of operation, Middendorf and Langerthal joined the school "family."

---

[2] Christoph had provided sanctuary to a French soldier who had the plague, and Christoph died soon after of the disease himself.

The school also included a system of student government, which was described by George Ebers, a student in the school:

> *"We formed one large family, and if any act really worthy of punishment was committed by any pupil, Barop summoned us all, formed us into a court of justice, and we examined into the affair, fixing the penalty ourselves. Froebel regarded these meetings as a means of coming into the unity with life."*
>
> **— quoted in Aborn, "Friedrich Froebel: Apostle of Childhood Education"**

At this point Froebel's life was once again upset. In 1818, he married Henrietta Wilhelmine Hoffmeister, whom he had known at the University of Berlin. She had been married before but divorced her husband who had not treated her well. In 1826 Langerthal married Henrietta's foster daughter Ernestine.

Froebel's sister-in-law flew into a rage and withdrew her financial support of the school. She settled in a nearby village, embittered and resentful of her loss. Froebel was beset with other problems, as his teaching assistants disagreed on philosophy and methodology. Froebel closed himself off from advice, and the school neared collapse. Another brother of Froebel, Christian (whose daughter Albertine married Middendorf) gave some financial support to the school, and the enrollment grew to 60 children.

George Ebers described his memories of the school:

> *"We took long walks up the mountains or in the forest, the older pupils acting as teachers. We discovered every variety of insect on the bushes and in the moss, the turf, the bark of trees, on the flowers and blades of grass. We listened to the note of birds; and how many trees we climbed, what steep cliffs we also climbed, through what crevices we squeezed, to add a rare egg to our collection. Our teachers' love for all animate creation had made them impose bounds on our zeal, so we were required always to leave one egg in the nest, and if it contained but one not to molest it."*
>
> **— quoted in Aborn, "Friedrich Froebel: Apostle of Childhood Education"**

Froebel remained inflexible and authoritarian in his administrative style. His nephews made public charges against him, still resentful of what they perceived to be Froebel's slight of their mother. They charged that the school was a centre of radicalism and treason. The school was already suspect because of its progressive approach to education and the long hair of the boys (in German tradition) and male teachers! The Prussian government cleared the school of these charges after a thorough investigation, but the school's reputation was damaged. The school plunged into debt, and the enrollment sank to five in 1829. Froebel's brother took over and Froebel left.

Immersed in deep despair, Froebel went to Switzerland in 1831 and was able to interest some Swiss nobles in his ideas. He set up another school, but public charges against him from disgruntled former teachers, opposition from the Catholic church and his autocratic ideas forced the school's closure.

## Burgdorf at Mid Life

Froebel travelled to Burgdorf, near Berne, the site of the original Pestalozzi school. Here a strong local government protected him as he set up another school in 1835. In this situation he developed two main ideas:

1. Very small children needed an *orderly* set of experiences calculated to awaken their abilities, stimulate their mental activities and produce an inner organization.
2. Mothers needed specific training to help their young children at home so they could provide beginning basic education.

To support these beliefs, he developed his ideas into a book called *Mother Play and Nursery Songs* (sometimes called *Mother's Songs, Games and Stories*), published in 1844. Organized series of games, songs and pictures were presented to help mothers educate their children. In each instance there was a motto to guide the mother, a verse with music and a picture to illustrate the activity. It was a precursor to activity books of songs, dances and finger plays still common in early childhood programs.

## The Origin of Kindergarten

Renewed by a specific interest in young children, Froebel went to Berlin to study and develop his plans for schools for younger children. Soon afterward, he rented an abandoned mill in Blankenburg and opened a school called *Kleinkinderbeschaftigungsanstalt* (translates as an "institution where small children are occupied").

Imagine a man of 55, a failure in everything he had done. The village called him an old fool who played with children. His wife was an invalid and died soon afterward in 1839. His nephews continued to attack him. *But at last he had found his passion and talent.*

There were about 50 children from one to seven years of age, and Froebel developed materials and equipment for them to use in their learning. One day in talking with Middendorf about his school, Froebel came to see his community as a garden in which children could grow and learn. From then on the word **kindergarten** was used to identify that type of program for young children:

> *"Eureka! I have it! Kindergarten shall be the name of the new Institution."*
> — ***Autobiography***

Froebel wanted his school to be seen as a place children could fully develop. The term "kindergarten" allowed him to avoid using the word "school," and this distinction was important to him, as he wanted the kindergarten to be different from a traditional school. His image of a garden and the natural growth of children developed not only from his own ideas but also the nature images described by people like Comenius, Rousseau and Pestalozzi.

Before choosing the word kindergarten, Froebel had thought of the German equivalents of "institute for the self teaching of little children," "playschool" and "school for the psychological training of little children by means of play and occupations." He did not want the word "school" as it implied schooling as "putting in." Rather he wanted the new name to reflect the cultivation of children's capacities and thought of "nursery school for little children" which conveyed his sense of a nursery that gardeners use to nurture plants.

For the next seven years, Froebel worked with the children and developed a rich assortment of teaching materials and experiences for children. The equipment and activities were produced and distributed throughout Germany and the rest of Europe for schools and mothers.

## Later Life

**Luise Levin was one of Froebel's first students in his training program for teachers. She helped him set up more schools and disseminate Froebel teaching materials. They were married in 1851, just a year before his death. (From Edward Wiebe's *Paradise of Childhood,* 1896.)**

In 1844 Froebel left the school to expound on and promote his kindergarten ideas in the European community. Travelling widely with Middendorf, he also set up a training program for teachers. His first group of students was all men, but in the second year, he had some female students; he then became convinced that women made better teachers of young children than men and should provide the starting points for a child's education. This idea was initially received with great laughter and ridicule because women were not seen as capable of working professionally outside the home.

Froebel persevered, opening the first Training College for women in central Europe. The feminization of the role of early childhood educators and the emergence of women in professional roles were two converging outcomes of these early days of educating teachers of young children.

He wanted applicants to have a good educational background, a love of childhood and play, a joyful view of life and skills with children. The training program was a mix of theory and practice with children. Quality early childhood preparation programs today would still reflect these basic elements.

One of these first students of the Training College was Luise Levin, who was 30 years younger than Froebel. Her family had been friends of his family. Froebel found understanding and companionship with Levin, and they became romantically linked. Levin had had a life full of hardships and heavy family responsibilities. Her only education before attending the Training College had focused on the domestic arts expected of women. Their liaison created an even greater schism between Froebel and his family members who were scandalized by his relationship with the young woman.

Though Froebel's ideas spread, there was also strong opposition from people who saw no need for early education; they believed that play would create loafers and sluggards and not prepare children adequately for schoolwork to follow.

**Former students of Froebel gathered in 1924 late in their own lives to honour Froebel. They are standing in front of the monument then located in Schweina. (Photo courtesy of Dr. Matthias Brodbeck, Bad Liebenstein, Germany.)**

Froebel and Luise Levin set up more training schools with the financial support of the Baroness Von Marenholtz Bulow who dedicated her life and monetary resources to spread the kindergarten movement. Her only son had died early in life after a long illness which she blamed on the severity of the education he received.

The following is her memory of her first meeting with Froebel:

*"My landlady . . . told me that a few weeks before, a man had settled down on a small farm near the springs, who danced and played with the village children, and therefore went by the name of 'the old fool'. Some days after I met on my walk this so-called 'old fool.'" A tall, spare man, with long gray hair, was leading a troop of village children between the ages of three and eight, most of them barefooted and but scantily clothed, who marched two and two up a hill, where, having marshalled them for a play, he practiced with them a song belonging to it. The loving patience and abandon with which he did this, the whole bearing of the man while the children played various games under his direction, were so moving, that tears came into my companion's eyes as well as into my own, and I said to her, 'This man is called an old fool by these people; perhaps he is one of those men who are ridiculed or stoned by contemporaries, and to whom future generations build monuments.'"*

— from ***Reminiscences of Friedrich Froebel***

And future generations did build monuments!

Froebel's nephews did not cease trying to discredit their uncle. Exhausted, Froebel retired to teach in a school funded by the Baroness. A year

**Froebel's Gravestone. Kindergarten children in 1992 visiting the tomb of Froebel, 201 years since his birth. (Photo courtesy of Dr. Matthias Brodbeck, Bad Liebenstein, Germany.)**

Bad Liebenstein: Fröbeldenkmal im Marienthaler Wäldchen

**Wilhelm Middendorf, Froebel's close friend and colleague, planned the memorial to Froebel using the sphere, cube and cylinder, the basic three shapes in Froebel's system. Ernst Luther, a relative of Martin Luther, built the statue as a living memorial to Froebel. Luther had visited Froebel in 1817 at his school in Keilhau. From 1852 – 1872 it was the Froebel tombstone. It now stands in Froebelsruh, a place Froebel enjoyed visiting. (Photo courtesy of Dr. Matthias Brodbeck, Bad Liebenstein, Germany.)**

before Froebel's death, the Prussian government officially outlawed kindergartens and the training programs, claiming that they fostered revolutionary ideas. They were condemned for the education of female teachers and for their socialistic and atheistic leanings. The order was not revoked until 1860.

In 1851, he and Luise were married in Bad Liebenstein in a festive wedding that included a children's play. Middendorf was the groomsman, and the Baroness was the bridesmaid. At the end of the festivities, Froebel said, "Now we will go to work with new power," and he enthusiastically taught the next morning. Even in his later life, Froebel continued to teach. His wife, Luise, said, "Froebel loved to teach, even whilst in the act of walking."

Froebel died at the age of 70 after a short illness. His longtime friend Middendorf planned and erected a monument to Froebel incorporating three of his main "gifts" for children: the sphere, cube and cylinder. It was built by Ernest Luther, a descendent of Martin Luther. Inscribed on the monument were the words from the poet Schiller that had so intrigued Froebel as a young man:

> *"Come, let us live for our children."*

The Baroness continued Froebel's ideas in collaboration with Luise Levin. Middendorf intended to join them, but he died within a year of his close friend Froebel. Luise continued her active kindergarten work for 33 years after Froebel's death.

**Froebel Training for Teachers. Bedford Kindergarten and Training College in Bedford, England continued the Froebel traditions. This is a photo of the staff and students in 1886. (Courtesy of De Montfort University, Bedford with thanks to Richard Smart, Head of History at Bedford and College Archivist and Colin Caselton-Bone, Department of Learning Technologies.)**

## The Education of Man

In 1826 while still at Keilhau, Froebel wrote *The Education of Man,* his major philosophical and theoretical writing on education. Froebel saw the universe as a whole, as unity, as oneness, and called this concept "god." This was not the personal God of a Hebrew-Christian tradition. He saw god as an "all pervading, energetic living, self-conscious and eternal unity." His goal was to bring children closer to god, to this unity. All his earlier studies focused on this, and the concept resurfaced at the core of his educational theory.

Froebel believed that children came to realize themselves only through self activity or self occupations, not through the traditional format of children responding to static subject matter. Education, therefore, had to be based on the spontaneous interests and activities of children.

The role of the teacher was to become a guide and to protect the child from things that would weaken, warp or hinder the process of learning. The teacher needed to create an environment that would stimulate and further the child's education and learning. In order to do this, the teacher needed to introduce specific experiences and activities for the child. Rousseau had also been concerned with protecting the child from a "negative" environment, but Froebel had found removing and isolating children from society did not work.

This same duality and tension exists in our programs today, as we try to balance a pre-set curriculum with the different needs of children.

In Froebel's educational model, instruction and teaching were not synonymous with imparting knowledge. Froebel believed education had to balance a respect for the individuality of children and the need for an organized, articulated program.

Froebel believed that teachers and parents **must** be aware of a child's development in order to teach and to provide an appropriate environment:

> *". . . note the moment, the proper place, for the introduction of a new branch of instruction. The whole attention of the teacher must be directed to these budding points of new branches of instruction."*
>
> — ***The Education of Man***

*What makes children ready?*

*Who decides when children will learn to read and write? Learn any new skill or knowledge?*

*How much is curriculum today based on a sound knowledge of child development?*

*Why have "readiness" programs reached down into earlier years?*

Froebel was also clear in his belief that teachers and parents were not to rush children's development.

## Stages of Development

Froebel articulated three stages of development and early growth. Though he gave rough estimates of ages for these, he warned that these stages were not strictly age-dependent.

1. **infancy stage birth – 3 years**
   - relied on mother and family,
   - experienced oneness (unity) in family situation,
   - learned that each person is unique but also a member of a whole,
   - mother responsible for education in these early stages,
   - *Mother Play and Nursery Songs* used to assist mothers at this stage.

XII.

## Pat-a-Cake

CAN such a simple game
Some deeper meaning claim?
Yes; and the meaning's here—
A meaning wise and clear.
So many things must join with free good-will,
At the right moment task and share fulfil;
If the good work is to succeed and win
The joy we hope when we fresh work begin.

BABY wants to try and make us
Such a cake as he can bake us.
Pat your cake; I'll show you how.
Baker says, "It's quite time now;
Bring the dough, as you are told,
Ere my oven gets too cold."
Baker, here is a nice large cake
You for Baby so kindly will bake.
Deep in the oven, my little one,
Push in your cake; it will soon be done.

34

Patsche-Kuchen.

„Mag euch wohl ein höh'rer Sinn
In dem Patsche-Kuchen liegen? —
O, wohl liegt er klar darin:
Willig muß sich Mehres fügen,
Jeder euch zu rechter Zeit
Sein an seinem Theil bereit,
Soll das Werk gelingen
Und uns Freude bringen."

Kindchen! wollen es versuchen,
Und zu backen einen Kuchen:
Patsche, patsch' den Kuchen glatt,
Der Bäcker sagt: „Nun ist es satt;
Bringt mir doch den Kuchen bald,
Sonst wird ja der Ofen kalt." —
„„Bäcker! hier ist mein Kuchen fein,
Back' ihn schön für mein Kindchen klein.""
„Bald soll der Kuchen gebacken sein,
Tief in den Ofen schieb' ich ihn ein."

Picture 10.

35

**Froebel developed the game Pat-a-Cake into a complex educational activity to help children learn about unity and interdependence of nature and human beings. (From Froebel's *Mother's Songs, Games and Stories* published in 1900 by Rice in London.)**

**Illustrations added to the meaning of the activity and created a visual message. (From Froebel's *Mother's Songs, Games and Stories* published in 1900 by Rice in London.)**

Froebel had approximately the same ages in this stage as Piaget, who developed his theory from a psychological perspective and extensive research.

2. **child stage 3 – 7 years of age**
   - began when child came to represent the internal world in outward ways; children could express inner feelings in language and through art,
   - play would be the basic technique of learning and development,
   - Froebel's whole set of kindergarten materials developed for this age group,
   - rhythm, dancing, music, language, and drawing would be important.
3. **boyhood 7 – 10 years of age**
   - more formal instruction at this point; activity turned to production of things; other children played an increasingly important role in children's learning about the social world.

In his writings and in his work with children, Froebel concentrated primarily on the first two stages.

**Teacher and student teacher singing action songs with children at the Crescent School Kindergarten about 1898. (Courtesy of De Montfort University, Bedford with thanks to Richard Smart, Head of History at Bedford and College Archivist and Colin Caselton-Bone, Department of Learning Technologies.)**

**Children from the Froebel House School in Bedford, England in the late 1800's dance around the May pole. (Courtesy of De Montfort University, Bedford with thanks to Richard Smart, Head of History at Bedford and College Archivist and Colin Caselton-Bone, Department of Learning Technologies.)**

*Would modern psychology view Froebel's stages of development as accurate? What about his idea of continuity of development?*

These three stages were continuous, with no sudden breaks in the process:

> *"In his entire cultivation, it is highly important that his development should proceed continuously from one point, and that this continuous progress be seen and ever guarded. Sharp limits and definite subdivisions within the continuous series of the years of development . . . are therefore highly pernicious, and even destructive in their influence."*
>
> — ***The Education of Man***

Long before psychologists were to develop theories about developmental stages, Froebel stated that the needs of each stage must be fully met. The complete development in each stage was essential to the attainment of the next stage. As a consequence, education was not primarily for teaching but for **development**:

> *"How different could this be in every respect, if parents were to view and treat the child with reference to all stages of development and age, without breaks and omissions; if, particularly, they were to consider the fact that the vigorous and complete development and cultivation of each successive stage depends on the vigorous, complete and characteristic development of each and all preceding stages of life!*
>
> *The boy has not become a boy, nor has the youth become a youth, by reaching a certain age, but only by having lived through childhood."*
>
> — ***The Education of Man***

## Symbolism in Program Ideas

*Froebel's concept of unity or interconnectedness of the elements of the world affected all his educational ideas. How could you focus on this goal through a project on dairy products or bread? What experiences might you envision?*

Symbolism was very strong in Froebel's mind and practice. He often saw children taking objects and pretending that they were other objects. A stick would become a horse. A tree might be a giant. He felt that the process could be reversed by giving children objects that had certain cosmic truths or realities. If children were properly exposed to them, they would learn the truths that were embedded in the objects. Pestalozzi focused on the knowledge gained through the senses, but Froebel was interested in the symbolic knowledge that the object contained.

His lifelong quest for an understanding of unity also played a central role in the children's program. How would children come to understand this abstract concept of unity? For very young children, rhymes like Pat-a-Cake would lead them to see the interconnection of elements of the world (sun, wheat, milling, baking). Gardening was a part of Froebel's program; each child had a small garden and shared with the other children a common garden of both vegetables and flowers.

**Children studying plants in the bright, sun-filled Conservatory at the Froebel kindergarten in Bedford, England. The photo was taken for the Glasgow Exhibition of 1901 to give visitors an idea of the kindergarten work. (Courtesy of De Montfort University, Bedford with thanks to Richard Smart, Head of History at Bedford and College Archivist and Colin Caselton-Bone, Department of Learning Technologies.)**

**Children learning to take care of plants at the Froebel kindergarten in Bedford, England in the early 1900's. Quote on back of photo reads: "Encouraging children to interest themselves in the life of plants, animals and other living things which they can find in the neighborhood—extract from 'The Froebel Gazette.'" (Courtesy of De Montfort University, Bedford with thanks to Richard Smart, Head of History at Bedford and College Archivist and Colin Caselton-Bone, Department of Learning Technologies.)**

Children would begin to understand the underlying unity of life as they saw connections in things that they could observe themselves. For example, if they saw a nest of young birds, the children would learn about egg hatching, places where nests are built, characteristics of different nests, food eaten by young birds, the effect of seasons on bird life, adaptations of nests, and protective devices of birds.

Froebel felt that the materials provided to children were "gifts" from god, and he called them just that. His first **gift** for the children was a set of several soft, coloured, crocheted balls. These were, of course, round with no corners or sharpness. With this symbol of unity, the children would experience a sense of "god," unity and connectedness:

> *"Starting from the ball, which is unity of form, its distinctness and simplicity, we can proceed to take hold of, and ennoble the whole life of the child."*
>
> **— from a letter of Froebel to his wife in 1838 included in Shirreff, *A Short Sketch of the Life of Friedrich Froebel***

Older children would actually crochet the balls.

The children would also experience the concept of unity with a wooden sphere. But for there to be unity, there must also be diversity, its opposite. The **cube** represented this concept of the diversity of the world. It was an object that had many edges, many corners, and many sides. It was exactly in opposition to the **sphere**.

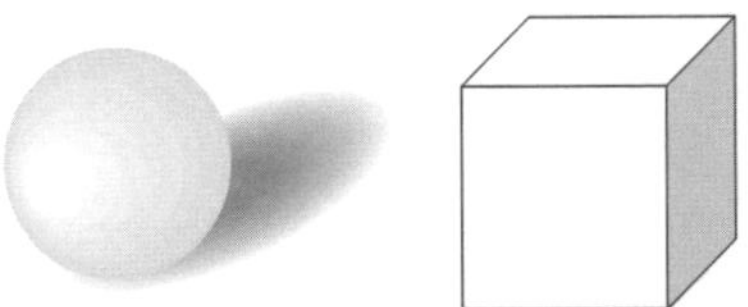

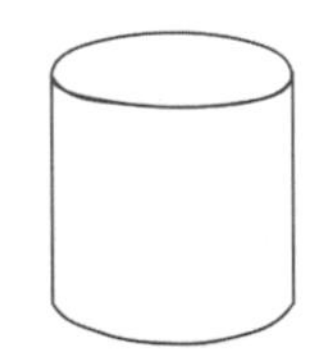

But another shape had to represent the dynamic equilibrium or reconciliation of opposites. The **cylinder** would represent this as it rolled like a sphere and stacked like a cube, demonstrating properties of both shapes and showing diversity within unity.

Along with the **gifts** were **occupations** that were activities to help children's development. Froebel worked to develop and modify these materials from 1835 to 1850. Though not new materials or experiences, their use in an educational program was radically new.

**Froebel created "circle time" to help children gain a sense of unity and interconnectedness. In this illustration children are learning about the ocean with sea shells in the middle of the circle. (From *Century Magazine,* January 1893,"Kindergarten Movement" by Talcott Williams.)**

Froebel created morning "circle time," allowing children a sense of unity in a time for songs and group experiences. This became a central part of the Froebel kindergarten program. As children sang, they created movements to illustrate the meaning of melody and words.

### The Snail Song

Hand in hand, as all can see,
Like a little snail go we;
Always nearer, always nearer;
Always closer, always closer;
Always tighter, always tighter —
Till in closest union stand
All we children, hand in hand.

**— *Pedagogics of the Kindergarten***

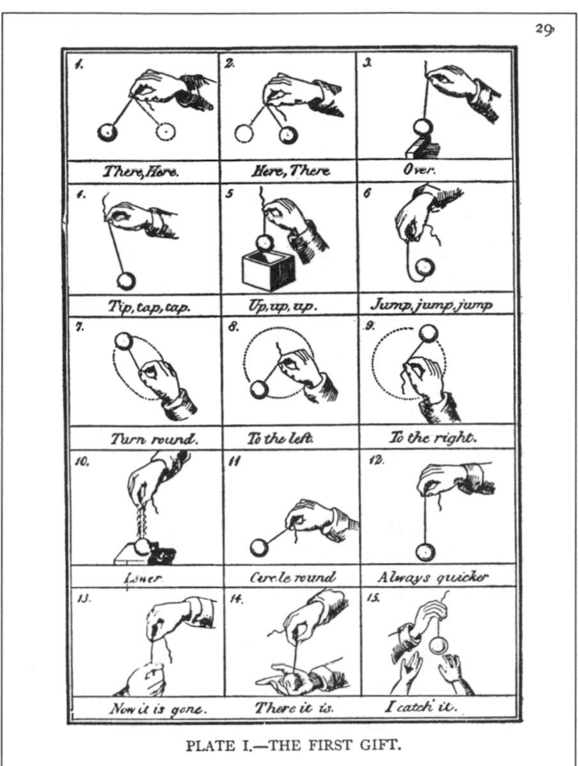


**Exercises with gift #1. In addition to learning colours, gift #1 helped children acquire concepts of direction and exercised the fingers, hands and arms as illustrated by these exercises. (From Von Norstrand's *Royal Gifts*, 1891.)**

## In-Depth Look at Gifts

### 1st Gift:

The six soft woollen balls were the colours of the rainbow's spectrum — red, orange, yellow, green, blue, and violet. In the box there were six strings of different colours that corresponded with the balls. The children could use them in many ways to stimulate their observation and self-expression. Each child would have his or her own box and the teacher was there to help with any problems. Froebel and his colleagues worked out more than 100 games with the balls, and teachers used children's ideas to develop more. Since the balls were identical except for their colour, child would learn to discriminate colour and form. In mathematical terms, the ball was a point and the number one. Children could also learn direction, train their eyes and exercise their fingers, hands and arms.

Songs were used to assist the children in the lessons. For example, "Take This Little Ball" would be sung with the children while they had a box of the crocheted balls.

*What are your thoughts on circle time and its current usage contrasted with Froebel's goal of children learning about unity and interconnectedness as they participated in circle time?*

**Gift #1. Froebel's first gift consisted of six coloured, crocheted balls to help children learn about unity, colour, form and the unit of one. They also helped with observation and hand-eye coordination. These kindergarten children were in a New York kindergarten about 1900. The teacher is at the right, sitting in the circle with the children. (Used with permission of the New York Public Library. From the photography collection, Miriam and Ira D. Wallach Division of Art, Prints and Photographs. Astor, Lenox and Tilden Foundations.)**

Songs like "Now Take This Little Ball" were developed to help children learn from the first gift. (From *Merry Songs and Games for Use of The Kindergarten* by C.B. Hubbard, 1881.)

# Gifts # 2 – 6

## Gift #2:

This gift contained a cube, a cylinder (added later in 1844) and a sphere as well as rods, string and hooks to allow ***the shapes to revolve***. In motion the shapes would be transformed into new forms such as the double cone and conoid (cone shaped figure).

These objects were also used in story time to act out people, animals and objects.

The gifts increased in complexity and variety from # 2 through #6.

**Gift #2. A wooden sphere (unity), a cube (diversity) and a cylinder (equilibrium) made up gift #2. (From the personal collection of Jennifer Wolfe. Photo taken by Kitty Ng.)**

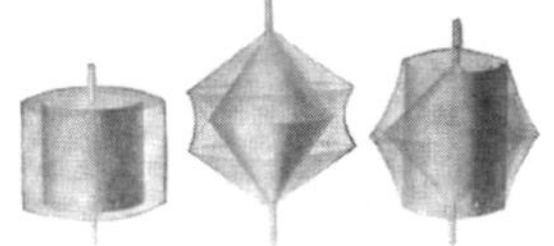

**Spinning Shapes. Shapes became "new" shapes as they spun quickly on strings attached to hooks. (From E. Wiebe's *Paradise of Childhood* published in 1910 by Milton Bradley & Co. of Boston, Massachusetts.)**

THE BOYS' CLASS AT JAMAICA PLAIN.

**Children at a Jamaica Plain Kindergarten used gift #2 on tables with grids to assist their manipulation of the materials. (From *Kindergarten News,* March 1894, "The "Kindergarten for the Blind" by Emilie Poulsson.)**

## Gift #3:

The third gift was a cube that subdivided into eight smaller cubes. Froebel saw an individual as a separate entity as well as part of a greater whole and believed the subdivided cube represented this concept. The separate parts were interdependent and joined together to complete the whole. To express some of the possibilities of the gift, the teacher might use a rhyme such as this:

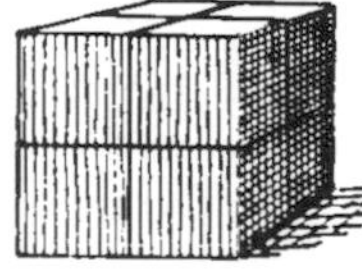

(From E. Wiebe's *Paradise of Childhood* published in 1910 by Milton Bradley & Co. of Boston, Massachusetts.)

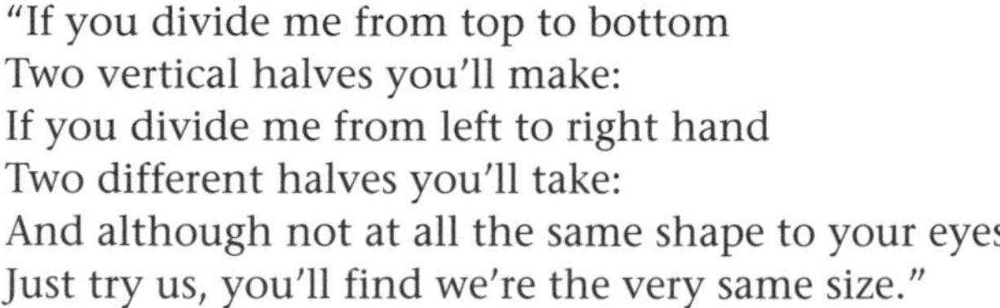

> "If you divide me from top to bottom
> Two vertical halves you'll make:
> If you divide me from left to right hand
> Two different halves you'll take:
> And although not at all the same shape to your eyes
> Just try us, you'll find we're the very same size."
>
> **— quoted in White, *The Educational Ideas of Froebel***

Children at the Bedford Froebel Kindergarten, Crescent School, using the Froebel gifts in 1898. Tables would have grids to aid in the use of the blocks. (Courtesy of De Montfort University, Bedford with thanks to Richard Smart, Head of History at Bedford and College Archivist and Colin Caselton-Bone, Department of Learning Technologies.)

## Gift #4:

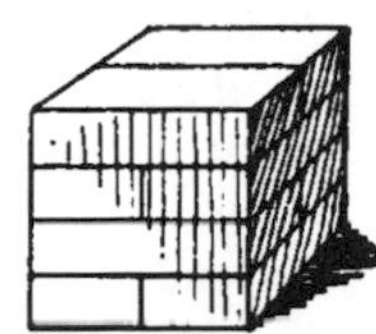

(From E. Wiebe's *Paradise of Childhood* published in 1910 by Milton Bradley & Co. of Boston, Massachusetts.)

Gift #4 was a cube, the same size as gift #3, which subdivided into eight rectangular, oblong solids. Froebel suggested a song such as this to accompany the play:

> "As cube I stand here in my place;
> As surfacc now, I show my face,
> Yet always am the same — I like this pretty game.
> Now without delay
> Divide me in your play;
> Making fleetly,
> But yet neatly,
> Two quite equal parts."
>
> **— quoted in *Pedagogics of the Kindergarten***

## Gift #5:

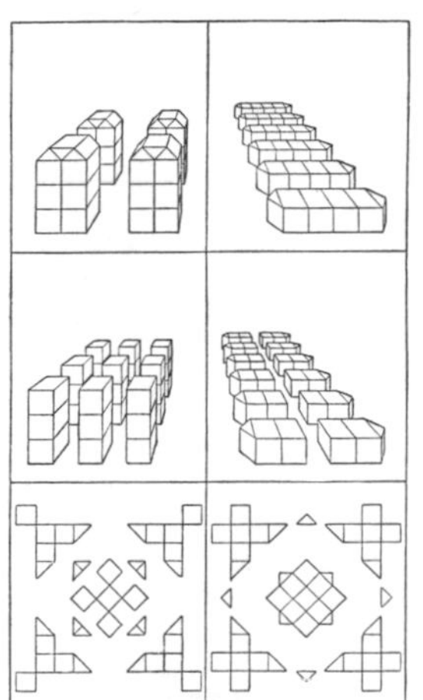

The 5th gift allowed exploration of diagonals, extending the possibilities for design, mathematics, and building. (From White's *The Educational Ideas of Froebel,* 1907.)

Gift #5 was a larger cube that subdivided into cubes, triangular half cubes and triangular quarter cubes. This gift introduced the concept of diagonals.

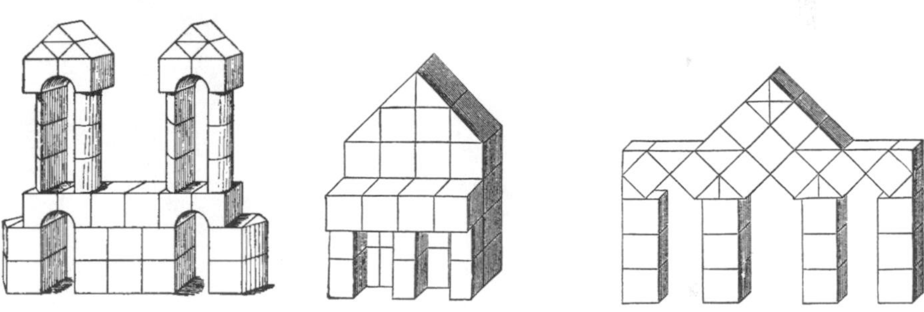

(From E. Wiebe's *Paradise of Childhood* published in 1910 by Milton Bradley & Co. of Boston, Massachusetts.)

## Gift #6:

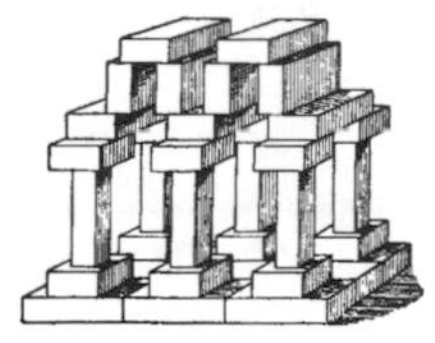

(From E. Wiebe's *Paradise of Childhood* published in 1910 by Milton Bradley & Co. of Boston, Massachusetts.)

Gift #6, another large cube, subdivided into 18 rectangular, oblong solids, 12 flat, square blocks and 6 narrow columns.

(From Kraus-Boelte, M. & Kraus, J., *The kindergarten guide: An illustrated hand-book, designed for the self-instruction of kindergarteners, mothers and nurses. First volume: The gifts.* New York: E. Steiger & Co.)

## Gift #7:

**Parquetry**. A collection of square and triangular tablets of wood or cardboard that focused on the study of *planes* and *surfaces; these were also called* ***Parquetry Tablets.*** These flat shapes were based on the surfaces represented in gifts #2-6. They were scaled to the grids on the kindergarten tables. The tablets allowed the creation of two-dimensional pictures representing objects as well as patterns. Geometric concepts and even the Pythagorean Theorem could be investigated.

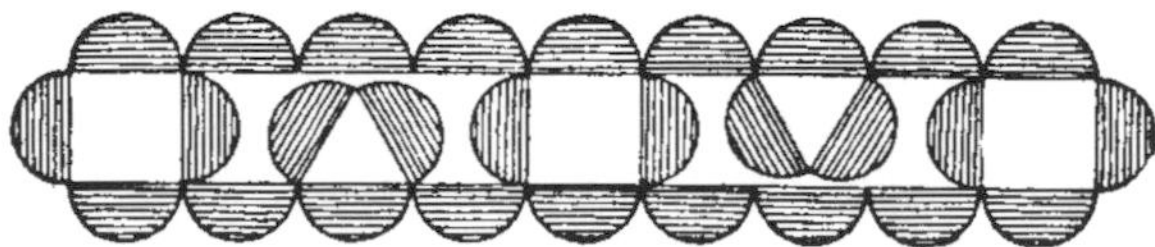

Tablets — also called Parquetry. (From E. Wiebe's *Paradise of Childhood* published in 1869 by Milton Bradley & Co. of Springfield, Massachusetts.)

Stained wood parquetry tablets made by J. L.. Hammett, 1880. Pieces are 4.5 cm x 2.5 cm or smaller. (Used with permission. From the collection of architectural toys and games, Centre Canadien d'Architecture/Canadian Centre for Architecture, Montreal. Acquired thanks to Bell Canada.)

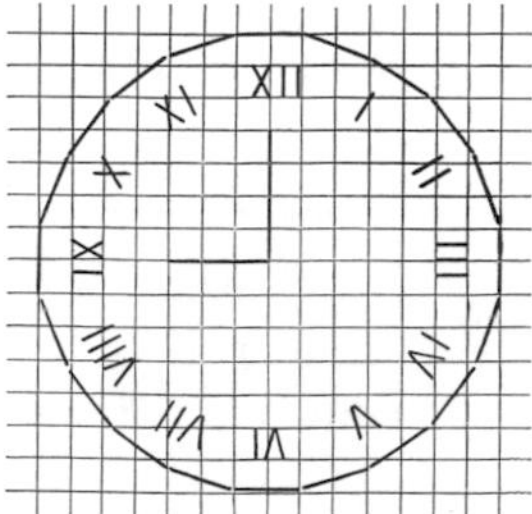

(From Kraus-Boelte, M. & Kraus, J., *The kindergarten guide: An illustrated handbook, designed for the self-instruction of kindergarteners, mothers and nurses. First volume: The gifts.* New York: E. Steiger & Co.)

## Gift #8:

**Sticks and Rings.** A collection of sticks and circles of different diameters and made of wire; with the 8th gift, the child could bisect the circle or divide it into more segments. This gift included whole circles, half circles and quarter circles which could be used to show *representation of a curved line*. The sticks were of various lengths; the focus of this gift was lines-both straight and curved. The fixed, straight lines could form the outlines of objects.

(From E. Wiebe's *Paradise of Childhood* published in 1869 by Milton Bradley & Co. of Springfield, Massachusetts.)

Straight and curved sticks and rings were used to teach form and proportion and also helped prepare children for drawing. The circular rings lent themselves well to forms of beauty and to symmetrical designs. (From Von Nostrand's *Royal Gifts*, 1891.)

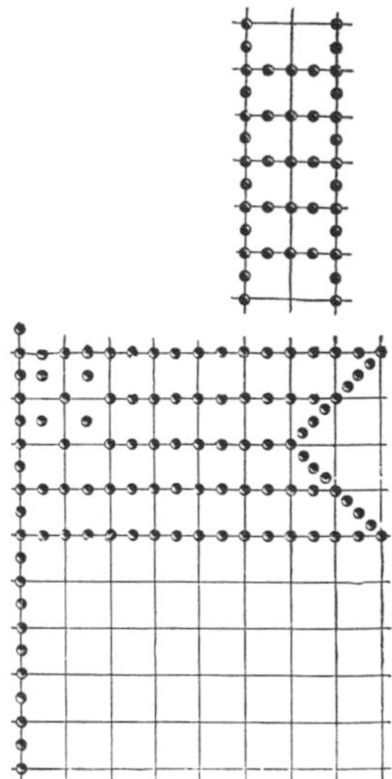

Gift #9 (From Kraus-Boelte, M. & Kraus, J., *The kindergarten guide: An illustrated hand-book, designed for the self-instruction of kindergarteners, mothers and nurses. First volume: The gifts.* New York: E. Steiger & Co.)

## Gift #9:

Natural objects such as beans, lentils, seeds, pebbles; the tip of such objects represented the *point.*

---

Note: There is some discrepancy in the numbering of these final gifts in different references. Froebel himself did not specify a sequence of these latter gifts. Different numbering systems have been used, and some gifts are combined into one unit.

---

### Usage of Gifts

The gifts were specific materials that were manipulated in specific ways.

There were three different ways to use gifts
# 3 – 6, and children gained experience with all three modes:

- **forms of life** (representation of things from the child's environment such as bridges, chimneys, and boats)

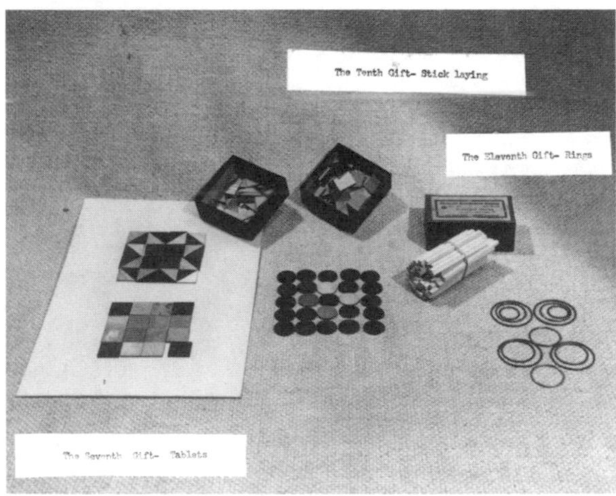


Froebel Gifts. Stick laying, rings and tablets (parquetry). (Used with permission of the ACEI and the ACEI Archives, Special Collections, University of Maryland.)

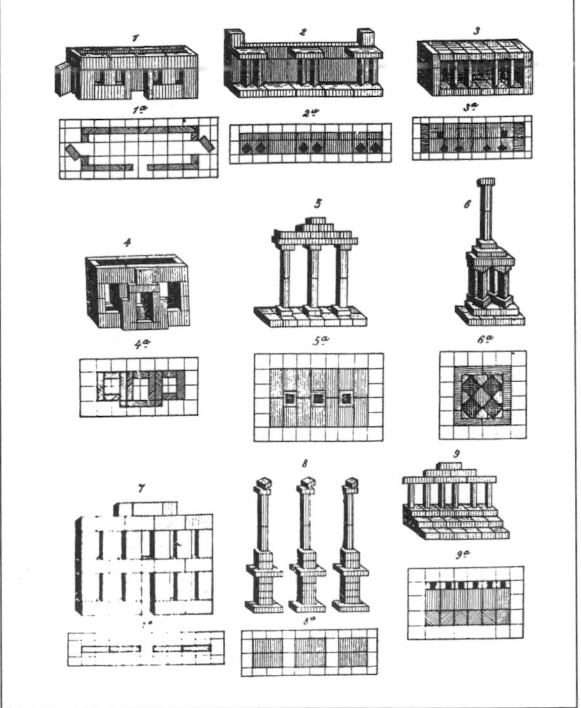

Forms of Life. Children built objects from their environment as "forms of life" with gifts #3 – 6. These are forms of life from gift #6 and include houses, columns, and monuments. (From Von Nostrand's *Royal Gifts,* 1891.)

*Look at the three photos and see if you can find the forms of knowledge, forms of beauty and forms of life in each of them.*

- **forms of beauty** (symmetrical designs where any change on one side corresponded to an equivalent change on the other side; intended to sensitize children to aesthetics)
- **forms of knowledge** (math properties and relationships of number, addition, subtraction, multiplication and division).

**Forms of Life, Beauty and Knowledge. The gifts could be used to explore objects from the environment (forms of life), symmetrical designs (forms of beauty) and mathematical properties (forms of knowledge). These photos show the three usages with gift 7 (Parquetry), gift 8 (Rings) and gift 9 (Points). (Photos taken by Jennifer Wolfe.)**

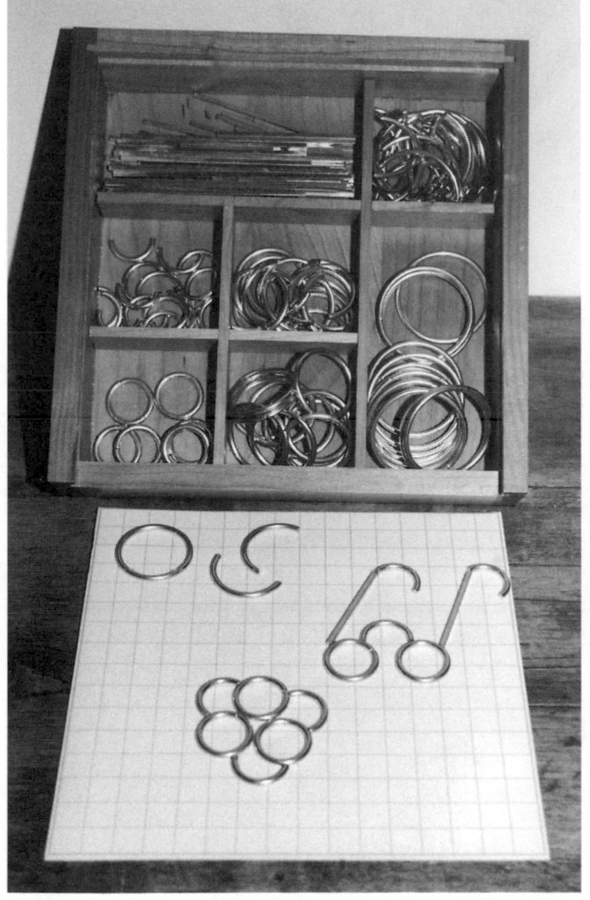

Froebel stated that children should never just learn to say the numerals because numerals were "empty and meaningless" without real objects to count. The forms of knowledge provided concrete mathematical activities.

**Let the children form a large square of 144 cubes, and beginning at one corner, separate them as in the following diagrams, forming squares in the following order, and repeating,—**

| The square of | The square root of |
|---|---|
| 1 is 1 | 1 is 1 |
| 2 is 4 | 4 is 2 |
| 3 is 9 | 9 is 3 |
| 4 is 16 | 16 is 4 |
| 5 is 25 | 25 is 5 |
| 6 is 36 | 36 is 6 |
| 7 is 49 | 49 is 7 |
| 8 is 64 | 64 is 8 |
| 9 is 81 | 81 is 9 |
| 10 is 100 | 100 is 10 |
| 11 is 121 | 121 is 11 |
| 12 is 144 | 144 is 12 |

**Concrete Mathematical Experiences — Squares and Square Root. The blocks could be used to help children understand the nature of squares and square roots. One hundred and forty-four cubes would be laid out to assist children's understanding of these abstract concepts. (From Ronge, J. & Ronge, B. (1855). *A Practical Guide to the English Kinder garden* [sic]. London: J. S. Hodson.)**

The low tables children used were squared on the top, and grids like graph paper were added to make the use of the small blocks more effective. There was a very specific way to take each gift out of the box, rather than just dumping the blocks out on the table. Likewise, the gift was reconstructed and returned to the box. Unity became diversity and was returned to diversity.

**Clay modeling was one of the Froebel occupations. In this illustration, children are making cylinders, one of the basic shapes in Froebel's method. (From *Century Magazine,* January 1893, "Kindergarten Movement" by Talcott Williams.)**

---

Froebel Gifts are no longer produced in large quantities but sets for educational and study purposes are available from:

Uncle Goose Toys
407 Richmond NW
Grand Rapids, MI 49504
U.S.A.
Website: http://www.unclegoose.com/

Uncle Goose Toys also has produced a CD-ROM by Scott Bultman. This is a multimedia guide to the Froebel Gifts and could be used as a study guide or a teaching tool for college or university classes.

Froebel Foundation USA
407 Richmond NW
Grand Rapids, MI 49504
U.S.A.
Website: http://www.froebelfoundation.org/

The nonprofit Froebel Foundation USA was established to promote and disseminate the ideas of Froebel. The Foundation has a bookstore of Froebel-related books, organizes workshops on the use of Froebel gifts, publishes a newsletter (the *Kindergarten Messenger*), is developing a documentary video on Froebel sites in Germany, and is planning to open the first Froebel school/teacher training facility in the U.S.A. in 60 years.

---

## Occupations

In contrast to gifts, which were materials manipulated in specific ways, **occupations** were planned experiences to train children's eyes, hands and minds and to allow children to work with malleable materials. They were designed to help the children synthesize and then creatively express the impressions that were received through the gifts. The gifts were thus transformed and put to practical use through the occupations:

- perforating (ancient art form) — cardboard cards on soft pads were pricked with a darning needle to create designs and pictures (included darning needle used with a cushion as a backing behind the cardboard). Moving from the example of a point in natural objects, children expressed the concept of point in this occupation. The finished design could be held up to the light or put between coloured tissue papers for another effect. The perforating was a kind of drawing or tracing with points.

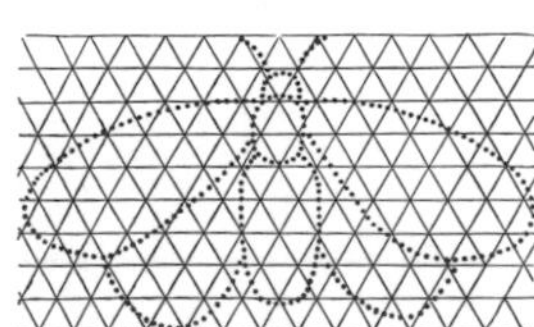

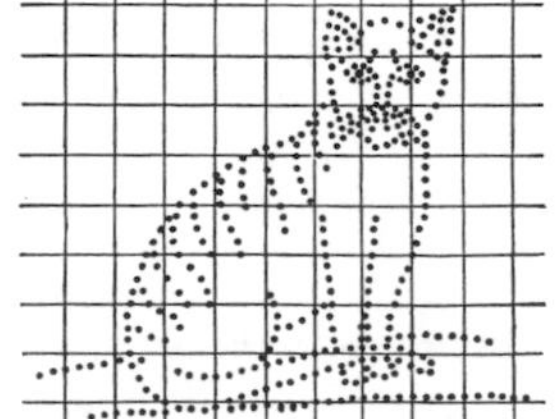

**(From Kraus-Boelte, M. & Kraus, J.,** ***The kindergarten guide: An illustrated hand-book, designed for the self-instruction of kindergarteners, mothers and nurses. Second volume: The occupations.*** **New York: E. Steiger & Co.)**

**(From E. Wiebe's** ***Paradise of Childhood*** **published in 1910 by Milton Bradley & Co. of Boston, Massachusetts.)**

- sewing/embroidery — coloured yarn sewed into cardboard that was perforated with a pattern; large yarn needles with blunt points; this occupation was considered to be drawing with threads

**(From Kraus-Boelte, M. & Kraus, J.,** ***The kindergarten guide: An illustrated hand-book, designed for the self-instruction of kindergarteners, mothers and nurses. Second volume: The occupations.*** **New York: E. Steiger & Co.)**

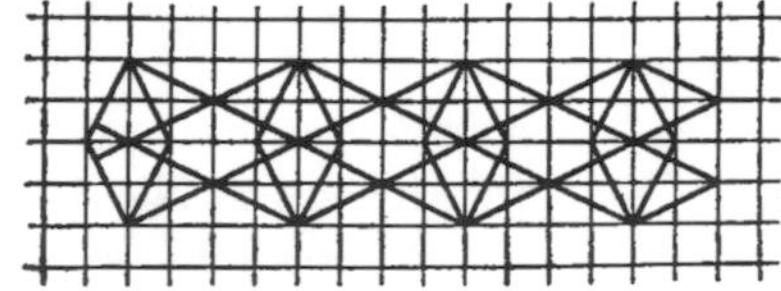

**(From E. Wiebe's** ***Paradise of Childhood*** **published in 1910 by Milton Bradley & Co. of Boston, Massachusetts.)**

- drawing — on dotted paper and freehand; child often started by drawing on frosted window panes; grid paper would often be used

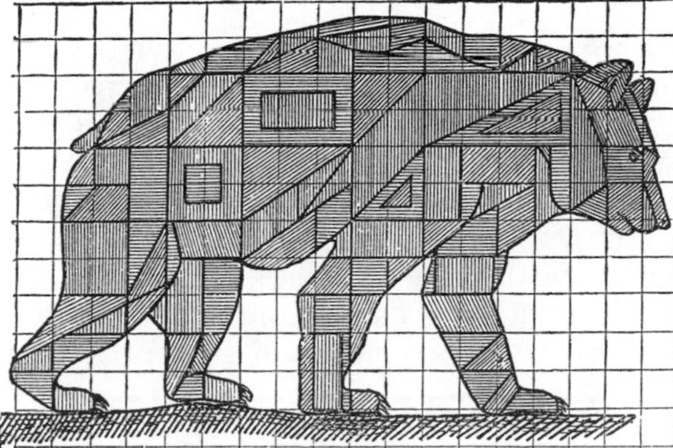

**(From Kraus-Boelte, M. & Kraus, J., *The kindergarten guide: An illustrated hand-book, designed for the self-instruction of kindergarteners, mothers and nurses. Second volume: The occupations.* New York: E. Steiger & Co.)**

- interlacing paper strips

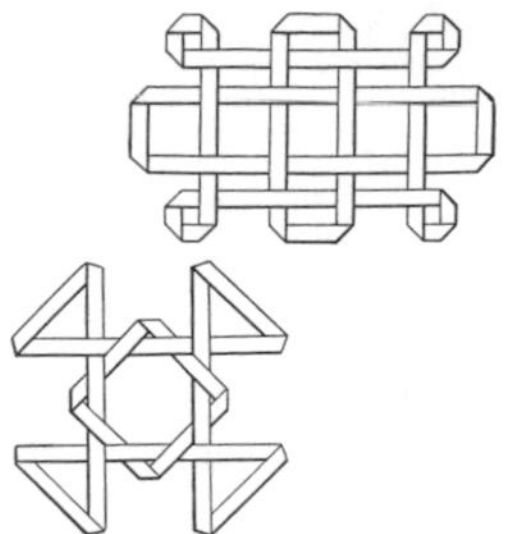

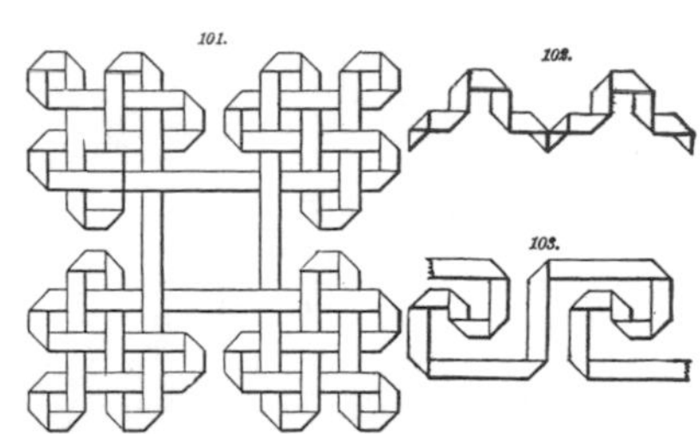


**(From Kraus-Boelte, M. & Kraus, J., *The kindergarten guide: An illustrated hand-book, designed for the self-instruction of kindergarteners, mothers and nurses. Second volume: The occupations.* New York: E. Steiger & Co.)**

- mat weaving — this early form of weaving was used to create patterns and learn number and grouping

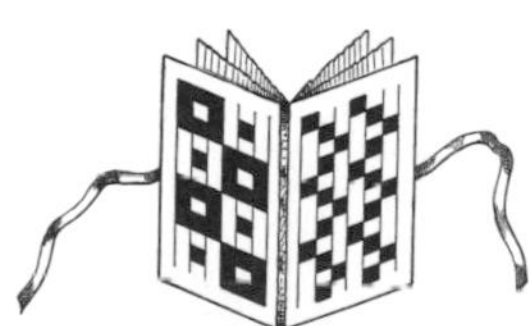

**(From Kraus-Boelte, M. & Kraus, J., *The kindergarten guide: An illustrated hand-book, designed for the self-instruction of kindergarteners, mothers and nurses. Second volume: The occupations.* New York: E. Steiger & Co.)**

**Weaving. The Milton Bradley Company produced the Froebel gifts and occupations for distribution in North America. (Covers From the personal collection of Jennifer Wolfe. Photo taken by Kitty Ng.)**

**Weaving. (From E. Wiebe's *Paradise of Childhood* published in 1869 by Milton Bradley & Co. of Springfield, Massachusetts.)**

- silhouetting — form of paper cutting where figures or profiles were cut out of black paper without previously being outlined

---

The word "silhouette" was derived from Etienne de Silhouette who was the French Minister of Finance in 1759. He enacted strict economic fiscal restraints that angered the nobles who felt that such "reforms" were cheap, capricious and petty. He was forced to resign after nine months but the phrase "a la Silhouette" (according to Silhouette) evolved to refer to anything cheap or plain. Shadow portraits made by tracing the outline of a profile and filling in with black or by cutting out the outline in black paper became known as portraits a la silhouette. They were substitutes for more expensive portraits. Soon they just became known as silhouettes.

---

- paper cutting and pasting — focused on separation of surfaces

**From Kraus-Boelte, M. & Kraus, J., *The kindergarten guide: An illustrated hand-book, designed for the self-instruction of kindergarteners, mothers and nurses. Second volume: The occupations.* New York: E. Steiger & Co.)**

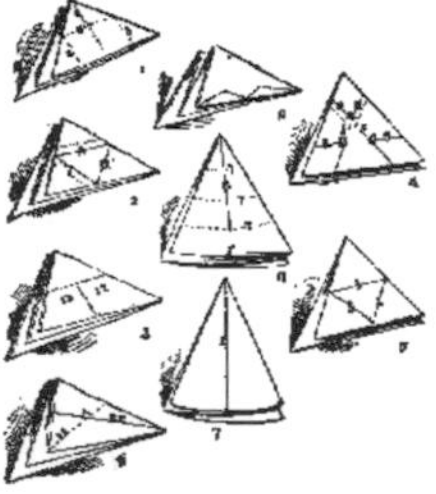

**(From C. Stockham and E. Kellogg's *Mother's Portfolio* published in 1889 by Alice Stockham & Co. in Chicago, Illinois.)**

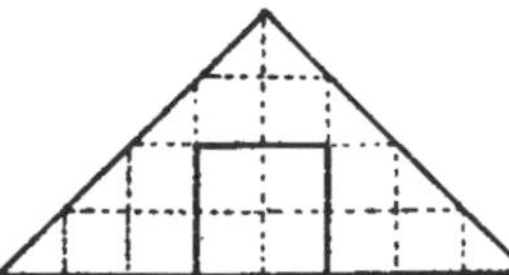

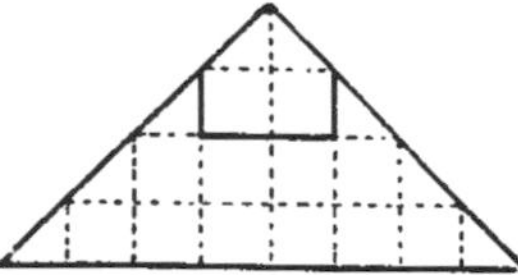

**(From E. Wiebe's *Paradise of Childhood* published in 1910 by Milton Bradley & Co. of Boston, Massachusetts.)**

- paper folding — helped children appreciate ordinary materials and required no tools; focused on surfaces

108 PLATES IX. AND X.

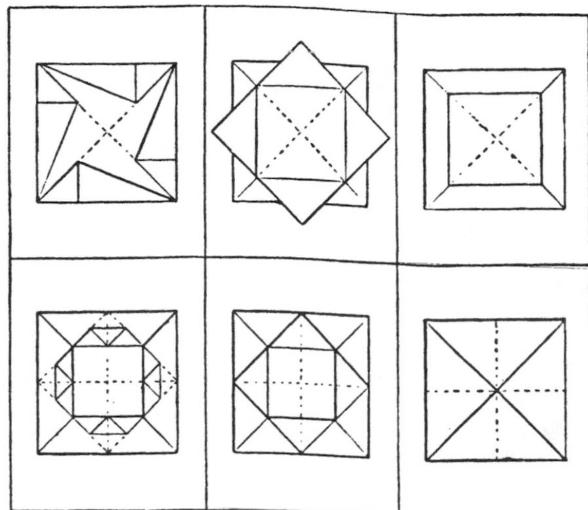

PLATE IX.—OBJECT PAPER-FOLDING.

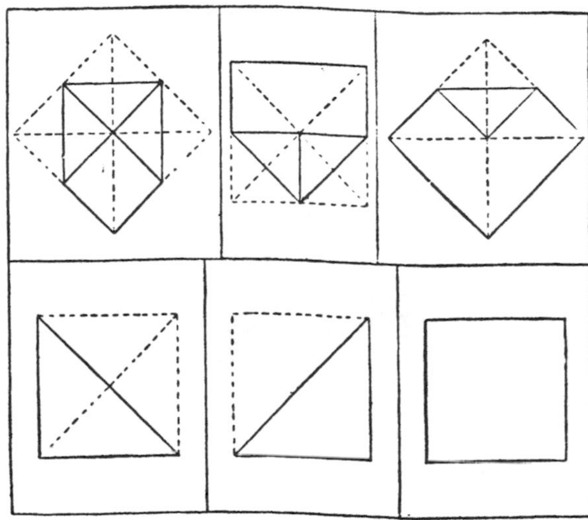

PLATE X.—SYMMETRICAL PAPER-FOLDING.

**Paper folding was an important occupation in the kindergarten because of the artistic work as well as the application of geometric concepts. (From White's *The Educational Ideas of Froebel,* 1907.)**

**Children in the Froebel kindergarten in Bedford, England participated in paper folding. (Courtesy of De Montfort University, Bedford with thanks to Richard Smart, Head of History at Bedford and College Archivist and Colin Caselton-Bone, Department of Learning Technologies.)**

**(From C. Stockham and E. Kellogg's *Mother's Portfolio* published in 1889 by Alice Stockham & Co. in Chicago, Illinois.)**

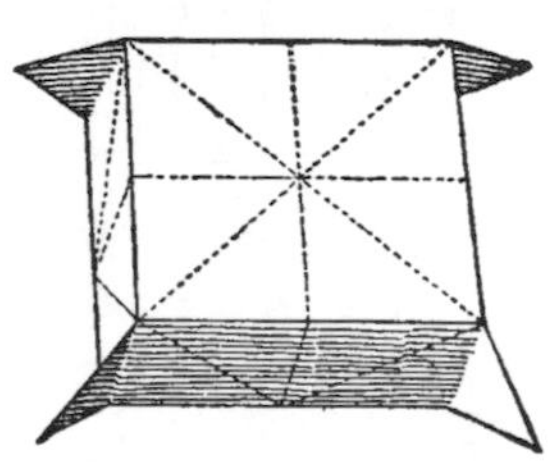

**(From E. Wiebe's *Paradise of Childhood* published in 1910 by Milton Bradley & Co. of Boston, Massachusetts.)**

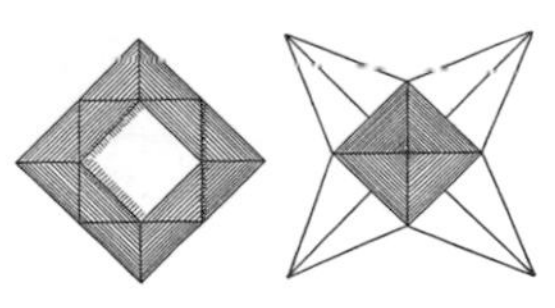

**(From Kraus-Boelte, M. & Kraus, J., *The kindergarten guide: An illustrated hand-book, designed for the self-instruction of kindergarteners, mothers and nurses. Second volume: The occupations.* New York: E. Steiger & Co.)**

- painting — combined form, light, shade and colour

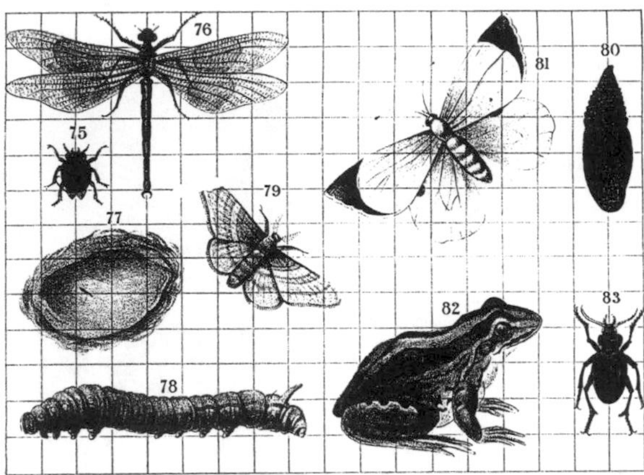


(From Kraus-Boelte, M. & Kraus, J., *The kindergarten guide: An illustrated hand-book, designed for the self-instruction of kindergarteners, mothers and nurses. Second volume: The occupations.* New York: E. Steiger & Co.)

- pea work with sticks (dried peas were soaked first) — thin round sticks were used; clay or wax balls, cork cubes and wires increased the possibilities for construction; allowed the creation of outlines of surfaces and skeletons of solid bodies

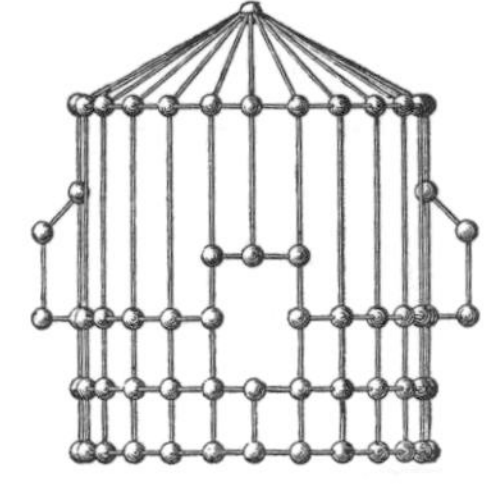

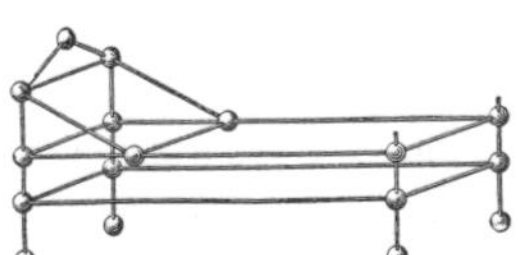

(From Kraus-Boelte, M. & Kraus, J., *The kindergarten guide: An illustrated hand-book, designed for the self-instruction of kindergarteners, mothers and nurses. Second volume: The occupations.* New York: E. Steiger & Co.)

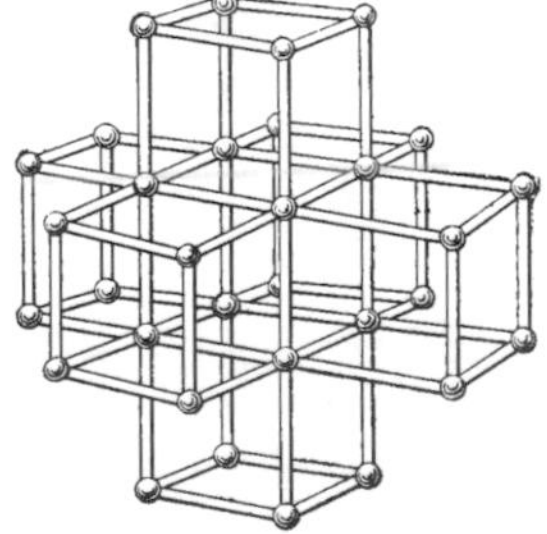

(From E. Wiebe's *Paradise of Childhood* published in 1910 by Milton Bradley & Co. of Boston, Massachusetts.)

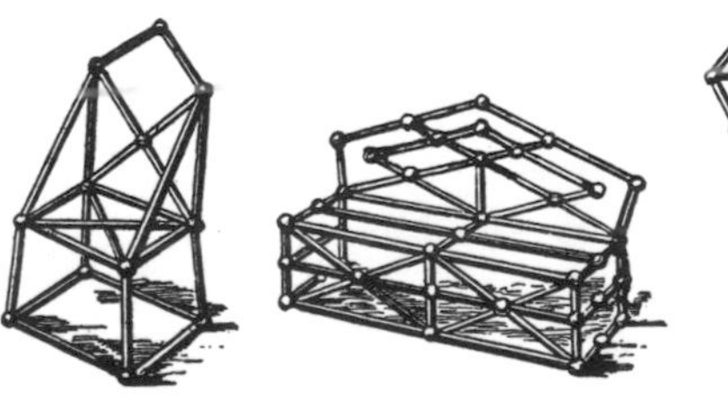

Pea work with sticks used soaked peas with sticks (gift #8) to create two- and three-dimensional designs. Sometimes clay or cork was used in place of peas and wires, instead of sticks. (From Von Nostrand's *Royal Gifts*, 1891.)

---

Many toys have been developed along these lines including the well-known Tinker Toys. Educational toys on the market (Ikoso and Zometools) today also emulate this occupation.

Zometool
1526 South Pearl Street
Denver, Colorado 80211 U.S.A.
Website: http://www.zometool.com

Ikoso
85210 Willamette St.
Eugene, Oregon 97403 U.S.A.
Website: http://www.ikoso.com

---

- cardboard modeling — cardboard was cut and then folded; hollow surface bodies were represented; focus on surface as a step between plane and solids

**Children doing cardboard paper modelling at the Bedford Kindergarten in 1901. Quote on the back by E. F. Galloway, a graduate of the teacher training program: "Paper folding and cutting, paper and cardboard modeling are extremely useful in the teaching of physical science and mathematics." (Courtesy of De Montfort University, Bedford with thanks to Richard Smart, Head of History at Bedford and College Archivist and Colin Caselton-Bone, Department of Learning Technologies.)**

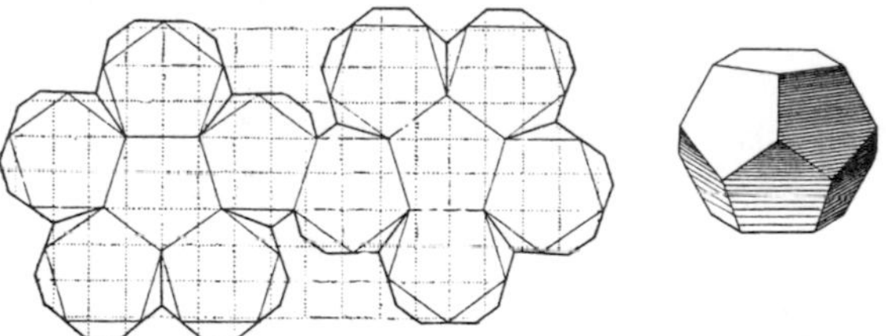

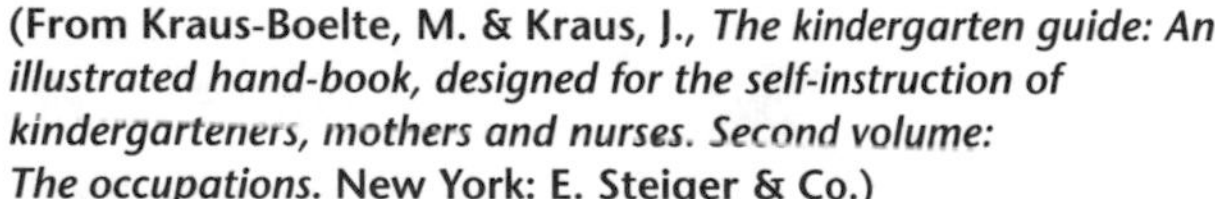

**(From Kraus-Boelte, M. & Kraus, J., *The kindergarten guide: An illustrated hand-book, designed for the self-instruction of kindergarteners, mothers and nurses. Second volume: The occupations.* New York: E. Steiger & Co.)**

- clay, beeswax and putty modeling — clay was mixed with oil to keep it supple; intended to create shape from a shapeless material

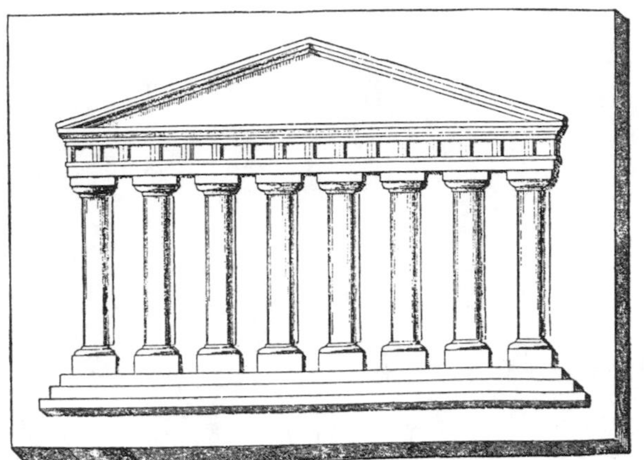

(From Kraus-Boelte, M. & Kraus, J., *The kindergarten guide: An illustrated hand-book, designed for the self-instruction of kindergarteners, mothers and nurses. Second volume: The occupations.* New York: E. Steiger & Co.)

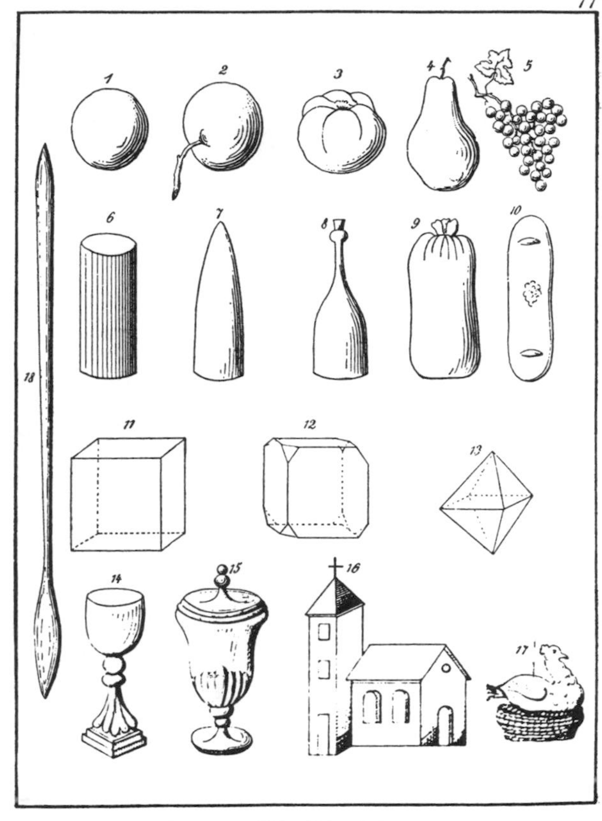

PLATE XXII.—THE TWENTIETH GIFT.

**Children used clay (or sometimes wax) to create new forms. The child would begin with the sphere, cube and cylinder. (From Von Nostrand's *Royal Gifts.*)**

- sand play (sand table or sand garden with both wet and dry sand)
- linking, jointed slats (flat sticks with brass hinges or rivets on the ends) — focused on edges to create different forms

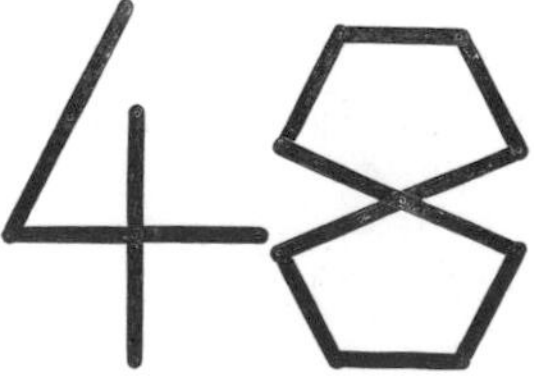

(From Kraus-Boelte, M. & Kraus, J., *The kindergarten guide: An illustrated hand-book, designed for the self-instruction of kindergarteners, mothers and nurses. Second volume: The occupations.* New York: E. Steiger & Co.)

- intertwining slats/interlacing slats — uncoloured or coloured birch or oak slats

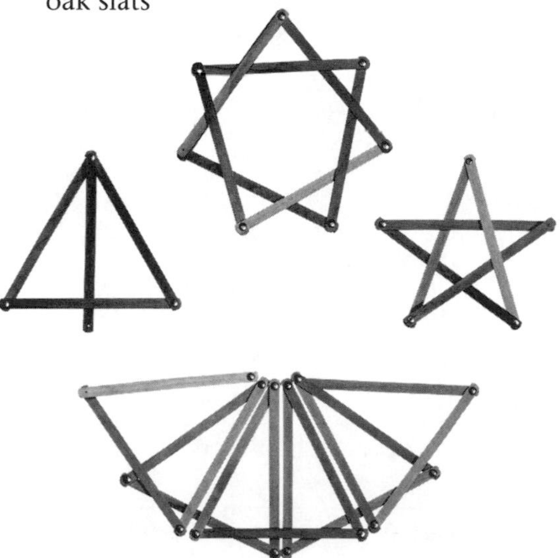

**Jointed slats manufactured by Milton Bradley and Co. in 1880. Each wood slat was 107 cm high. (Used with permission. From the Collection of architectural toys and games Centre Canadien d-Architecture/Canadian Centre for Achitecture, Montreal. Acquired thanks to Bell Canada.)**

- paper chain making — developed from paper cutting
- straw chains (Daisy chains on heavy thread)
- rolled strip work with coloured paper
- bead stringing with wooden beads
- pegboards

**This display of Froebel occupations has an obvious American perspective with the drawing of George Washington. (Used with permission of the ACEI and the ACEI Archives, Special Collections, University of Maryland.)**

*What "modern" toys or educational materials have their origin in Froebel's gifts or occupations?*

*Where do you think Froebel got his ideas for the gifts and occupations?*

There was a focus on **points** (beads, perforating), **lines** (interlacing, weaving, drawing, embroidery), **surfaces** (paper folding, paper cutting, painting, parquetry) and **solids** (clay, cardboard work).

Many of these were ancient art forms, redefined for use with young children. Most of these "occupations" can be seen in early childhood programs today.

Though not "new" experiences, this was the first time that these kinds of activities were ***systematically*** organized in programs for young children.

The following is a comparison of the gifts and occupations in terms of their dimensions:

| | Learning Mode | Activity | Results | Focus |
|---|---|---|---|---|
| gifts | analytic | rearrangements | short-lived results | focus on the solid, then the line and finally the point |
| occupations | synthetic | transformations | permanent results | focus on the point, then the line and finally the solid. |

### Mother Play and Nursery Songs

The book had songs, stories, and games, but these were done with a broader goal of seeing "unity."

For example with the rhyme pat-a-cake, children would learn about the contributions of the baker, the source of wheat and the dependence of the wheat on sun and rain; but they would also see the inter-connected nature of it all.

**Children in the Froebel Kindergarten in Bedford, England participated in carpentry classes twice a week. (Courtesy of De Montfort University, Bedford with thanks to Richard Smart, Head of History at Bedford and College Archivist and Colin Caselton-Bone, Department of Learning Technologies.)**

*Froebel was always studying and modifying his ideas. How do you think he would have adjusted his programs to incorporate our current knowledge of children?*

**Bedford Froebel Kindergarten in the early 1900's included a mix of Montessori apparatus, a sand "heap," and a child-sized playhouse (a "Wendy House") built by the children themselves. (Courtesy of De Montfort University, Bedford with thanks to Richard Smart, Head of History at Bedford and College Archivist and Colin Caselton-Bone, Department of Learning Technologies.)**

**Taken in the early 1900's at the Bedford Froebel kindergarten. Quote on the back by Miss Walmsley and recorded in the Froebel Gazette: "We sometimes hear that it is said we do nothing but play at the kindergarten. This is in one sense a most untrue, and yet in another sense, a most true statement. If play means to fritter time away aimlessly, that we do not do—the statement is utterly false. If on the other hand it means that we recognize that the further life of a child rests upon his play activities, and therefore we make right use of these play activities in order to prepare the child for a sound healthy life, then we do play in the highest sense of the word." (Courtesy of De Montfort University, Bedford with thanks to Richard Smart, Head of History at Bedford and College Archivist and Colin Caselton-Bone, Department of Learning Technologies.)**

## Child Study at the Centre

Froebel deeply respected the life of a child and wanted to ensure that childhood was studied and built upon in the kindergartens.

He believed it was vital that

> *"the life of a childhood be recognized, acknowledged, and actually considered and treated in life relatively as a whole in its worth and dignity."*
>
> **— *Education by Development***

> *"What, now, shall the school teach? But the knowledge of this nature and these requirements can be derived only from the observation of the character of man in his boyhood."*
>
> **— *The Education of Man***

## Play

Play was central to Froebel's concepts of learning for children. He eloquently expressed the meaning of play for young children:

> *"Play is the highest phase of child development — of human development at this period: for it is self-active representation of the inner — representation of the inner necessity and impulse.*
>
> *It gives, therefore, joy, freedom, contentment, inner and outer rest, peace with the world.*
>
> *Is not the most beautiful expression of child-life at this time a playing child?*
>
> *. . . play at this time is not trivial, it is highly serious and of deep significance.*
>
> *. . . the spontaneous play of the child discloses the future inner life of the man."*
>
> **— *The Education of Man***

## The Family and Community

Froebel did not limit the programming for children to the schoolroom. Teachers were encouraged to take children on field trips into the community to explore their immediate world:

> *"Parents and teachers should remember this — take the little ones at least once a week for a walk — not driving them out like a flock of sheep, nor leading them out like a company of soldiers, but going with them as a father with his sons, and acquaint them more fully with whatever the season or nature offers them."*
>
> ***— The Education of Man***

Small group field trips with plentiful opportunities to explore the environment are still the most effective way for children to learn. Small groups allow ample time for discussion and questioning. They can and should be at the heart of programs for young children, allowing the children to investigate the real world around them.

Nature study was a revelation of god/unity and played a large part in the program.

Froebel also maintained that there must be a balance and cooperation between family and community. He believed that the family was a part of the life of a community and that it was important to acknowledge and support

> *"the constant reciprocal relation between the two."*
>
> ***— Education by Development***

## Goals of Education

*What aspects of Froebel's kindergarten practice do you still see in early childhood programs?*

What is education? What are the goals for children? These questions are reiterated from Plato to the present. Is autonomous thinking a goal?[4]

Froebel insisted thinking be at the heart of education for children:

> *"To lead children early to think, this I consider the first and foremost object of child-training."*
>
> ***— The Education of Man***

## Froebel Education in the United States

As early as 1836, Froebel prophetically predicted that the United States would be a more fertile ground for his kindergarten ideas.

---

[4] See appendix to *Number in Preschool and Kindergarten* by Constance Kamii for an in-depth discussion of the goals of education—autonomous versus heteronomous thinking.

The kindergarten ideas of Froebel spread in North America through the work of Elizabeth Peabody, Mary Peabody Mann, Susan Blow and Kate Douglas Wiggin.[5] Elizabeth Peabody had taught with Bronson Alcott at his Temple School in Philadelphia.

---

Elizabeth was the oldest of three sisters. Her younger sister, Sophia, married Nathaniel Hawthorne, author of *The Scarlet Letter*, and her sister Mary married Horace Mann, a renowned educator and politician. Louise Tharp tells the story of these three remarkable women in *The Peabody Sisters of Salem. Pioneers of the Kindergarten in America* by the Committee of Nineteen (of the International Kindergarten Union) also provides accounts of Peabody and other early kindergarten leaders in the U. S. Other biographies of Peabody include *Elizabeth Palmer Peabody* by Ruth Baylor (1965) and more recently, B. Ronda's *Elizabeth Palmer Peabody: A Reformer on Her Own Terms (1999)*. An 1862 article by Peabody, "What is a Kindergarten," in the *Atlantic Monthly* magazine is a clear representation of her ideas of the emerging kindergarten movement in the United States. Peabody wrote "The Origin and Growth of the Kindergarten" in 1882. There is a chapter on Peabody in Agnes Snyder's *Dauntless Women in Childhood Education.*

---

Froebel's ideas appealed to people disenchanted with the prevalent school attitude vividly described by William Heard Kilpatrick:

> *"We'll all take our places, and show no wry faces.*
> *We'll all say our lessons distinctly and slow.*
> *For if we don't do it, our teachers will know it;*
> *And into the corner we surely must go."*
>
> — ***Froebel's Kindergarten Principles Critically Examined***

**Edward Wiebe's *Paradise of Childhood* (1869) and C. Stockham and E. Kellogg's *Mother's Portfolio* (1889) introduced Froebel's ideas to a North American audience. (From the personal collection of Jennifer Wolfe. Photo by Kitty Ng.)**

Froebel's method increased in popularity when Milton Bradley heard Elizabeth Peabody speak. His interest piqued by her impassioned words about the Froebel methods and materials, Bradley agreed to publish in 1869 Edward Wiebe's *Paradise of Childhood: A Practical Guide to Kindergartners*. Wiebe, who had trained directly under Luise Froebel and taught kindergarten in Germany, lived in Bradley's hometown of Springfield, Massachusetts and taught music. Bradley's father had actually used Froebel-like materials in Milton's own education.

[5] Wiggin was also the author of *Rebecca of Sunnybrook Farm*. Biographical material on Kate Wiggin and Susan Blow can be found in Agnes Snyder's *Dauntless Women in Childhood Education.*

Milton Bradley had made his fortune selling game kits (*Games for Soldiers*) to Union soldiers in the U.S. Civil War. Milton Bradley then began manufacturing Froebel kindergarten gifts and occupations for wider distribution. His company actually produced "improved" lines of gifts and occupations that varied from the originals. E. Steiger Company also produced the Froebel materials in North America.

The kindergarten "firsts" happened quickly.[6] The first U.S. kindergarten opened in Wisconsin in 1856 organized by Margarethe Meyer Schurz[7], a student of Froebel; it had classes in German. Elizabeth Peabody organized the first English kindergarten in Boston in 1860. The first public school kindergarten was in St. Louis in 1873 under Susan Blow with William Harris as superintendent.

Many books were published with instructions on how to use the gifts and occupations in an American context (e.g. *Kindergarten Culture in the Family* and *Kindergarten: A Complete Sketch of Froebel's System of Early Education, Adapted to American Institutions.*) Froebel's own *Mother Play* was not translated into English until 1878. Other books contained action songs for children. Susan Blow provided the introduction to a book by another kindergarten leader from St. Louis. Clara Hubbard's 1881 *Merry Songs and Games* had songs for the ball, cube, circle time, the senses, seasons, occupations, and nature. The zeal of Froebel's followers is shown in the introduction by Blow:

> *"Through the whisperings of the wind and the glory of the light, through the love of father and mother, and the voiceless longings of his own soul he may be pointed to God."*

**Songs for Circle Time. Children sang songs as they sat in "circle time" to help them learn about unity. (From *Merry Songs and Games for Use of The Kindergarten* by C.B. Hubbard, 1881.)**

[6] Different start dates for these openings are indicated in the research literature because of poor or nonexistent record keeping in these early kindergartens.

[7] See biographical information on Margarethe Meyer Schurz in Agnes Snyder's *Dauntless Women in Childhood Education.*

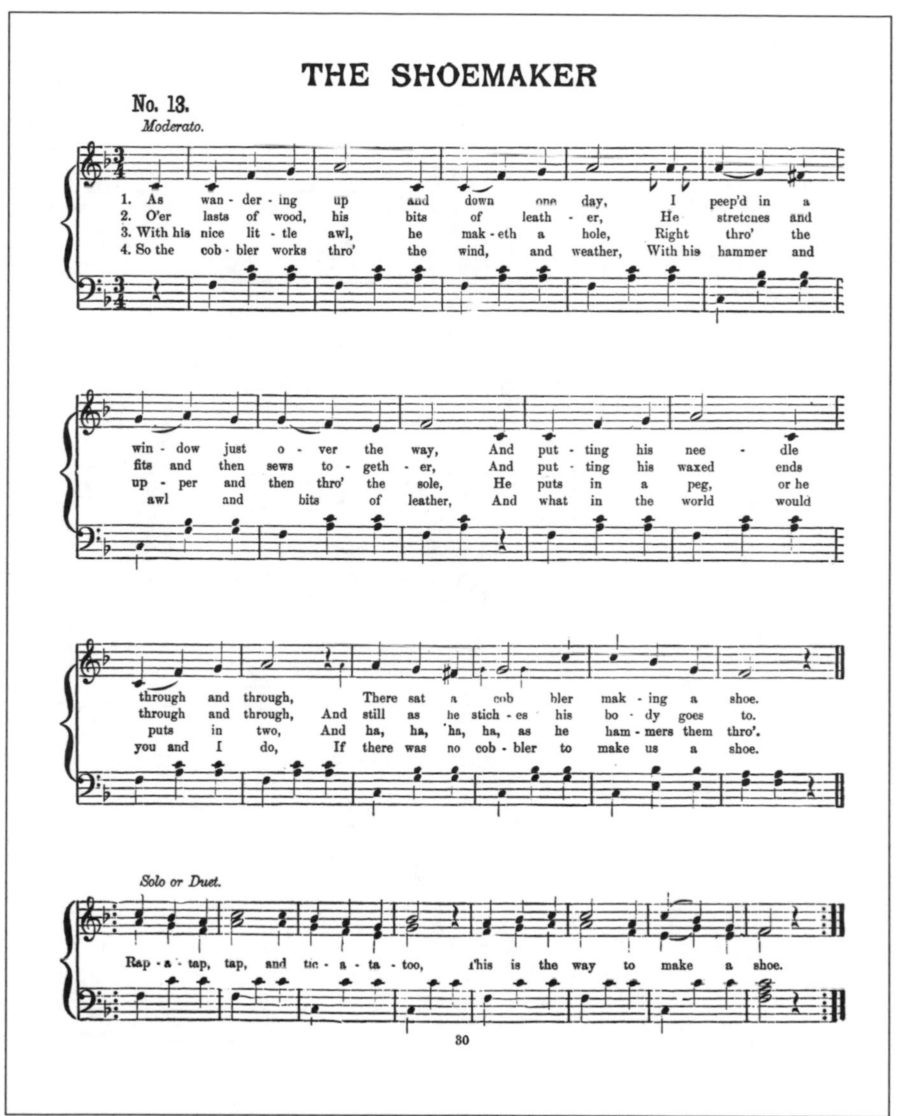


**Songs were developed to help children learn about various jobs and work that the children might see around them. (From *Merry Songs and Games for Use of The Kindergarten* by C.B. Hubbard, 1881.)**

**Teaching songs were created to assist children learning the concepts of the gifts. These two songs revolve around Gift #1 and #2. (From *Merry Songs and Games for Use of The Kindergarten* by C.B. Hubbard, 1881.)**

Milton Bradley Company published many of the books related to Froebel kindergarten education, and there was even a whole book about the occupations of paper folding and cutting (*Paper and Scissors in the Schoolroom*).

In 1887 Teachers College of Columbia University opened with its kindergarten department as a major component. Mary Peabody Mann and Elizabeth Peabody wrote the first American kindergarten text in 1863, entitled *The Moral Culture of Infancy and Kindergarten.*

The Philadelphia Centennial Exposition in 1876 highlighted kindergarten materials and spurred the growth of the kindergarten movement. In addition to the displays of kindergarten materials, the province of Ontario exhibited in the Main Exhibition Hall under the leadership of Egerton Ryerson. Unlike many of the exhibits that focused on children's work and the results of education, the Ontario exhibit highlighted the process, the teaching tools, the visual aids and the practical workings. The exhibit won praise from critics and received major awards and medals.[8]

**The Canada Log House had a kindergarten exhibit showing Froebel gifts. (From *Centennial Portfolio: A Souvenir of the International Exhibition at Philadelphia* by Thompson Westcott, 1876.)**

[8] The Ontario exhibit is described in McDonald and Chaiton's *Egerton Ryerson and His Times* and shown in an engraving in Hodgins's *The Story of My Life by the Late Rev. Egerton Ryerson, D.D., LLD.*

**Women's Pavilion, Centennial Exhibition, 1876. There was a small building, The Kindergarten Cottage, next to the Women's Pavilion, which housed one of the kindergarten exhibits. It was often overlooked in the guidebooks, and is not evident in this illustration. (From *What is the Centennial? And How To See It* by Thomas Dando, 1876.)**

**Inside the Kindergarten Cottage. In the demonstration kindergarten, children sat at tables with grid lines and used the gifts and occupations of Froebel. The illustrator, Hyde, included an alphabet block that would not have been part of the Froebel materials. (From Norton's 1877 *Frank Leslie's Historical Register of the United States Centennial Exposition, 1876.*)**

**Main Exhibition Building. The Centennial of 1876 celebrated the 100th anniversary of the Declaration of Independence in the U.S. and was held on 8 hectares (10 acres) in Philadelphia. There were at least seven kindergarten exhibits, including one in the Main Exhibition Building. (From *What is the Centennial? And How To See It* by Thomas Dando, 1876.)**

**Kindergarten Cottage. A model Froebel kindergarten was held in the Kindergarten Cottage next to the Women's Pavilion at the Philadelphia Centennial Exposition. (Used with permission of the Library of Congress, Washington, D.C LC-USZ62-29903.)**

**[See end of chapter for an 1890 catalogue and price list of Froebel gifts and occupations.]**

**Froebel Kindergarten in Bennington, Vermont. This photo was taken by Madison E. Watson in 1896 and shows children using the 2nd gift of Froebel. It was on the cover of *The Benningtonian*, a newsletter/fundraiser put out by the Bennington Kindergarten Association. (Photo courtesy of Images from the Past, Bennington, Vermont.)**

**One of the world's most influential architects, Frank Lloyd Wright, benefitted from a Froebel education as a young child. Wright attributed his sense of colour and design to the work with Froebel's gifts and occupations. (Used with Permission of the Library of Congress, Washington, DC. LC-USZ62-36384.)**

## Frank Lloyd Wright's Inheritance from Froebel

Frank Lloyd Wright, one of the foremost architects of the 20th century, had a Froebel education when he was young. The Froebel exhibit at the Philadelphia Centennial Exposition in 1876 fascinated Wright's mother. In the same year, when Frank was seven years old, she travelled to Boston to see Froebelian kindergartens and the Milton Bradley store that had a complete line of the kindergarten gifts and occupations. Though older than most kindergarten children, Wright was immersed in kindergarten materials.

The gifts and occupations stood in stark contrast to the gingerbread gimcrackery, showy but useless toys that prevailed at the time. The materials were simple and crystalline in shape.

Frank Lloyd Wright attributed his sense of line, form and colour to these early experiences. He expressed eloquently the impact of the gifts and occupations on his work.

In his autobiography, Wright said,

> *"The strips of coloured paper, glazed and 'matte,' remarkably soft brilliant colours. Now came the geometric by-play of these charming checkered colour combinations! The structural figures to be made with peas and small straight sticks; slender constructions, the joinings accented by the little green pea-globes. The smooth shapely maple blocks with which to build, the sense of which never afterward leaves the fingers: form became feeling.*
>
> *And the exciting cardboard shapes with pure scarlet face — such scarlet! Smooth triangular shapes, white-back, and edges, cut into rhomboids, with which to make designs on the flat table top. What shapes they made naturally if only you would let them!*
>
> *Adding thickness, getting 'sculpture' thereby, the square became the cube, the triangle the tetrahedron, the circle the sphere. These primary forms and figures were the secret of all effects . . . which were ever got into the architecture of the world."*
>
> ***— Frank Lloyd Wright: An Autobiography***

Some of Wright's architectural designs were actually based directly on the Froebel block designs.[9]

- Imperial Hotel in Tokyo was based on the block pattern for a farmyard using **gift #6.**

**The design of his Tokyo's Imperial Hotel is reminiscent of the farmyard block design of Froebel. (Used with permission. Photo copyright 1999 The Frank Lloyd Wright Foundation, Scottsdale, Arizona.)**

**Froebel's Farmyard Block Design. This block design was made with Froebel's gifts. (From the personal collection of Jennifer Wolfe. Photo by Kitty Ng.)**

[9] See "The education of a genius" by D. DeNevi in *Young Children*, March 1968 as well as Brosterman's *Inventing Kindergarten.*

**Froebel's Organ and Lumber Pile. These block design was made with Froebel's gifts. (From the personal collection of Jennifer Wolfe. Photo by Kitty Ng.)**

- Midway Gardens in Chicago was formed upon the block designs of the organ and pile of lumber.

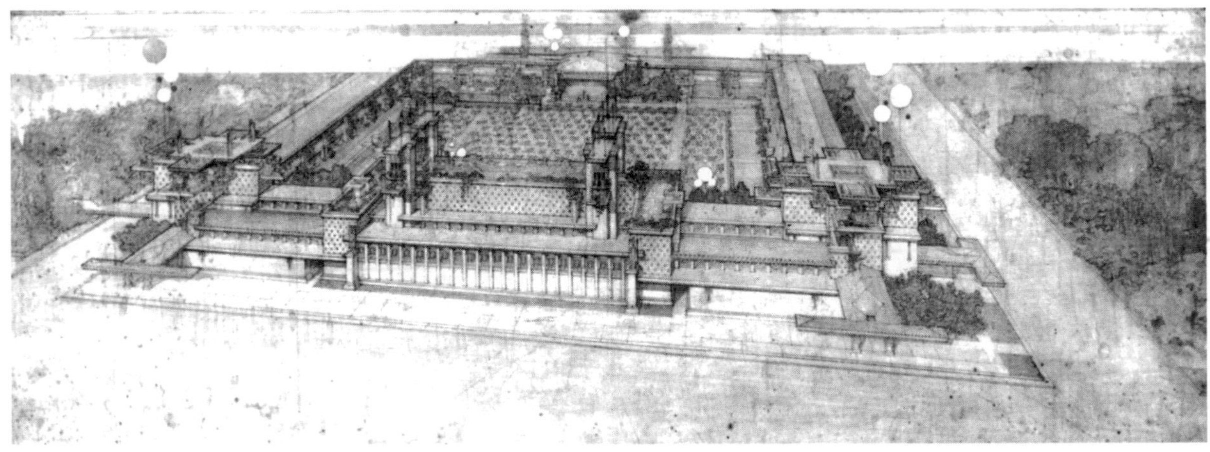

**Frank Lloyd Wright used the organ and lumber pile block designs from Froebel's gifts to design Midway Gardens in Chicago. (Used with permission. Photo copyright 1999 The Frank Lloyd Wright Foundation, Scottsdale, Arizona.)**

- Unity Temple in Chicago and Wright's studio in Oak Park, Illinois were based on the newsstand block pattern using **gift #6**.

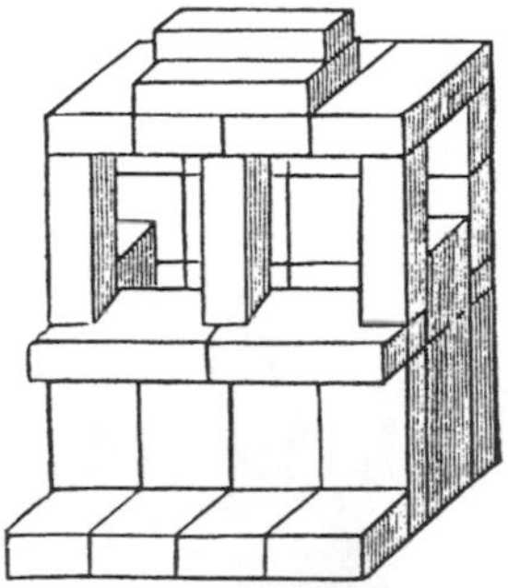

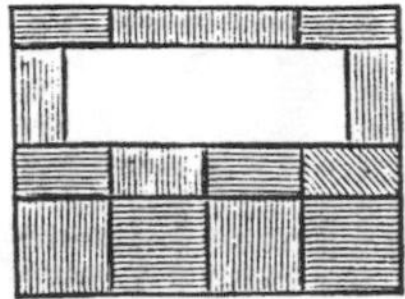

**The newstand from gift #6 provided an inspiration for Wright to design Unity Temple. (From Kraus-Boelte, M. & Kraus, J., *The kindergarten guide: An illustrated hand-book, designed for the self-instruction of kindergarteners, mothers and nurses. First volume: The gifts.* New York: E. Steiger & Co.)**

**Unity Temple. (Used with permission. Photo copyright 1999 The Frank Lloyd Wright Foundation, Scottsdale, Arizona.)**

The building legacy continued with Wright's son, John Lloyd Wright. He got the vision for the toy Lincoln Logs (Log Builders) when he saw the construction techniques used in the Imperial Hotel on a trip to visit his father in Tokyo. These were first manufactured in 1916.[10]

**Lincoln Logs With Wheels. Later sets of Lincoln Logs allowed the building of more elaborate structures. (Used courtesy of Joseph W. Lauher, Stony Brook, New York)**

**Lincoln Logs Instruction Book. The son of Frank Lloyd Wright first marketed Lincoln Logs in the early 1920's. (Used courtesy of Joseph W. Lauher, Stony Brook, New York)**

[10] An earlier version of building logs was produced by Joel Ellis in 1866.

**Lincoln Logs Today. (Photo taken by Jennifer Wolfe.)**

*The Froebel kindergarten background in the area of design affected Frank Lloyd Wright and many others in the arts. What materials do you use now that you think might aid children in developing a sense of design?*

American architect and engineer Buckmister Fuller, French architect Le Corbusier and Russian painter Wassily Kandinsky had Froebel materials and methods in their childhoods and were influenced directly by the blocks and designs.

## Froebel Education in Canada

Kindergartens in Canada also had a Froebelian origin. The second public school kindergarten in North America (Louisa Street Public School) opened in Toronto in 1882 through the efforts of James and Ada Marean Hughes. James Hughes went to St. Louis, Missouri to visit the kindergartens there and recommended incorporating kindergartens into Ontario. Susan Blow was invited to illustrate and explain the kindergarten program. Training programs, often with model kindergartens attached to them, were set up for kindergarten teachers. In 1887 the province of Ontario was one of the first governments in the world to officially support kindergartens as part of the public school system. Before 1900 there were 120 kindergartens in Ontario, and they spread quickly throughout eastern Canada. Large classes prevented the full and effective utilization of Froebel's ideas and materials.

Kindergarten-primary programs were introduced in 1915 in Ontario to provide continuity in early childhood programming, but instead the more academic primary grades affected the kindergarten philosophy.[11]

In 1925, The University of Toronto established the Institute of Child Study.

---

[11] See chapter 9 for Patty Smith Hill's work in the United States to unify kindergarten-primary programming.

There is a Canadian Froebel Education Centre that was established in 1990 by Barbara Corbett though the Froebel Kindergarten was set up in 1970. The Centre has three divisions:

Kindergarten (ages 3 – 7 years)
Froebel School (grades 3 – 8)
Froebel Institute (teacher training)

The Froebel Education Centre
1576 Dundas Street West
Mississauga, Ontario L5C 1E5 Canada

Their web site URL is:
http://www.froebel.com

Many of Froebel's ideas and principles still permeate the children's program with Opening Circle (seen not as a teaching circle but a nurturing circle), gifts, art, occupations and a focus on children's full development within a play focus.

However, the program has adapted to the times, as Froebel encouraged people to do. A letter from Natalie Crawford of the Froebel Education Centre contained the following quotation:

> *"To be a true Froebelian one must follow 'the spirit' of his work. It is not to be committed to the form of the work. Form itself is an empty shell. Many, since his time, have made the mistake of following the form and neglecting the spirit of his work."*
>
> **— Corbett, as cited in N. Crawford, personal communication, April 20, 1999**

The resource teacher for the gifts and occupations describes her current use of the materials:

> *"We use the Froebel gifts as we understand Froebel himself intended them to be used. We use the original nine gifts in the course of the year, not necessarily in sequence, and the occupation relates to whatever gift is being played with at the time. Sometimes we use extensions of the gift. For example, the youngest children would not play with the sphere, cube and cylinder of the second gift, instead they would play with beads of the same shapes. Likewise with the tablets of the seventh gift, the youngest children would first play with much larger squares and triangles. I have found Zometool a wonderful modern extension of peawork, the occupation connecting the line of the eighth gift to the point of the ninth gift."*
>
> **— from personal communication with Finella Scholtz, October 17,1999**

**The "father" of kindergarten. Friedrich Froebel wanted children to grow in an environment that would nurture their capabilities—a garden for children. He gave the name "kindergarten" to his dream. (Used with Permission of the Library of Congress, Washington, DC. LC-USZ62-36384.)**

## Groundwork for the Future

Froebel had remarkable sensitivity and insight into children and their lives and growth. He had a rare understanding of the vulnerability of childhood and of the key role adults assume in nurturing the child. He not only developed materials and experiences for young children but also raised the profile of early childhood education for centuries to come. Organized and articulated curriculum, respect for the individuality of children, a balance of child focus and knowledge focus, and a play orientation were all hallmarks of his programs of *gardens for children*.

In *Froebel's Kindergarten Principles Critically Examined* (1916), William Heard Kilpatrick honoured Froebel's place in history:

> *"Froebel saw education in far larger terms than the mere memorizing of set intellectual tasks or even the acquiring of the formal school arts. As the embodiment of this vision, the kindergarten will remain a permanent monument to an epochal step in the history of education."*

KINDERGARTEN MATERIAL.

In the limited space at our disposal it is impossible to give a complete explanation of the varied material used in a Froebel Kindergarten, but the following enumerations and brief description will serve to give a general idea of the various occupations, and the usual price of the principal material is given that those who are not Kindergartners may be able to form an estimate of the expense. A more full catalogue may be obtained by addressing any large dealer in school supplies, or manufacturer of Kindergarten material.

FIRST GIFT.

The first gift consists of six soft balls about $1\frac{1}{2}$ inches diameter, and usually made of wool or hair, covered with a netting of worsted in the three primary and three secondary colors. A trained Kindergartner should be competent to make these for herself, and will not be satisfied with the inferior goods often offered by dealers.

SECOND GIFT.

The second gift consists of a sphere, cylinder and cube, provided with the necessary staples and holes for suspending in the air, an additional plain cube, two rattan axles for revolving the forms, and two posts and a cross beam for suspending them.

All in a neat wooden box properly constructed for supporting the posts and beam.

Price, $0.60 ; Postage, $.09

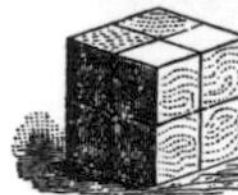

THIRD GIFT.

Eight rock maple cubes one inch square, in a neat, strong, varnished wooden box with slide cover,

Price, $0.20 ; Postage, $.05

FOURTH GIFT.

Eight oblong blocks of rock maple, each two inches long, one inch wide and one-half inch thick.

In neat, strong, varnished wooden box with slide cover,

Price, $0.20 ; Postage, $.05

**1890 catalogue and price list of Froebel gifts and occupations. These pages reproduced from E. Barnard's *Kindergarten and child culture papers: Papers on Froebel's kindergarten with suggestions on principles and methods of child culture in different countries.* (Reprinted from *American Journal of Education.*) Illustrations on the next three pages are all from this source.**

The New Educators *looks at the lives and ideas of Rousseau, Locke, Wollstonecraft and Froebel. It is available from:*
*Insight Media*
*2162 Broadway*
*New York, New York 10024-0621*
*U.S.A.*

*Extensive archival information on Froebel as well as the Froebel Society (and its successor the National Froebel Foundation) is available in the Froebel Archive for Childhood Studies:*

*Froebel College*
*University of Surrey Roehampton*
*Roehampton Lane*
*London, England*
*SW15 5PJ*
*www.roehampton.ac.uk/froebel/archive.asp*

*Froebel Web is an online resource:*
*http://froebel.50megs.com/weblinks.html*

**The gifts and occupations of Froebel were described in an 1890 book, *Kindergarten and child culture papers: Papers on Froebel's kindergarten with suggestions on principles and methods of child culture in different countries.* (Reprinted from *American Journal of Education.*)**



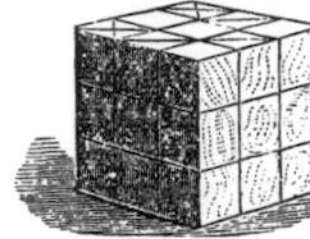

FIFTH GIFT.

A cube (3 x 3 x 3 inches) consisting of 21 whole cubes (1 cubic inch), six half cubes and 12 quarter cubes.

In varnished wooden box with slide cover, Price, $0.40; Postage, $.15

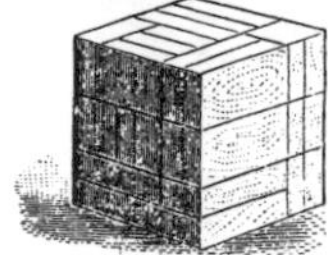

SIXTH GIFT.

Large cube, consisting of 18 whole, and three lengthwise and six breadthwise divided oblong blocks. In wooden box, slide cover, Price, $0.40; Postage, $.15

The above blocks should be made with great accuracy from the most thoroughly seasoned hard rock maple.

SEVENTH GIFT.

The Seventh gift consists of quadrangular and triangular tablets usually of wood, although a heavy card-board serves the purpose fairly, at a much less price, while they retain their corners. If of wood they should be finely polished, and are desirable in light and dark woods.

| | Price. | Postage. |
|---|---|---|
| A. Eight squares, one inch on each side, in wooden box, | $0.25 | $.02 |
| A. 2. Sixteen squares, as above, | .35 | .03 |
| B. Sixty-four half squares, one inch on each leg. Wooden box, | .50 | .03 |
| C. Twenty-four equilateral triangles, one inch each side. Wooden box, | .40 | .02 |
| C 2. Fifty-four equilateral triangles, as above, | .50 | .03 |
| D. Sixty-four obtuse-angled triangles. Acute angles 30°. Wooden box, | .60 | .03 |
| E. Fifty-six right-angled triangles, 30° and 60°. Wooden box, | .60 | .04 |

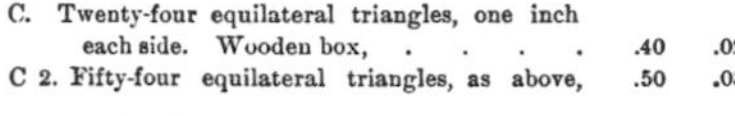

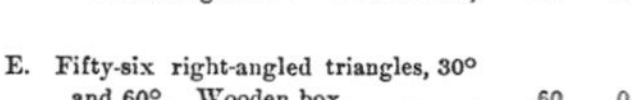

The tablets for the seventh gift are also made in very heavy and solid paper board, each form and quantity as indicated above in A, B, C, D, E, in a paper box. The whole set, Price, $1.00; Postage, $.08

*Kindergarten Parquetry.*—Those occupations in which something permanent can be made, are the most interesting, and seem to be more productive of good.



It is owing largely, no doubt, to this feature, that the weaving and braiding is now the most popular occupation in the school and family. With this thought in mind, a new occupation has been devised in connection with the Seventh Gift which is termed Kindergarten Parquetry, and which has been received with favor by leading Kindergartners.

It consists of colored paper similar to the weaving and braiding papers, but cut accurately to the forms and sizes of the tablets in the Seventh Gift. A pupil having designed with the tablets a figure which is deemed worthy of preservation, is allowed to reproduce it permanently, by pasting papers of corresponding forms on to a heavy paper or card-board. These triangular papers are sold with the backs gummed like postage stamps, and also plain.

For Kindergartens the plain is perhaps preferred by the majority, as the occupation of gumming neatly affords the best possible practice in manual dexterity. But for home use where less supervision is available the gummed papers are more desirable.

A box containing one thousand pieces, assorted forms gummed, is sold for forty cents, and the same without gum for twenty-five.

**The gifts and occupations of Froebel were described in an 1890 book, *Kindergarten and child culture papers: Papers on Froebel's kindergarten with suggestions on principles and methods of child culture in different countries.* (Reprinted from *American Journal of Education.*)**



EIGHTH GIFT.

*Sticks for Stick Laying.*—This Gift consists of wooden sticks, which are cut to various lengths, and used to teach numerical proportions and for producing elementary forms, preparatory to drawing.

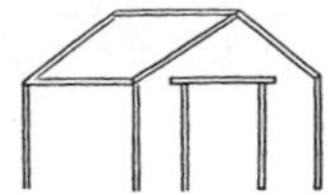

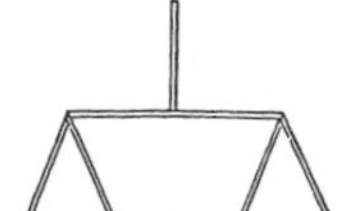

That which is usually called the multiplication table is taught by means of this Gift, by actual observation. Instruction in reading according to the phonetic method, as well as imitation of all letters of the alphabet, together with Roman and Arabic numerals, are taught in connection therewith, preparatory to the instruction in writing.

The sticks for this Gift, if colored red, yellow, blue, purple, orange and green, are very attractive and useful.

NINTH GIFT.

*Rings for Ring Laying.*—This Gift consists of whole and half wire rings for laying figures embodying circles. A continuation of the Eighth Gift and preparatory to drawing and designing.

The rings as ordinarily made are not soldered at the joints, and hence are not rings in the proper sense of the term.

They may be obtained soldered, but of course are more expensive.

A box with 36 whole rings and 72 half rings, assorted sizes, not soldered, sells for fifty cents, and if soldered, for about seventy cents.

TENTH GIFT.

*Drawing.*—This material is slates and paper properly netted in squares.

The paper formerly used was ruled into squares over the entire surface, and the ruling was very inaccurate.

Recently drawing paper and books have been introduced in which the lines are accurately engraved and printed, and each small sheet or page has a plain margin. These features add to the value of this material.

Still more recently slates ruled in the same way have been made as shown in cut on the following page, which are received with great favor because positive corners are thus provided for counting from in dictation.



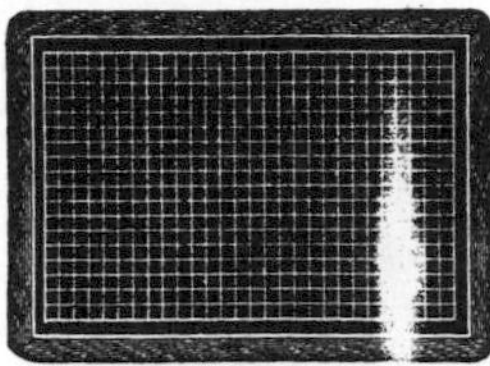

ELEVENTH GIFT.

The Eleventh Gift or occupation is perforating, and the material consists of ruled papers and cards, a heavy needle in a handle, and a felt cushion or pad on which to lay the paper or card.

TWELFTH GIFT.

*Embroidering.*—This material is varied, consisting of cards, plain or perforated, silks or worsteds and needles. Cards ready pricked in various geometrical patterns are largely used in this occupation by many Kindergartners.

THIRTEENTH GIFT.

*Cutting Paper.*—Squares of papers are folded and cut in various ways, producing symmetrical designs. The child's natural propensity to destroy with scissors is here guided in such an ingenious manner that the most astonishing results are produced. The usual material is plain squares of white or colored paper which, after having been properly folded, are marked by the teacher, to guide the pupils in cutting.

A modification of the above consists in the use of papers having guide lines ruled on one side serving the same purpose as the ruled lines on the netted drawing papers, and enabling the pupils to do for themselves much which was formerly done by the Kindergartner.

The Following diagrams represent the ruled cutting papers.

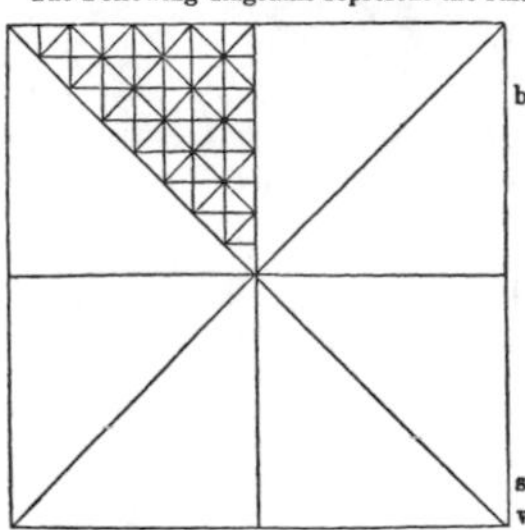

Fig. 1.

Fig. 1 represents the ruled paper before being folded.

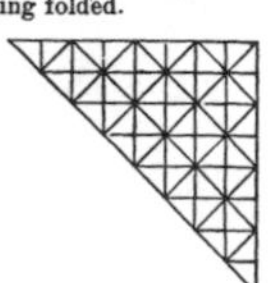

Fig. 2.

Fig. 2 is one of the triangular surfaces which is on the outside when folded.

**The gifts and occupations of Froebel were described in an 1890 book, *Kindergarten and child culture papers: Papers on Froebel's kindergarten with suggestions on principles and methods of child culture in different countries.* (Reprinted from *American Journal of Education.*)**

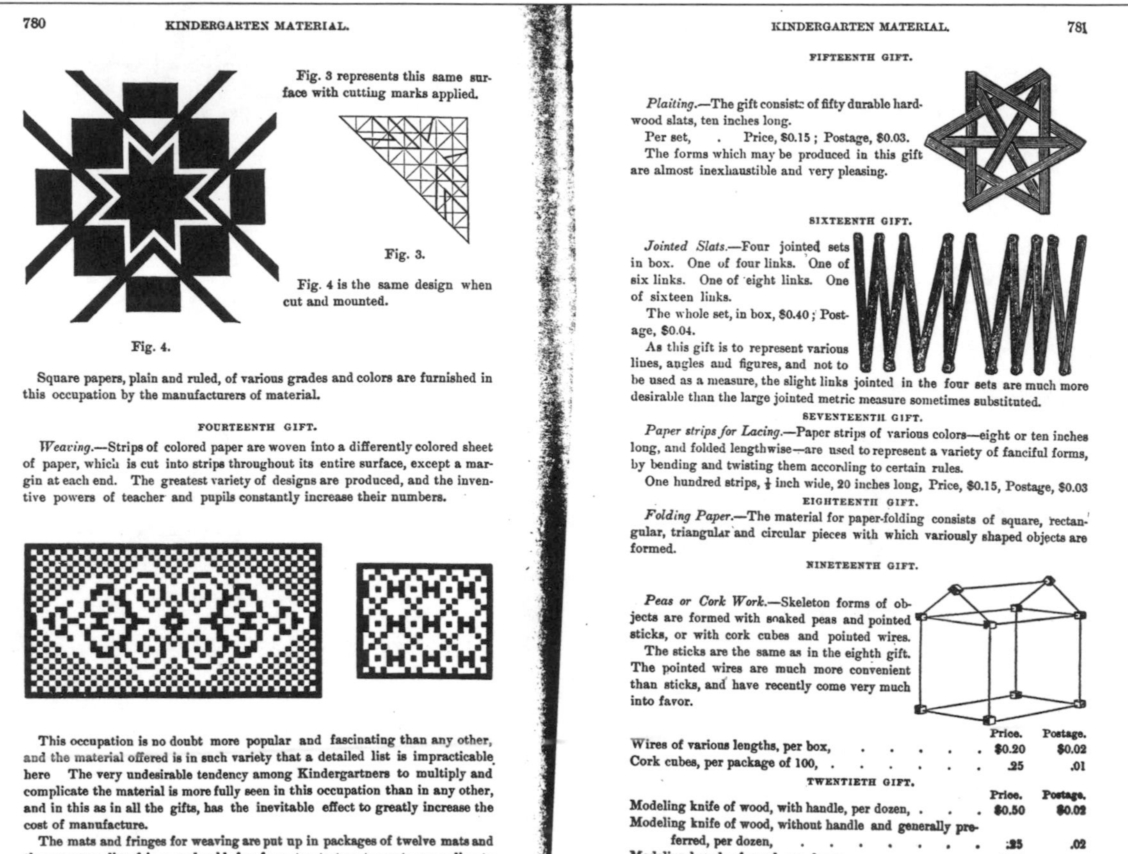

780 KINDERGARTEN MATERIAL.

Fig. 3 represents this same surface with cutting marks applied.

Fig. 3.

Fig. 4 is the same design when cut and mounted.

Fig. 4.

Square papers, plain and ruled, of various grades and colors are furnished in this occupation by the manufacturers of material.

FOURTEENTH GIFT.

*Weaving.*—Strips of colored paper are woven into a differently colored sheet of paper, which is cut into strips throughout its entire surface, except a margin at each end. The greatest variety of designs are produced, and the inventive powers of teacher and pupils constantly increase their numbers.

This occupation is no doubt more popular and fascinating than any other, and the material offered is in such variety that a detailed list is impracticable here The very undesirable tendency among Kindergartners to multiply and complicate the material is more fully seen in this occupation than in any other, and in this as in all the gifts, has the inevitable effect to greatly increase the cost of manufacture.

The mats and fringes for weaving are put up in packages of twelve mats and the corresponding fringe, and sold for from ten to twenty cents, according to size and quality.

KINDERGARTEN MATERIAL. 781

FIFTEENTH GIFT.

*Plaiting.*—The gift consists of fifty durable hardwood slats, ten inches long.

Per set, . Price, $0.15 ; Postage, $0.03.

The forms which may be produced in this gift are almost inexhaustible and very pleasing.

SIXTEENTH GIFT.

*Jointed Slats.*—Four jointed sets in box. One of four links. One of six links. One of eight links. One of sixteen links.

The whole set, in box, $0.40 ; Postage, $0.04.

As this gift is to represent various lines, angles and figures, and not to be used as a measure, the slight links jointed in the four sets are much more desirable than the large jointed metric measure sometimes substituted.

SEVENTEENTH GIFT.

*Paper strips for Lacing.*—Paper strips of various colors—eight or ten inches long, and folded lengthwise—are used to represent a variety of fanciful forms, by bending and twisting them according to certain rules.

One hundred strips, ½ inch wide, 20 inches long, Price, $0.15, Postage, $0.03

EIGHTEENTH GIFT.

*Folding Paper.*—The material for paper-folding consists of square, rectangular, triangular and circular pieces with which variously shaped objects are formed.

NINETEENTH GIFT.

*Peas or Cork Work.*—Skeleton forms of objects are formed with soaked peas and pointed sticks, or with cork cubes and pointed wires.

The sticks are the same as in the eighth gift. The pointed wires are much more convenient than sticks, and have recently come very much into favor.

| | Price. | Postage. |
|---|---|---|
| Wires of various lengths, per box, . . . . . . | $0.20 | $0.02 |
| Cork cubes, per package of 100, . . . . . . . | .25 | .01 |

TWENTIETH GIFT.

| | Price. | Postage. |
|---|---|---|
| Modeling knife of wood, with handle, per dozen, . . . . | $0.50 | $0.02 |
| Modeling knife of wood, without handle and generally preferred, per dozen, . . . . . . . . | .25 | .02 |
| Modeling boards of wood, per dozen, . . . . . . | 1.50 | |
| Clay, prepared, per pound, . . . . . . . | .05 | |

## Friedrich Froebel — References for Further Study


Aborn, C. (1937). Friedrich Froebel: Apostle of childhood education. *Childhood Education, XIII* (5), 211-215.

*Annual report of the New York Kindergarten Association, 1890 – 1903.* (1890-1903, bound together). New York: The De Vinne Press.

Arnold, J. C. (1914). *Notes on Froebel's Mother Play and Songs.* Chicago: The National Kindergarten College.

Barnard, H. (Ed.). (1890). *Kindergarten and child culture papers: Papers on Froebel's kindergarten with suggestions on principles and methods of child culture in different countries.* Hartford, CT: no publisher. Reprinted from *American Journal of Education.*

Baylor, R. (1965). *Elizabeth Palmer Peabody: Kindergarten pioneer.* Philadelphia: University of Pennsylvania Press.

Blow, S. (1898). The mottoes and commentaries of Friedrich Froebel's *Mother play*. New York: D. Appleton.

Blow, S. (1905). *Symbolic education.* New York: D. Appleton.

Blow, S. (1912). *Letters to a mother.* New York: D. Appleton.

Blow, S. (Ed. & Trans.). (1923). *The songs and music of Friedrich Froebel's Mother play.* New York: D. Appleton.

Bowen, H. C. (1887, May). Hints to Froebel Students. *Journal of Education, IX*, 229-232.

Bowen, H. C. (1901). *Froebel and education by self-activity.* London: William Heinemann.

Bowen, H. C. (1911). *Froebel and education through self-activity.* New York: Charles Scribner's Sons.

Brosterman, N. (1997). *Inventing kindergarten.* New York: Harry N. Adams Inc.

Cavallo, D. (1979). The politics of latency: Kindergarten pedagogy, 1860-1930. In B. Finkelstein (Ed.), *Regulated Children/Liberated Children: Education in psychohistorical perspective.* New York: Psychohistory Press, Publishers.

Cohen, B. (1969). *Educational thought.* London: Macmillan.

Committee of Nineteen. (1924). *Pioneers of the kindergarten in America.* New York: The Century Co.

Cooke, E. (1904). Is development from within? Did Froebel's conception differ from Darwin? *Child Life, VI* (24), 185-192.

Cooke, E. (1904). Is development from within? Did Froebel's conception differ from Darwin? *Child Life, VII* (25), 14-23.

Corbett, B. (1979). *A garden of children.* Mississauga, Canada: The Froebel Foundation.

Corbett, B. (1989). *A century of kindergarten education in Ontario.* Mississauga, Canada: The Froebel Foundation.

Costantino, M. (1991). *Frank Lloyd Wright.* London: Bison Books.

Crawford, A. (1890, November). The kindergarten in Ottawa, Canada. *The Kindergarten, III* (3), 150.

Dando, T. (1876). *What is the Centennial? And how to see it.* Philadelphia: Thomas Dando Press.

DeNevi, D. (1968, March). The education of a genius: Analyzing influences on the life of America's greatest architect. *Young Children*, 72-75.

Devereaux, A. (Arranged by). (1895). *Outline of a year's work in the kindergarten.* Boston: J. L. Hammett.

Douai, A. (1872). *The kindergarten: A manual for the introduction of Froebel's system of primary education into public schools.* New York: E. Steiger.

Downs, R. (1978). *Friedrich Froebel.* Boston: Twayne Publishers.

Eliot, H., & Blow, S. (Eds. & Trans). (1912). *The mottoes and commentaries of Friedrich Froebel's mother play.* New York: D. Appleton.

Findlay, M. E. (1900). The kindergarten movement in America. *Child Life, 11* (7), 158-163.

Fletcher, S., & Welton, J. (Trans). (1912). *Froebel's chief writings on education.* London: Edward Arnold.

Franks, F. (1903). Some notes on current objections to the kindergarten. *Child Life, V* (19), 121-126.

Froebel, F. (1889). *Autobiography.* (E. Michaeles & H. Moore, Trans.). Syracuse, NY: C. W. Bardeen.

Froebel, F. (1900). *Mother's songs, games and stories.* London: Rice.

Froebel, F. (1902). *Education by development.* (J. Jarvis, Trans.). New York: D. Appleton.

Froebel, F. (1907). *The education of man.* (W. N. Hailmann, Trans.). London: Appleton. (Original work published 1826)

Froebel, F. (J. Jarvis, Trans.). (1925). *Pedagogics of the kindergarten.* New York: D. Appleton and Company.

Froebel, F. (1976). *Mother's Songs, games and stories.* (F. Lord, Trans.). New York: Arno Press. (Reprint from Students' Edition, published 1914).

Goldammer, H. (1882). *The gifts of the kindergarten.* New York: E. Steiger & Co.

Goldammer, H. (1882). *The occupations of the kindergarten.* New York: E. Steiger & Co.

Hailmann, W. N. (1873). *Kindergarten culture in the family and kindergarten: A complete sketch of Froebel's system of early education, adapted to American institutions for the use of mothers and teachers.* New York: American Book Company.

Hailmann, W. N. (Trans.). (1887). *The education of man by Friedrich Froebel.* New York: D. Appleton.

Harrison, E., & Woodson, B. (1903). *The kindergarten building gifts.* London: J. Curwen & Sons, Ltd.

Hayward, F. A. (1979, first published in 1904). *The educational ideas of Pestalozzi and Frobel[sic].* Westport, CT: Greenwood Press, Publishers.

Heerwart, E. (1897). *Froebel's theory and practice.* London: Charles and Dible.

Heinemann, A. (Ed.). (1893). *Froebel letters.* Boston: Lathrop.

Herford, W. (1894). *The student's Froebel. Part II. Practice of education.* London: Libister and Company Limited.

Herford, W. (1899). *The student's Froebel. Part I: Theory of education.* London: Libister and Company Limited.

Hewes, D. (2001). *W.N. Hailmann: Defender of Froebel.* Grand Rapids, MI: The Froebel Foundation.

Hodgins, J. S. (Ed.). (1883). *The story of my life by the late Rev. Egerton Ryerson, D.D., LLD.* Toronto, Canada: William Briggs.

Hoffman, H. (1874). *Kindergarten toys, and how to use them. A practical explanation of the first six gifts of Frobel's [sic] kindergarten.* New York: E. Steiger.

Hubbard, C. B. (1881). *Merry songs and games for use of the kindergarten.* St. Louis, MO: Balmer & Weber.

Hughes, J. (1899). Froebel's educational laws for all teachers. New York: D. Appleton.

Jarvis, J. (Trans.). (1895). *Friedrich Froebel's pedagogics of the kindergarten.* New York: D. Appleton.

Jarvis, J. (Trans.). (1899). *Friedrich Froebel's education by development.* New York: D. Appleton.

Johnston, M. (n.d.) If education is life. *Alabama School Journal.* One page handout from Marietta Johnson Museum, Fairhope, Alabama.

Kamii, C. (1982). *Number in preschool and kindergarten: Educational implication of Piaget's theory.* Washington, DC: National Association for the Education of Young Children.

Kaufmann, E. (1989). *9 commentaries on Frank Lloyd Wright.* Cambridge, MA: The MIT Press.

Kilpatrick, W. H. (1916). *Froebel's kindergarten principles critically examined.* New York: The MacMillan Co.

Kirby, S. (1896). *Kindergarten papers.* New York: The Butterick Publishing Co.

Kraus-Boelte, M., & Kraus, J. (1877). *The kindergarten guide: An illustrated hand-book, designed for the self-instruction of kindergarteners, mothers and nurses. First volume: The gifts.* New York: E. Steiger & Co.

Kraus-Boelte, M., & Kraus, J. (1889). *The kindergarten guide: An illustrated hand-book, designed for the self-instruction of kindergarteners, mothers and nurses. Second volume: The occupations.* New York: E. Steiger & Co.

Lascarides, V.C. & Hinitz, B. (2000). *History of Early Childhood Education.* New York: Falmer Press.

Lawrence, E. (Ed.). (1969). *Froebel and English education.* New York: Schocken.

Liebschner, J. (1991). *Foundations of progressive education: The history of the National Froebel Society.* Cambridge, England: The Lutterworth Press.

Liebschner, J. (1992). *A child's work: Freedom and guidance in Froebel's educational theory and practice.* Cambridge, England: The Lutterworth Press.

Lilley, I. (1967). *Friedrich Froebel.* Cambridge, MA: University Printing House.

MacVannel, J. A. (1909). The materials of the kindergarten. *Teachers College Record, X* (5), 343-370.

Manning, E. A. (1884). What Froebel did for young children. *Health Exhibition Literature, XIII,* 78-87.

Manson, G. (1953, June). Wright in the nursery. *Architectural Review, CXIII,* 349-351.

Manson, G. (1958). *Frank Lloyd Wright to 1910.* New York: Van Nostrand Reinhold Co.

McDonald, N., & Chaiton, A. (Eds.). (1978). *Egerton Ryerson and his times.* Toronto, Canada: Macmillan of Canada.

Michaels, E., & Moore, H. K. (1891). *Froebel's letters on the kindergarten.* London: Swan Sonnenschein & Co.

Moore, N. (1879). *A kindergartner's manual of drawing.* Springfield, MA: The Milton Bradley Company.

Murray, E. R. (1914). *Froebel: A pioneer in modern psychology.* Baltimore, MD: Warwick & York, Inc.

Murray, E. R. (n.d.). *A story of infant schools and kindergartens.* London: Sir Isaac Pitman & Sons.

New York Kindergarten Association. *Annual Reports, 1890-1903.* New York: The De Vinne Press.

Norton, F. (Ed). (1877). Frank Leslie's historical register of the United States Centennial Exposition, 1876. New York: Frank Leslie's Publishing House.

O'Brien, R. (1990). *The story of American toys.* New York: Abbeville Press.

Peabody, E. (1862, November). What is a kindergarten? *Atlantic Monthly, 10,* 586-593.

Peabody, E. (1882). The origin and growth of the kindergarten. *Education, 2,* 507-527

Peabody, E. (Ed.). (1878). *Mother play and nursery songs by Froebel.* Boston: Lathrop.

Peltzman, B. R. (1998). *Pioneers of early childhood education: A bio-bibliographical guide.* Westport, CT: Greenwood Press.

Plaisted, L. (1913). *Handwork and its place in early education.* Oxford, England: Oxford University Press.

Priestman, B. (1946). *Froebel education to-day.* London: University of London Press Ltd.

Prochner, L. & Howe, N. (2000). *Early childhood education and care in Canada.* Vancouver: UBC Press.

Ronda, B. (1999). *Elizabeth Palmer Peabody: A reformer on her own terms.* Cambridge, MA: Harvard University Press.

Ronge, J., & Ronge, B. (1855). *A practical guide to the English kinder garden* [sic]. London: J. S. Hodson.

Salmon, D., & Hindshaw, W. (1904). *Infant schools: Their history and theory.* London: Longmans, Green & Co.

Shapiro, M. S. (1983). *Child's garden: The kindergarten movement from Froebel to Dewey.* University Park, PA: The Pennsylvania State University Press.

Shea, J. (1960). *It's all in the game.* New York: G. P. Putnam's Sons.

Shirreff, E. ( 1887). *A short sketch of the life of Friedrich Frobel [sic].* London: Chapman and Hall, Limited.

Shirreff, E. (1889). *The kinder-garten: Principles of Frobel's [sic] system and their bearing on the education of women: Also remarks on the higher education of women.* Syracuse, NY: C.W. Bardeen.

Shirreff, E. (1895). *The kindergarten at home: A practical hand-book for mothers and teachers.* London: Abbott, Jones & Co.

Shute, M. (1943). Come, let us live with our children. *Childhood Education, 19* (9), 387-389, 432.

Smith, N. A. (1900). *The message of Froebel and other essays.* Springfield, MA: Milton Bradley Company.

Snideer, D. (1900). *The psychology of Froebel's play-gifts.* St. Louis, MO: Sigma Publishing Co.

Snyder, A. (1972). *Dauntless women in childhood education.* Washington, DC: Association for Childhood Education International.

Stockham, C., & Kellogg, E. (1889). *Mother's portfolio.* Chicago: Alice B. Stockham & Co.

Tafel, E. (1979). *Apprentice to genius: Years with Frank Lloyd Wright.* New York: McGraw-Hill Book Co.

Talcott, W. (1893, January). The kindergarten movement. *Century Magazine, XLV,* 369-379.

Tenenbaum, S. (1951). *William Heard Kilpatrick.* New York: Harper & Brothers.

Tharp, L. (1950). *The Peabody sisters of Salem.* Boston: Little, Brown & Co.

The Froebel Kindergarten Foundation. (1980). *The Froebel gifts: A manual for kindergartners and teachers.* Mississauga, Canada: Froebel Kindergarten Foundation.

The kindergarten in Canada. (1905, February). *Kindergarten Magazine, XVII* (6), 325-326.

The kindergarten in Canada. (1905, April). *Kindergarten Magazine, XVII* (8), 495-503.

Van Norstrand, F. P. (1891). *Royal gifts for the kindergarten: A manual for self instruction in Friedrich Froebel's principles of education along with a collection of songs, games and poems for the home, the kindergarten and the primary school.* Chicago: Standard-Columbian Company.

Vanderwalker, N. (1971). *The kindergarten in American education.* New York: Arno Press & The New York Times. (Original work published 1908)

Von Marenholtz-Bulow, B. (M. P. Mann, Trans.). (1877). *Reminiscences of Friedrich Froebel.* Boston: Lothrop, Less & Shepard Co.

Weaver, E. (1893). *Paper and scissors in the schoolroom.* Boston: Milton Bradley Company.

Weber, E. (1969). *The kindergarten: Its encounter with educational thought in America.* New York: Teachers College Press.

Westcott, T. (1876). *Centennial portfolio: A souvenir of the international exhibition at Philadelphia.* Philadelphia: Thomas Hunter, Publisher.

Weston, P. (2000). *Friedrich Froebel: his life, times & significance.* London: University of Surrey Roehampton.

Weston, P. (2002). *The Froebel Educational Institute: The origins and history of the college.* London: University of Surrey Roehampton.

White, J. (1907). *The educational ideas of Froebel.* London: W.B. Clive, University Tutorial Press.

Wiebe, E. (1869). *Paradise of childhood.* Springfield, MA: Milton Bradley & Co.

Wiebe, E. (1896). *Paradise of childhood.* Springfield, MA: Milton Bradley & Co.

Wiebe, E. (1910). *Paradise of childhood.* Boston: Milton Bradley & Co.

Wiggin, K. D. (1893). *The kindergarten.* New York: Harper & Bros.

Wiggin, K. D., & Smith, N. A. (1896). *Froebel's occupations.* Boston: Houghton, Mifflin & Co.

Wiggin, K. D., & Smith, N. A. (1898). *Froebel's gifts.* Boston: Houghton, Mifflin & Co.

Woodham-Smith, P., Slight, J. P., Priestman, O. B., Hamilton, H. A., & Isaacs, N. (1952). *Friedrich Froebel and English Education.* London: Routledge & Kegan Paul.

Wright, F. L. (1943). *Frank Lloyd Wright, an autobiography.* New York: Dvell, Sloan & Pearce.

# **Chapter 6** — *Robert Owen*

**1771 – 1858**

*"To effect any permanently beneficial change in society, I found it was far more necessary to act than to speak."*

— **"Address Delivered To The Inhabitants of New Lanark," 1816, in *Selected Works of Robert Owen Volume 1***

*Children were to be "trained and educated without punishment or any fear of it, and were while in school by far the happiest human beings I have ever seen. . . . Punishment . . . will never be required, and should be avoided as much as giving poison in their food."*

*"When beginning to be tired of play in their playground, they should be taken within the school room, and amused by the teacher, by showing and explaining them some useful object within their capacity to comprehend. . . . The schoolroom for infant instruction was furnished with paintings. . . . with maps, and often supplied with natural objects from the gardens, fields, and the woods . . . with these infants everything was made to be amusement."*

— ***Life of Robert Owen, by Himself***

In the 1820's, England was a gloomy place. The factory system had been seen as the great boon to progress and wealth, but its price on society was tremendous. Factory policies were under the sole discretion of the factory owners, and inhumane practices in the factories were accepted as the natural order of events. It was believed the poverty of factory workers resulted from their laziness, ignorance and overindulgence. Poverty, in this view, was a natural part of the order of the world and a consequence of sinful behaviour.

The industrial revolution was at its peak. Inventions such as the spinning jenny (a framed machine for spinning more than one strand of yarn at a time) were replaced by large water-driven spinning machines. Samuel Crompton combined the jenny and the water frame to create the mule (a cotton spinning machine that could spin stronger warp threads as well as the finer weft threads), and spinning soon became solely a factory industry.

*What are current examples of exploitation of people in the workforce? Does child labour still exist? In what forms?*

In the factories at that time, 16-hour working days were common, and children were a significant part of the workforce — it was typical for five- and six-year-old boys and girls to be working long days. Children were cheap labour, and their small hands could easily clean the machines. Child labour, in fact, was seen as an essential component of profitable mills. Physical and sexual abuses were prevalent at the time, and physical diseases including cholera, rickets, and tuberculosis were rampant. The harsh living and working conditions took their toll on the citizens: a quarter of the children in this time died before the age of one, while the average life expectancy was 30 years.

Increasingly, workers were enraged by the terrible conditions and took to the streets in protest. Mills were burned to the ground. Protests against advances in technology mushroomed as workers lost their jobs. The ones with jobs worked under horrendous and unlivable situations. Progress resulted in suffering, with the poor pitted against the rich. The costs of progress seemed inescapable.

Amidst all this misery, one place in Britain showed a different outcome and was seen as a beacon in the storm. In the isolated mountains of Scotland, a good day's wagon ride from Glasgow, there was a small factory community called New Lanark. A constant flow of visitors came to see it: 20,000 people signed the guest book between 1815 and 1825. A whole assortment of reformers, writers, businessmen and world leaders came to see something very different from the rest of the British factory system.

What did they come so far to see in the tiny community? They saw evidence that the horrendous conditions in the factory system were not inevitable after all, that people were poor only because they lacked opportunity and education.

In New Lanark, factory workers had individual homes of two rooms each. Coal was provided to the homes for heat and cooking, garbage was collected, the streets were cleaned, there were pleasant green spaces to enjoy, and gas lighting was provided in the town. Free medical care and a Sickness Fund were available to the citizens. When U.S. President Thomas Jefferson cut off all trade with Europe in 1806, the ensuing cotton crisis stopped the mill in New Lanark for four months, but workers at New Lanark were still paid full wages. Workers were not punished.

Another remarkable difference was the way the children of New Lanark were treated. No children worked in the factories until age 10 or 11, and if they did work at those ages, the children worked half days only. Children learned in the outdoors as well as from kind teachers; children were in a schoolhouse for both work and play. The older children tended gardens. At New Lanark it was believed that children could learn best from example rather than from warnings or advice.

Those who came to see New Lanark were astounded. The pleasant atmosphere was dramatically different from the situation in other factory towns in Britain and was beyond the imagination of the visitors. Adding to the astonishment was the fact that even with all these added expenses of caring for the factory workers, the mills of New Lanark were financially profitable.

The key to this remarkable "experiment" was **Robert Owen.** He was a man full of energy, vision, practicality, achievement and common sense.

**Owen was born in Wales, and moved first to England and then to Scotland. Later in his life he went to the United States.**

## Early Life

Robert Owen was born in Newtown, Montgomeryshire, Wales, on May 14, 1771. Newtown was a small market town of about 1,000 people in the wooded banks of the upper Severn Valley. Inhabitants spoke a dialect that was a mixture of Welsh and English. His parents were very poor, and opportunities for their seven children were limited. Robert was the youngest child, though two had died in infancy. He was respected by his parents and raised without any of the corporal punishment customary in many other homes. His father, Robert, was a saddler, iron monger (seller, dealer and trader) and village postmaster.

In 1762 Newtown had established a First Benefit's Society. The Society charged members weekly subscriptions and gave free medical care, sick pay, a pension at 60 years of age, and even a free burial. Growing up in a town that had pioneered such a program likely affected Owen's belief in what a society could and should offer its members.

Owen was an intelligent child and was good at music, dance and sports. He had an early dislike of the negative effects of competition. Owen read avidly, using the libraries of the town's doctor, lawyer and clergyman. By age seven, he had learned as much as the local teacher could teach and became a pupil/assistant (called an usher) teaching the younger children. This work gave him insight into children's learning problems as well as an early interest in education.

He continued to read voraciously, reading such classics as *Robinson Crusoe, Paradise Lost*, and *Pilgrim's Progress*. During summer holidays Owen stayed at the farms of his mother's relations. He was an athletic child but disliked the competition and prizes in sports because they made the losers so unhappy. By age nine, he left school, feeling he had learned all the local school could teach him, and went to work in the local draper's (retail merchant who dealt in cloth) and grocer's shops.

In 1781, Owen left for London with stagecoach money and a small amount of additional cash. He was only ten years old and was going to a large city that only a year earlier had suffered a week of riots during which mobs took control of the streets and hundreds of citizens were killed. The social unrest had resulted from problems with rapid urbanization and industrialization and from workers' objecting to inhumane conditions in the factories.

A dramatized video account of Owen's life, *The Life of Robert Owen*, can be obtained from:

The Robert Owen Memorial Museum

The Cross,
Broad Street,
Newtown, Powys,
SY16 2BB
Wales

From that time on, Owen was financially independent from his parents and returned to Newton only for brief visits. In Lincolnshire (in eastern England on the North Sea) Owen was apprenticed to a draper named James McGuffog. Owen's older brother William, a saddler, obtained this position for him. Owen received sound business training and was regarded as a son by his childless employer. He stayed four years and benefitted from McGuffog's expertise in business and fabrics; he also made extensive use of his employer's library, reading about five hours each day.

He went to London to work in a drapery house and then to a wholesale drapery in Manchester where he stayed until he was 18. These early experiences gave him extensive knowledge of fabrics, textiles, and bookkeeping in both wholesale and retail business. He also acquired habits of industry, order and attention to detail in business.

Owen then borrowed money from his brother William to set up his first business of making spinning mules. This business lasted only a few months when Owen discovered his partner, John Jones, lacked business ability. Owen took his share of the company assets and entered into his own yarn-spinning and sales venture.

## Jones and Owen

Respectfully inform the Public, that they have opened a Warehouse near the New Bridge, Dolefield, for making WATER PREPARATION and MULE MACHINES, and flatter themselves from their strict Attention to Business, and the experienced Hands they employ, that they shall be able to finish work in such a manner as will merit the future Favours of those that employ them.

**Ad in the *Manchester Mercury* from January 18 – 25, 1791**
**Included in article by W.H. Chaloner**

## Superintendency of a Factory Wanted

A PERSON to superintend and conduct an extensive MULE FACTORY, to whom any salary will be allowed proportionate to Merit.

No one need apply, whose Character, in regard to Morals, as well as Capacity and Steadiness, is not every way respectable.

For Particulars apply to Mr. Drinkwater, at his Warehouse in Manchester, on Tuesdays, Thursdays or Saturdays from eleven to two o-clock.

**Ad in the *Manchester Herald*, April 1792**
**Included in article by W.H. Chaloner**

About a year later, Owen saw an ad for the manager of Drinkwater's Bank Top Mill in Manchester, a booming factory town that doubled in population between 1780 and 1800. Drinkwater's mill was the first in Manchester to be powered by a rotary steam engine. This mill had 500 workers, and the manager would have total responsibility for the mill's production, from cotton to yarn. Owen got the job using what could only be described as chutzpah (Yiddish word meaning bold self-confidence, brazen nerve, and gall).[1]

[1] The humorous Yiddish story to explain it involves a person who kills both his parents and then pleads to the court for leniency because he is an orphan. That is chutzpah.

Owen's account of the initial meeting between him and the mill owner, Peter Drinkwater, is recounted in the autobiography of his son Robert Dale Owen. This anecdote portrays Owen's confidence and sense of self:

> *"A sudden impulse induced him to present himself, an applicant for the place.*
>
> *'You are too young,' was Mr. Drinkwater's curt objection.*
>
> *'They used to object to me,' said my father, 'on that score four or five years ago; but I did not expect to have it brought up now.'*
>
> *'Why, what age are you?'*
>
> *'I shall be twenty in May next.'*
>
> *'How often do you get drunk in the week?'*
>
> *My father blushed scarlet. 'I never,' he said indignantly, 'was drunk in my life.'*
>
> *This seemed to produce a good impression. The next question was: 'What salary do you ask?'*
>
> *'Three hundred a year.'*
>
> *'Three hundred a year! Why, I've had I don't know how many after the place here, this morning; and all their askings together wouldn't come up to what you want.'*
>
> *'Whatever others may ask, I cannot take less.' "*
>
> **— Robert Dale Owen, *Threading My Way***

During this period, Owen lived in the same boarding house as Robert Fulton and even lent him some money for his naval engineering projects. Robert Fulton was an American inventor, engineer and painter who built the first commercially successful steamboat.

It was a characteristic Owen interchange, and it worked! At 20 years of age he became the "boy wonder" of the textile world. He had never before entered a large factory, yet at this point he became the head of one of the most up-to-date mills in the country, in charge of the whole operation except the final marketing of the product. The mill was a great success with improved quality of yarn *and* improved working conditions in the mill. Within six months, Drinkwater offered Robert Owen one-quarter ownership of the business. Soon afterward, Owen was running another Drinkwater mill in Cheshire as well.

Owen was concerned with both the scientific and philosophical issues of the day. In 1793 he was elected a member of the Manchester Literary and Philosophical Society (known as the "Lit and Phil") where the ideas of leading philosophers such as Jean-Jacques Rousseau, Jeremy Bentham and Thomas Paine were discussed. Owen himself contributed several papers including "The Connection Between Universal Happiness and Practical Mechanics" and "The Origin of Opinions with a View to the Improvement of the Social Virtues." Many members of the Society were leaders in the movements for political and social reform. Owen's chief friend was John Dalton, creator of the modern atomic theory.[2]

---

[2] The atomic theory maintains that matter is composed of tiny individual particles in constant motion; it was originally proposed in the 5th century B.C.E. but ignored until Dalton's work in 1808.

Owen was active in the community and was a committee member of the Board of Health for Manchester. In this role he worked to improve the health and working conditions in all factories. After leaving the Drinkwater Mill in 1794, he entered into another business venture at the Chorlton Twist Company in Manchester, which made cotton threads for weaving.

## New Lanark

On some business trips to Glasgow, Owen was introduced to Anne Caroline Dale, whose father David was a city banker and leading industrialist. Caroline invited Robert Owen to see her father's cotton mills on the Falls of Clyde in New Lanark, Scotland. Dale had built the mills in 1785 in this remote ravine. Caroline and Robert quickly became involved romantically. Owen was an unlikely candidate to marry her as he was not Scottish and did not belong to the Scottish Presbyterian church. However, he gained Dale's respect though his obvious business acumen, and Robert and Caroline were married in 1799.

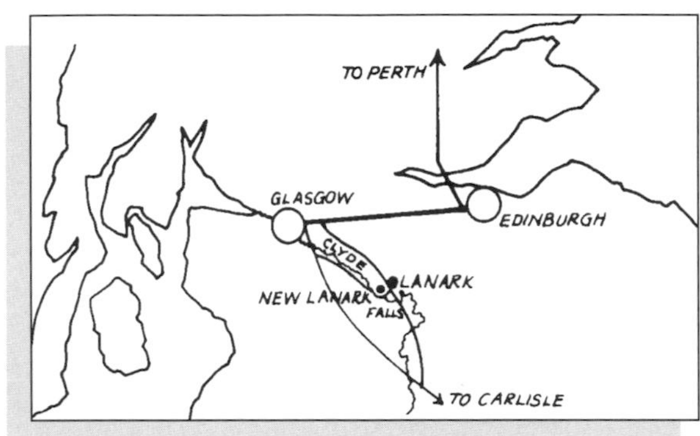


**New Lanark. Owen's community was built in New Lanark on the Clyde River southeast of Glasgow.**

Owen borrowed money and bought the mills from David Dale in New Lanark, and Caroline and Robert moved there. They had eight children who grew up with their father's love of books, music, sports, fresh air and play. Subsequent generations of Owens retained both names — Dale and Owen.

**Portrait of Robert Owen by Mary Ann Knight around 1810 when Owen was preparing to erect the school buildings at New Lanark. (Used with permission of Scottish National Portrait Gallery Ph 1606.)**

**New Lanark. Robert Owen's social and economic experiment as seen in 1818. (Illustration courtesy of New Lanark Conservation Trust.)**

When Robert Owen bought the mills in New Lanark, there were 2,000 employees. Five hundred of them were children of five and six years of age and working 13 hours a day! Though these statistics are horrendous, Dale was considered an enlightened mill manager compared to others of the time. He did provide after-work education for poor children. Within a year, Owen had changed the mills. Within five years, they were completely transformed, and within 10 years, they were world famous.

*Owen reacted against the exploitation of workers in the mills and created a radically different environment for the people. How did he arrive at this new social vision?*

Owen also made a fortune. The expenses of caring for workers paid off in higher worker productivity and improved quality of yarn; moreover, markets developed around the world for the cotton yarn, and the value of the mills increased dramatically.

## The Promise of the Future

Robert Owen not only made the mills financially successful. He wanted to make the spinners into better people. To this end he dramatically improved the living and working conditions of the workers. Like the hero of his youth, Robinson Crusoe, Owen sought to create a new community. New Lanark became his metaphorical island.

*What examples exist in your community for workplace child care? What are some advantages of such child care facilities?*

At the centre of his social reforms were the children's programs. Owen set up a quality-based system of child care and a school for children whose parents were at work in the factory. It was the first workplace child care/ education in western society. That was in 1816.

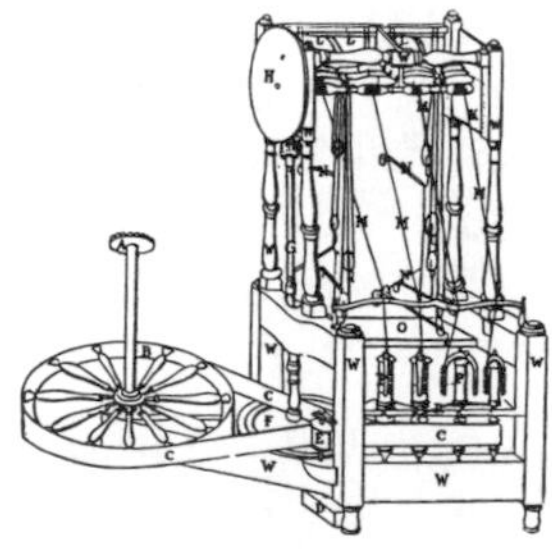

**Arkwright's Spinning Frame. Richard Arkwright patented his spinning frame in 1769, and it was used in factories like New Lanark. The mechanized process allowed greater output while requiring fewer skilled spinners. The spinning frame had a series of geared rollers that imitated the work of hand spinners. The gearing mechanisms were like those in a clock; Arkwright worked with John Kay, a clockmaker, to produce his invention. The spinning frames at New Lanark were driven by water power from the falls at New Lanark. (Used courtesy of the New Lanark Conservation Trust, New Lanark, Scotland.)**

Reading Owen's writings today, one is impressed with the relevance of and modern slant to his ideas. In the introduction to the Penguin Classics edition of *A New View of Society*, Professor Gregory Claeys says,

> *"Each generation finds something surprisingly modern in Owen's writings, and our own is no different. Today his emphasis upon feminism and upon 'green' issues, like the balancing of parks and gardens within urban areas, strike us as distinctly contemporary. His demand for the humane treatment of the labor force has never lost its relevance. Nor has his stress on infant education. His ideas on co-operative ownership and profit-sharing are again increasingly popular."*

Owen was the eternal optimist, as his life history proves. He never faltered from his belief that society could be improved with the concerted efforts of people to reduce poverty, crime and misery. Education was at the very core of these changes:

> *"It is, therefore, the interest of all, that everyone, from birth, should be well educated, physically and mentally, that society may be improved in its character, that everyone should be beneficially employed, physically and mentally, that the greatest amount of wealth may be created, and knowledge attained, that everyone should be placed in the midst of those external circumstances, that will produce the greatest number of pleasurable sensations, through the longest life, that man may be made truly intelligent, moral and happy, and be, thus, prepared to enter upon the coming Millennium."*
>
> **— quoted in *The Story of Robert Owen* by New Lanark Conservation Trust**

This statement was written in 1841, and it reflects Owen's deep interest in child education and child care. Education was the primary force in the goal to achieve a better quality of life. He saw education in is broadest connotation — the influences on a person from birth to death.

## Educational Programs

The Institution for the Formation of Character. The educational program for children and adults opened in 1816 and the building still stands today. (Illustration courtesy of New Lanark Conservation Trust, New Lanark, Scotland.)

Front View of The New Institution for the Formation of Character. (Used courtesy of the New Lanark Conservation Trust, New Lanark, Scotland.)

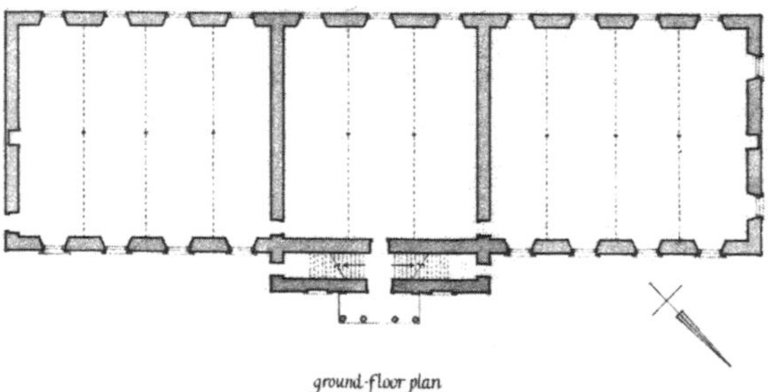


Ground Floor Plan for The New Institution for the Formation of Character. (Used courtesy of the New Lanark Conservation Trust, New Lanark, Scotland.)

The Institution for the Formation of Character (formally opened on New Years Day, 1816) was a two-story building in which programs for all ages, from young children to adults, were conducted. The Nursery had children from one to three years old; the Infant School had children from three to six years old and a program for seven to 12 year olds. Each group had a room of its own. In the evenings there were educational and recreational programs for adults, anyone old enough to work.

A second building (now called The School for Children) was completed in 1817. It had been planned to include a community kitchen and dining room. This building provided further facilities for adult education and recreation, as the population of New Lanark was up to 2,500 people.[3]

A tremendous amount of thought was put into the programs. Owen had viewed Pestalozzi's programs for children and was familiar with the writings of Pestalozzi and Rousseau. He had also seen a program run by Philipp Emanuel von Fellenberg in Hofwyl, Switzerland, which focused on the integration of all areas of development (mental, moral and manual) and on the education of all classes of society. In fact, due to Owen's interest in educational reform, his sons Robert Dale and William attended the Fellenberg school in 1818 for three years.

Owen had also studied the ideas of British educational leaders Andrew Bell and Joseph Lancaster and brought both men to Scotland in 1812. Andrew Bell (1753 – 1832) and Joseph Lancaster (1778 – 1838) developed the

[3] After the time of Robert Owen, the Institution became the centre of social and recreational pursuits, and The School for Children provided day classes. In 1875 the Parish School Board took over responsibility for local education from the Mill Company. They opened a new school at the edge of New Lanark in 1884, and it remains today the New Lanark Primary School.

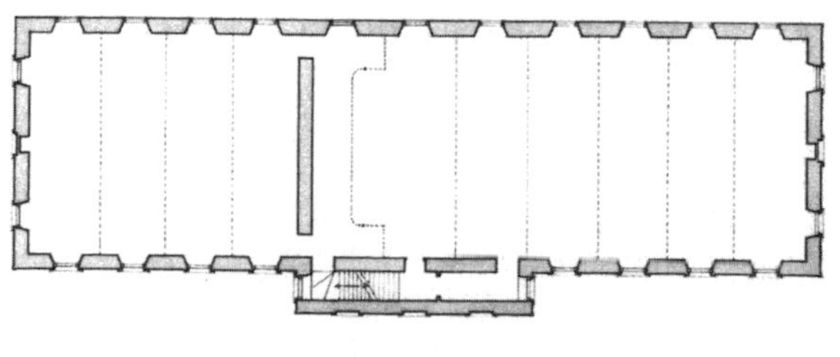


**First Floor Plan for The New Institution for the Formation of Character. (Used courtesy of the New Lanark Conservation Trust, New Lanark, Scotland.)**

monitorial system of elementary education to aid in teaching, with limited facilities, children living in poverty.[4]

Older students would instruct younger students and would eventually become teachers themselves. Bell and Lancaster were embroiled in a bitter controversy: Bell's system received the support of the established church and Lancaster's did not, as he was a Quaker. The ruling class saw the system as a way to keep large numbers of poor children in one place without incurring the cost of trained teachers. Owen was impressed with some of the ideas but not with the rigidity of the system, the narrow emphasis on reading, writing and arithmetic, or the huge, impersonal rooms. His infant schools were to be different, working toward the full development of each person. Reading and writing were instruments rather than ends in themselves.

Owen's own educational ideas were outlined in several books he wrote including *Book of the New Moral Order* and *A New View of Society:*

> *"The constitution of every infant is capable of being formed or matured, either into a very inferior or a very superior being according to the qualities of external circumstances allowed to influence that constitution from birth.*
>
> *To a great extent the character is made or marred before children enter the usual schoolroom."*
>
> **— *Life of Robert Owen, by Himself***

Owen took an active role in the definition and workings of the Institution for the Formation of Character. In 1814 he hired James Buchanan, a former weaver and gifted natural educator who had a great rapport with children, to help him develop the school. Buchanan developed extensive programming materials for the children and used his flute to gain children's attention. Molly Young, a worker from the cotton mills, became Buchanan's assistant.

## Seven Key Approaches

Seven main rules and approaches to children were laid out clearly.

**Children were not punished.**

Children were not to be scolded or punished; instead, natural consequences would guide children. Owen felt artificial incentives, whether punishments or rewards, harmed and created weaknesses in both children and adults. The pleasure of learning would become the needed incentive. Children would naturally strive for self-improvement:

> *"Punishment ... will never be required, and should be avoided as much as giving poison in their food."*
>
> **— *Life of Robert Owen, by Himself***

---

[4] See *The Lancasterian System of Education* by Joseph Lancaster and *Experiment in Education* by Andrew Bell.

*Do either Canada or the United States have a system of quality-based child care or education for children whose parents work? Certainly Owen's motivation for establishing child care at his mill was partially economic, but he was a philosopher and social activist who saw child care in a wider framework and believed it to be essential to economic and social progress.*

Robert Dale Owen described this focus on self-discipline that did not rely on artificial or outside restraint:

> *"Let us suppose a set of children overawed by fear and stimulated by hope of reward, kept, which is but seldom the case, during the presence of their teacher in what is called' 'trim order,' apparently all diligence and submission; will these children, we ask, when the teacher's back is turned, and this artificial stimulus ceases to operate, continue to exhibit the same appearance? Or are they not much more likely to glory in an opportunity of running to the opposite extreme, and thereby exonerate themselves of a restraint so irksome?"*
>
> **— from *An Outline of the System of Education at New Lanark* by Robert Dale Owen**

As children got older, they would participate in self-government, and teachers would become more of advisors.

**Teachers must be kind.**

Teachers were to use unceasing kindness in tone, look, word and action to all children without exception:

> *"always to speak to them with a pleasant countenance, and in a kind manner and tone of voice."*
>
> ***— Life of Robert Owen, by Himself***

**Instruction was based on children's experiences.**

Instruction was to be through the inspection of realities and their qualities, with these to be explained by familiar conversations between the teachers and the children; small group interaction was encouraged:

> *"The children were not to be annoyed with books; but were to be taught the uses and nature or qualities of the common things around them, by familiar conversation when the children's curiosity was excited so as to induce them to ask questions."*
>
> ***— Life of Robert Owen, by Himself***

*The arts were a major part of the program at New Lanark. How have you incorporated arts in children's programs? Are they as important as other curriculum areas?*

**Dance, rhymes, singing and music were a large part of the program.**

> *"The infants and young children, besides being instructed by sensible signs,—the things themselves, or models or paintings, — and by familiar conversation, were from two years and upwards daily taught dancing and singing."*
>
> ***— Life of Robert Owen, by Himself***

The following is an example of one of the rhymes, developed by Buchanan, that would be used for teaching concepts:

"Hark to me and silence keep,
And you will hear about the sheep;
For sheep are useful and you know
That on their backs the wool does grow.
The sheep are taken once a year
And plunged in water cool and clear
And there they swim and never bite
While men do wash and clean them white."

The children learned dances of many countries to increase their understanding and appreciation of other people and wore the appropriate costumes when they did the dances. The inclusion of dancing was unprecedented in other schools. Owen attached so much importance to it that he paid the dancing teacher, David Budge, a salary equal to that of the academic subject teachers. Many people were aghast at his supporting the arts to this degree.

*The New Institution for the Formation of Character provided free school uniforms. What do you think are the advantages and disadvantages of school uniforms?*

An engraving of a dancing class by G. Hunt in 1825 shows the children of Owen's school in white tunics, dancing to a live string trio. The Roman tunic-like cotton garments allowed freedom of movement and spirit and were provided for the children as school uniforms. The children received clean tunics three times per week. The animal murals on the wall were painted by Miss Whitwell, a teacher in the school.

**The Children's Program. Engraving by G. Hunt showing the school at New Lanark. (Illustration courtesy of New Lanark Conservation Trust.)**

**The questions of children were to be answered in kind and rational ways.**

**Outdoor time was to be used whenever the children's minds were fatigued, not at any pre-determined time.**

> *"They should be out of doors in good air at play, as much as the weather and their strength will admit."*
>
> — ***Life of Robert Owen, by Himself***

**Children would be helped to become familiar with garden production, fields, woods, domestic animals and natural history.**

In 1819 the Duke of Kent's physician wrote a report on Owen's Institution:

> *"The youngest, or infant class, under the age of five, are of course occupied only in the amusements which are suitable to their age, playing about in the area before the school when the weather admits it, under the charge of a male and female superintendent, and whose principal office it is to encourage amongst them habits and feelings of good-will and affection towards each other.*
>
> *Our party walked down to the village, and entered the children's playground. There were some bowling hoops, some drumming on two sticks — all engaged in some infantine amusement or other. Not a tear — not a wrangle.*
>
> *From the playground we entered a large room for the purpose of play and amusement, when the weather will not permit them to be out of doors. Here the most unrestrained liberty is given for noise or amusement."*
>
> **— quoted in Siraj-Blatchford, *Robert Owen: Schooling the Innocents***

New Lanark is now a historical site and museum. Cotton mills actually continued in production until 1968.

Web site:

http://www.newlanark.org
http://www.robert-owen.com

Address:

The New Lanark Conservation Trust
New Lanark Mills
Lanarkshire,
ML11 9DB
Scotland

## Other Innovations in Education

The school demonstrated other innovative methods and approaches. Information presented to children needed to have value or use in the children's lives and help them understand the world. The teachers used small blocks of wood and other manipulatives to help children learn math. Children were introduced to natural history, geography, history, geology and botany through visual aids and materials. One type of lesson involved a world map without place names or words. One child pointed to a part of the map with a pointing stick, and the other children posed questions about the location. Whichever child figured out the location had the stick passed to him or her, and the game continued:

> *"The lookers-on were as much amused, and many as much instructed as the children, who thus at an early age became so efficient, that one of our Admirals, who had sailed round the world, said he could not answer many of the questions which some of the children not yet six years old readily replied to, giving the places most correctly."*
>
> — ***Life of Robert Owen, by Himself***

When visual aids were not available, they were created. For example, the school used large canvasses on rollers that were printed with subjects of natural history. Travel brochures, maps, paintings, and even a phrenologist's[5] model of a head became part of the teaching materials.

---

Phrenology played a central role in the amazing life of Sarah Edmonds from Moncton, New Brunswick, Canada. She enlisted in the Union Army during the U.S. Civil War disguised as Franklin Thompson. She passed as a man fighting in the First Battle of Bull Run and disguised as a slave, she went behind enemy lines as a spy. No physicals were required, and personal hygiene was a private matter even for soldiers. When she volunteered to spy, only the contours of her head were examined in a phrenological exam. She passed this "test" and was deemed to be of good character and sound mental frame to work as a spy. She published her exploits in a book called *Nurse and Spy in the Union Army.*

---

Learning grammar was made fun by personifying parts of speech in pictures (for example, Corporal Adverb, General Noun, Colonel Verb), and word and picture cards aided emerging reading skills.

Nature walks were encouraged; field trips were common and used for educational reasons. If weather was inclement, teachers brought natural objects such as flowers and animals into the classroom. The school contained the first school playground in the world. Teacher-student ratios were low, and Owen supported the need for both male and female teachers to provide a balance in children's lives.

Robert Dale Owen described his father's educational system in "An Outline of the System of Education at New Lanark" (1824).[6] Teachers adapted lessons to meet needs of different age groups, used extensive visual aids and began with actual objects rather than symbolic representations. New information was introduced by comparing it to and integrating it with knowledge children already had. For example, children would be introduced to the idea of minerals changing over time after first discussing how animals and vegetables grow and change. The fundamental source of information acquisition — the senses — would be described to the children as follows:

> *"We certainly do not know how our senses get these impressions, but we know that they do get them; for we see things with our eyes, hear with our ears, feel with our fingers and other parts of our bodies, smell with our noses, and taste with our mouths. If we could not see, hear, smell, taste or feel, we could know nothing of what is about us; so that every thing we know, we know by our senses. We could not think at all if we knew nothing, and we always think according to what we know, or according to these impressions.*

---

[5] Phrenology was a theory that maintained that the shape of a person's skull showed the kind of mind and character the person had. It was based on a theory by Dr. Franz Josef Gall.

[6] A section of Robert Dale Owen's "An Outline of the System of Education at New Lanark" is contained in Karen Altfest's *Robert Owen as Educator.* The entire outline is in Robert Dale Owen's *Robert Owen at New Lanark.*

> *Therefore these impressions give us thoughts, and after we have thought, then we move about or act. So that you see the impressions which we receive by our senses, cause us to move about or act."*

Subjects were studied based on children's own life experiences. In addition to learning about different subject areas, the children were taught how everything connects to the world and experience: "All knowledge belongs either to an *art* or a *science*. Whatever tells us of the nature and properties of any substance, is a *science*. Whatever teaches us how to produce any thing, is an *art*."

As we review programs today, it is important to remember Owen's words and see if ***"children's minds and feelings are duly considered or attended to."***

Owen had an unusual sense of children and their feelings:

> *"I have long thought that the minds and feelings of young children are seldom duly considered or attended to, and that if adults would patiently encourage them to express candidly what they thought and felt, much suffering would be saved to the children, and much useful knowledge of human nature would be gained by the adults."*
>
> ***— Life of Robert Owen, by Himself***

*Do you know a current entrepreneur with a social vision? What has that person done?*

As well as the school classes in the day, evening school for older children and adults was provided. Older children who did work in the factory had shorter workdays to allow them to attend school. The school was seen as central to the community, and, in addition to classroom instruction, was also used for many community events such as concerts, lectures and dances. In essence, New Lanark had day care, school, adult education and a community cultural centre.

*Robert Owen's view that a healthy environment would produce healthy, productive people is very different from the ideas of Rousseau or Pestalozzi who believed the child's development and character would later create changes in society. This issue continues today. Do we create resilient children and youth? Or do we make changes to the institutions that exist? Or is it some of both that creates long-term change?*

The school programs were in stark disparity to the narrow-focused and brutalizing schools in Great Britain. The idea of educating poor children and adults met with hostility long into the $19^{th}$ century. Imagine the contrast between the harsh schools of the day and children singing and dancing at New Lanark!

Owen had a vision. He did not intend to be simply a philanthropist, giving money to charitable causes. He wanted to test out his ideas and theories on the advancement of humanity as a whole. He was convinced that a "man" was no better than his environment and that if the environment changed, people would change. Education was the key to his ideal society; the New Institution and New Lanark would serve as examples to other industrial communities.

## New Thoughts and Plans

In 1815, Owen wrote *Observations on the Effect of the Manufacturing System,* in which he condemned the exploitation of young children as cheap labour and advocated a national system of education. He visited Newgate Prison in 1817 with Elizabeth Fry, a Quaker activist who worked with female prisoners. Fry had also established a school for the women's children. Owen cited the astonishing improvements she had achieved as proof that ignorance and misery could disappear

> *"under the influence of a persevering well-directed kindness"*

and that

> *"the most deep-rooted and long continued habits of depravity may be easily and speedily overcome by a system of kindness."*

**Robert Owen in 1823, a few years before going to the United States. (Illustration courtesy of New Lanark Conservation Trust.)**

Though things were different in New Lanark, the situation in most of England had worsened. People did not follow Owen's suggestions about making the poor productive. He was advocating Villages of Unity and Mutual Co-operation; in each there would be a farm and factory that would form a self-sustaining unit. Villages of 1,200 persons would live co-operatively on 1,000 – 1,500 hectares of land, and these units would form the basis for a re-organization of society. Owen felt that poor people needed a chance to work and that if they were put in the right environment, their circumstances could change. He felt that the new era would bring equality of the sexes and cessation of war.

Villages would have all services and green spaces

> *"surrounded by gardens and an abundance of space in all directions to keep the air healthy and pleasant: they will have walks and plantations before them, within the square, and well-cultivated grounds, kept in good order around, as far as the eye can reach."*
>
> — **New Lanark Trust,**
> ***The Story of Robert Owen***

The ruling nobles of England had asked Owen's advice but were taken aback by the idea of a a planned social community. It was anathema in their world of laissez-faire capitalism. His ideas were ignored; however, he kept advocating and promoting the beliefs and the plans. There was even government money set aside for a trial community, but his ideas were ultimately too far removed from the reality of the day. The money was not given.

## Across the Ocean to New Harmony

**New Harmony Plan. This is a copy of an old print of the proposed village at New Harmony, Indiana. This plan was created in about 1825, before Owen came to the United States. Owen often used visual arts to explain ideas and had an engraving done of his planned village to present to interested audiences. When he lectured and talked in the U.S., he also had a two-metre (six-foot) square model of his ideal community. (Used with Permission of the Library of Congress, Washington, DC. LC-USZ62-55096.)**

Owen was not discouraged! He had made a fortune and still wanted to try out his ideas for a Village of Co-operation as a way to create a more perfect society. He sold his interest in New Lanark in 1825 to Charles and Henry Walker, sons of one of his Quaker partners. He retained a financial interest until 1828.

Owen left New Lanark to build his ideal community of the future in which citizens would learn new ways of living and associating with each other. He headed across the Atlantic to the United States, as he believed the "new world" would be more supportive of his social experiment, and land was much less expensive. In the Midwest, a number of utopian communities were being established. Owen hoped that the more open views of the United States would assist in the development of the community. The 20,000-acre community was called New Harmony and was established on the Lower Wabash River in Indiana, near the Illinois border. It was the second utopian community in the same location; Johann Rapp[7] and the Harmony Society founded the first in 1814.

**Watercolour painting of New Harmony in 1832, by Karl Bodmer. Karl Bodmer (1809 – 1893) was a Swiss artist who travelled with naturalist Prince Alexander Philip Maximilian of Wied as he explored the natural history and native people of the Upper Missouri River region from 1832 – 1834. The expedition stopped in New Harmony in October 1832 to meet with Thomas Say, an entomologist who advised them on western travel. A complete collection of Bodmer's work can be seen in *Karl Bodmer's America* published by the Joslyn Art Museum and The University of Nebraska Press. (Photo of painting used with permission of Joslyn Art Museum, Omaha, NE; Gift of Enron Art Foundation JAM.1986.49.368.)**

Owen and his partner William Maclure (1763 – 1840) planned a Community of Equality, an intentional community set up to realize social goals and marshal in a new society in the new world. Maclure was a leading American scientist,

[7] Rapp and his followers relocated to Pennsylvannia.

**William Maclure, scientist and educator, worked with Owen in New Harmony. Maclure, with a Pestalozzian background, was responsible for the educational programs. In this photo he is holding a goniometer, which was used for measuring the angles of solids such as crystals. (Used with permission of the Ewell Sale Stewart Library. The Academy of Natural Sciences, Philadelphia, PA. Photo taken by CW Peale.)**

philanthropist, educational leader and social reformer. His life paralleled Owen's in that he too had acquired a fortune and focused on educational ideas. Owen used his own money ($95,000 in 1825 U.S. dollars) to purchase New Harmony; he was that committed to his goals.

En route to Indiana, Owen gave lengthy speeches in Washington, D.C. with President James Monroe and President-elect John Quincy Adams in the audience. He carried with him a huge model, almost 2 metres long, of his envisioned community. In Washington, the model sat in the anteroom of the White House where its advantages were publicized. Owen even met with both Choctaw and Chickasaw Native chiefs along with their interpreters to describe his view of society.

In his February 25, 1825 speech to the House of Representatives, Owen articulated his utopian goals:

> *"The great object intended to be attained, by the various institutions of every age and country, was, or ought to be, to secure happiness for the greatest number of human beings. That this object could be obtained only, 1st, by a proper training and education from birth, of the physical and mental powers of each individual; 2nd, by arrangements to enable each individual to procure, in the best manner, at all times, a full supply of those things which are necessary and the most beneficial for human nature; and, 3rd, that all individuals should be so united and combined in a social system, as to give to each the greatest benefit from society."*
>
> — O. Johnson, ***Robert Owen in the United States***

**New Harmony Street. (Used with permission of the State Historical Society of Wisconsin. Whi (Neg)3167.)**

## Education in New Harmony

Education would unite the social and economic aspects of Owen's social reconstruction. He entrusted the educational program to Maclure who had visited Pestalozzi several times and had spent time with Owen at New Lanark. Maclure's vision for education was stated in one very long sentence in his book *Epitome of the Improved Pestalozzian System:*

> *"The great and fundamental principle is never to attempt to teach children what they cannot comprehend, and to teach them in the exact ratio of their understanding it, without omitting one link in the chain of ratiocination, proceeding always from the known to the unknown, from the most easy to the most difficult, practicing the most extensive and accurate use of all the senses, exercising, improving and perfecting all the mental and corporeal faculties by quickening combination, accelerating and carefully arranging comparison, judiciously and impartially making deduction, summing up the results free from prejudices and cautiously avoiding the delusions of imagination, the constant source of ignorance and error."*
>
> **— quoted in Monroe, *History of the Pestalozzian Movement in the United States***

New Harmony is now a historic site:

Historic New Harmony, Inc.
P.O. Box 579
New Harmony, Indiana 47631
U.S.A.

http://ulib.iupui.edu/kade/newharmony/home.html

Francis Joseph Neef (1770 – 1854), a colleague of Pestalozzi, was brought to New Harmony along with Pestalozzian educators Phiquepal d'Arusmont and Marie Duclos Fretageot as part of the "Boatload of Knowledge" to assist with the setting up of schools. The group got its name as the members met in Pittsburgh to board the keelboat "Philanthropist" for the trip down the Ohio River to New Harmony. The trip unexpectedly took much longer as the boat got caught for a full month in ice near Beaver, Pennsylvania. In addition to educational leaders, the group had well known scientists such as Thomas Say (entomologist and conchologist) and Charles Alexandre Lesueur (naturalist). The boat often stopped enroute, and prospective members of New Harmony were interviewed.

Neef followed many of Pestalozzi's methods and approaches and applied them at New Harmony. Owen himself had visited Pestalozzi in 1818 in Yverdon and studied his teaching methods. Neef was head of the schools, with Maclure acting as overall supervisor of the educational programs. Neef was skilled in languages and music and brought a good sense of humour to the lessons. He once heard a boy use profane language and admonished him. The boy then asked why Neef swore and was told, "Because I am a damned fool. Don't you be one too" (quoted in Monroe's *History of the Pestalozzian Movement in the United States).*

---

The following is an excerpt from a letter to the American Journal of Education in 1826 describing the educational setting:

> *"Among the public buildings are a large hall about 100 square feet; the lower part for lecture and reading rooms, dancing, and music; the upper part for a library, a museum of natural history, cabinets of mineralogy, & c.*
>
> *Upwards of a hundred packages of books, &c., have just arrived via New Orleans. The works are the most useful and the most splendid that could be procured on natural history, antiquities, architecture, agriculture, & c. There is besides an extensive collection of paintings and prints.*
>
> *Our teachers are Messrs. Neef , Phiquepal, T. Say, and several other eminent foreigners. We do not hesitate to say that this place offers advantages for education which are not surpassed, if equaled in any part of this country."*
>
> **— "Mr. Owen's School at New Harmony," 1826**

**The Infant School at New Harmony was housed in the Community House Number Two. It was built between 1817 – 1822 and was originally a Harmonist communal dwelling. (Used with permission of the Indiana State Museum & Historic Sites.)**

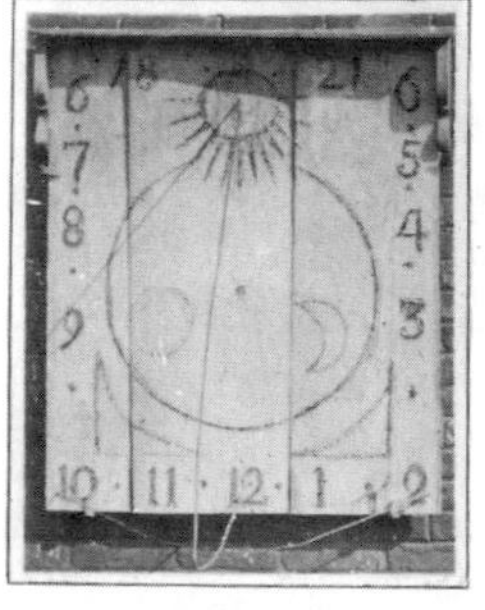

**Education materials at New Harmony. (Used with permission of the State Historical Society of Wisconsin. Whi (Neg)3167.)**

**Workingmen's Institute Library. William Maclure established the Workingmen's Institute Library to help with adult education in New Harmony. (Used with permission of the State Historical Society of Wisconsin Whi (Neg)3167.)**

There were three schools in New Harmony: an infant school for children two to five years, a higher school for children from 5 – 12 and a school for adults.

The schools represented the ideas of Pestalozzi and paralleled much of the educational practice at New Lanark:

- Students went from the known to the unknown, from the simple to the complex.
- Books were abolished from the lower grades, and instruction was given orally.
- Nature and geography were taught in the field.
- Music, art, dance and gymnastics were important elements in the school.
- Equal education was offered for boys and girls and men and women.
- Corporal punishment, felt to be degrading to children, was forbidden.

Rating scales (0 – 100) were developed to measure children's progress in academic achievement, work habits and social skills.

Robert Dale Owen described the approach of leading children to learning that was encouraged at New Harmony:

> *"The mind of man is a valve that opens outwardly, and the application of external force may crush it but it cannot open it. It can be opened only by gentleness and reason, and he betrays a most injurious ignorance of his nature who imagines the contrary."*
>
> **— quoted in Thomson's *The Educational Work of Robert Dale Owen;* from *The New Harmony Gazette,* May 7, 1818**

An extensive trades department taught such professions as taxidermy, printing, carpentry, and shoemaking.

Lecture halls, a reading room and a museum of natural history and mineralogy were set up. Maclure was particularly interested in adult education and helped establish libraries for workers. The Workingmen's Institute at New Harmony was one of these libraries.

## The Demise of Owen's New Harmony

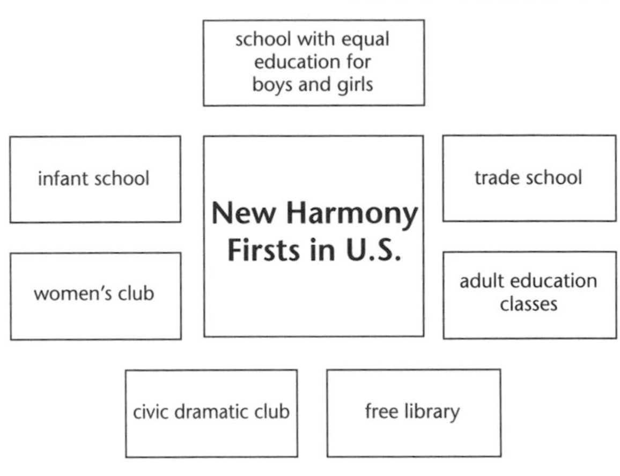


Unfortunately, Owen's utopian community could not and did not succeed. Problems developed because of lack of advance planning and orientation for newcomers, unregulated open admission and lack of precautions against fraud. In addition, the original housing was inadequate and there was a dearth of skilled trades people. Owen and Maclure disagreed on educational practice with Owen advocating increased uniformity of methods.

Owen also never developed a clear policy on ownership of land. It is interesting to note that Owen had been an efficient and effective manager in New Lanark but was not as effective in New Harmony. Rival communities sprang up, and followers disagreed among themselves and with Owen. The community had many knowledgeable people but lacked key practical skills. New Harmony under Owen lasted only three years.

Owen sold the land, having now lost four-fifths of his New Lanark fortune. He remained optimistic, and in many ways New Harmony did not fail. Some of the original idealists remained and made significant contributions in many fields of endeavour. The town remained as a strong intellectual centre even after Owen left, and New Harmony was a site of many firsts for the United States. It may have been the end of Owen's experiment, but it remained a community with high intellectual, educational and social ends. It remained a model for the future.

## His Optimism Continues

Robert Owen approached newly elected United States President Andrew Jackson, Mexican President Guadalupe Victoria and Mexican General Santa Anna with his ideas, hoping to gain their support for his ideas on social reform. Turned down, he still was not discouraged.

He returned to England after his wife and two daughters (Anne and Mary) died within two years. He and his wife had drifted apart over the years, often arguing about organized religion and his frequent absences from home. Owen did not even attend her funeral.

Owen continued to work for a more just and fair society and became known as a leader of the working class. For another 20 years he unceasingly fought for better working conditions and improved educational systems. He set up the Institution for Removing Ignorance and Property, edited *The Crisis* and created an alternative currency in labour notes. Near the end of his life he was working on a new school system for his birthplace of Newtown, Wales. His autobiography, *The Life of Robert Owen* was written when he was well over 80 years.

He died at the age of 87 in Newtown with his son Robert Dale Owen at his side. Just before his death, a visiting clergyman asked if he regretted wasting his life on fruitless endeavours. He countered with his claim that he had given important truths to the world. They were just disregarded because of lack of understanding. He knew he had been ahead of his time. Owen was eternally hopeful that **"man is the creature of circumstances."**

**Robert Owen Statue in Newtown, Wales, his birthplace. (Used with permission of The Robert Owen Memorial Museum.)**

## Owen Family Legacies

Owen's children extended his influence by translating his utopian dreams into practical campaigns for an improved society.

Owen's eldest son, Robert Dale Owen,[8] was in the Indiana legislature and then became a United States Congressman and an advocate for women's rights especially in the areas of property, birth control and state-funded education. In a letter to President Abraham Lincoln in 1862 Robert Dale Owen wrote about the affliction of slavery in the United States, demanding that Lincoln *"extirpate the blighting curse"[of slavery]* and *"let them [the slaves] breathe free."* This demand was likely one of the strongest influences on Lincoln as he issued the Emancipation Proclamation, declaring slaves to be free. Robert Dale also worked to re-settle freed slaves and introduced a bill to establish the Smithsonian Institute in Washington, D.C., which still exists as a research and education centre as well as an extensive set of museums. Robert Dale also was a *charges d'affairs* (diplomatic position in absence of the ambassador) in Naples, Italy.

David Dale was appointed U.S. Geologist, carrying out the first official geological surveys of Indiana, Kentucky, and Arkansas. He also helped his brother Robert Dale draw up plans for the Smithsonian. David Dale married Neef's daughter Caroline.

William Owen died in midlife at the age of 40 but founded the Thespian Society that gave life to the theater at New Harmony for a century. He was co-editor of the *New Harmony Gazette*. William also helped establish the Posey County Agricultural Society to stimulate quality agricultural products and livestock and was the director of the State Bank of Indiana.

Owen's youngest son, Richard, also a geologist, followed his brother David as Indiana State Geologist and was the first geologist to explore the northern shores of Lake Superior. Richard also worked for reform of military prisons. While in the Civil War he was known for his kindness to Confederate prisoners. Later he was a professor of natural history at Indiana University and was elected the first president of Purdue University.

---

[8] The autobiography of Robert Dale Owen, *Threading My* Way, and Richard Leopold's biography of Robert Dale Owen, *Robert Dale Owen,* provide extensive insight into Robert Owen. A Ph.D. dissertation by Keith Thomson called *The Educational Work of Robert Dale Owen* focuses on both his life and educational endeavours.

*Owen's children also made tremendous contributions to society. How do parents affect children's values? How did your parents affect your values?*

Jane Dale Owen, Owen's only surviving daughter, began a seminary for "young ladies" with science classes taught by her brother David Dale. She married Robert Fauntleroy, a scientist and Coast Guard officer who also worked with David Dale and Robert Dale to build up a castor bean business in New Harmony.

A grandchild, Horace Pestalozzi Owen, was also active in education throughout his life.

## Owenite Communities Spread

There were other Owenite communities founded in Britain, Ireland, Continental Europe, Canada and the United States, but New Harmony was the largest.

One of the U.S. Owenite communities was started in Yellow Springs, Ohio in 1825 through the active plans of the local Owenite Society. Owen visited and gave his support to the project, which intended to duplicate New Harmony. Internal disagreements caused the demise of the colony. Despite the efforts of Maclure to save it, the community lasted only two years.

Antioch College later started in Yellow Springs in 1853 with Horace Mann as its first president. A world famous educator and antislavery activist, Mann envisioned a program that focused not just on the intellect but also on a social conscience and overall competency skills. Mann supported co-education as a key to successful learning. Mann was married to Mary Peabody, a leader in the kindergarten movement along with her sister Elizabeth. G. Stanley Hall (see chapter 7) also taught at Antioch. It is interesting to see how a small town became a centre of "enlightened and progressive" ideas.

The Toon O'Maxwell was an Owenite community established near what is now Sarnia, Ontario at the south end of Lake Huron. Henry Jones of Exeter, England founded the colony around 1828 after visiting New Lanark and Robert Owen. Jones's brother was married to the wife of the Governor of Upper Canada, and this association enabled him to obtain the land for his utopian plan. Jones recruited families in Scotland who were willing to join him in Canada. They constructed log buildings for living quarters and for farm shelters. The school was a central and key part of the plan. The colony lasted only two years due to the harsh conditions, individuals' preference for family ownership, and some devastating fires.

All of the educational ideas were part of Owen's view that education would lead to social improvements in all of society. He spent his entire fortune developing and acting on his ideas.

## Infant Schools in North America

Infant schools modelled after New Lanark did develop in North America, along the eastern seaboard in both Canada and the United States. There was a tremendous variety of children and families, and the programs reflected the people who used the schools. The history of infant schools also shows the impact of social-economic factors on children's programs.

Schools following Owen's ideas and methods were seen as a way to encourage social reform through the early education of poor children and also as a way to introduce educational reform into the elementary schools. Typical schools were still focusing on mechanical learning with harsh disciplinary methods.

---

*From reading the novels of Louisa May Alcott, do you think her father had an influence on her writing and career as a writer?*

The infant schools flourished between 1825 and 1835 under the leadership of Amos Bronson Alcott, the father of Louisa May Alcott (author of *Little Women, Little Men, Jo's Boys)*. Bronson Alcott (1799 – 1888) was an educational and social reformer, a transcendentalist, and writer. Elizabeth Peabody (see chapter 5) taught in Alcott's infant school in Boston and may have provided the model for the character "Jo" in *Little Women*. The Temple School focused on encouraging the integrated development of intellectual, physical and emotional aspects of the child. The school was criticized as too "liberal" and was forced to close though other schools were founded on Alcott's ideas. He wrote for the *Dial* magazine, co-founded a cooperative vegetarian community, and was an ardent abolitionist. He wrote *Observations on the Principles and Methods of Infant Instruction and Record of a School* among other publications. *Pedlar's Progress* by Odell Shepard and *A. Bronson Alcott* by Sanborn and Harris are biographies of Alcott. Bronson's work in the context of the history of American education is detailed in *American Education* by Lawrence Cremin.

---

**Bronson Alcott was a key leader in establishing infant schools in North America. Photo taken between 1860 – 1870. (Used with permission of Concord Free Public Library.)**

These infant schools were open programs with many opportunities for motor play, music, dance, and first-hand and sensory experiences with a focus on the "whole child." Corporal punishment was banned in the infant schools, and play was seen as central to childhood learning. Many of these infant schools reflected the educational methods and ideas of Pestalozzi.

What happened to them? By 1840 most had disappeared. They were too costly, and the opposition to early education was growing. Teachers found it difficult to adjust to these new methods, and there were pressures to adhere to mainstream school expectations if the schools were to receive government funding.

*Women's roles are no less contentious today; day care is not yet seen as a support service, nor is it high on the political agenda. What about family values? Morals? Will group child care undermine social, cultural and economic systems and destroy the family unit? According to research, the answer is no, but the questions continue to be raised.*

*How was Owen both a product of his time and ahead of his time? How was he able to see beyond current conditions to envision a different society?*

*Like Comenius and many of the historical figures studied, Owen never gave up his ideals and work for a better society. What do you think kept him optimistic?*

The Victorian idea that women should stay at home caring for children also discouraged people from sending their children to the schools. Though women were initially needed in the industrialized centres, immigrants replaced them as cheaper workers, and it became less common for middle-class women to work outside the home. The nuclear family and "Fireside Education" at home became the revered image. This idealized view was inaccurate even at the time because many women did have to work outside the home. There were also some medical reports that early schooling would destroy "jelly-like young brains."

It is interesting to note that while infant schools declined, kindergartens flourished. Though similar in approach, the part-time nature of kindergartens allowed the pre-eminence of "mother-care" to be maintained. Kindergartens were never seen as supplanting the mother's role or competing with the family.

Robert Owen did not fail in his endeavours despite the challenges and difficulties he faced. His work with infant schools and creating a better society provided beacons for future social reformers and educators. It is no wonder that H.G. Wells, in his 1926 book, *The Outline of History,* listed Robert Owen as one of the top ten people who had most influenced the thinking of people. Owen had a vision of a new society with education at its centre.

***Special Library Collection-Owen***
*University of Illinois at Urbana Library*
*Illinois Historical Survey*
*1408 W. Gregory Dr.*
*Urbana, Illinois 61801*
*U.S.A.*

*Robert Owen Collection*
*National Co-operative Archive*
*Co-operative College*
*Holyoake House*
*Hanover Street*
*Manchester*
*M60 0AS*

*United Kingdom*
*Owen Collection*
*Morisset Library*
*University of Ottawa*
*65 University*
*Ottawa, Ontario*
*K1N 9A5*

## Robert Owen — References for Further Study


Altfest, K. C. (1977). *Robert Owen as educator.* Boston: Twayne Publishers.

Bell, A. (1805). *An experiment in education.* London: Cadell and Davies.

Bellamy, J., & Saville, J. (Eds.). (1982). *Dictionary of Labour biography.* London: The MacMillan Press Ltd.

Bestor, A. E. (1970). *Backwoods utopias: The sectarian and Owenite phases of communitarian socialism in America: 1663 – 1829.* Philadelphia, PA: University of Pennsylvania Press.

Butt, J. (Ed.). (1971). *Robert Owen: Prince of cotton spinners.* Devon, England: David & Charles Publishers.

Carlson, H. (1992). Care and education of young children of pauper and working classes: New Lanark, Scotland, 1790 – 1825. *Paedagogica Historica, 28* (1), 9 – 34.

Carmony, D., & Elliott, J. (1980). New Harmony, Indiana: Robert Owen's seedbed for utopia. *Indiana Magazine of History, LXXVI* (3), 161 – 261.

Caughey, J. (1949). *Robert Owen.* Berkeley, CA: University of California Press.

Chaloner, W. H. (1954). Robert Owen, Peter Drinkwater and the early factory system in Manchester 1788 – 1800. *Bulletin of the John Rylands Library, 37 (1),* 78 – 102.

Claeys, G. (1987). *Machinery, money and the millenium: From moral economy to socialism.* Princeton, NJ: Princeton University Press.

Claeys, G. (Ed.). (1991). *Robert Owen: A new view of society and other writings.* London: Penguin.

Claeys, G. (Ed.). (1993). *Selected works of Robert Owen. Volume 1: Early writings. Volume 2: The development of socialism. Volume 3: The Book of the new moral order. Volume 4: The life of Robert Owen.* London: William Pickering.

Clayton, J. (1908). *Robert Owen: Pioneer of social reforms.* London: A.C. Fifield.

Cole, M. (1969). *Robert Owen of New Lanark.* New York: Augustus M. Kelley.

Cole, M., Butt, J., Watkins, W., & Harrison, J. (1971). *Robert Owen: Industrialist reformer visionary 1771 – 1858.* London: Robert Owen Bicentenary Assoc.

Co-operative Union Ltd. (1971). *Robert Owen and his relevance to our times: Addresses contributed during the Robert Owen bi-centenary summer school, 1971.* The Education Department. Loughborough, England: Co-operative Union Ltd.

Cremin, L. (1980). *American education: The national experience: 1783 – 1876.* New York: Harper & Row.

Croall, J. (1996, February 2). A share of happiness. *Times Educational Supplement*, 4153, 12.

Dallas, W. (1910, February). The Toon O' Maxwell: An Owenite settlement in Lambton County, Ontario. *Canadian Magazine of Politics, Science, Art and Literature, XXX* (4), 323 – 328.

Donnachie, I., & Hewitt, G. (1993). *Historic New Lanark.* Edinburgh, Scotland: Edinburgh University Press Ltd.

Edmonds, S. E. (1865). *Nurse and spy in the Union Army.* Hartford, CT: W.S. Williams.

Elliott, H. (1940). Our newest Indiana Shrine—New Harmony. *Indiana History Bulletin, 17* (2), 109 – 117.

Fretageot, N. (1934). *Historic New Harmony: A guide.* (No publisher noted).

Harrison, J. F. C. (1969). *Robert Owen and the Owenites in Britain and America.* London: Routledge & Kegan Paul.

Hielbroner, R. (1966). *The worldly philosophers.* New York: Simon & Schuster.

Johnson, O. (1970). *Robert Owen in the United States.* New York: Humanities Press.

Jones, L. (1890). *The life, times and labours of Robert Owen.* London: Swan Sonnenschein & Co.

Jones, P. (1860). *Life and journals of Kah-ke-wa-quo-na-by (Rev. Peter Jones).* Toronto, Canada: A. Green.

Kaplan, H., & Lankford, N. (1987). The history of education at New Harmony. *Contemporary Education, 58* (2), 106 – 110.

Lancaster, J. (1821). *The Lancasterian system of education: With improvements.* Baltimore: Lancasterian Institute.

Lascarides, V.C. & Hinitz, B. (2000). *History of Early Childhood Education.* New York: Falmer Press.

Leopold, R. (1940, reprinted 1969). *Robert Dale Owen.* New York: Octagon Books.

Maclure, W. (1826, February). An epitome of the improved Pestalozzian system of education as practiced by William Phiquepal and Madam Fretageot. *American Journal of Science and Arts, 10,* 145 – 156.

McLaren, D. (1983). *David Dale of New Lanark.* Glasgow, Scotland: Heatherbank Press.

Monroe, W. (1969). *History of the Pestalozzian movement in the United States.* New York: Arno Press & The New York Times. (Original work published 1907)

Morton, A. L. (1962). *The life and ideas of Robert Owen.* London: Lawrence & Wishart.

Morton, S. G. (1844, October). A memoir of William Maclure, Esq. Late president of the Academy of Natural Sciences of Philadelphia. *American Journal of Science and Arts, XLVII* (1), 1 – 17.

Mr. Owen's school at New Harmony. (1826, June). *American Journal of Education, 1,* 377 – 378.

Murray, E. R. (1912). *A story of infant schools and kindergartens.* London: Sir Isaac Pitman & Sons.

New Lanark Conservation Trust (no date). *The story of New Lanark.* Lanark, Scotland: New Lanark Conservation Trust.

New Lanark Conservation Trust. (1997). *The story of Robert Owen, 1771 – 1853.* Lanark, Scotland: New Lanark Conservation Trust.

Owen, R. (1920). *The life of Robert Owen, by himself.* London: G. Bell.

Owen, R. (1991). *A new view of society and other writings.* (G. Claeys, Ed.). London: Penguin Books.

Owen, R. D. (1874, reprinted 1967). *Threading my way.* New York: G. W. Carleton & Co.

Owen, R. D. (1972). An outline of the system of education at New Lanark. In *Robert Owen at New Lanark: Two booklets and one pamphlet, 1824 – 1838.* New York: Arno Press. (Original work published 1824)

Peltzman, B. R. (1998). *Pioneers of early childhood education: A bio-bibliographical guide.* Westport, CT: Greenwood Press.

Pence, A. (1990). The child-care profession in Canada. In I. Doxey (Ed.), *Child care and education: Canadian Dimensions*. Scarborough, Ontario: Nelson Canada.

Pence, A. R. (1986). Infant schools in North America 1825 – 1840. In S. Kilmer (Ed.), *Advances in Early Education and Daycare, 4* (pp. 1 – 25). Greenwich, CT: Jai Press.

Pitzer, D. (Ed.). (1997). *America's communal utopias*. Chapel Hill, NC: University of North Carolina Press.

Podmore, F. (1906). *Robert Owen: A biography*. London: George Allen & Unwin Ltd.

Prochner, L. & Howe, N. (2000). *Early childhood education and care in Canada*. Vancouver: UBC Press.

Salmon, D. (Ed.). (1932). *Practical parts of Lancaster's improvements and Bell's experiment*. Cambridge, England: Cambridge University Press.

Salmon, D., & Hindshaw, W. (1904). *Infant schools: Their history and theory*. London: Longmans, Green & Co.

Sanborn, F. B. (1877). A. Bronson Alcott. *Barnard's American Journal of Education, 27,* 225 – 236.

Sanborn, F. B., & Harris, W. (1893, reprinted in 1965). *A. Bronson Alcott: His life and philosophy, in two volumes*. New York: Biblo and Tannen.

Shepherd, O. (1968). *Pedlar's progress: The life of Bronson Alcott*. New York: Greenwood Press.

Silver, H. (Ed.). (1969). *Robert Owen on education*. Cambridge, England: Cambridge University Press.

Siraj-Blatchford, J. (1997). *Robert Owen: Schooling the innocents*. Nottingham, England: Educational Heretics Press.

Taylor, A. (1987). *Visions of harmony: A study in nineteenth-century millenarianism*. Oxford, England: Clarendon Press.

Thomson, K. (1948). *The educational work of Robert Dale Owen* (Doctoral Dissertation, the University of California).

# Chapter 7 — *John Dewey*

**1859 - 1952**

*The school must be "a genuine form of active community life, instead of a place set apart in which to learn lessons."*

— ***The School and Society***

*"Information severed from thoughtful action is dead, a mind-crushing load."*

*"No one has ever explained why children are so full of questions outside of the school... [yet there is a] conspicuous absence of display of curiosity about the subject matter of school lessons."*

— ***Democracy and Education***

*"A large part of the educational waste comes from the attempt to build a superstructure of knowledge without a solid foundation in the child's relation to his social environment."*

— ***University Record*, September 18, 1896**

*"Play is not to be identified with anything which the child externally does. It rather designates his mental attitude in its entirety and in its unity."*

— ***Elementary School Record*, February 1900**

Dewey's life spanned the period before the American Civil War to after the Second World War. Imagine the events in one lifetime! In the midst of tremendous technological changes and two world wars, Dewey was part of a fundamental shift in ideas, a shift he helped create. As one of the outstanding Western thinkers of the late 19th and 20th centuries, Dewey influenced ideas in fields as diverse as psychology, logic, aesthetics, religion and social and political thought and education.

He was one of the main proponents of **progressive education.**[1]
Key components of this movement included:

- the child's physical well being
- focus on the whole child
- curriculum developed from the interests and needs of children
- teacher as guide or facilitator
- co-operative learning and inquiry among children
- close home/school connections
- education for current life situations; effective living rather than accumulation of knowledge
- scientific study of child development
- the school as contributor to educational progress
- adaptability to change
- integrated curriculum.

These tenets were in stark contrast to those followed in schools of the time with their lack of individualized curriculum and their focus on subject matter, rote learning and harsh punishments.

[1] There has been recent renewed interest in practices derived from the progressive movement though rarely are the historical foundations recognized. See S. Semel and A. Sadovnik (Eds.), *"Schools of Tomorrow," Schools of Today.*

The Progressive Education Association published the journal *Progressive Education* from 1924 – 1957 though the organization began in 1919. This description was on the back cover of Vol. 1, No. 2:

"The Progressive Education Association believes in the right of each individual to the highest physical, mental, spiritual, and social development of which he is capable. Its advocates believe that every system of education, public and private, from kindergarten through college should carefully measure its pupils along these lines of development; that the ability to apply knowledge with intelligence and joy to the problems of everyday life should replace to a great extent expertness in passing examinations for book content alone; that education should use more and more laboratory methods which entail greater physical and mental freedom; that in the training of teachers the study of human nature and child reaction should have equal emphasis with methods of presenting facts."

An extensive description and explanation of the origins of the progressive education movement (also sometimes called experimental education) is by Eduard Lindeman, philosopher and past director of the New York School for Social Service:

> *"In the first place, experimental education represented a negative response to the deadly, stereotyped, ritualistic and doctrinaire form of education which prevailed everywhere in America where middle-class literature became dominant. In the second place, experimental education contributed positive response to ... liberalism and expressionism, especially self-expressionism.... Experimental education was, then, a ... revolt against cultural mediocrity. Naturally its influence was cast on the side of the individual. Like all movements involving the notion of freedom, its purpose was to allow the learner to expand, to discover his latent capacities, to break through the artificial barriers of conformity and formalism, and to reveal fresh, creative possibilities in his relationship to his environment."*
>
> **— from *Schools Grow* edited by Marjorie Schauffler and quoted in "Progressive Education and American Progressivism: Caroline Pratt" by Robert Beck**

Lawrence Cremin gave another definition of progressive education in *The Transformation of the School: Progressivism in American Education*:

> *"progressive education began as part of a vast humanitarian effort to apply the promise of American life — the ideal of government by, of, and for the people — to the puzzling new urban-industrial civilization that came into being during the latter half of the nineteenth century ... Progressive education began as Progressivism in education: a many-sided effort to use the schools to improve the lives of individuals."*

Schools were seen as fundamental levers for both social and political regeneration.

## Early Life

Dewey was born in 1859 into a climate of contrasting and stimulating new ideas. Charles Darwin's *Origin of Species*, Karl Marx's *Critique of Political Economy* and John Stuart Mill's *On Liberty* were all published in that year. It was the year John Brown, the American abolitionist, captured the U.S. arsenal at Harpers Ferry. America was also at the brink of the Civil War.

Dewey's ancestors had farmed in Vermont for three generations. John Dewey was the third of four children of Archibald Sprague Dewey and Lucina Rich. Shortly before John's birth, one of his older brothers died in a scalding accident. The family lived in Burlington, Vermont on Lake Champlain with a view to the Adirondacks and the Green Mountains. This area was very important in American history, and Archibald described to his children his memories of the gunboats on Lake Champlain during the War of 1812.

**Burlington, Vermont, on the shores of Lake Champlain, had a view of both the Adirondacks and the Green Mountains, and Dewey often skated on and swam in the lake. This photo was taken during the time Dewey was living in Burlington; it shows downtown Burlington and Lake Champlain. It was taken from atop the Old Mill, one of the buildings on the University of Vermont campus at the time. (Used with permission of the University of Vermont. Bailey-Howe Library. From the John Dewey Collection, Special Collections.)**

His father kept a grocery store and was known as a whimsical joker. He had a sign outside his store that read *Hams and Cigars — Smoked and Unsmoked*. He advertised a certain brand of cigars as *A good excuse for a bad habit.* His wheelbarrow was painted with a red sign — *Stolen from A. S. Dewey.*

His mother, Lucina Rich, 20 years younger than her husband, believed strongly in education. Her grandfather had been a United States Congressman and her father had been a member of the Vermont General Assembly. She worked tirelessly for the poor in Burlington, which had become an industrial centre of 15,000 people. Burlington was a mixed town of rich and poor and included Irish immigrants as well as French Canadian immigrants from Quebec. She surrounded young John with books and reading materials and constantly encouraged his educational pursuits. John's oldest brother, Davis, became an economist and his younger brother, Charles, worked in business.

**The University of Vermont, 1869. John Dewey entered the University of Vermont before he was 16 in 1875. It was the fifth oldest university in New England. This building was known as The Old Mill and was one of two buildings on the campus in Dewey's time. Dewey boarded in The Old Mill, which had dorms upstairs. (Used with permission of the University of Vermont. Bailey-Howe Library. From the John Dewey Collection, Special Collections.)**

During the Civil War Archibald was part of the Vermont cavalry and was separated from the rest of the family for six years. Toward the end of the war Lucina moved their family closer to the front in northern Virginia to be with Archibald, an action unheard of for a woman at the time.

In his boyhood and youth John Dewey saw his friends assuming a share in household chores and gaining exposure to both agricultural and industrial jobs. School did not equal the interesting world around him. He knew early that the most important learnings were outside the classroom and in stark contrast to the school emphasis on memorization and recitation.

Dewey pursued a classical high school education filled with Greek, Latin, French, English, and mathematics. He completed the four-year program in three years. He was fond of learning, books and the outdoors, swimming and skating on Lake Champlain. Dewey and his brothers spent summers at their grandfather's farm, hiking in the mountains and canoeing in Canada. He earned spending money by delivering papers after school and later through work in lumberyards.

Before he was 16 years old, he entered the University of Vermont, which was located in his hometown and was the fifth oldest university in New England. In 1875, when Dewey enrolled, there were only eight faculty and 94 students. Even though his family lived in Burlington, Dewey lived on campus in the third floor dormitory of the Old Mill, one of two buildings at the University of Vermont. He focused his studies on social and political philosophy and was fascinated by the intellectual debates of the day. Dewey took a course in physiology with a text by Thomas Huxley, Darwin's disciple, and was deeply affected by the arguments of scientific inquiry. He was intrigued by the ideas of evolution and scientific knowledge as they jostled with fundamentalist biblical interpretations.

**John Dewey's birthplace at 186 South Willard Street, Burlington, Vermont. (Used with permission of the University of Vermont. Bailey-Howe Library. From the John Dewey Collection, Special Collections.)**

**The Deweys lived at 14 George Street in Burlington from 1867 –1876. (Used with permission of the University of Vermont. Bailey-Howe Library. From the John Dewey Collection, Special Collections.)**

**The Museum (now Torrey Hall) was the Arts Building and Museum for the University of Vermont during Dewey's enrollment. The Old Mill was the only other building on campus. (Used with permission of the University of Vermont. Bailey-Howe Library. From the John Dewey Collection, Special Collections.)**

## Early Teaching Career

After graduating with high grades and Phi Beta Kappa academic honours, Dewey taught high school (for $40 a month) at Central Avenue High School for two years (1879 – 1881) in South Oil City, Pennsylvania. His cousin Clara Wilson was the principal of the school. There were only three faculty members, and Dewey taught Latin, algebra and natural sciences, also acting as assistant principal. A fellow boarder in his rooming house described him as serious, studious and reserved.

**John Dewey taught at Central Avenue High School in South Oil City, Pennsylvania. (Photo courtesy of Art Murphy, Venango County Genealogical Club, Oil City, Pennsylvania.)**

CENTRAL SCHOOL—South Oil City.

**Dewey taught Latin, algebra and natural sciences at Central High School. (Photo courtesy of Art Murphy, Venango County Genealogical Club, Oil City, Pennsylvania.)**

Dewey then taught one term (1881 – 1882) in the Lake View Seminary, a local district school in Charlotte, Vermont. He had no training in teaching and did not intend to follow a career in education. During this period Dewey embarked on independent studies in philosophy with one of the professors, H.A.P. Torrey from the University of Vermont, and published two scholarly articles — "The Metaphysical Assumptions of Materialism" and "The Pantheism of Spinoza." Torrey encouraged him to pursue graduate studies and even offered him a loan to study in Germany. He refused the offer and decided to apply to Johns Hopkins University.

**The Lake View Seminary, where Dewey taught and was the first principal. In 1895 the school became part of the public school system until 1949 when this photo was taken. The building is now a personal residence. (Used courtesy of Laurie Moser of Charlotte, Vermont. With assistance of Diane Dolbashian and the Charlotte Library.)**

**Lake View Seminary. (Used with permission of the University of Vermont. Bailey-Howe Library. From the John Dewey Collection, Special Collections. Photo taken by Horace Eldred.)**

## Graduate Study

Dewey borrowed $500 from an aunt and moved to Baltimore, Maryland to study with George Sylvester Morris and G. Stanley Hall at the newly founded Johns Hopkins University. Dewey majored in philosophy and minored in history and political science, maintaining his interest in social problems and current issues. He took every course G. Stanley Hall taught and worked in his experimental lab. When Dewey graduated from university, President Gilman advised him to get out and see people and not to live such a secluded life.

(From the personal collection of Jennifer Wolfe.)

G. Stanley Hall (1844 – 1924) was an American leader in child psychology and education who established an early psychology laboratory that was prominent in the field. He was once called "The Darwin of the Mind," as he influenced the study of human growth and thought as much as Darwin had influenced the understanding of evolution. In 1883 he published a pioneering work showing the "content of children's minds upon entering school" based on extensive research of what children knew before entering school. This research can be seen in Smith's *Aspects of Child Life and Education*. Clark University in Worcester, Massachusetts, where Hall was president, became a centre for child-study investigation, using questionnaires, child biographies and controlled experiments. Two early articles by Hall on child-study are "Child Study and Its Relation to Education" (1900) and "The Ideal School as Based on Child Study" (1901). Hall also founded the *American Journal of Psychology* and helped organize the American Psychological Association.

## University of Michigan

After attaining his Ph.D. from Johns Hopkins in 1884, Dewey went to the University of Michigan at the invitation of Morris and taught philosophy and psychology. He looked so young that he was sometimes mistaken for a freshman.

At this point in his academic career, Dewey came into direct contact with progressivism, which was the desire to apply the American dream to the new scientific, urban and industrialized society. Dewey and others wondered how democracy could function in this new frontier. The progressive movement of the time supported the use of human intelligence to make progress in social justice, education and other issues facing society and to address the problem of poverty.

Dewey also became interested in the obvious fact that schools were not adjusting to the latest findings in child development or to the needs of the rapidly changing society of the time. While at the University of Michigan, he was part of teams assessing the quality of instruction in secondary school programs. Through this involvement he was introduced to some of the practical problems of education. Dewey also helped found a Schoolmaster's Club that sponsored lectures for high school teachers on subjects such as attention and imagination. The Club explored issues relevant to both high schools and universities. He began to envision an experimental school to correct the disparity he saw between educational theory and practice.

John Dewey is not the same Dewey of the Dewey Decimal System. Melvil Dewey (1851 – 1931), a pioneer in library science, created the system of classification and cataloging of books that used numbers from 000 to 999 and decimal places that utilized general subject areas as organizers. The Dewey Decimal System is used in most public libraries. He also established the first library training college program, the Library Journal and the American Library Association.

Dewey published his first article on education, "Education and the Health of Women," in 1885. It questioned many of the assumptions about women and supported the need for women to exercise. His first textbook, *Psychology,* was published in 1886.

A few months after arriving in Ann Arbor, John Dewey met Harriet Alice Chipman, a third-year student at the University of Michigan who was finishing her degree after teaching school for several years. They were the same age and met in the boarding house in which they both lived. He married her at the end of his second year at the University of Michigan.

Alice Chipman's maternal grandparents had raised her after her parents died; her grandfather, Frederick Riggs, had been an agent for the Hudson's Bay Company. He was a staunch opponent of war, spoke the Chippewa language and championed native rights. Alice was strong minded and a suffragette. She believed that the essence of religion was in the lived life and not the church attendance:

> *"She had a brilliant mind which cut through sham and pretense to the essence of a situation; a sensitive nature combined with indomitable courage and energy, and a loyalty to the intellectual integrity of the individual which made her spend herself with unusual generosity for all those with whom she came in contact. Awakened by her grandparents to a critical attitude toward social conditions and injustices, she was undoubtedly largely responsible for the early widening of Dewey's philosophic interests from the commentative and classical to the field of contemporary life."*
>
> **— from Schilpp (Ed.), *The Philosophy of John Dewey***

Alice Chipman was also involved with social and educational issues. She had discussed many of the ideas with Dewey when he formulated his article on women's health. In 1885 she was part of a small group of women that fought to get a reading room for women in one of the University buildings. Alice also worked with other women to organize a sorority that was not a secret society. They created a college chapter of Sorosis, an international women's organization that had such members as Lucretia Mott (American feminist and social reformer), George Sand (French author, pseudonym of Amandine Aurore Lucie Dupin), and George Eliot (English novelist, pseudonym of Marian Evans). Alice Dewey also gave lectures at the Philosophical Society, including one on "Pantheism and Modern Science." She worked to support women who were isolated from social life at the university; she helped found the Women's League and held a weekly open house for women students.

**Dewey taught at the University of Michigan at the invitation of George Morris, replacing him as chair of the Department of Philosophy after Morris died. This photo was taken in 1890 and shows Dewey (centre front) with the editorial staff of *The Inlander*, the student monthly that he helped found. (Used with permission of the University of Vermont. Bailey-Howe Library. From the John Dewey Collection, Special Collections.)**

Alice and John married in 1886.[2] The Deweys eventually had three sons (Frederick Archibald, Morris and Gordon Chipman) and three daughters (Evelyn, Lucy Alice and Jane Mary); Morris and Gordon died in childhood while the Deweys were in Europe, Morris of diphtheria in 1895 and Gordon of typhoid in 1905. While travelling in Italy, the Deweys adopted an Italian child named Sabino.[3]

Dewey worked for a year (1888 – 89) at the University of Minnesota, before returning to the University of Michigan to be the chair of the Department of Philosophy when the previous chair of that department, his friend, colleague and teacher George Morris, died. Dewey hired two additional philosophy professors, Arthur Lloyd and George Mead, who both stimulated Dewey's emerging ideas.

Dewey co-founded *The Inlander*, a magazine of student writing, and he worked to ensure women were part of its editorial board. He also worked with other faculty members to improve the circumstances of graduate students who at that time were not taught separately from undergraduates.

## Chicago at the Turn of the Century

In 1894 Dewey accepted a new post at the University of Chicago (which had been endowed by John D. Rockefeller just two years previously) as head of the Department of Philosophy and Psychology. He assumed the position with the clear understanding from President William Rainey Harper that education (pedagogy) would be part of his department and that he could set up an on-campus laboratory school in which he could test his developing ideas and theories about education. The University of Chicago was primarily a research institution at the time, and Dewey made a strong argument that a School of Pedagogy should be part of this. The School of Pedagogy would not only prepare teachers and administrators for schools but would contribute to the development of education as a science. Normal schools also had demonstration schools to train teachers, but this laboratory school was to be a site for the scientific study of learning, curriculum, teaching and child development.

---

[2] While Alice married a university philosopher, her sister Augusta, a composer and writer, married a man who traveled with a circus road show. It was an unusual family.

[3] The Dewey children's names came from family and key friends/colleagues in their lives — including George Morris and Jane Addams. Evelyn co-authored a book with her father called *Schools of Tomorrow*, authored *New Schools for Old* (about rural education), and worked with the Bureau of Educational Experiments (see Chapter 11). She edited a book on infant development, called *Behaviour Development in Infants*, which surveyed the literature on pre- and post-natal activity. Evelyn also co-authored, with Katherine Glover, *Children of the New Day*, reporting on White House Conferences on Children. Sabino was a teacher in progressive elementary schools and designed educational equipment.

**Jane Addams with children at Hull House. Hull House opened in 1889, and its first organized activity was the establishment of a kindergarten. (Used with permission of the Chicago Historical Society, ICHi-09375.)**

**Jane Addams (1860 – 1935) was a pioneer American social worker. While providing specific services, Hull House also aimed to improve neighbourhood conditions as a whole. John Dewey was a trustee (board member) of Hull House and was influenced by the active social milieu and by the ideas of Jane Addams. Addams would later became a mentor for the young Lucy Sprague (see chapter 11). (Used with permission of the Chicago Historical Society. DN 84,134. Photographer: Chicago Daily News.)**

During this experimental period, Dewey developed what was called the **instrumental theory of knowledge**. He saw ideas as tools, or instruments, for the solution of immediate problems in the environment. He believed knowledge was not a static body of information to acquire. The Laboratory School would become the testing ground for his theories.

At the turn of the century, Chicago was a city of outstanding urban growth and of contrasts. It was the second largest city in the United States (after New York) in terms of rural migration and foreign immigration. Leaders of industry were extremely wealthy, while factories teemed with poverty-stricken workers, including children. Social reformists were beginning to organize. In Chicago Dewey saw raw, unrestricted industrialism and its effects on large segments of the population. The number of people working at the McCormick Reaper Works plant was greater than the total population of Chicago 50 years earlier. Manufacturing companies grew and profited without regard for human consequences, and individual businessmen made huge fortunes. Half of the school children left school before grade six, and only five per cent attended high school. The disparity between rich and poor was dramatic; while some children worked in factories to help support their families, Marshall Field (of department store fame) spent $75,000 on his son's birthday celebration.

Dewey became a trustee (board member) of Hull House, a settlement house started by Ellen Gates Starr and Jane Addams.[4] Settlement houses were typically urban social service agencies that functioned to improve social conditions in a community context. Today this might be called a community centre, family centre or neighbourhood centre. Hull House teemed with activity and programs — day care centre, college extension courses, public baths, concerts, gym, coffee house, science clubs, debating society, public library branch, women's club as well as numerous community action projects. Hull

[4] Jane Addams (1860 – 1935) was active in social reform work throughout her life and was a leader in women's suffrage and pacifist movements. She received the 1931 Nobel Peace Prize and wrote several books including *The Spirit of Youth and the City Streets* and *A New Conscience and an Ancient Evil.* She wrote two autobiographical books, *Twenty Years at Hull House* and *The Second Twenty Years at Hull House.* A biography of Addams is in *Woman Educators in the United States 1820 – 1993,* edited by Maxine Seller.

House worked to address the effects of the exploitation of minority and immigrant groups in Chicago. Hull House and the many thinkers and activists attracted to it affected Dewey's developing ideas. Dewey and Addams worked together and each benefitted from the reciprocity of their thinking.[5]

## The Dewey School — A Learning Community

John and Alice Dewey sought out a group of interested parents and started the university lab school in a house in 1896 with financial support from parents, friends and patrons. The only monetary contribution the University made consisted of tuition grants for children of graduate students. The school immediately attracted the attention of interested educators from around the world.

There is an amusing story of Dewey's search for portable, non-fixed desks for his new school. A school supply dealer bluntly told Dewey that he did not have the kind of desks Dewey wanted as he had desks that were only for listening, not for working!

The school was originally called The Dewey School though in 1901 its name was changed to the Laboratory School. It was established not only to test ideas and to train teachers but also to develop new ideas through practice:

> *"It has two main purposes: (1) to exhibit, test, verify, and criticize theoretical statements and principles; (2) to add to the sum of facts and principles in its special line."*
>
> — **"The University School"**

In addition, both Deweys wanted their own children to benefit from a new kind of schooling.

The spirit of experimentalism and the role of teachers at the school are also obvious from the following quotation:

> *"It is sometimes thought that the school started out with a number of ready made principles and ideas which were put into practice at once.... The teachers started out with question marks and if any answers have been reached, it is the teachers in the school who have supplied them."*
>
> — ***The School and Society***

Dewey promoted the multiple values of demonstration/laboratory schools to aid in the dissemination of new ideas and methods:

> *"We do not expect to have other schools literally imitate what we do. A working model is not something to be copied; it is to afford a demonstration of the feasibility of the principle, and of the methods which make it feasible."*
>
> — ***The School and Society***

[5] See *The Social Thought of Jane Addams*, edited by C. Lasch, chapter 16, "A Toast to John Dewey."

---

Memories after 30 Years

K. C. Mayhew and A. C. Edwards, who had both taught in the Dewey School, wrote a book called *The Dewey School* (1936). In it, former students of the Dewey School reminisced:

> *"...the building of the club-house — the real and practical work — helped us to see what architecture really is. We got far more out of that than out of books . . . . In the school we got firm foundations for life in every branch of usefulness. We learned to use our hands, our eyes, our heads and to accept responsibility. This is realizing fundamentals."*

***— Josephine Crane***

> *"The Dewey School gave us the opportunity to form practical, livable behavior patterns. The discipline we learned was a practical way of living congenially with our neighbors."*

***— Helen Greeley***

---

## The following basic principles were established:

- The child's early school experiences should reflect the home life (cooking, sewing, construction); academic skills would be an outgrowth of these activities/occupations.[6]
- Children would be part of a human community in school that would focus on co-operation.
- Learning would be focused on problems that children would solve (e.g. numbers would be learned through understanding relationships rather than memorizing multiplication tables).
- Motivation would be internal to the experiences and the child.
- The teacher's role would be to know the children and to choose stimulating problems for the children.

**(Photo by Jennifer Wolfe.)**

Dewey saw four natural and interconnected impulses (sometimes called native tendencies or instincts) in children that would motivate their learning:

1. social (communicating with others),
2. constructive (making things),
3. investigative and experimental (finding out about things), and
4. expressive (creating things).

In the first year, Dewey invited parents to meet to discuss issues and to learn more about the theory and practice in the school. In the second year, the parents formed a Parents' Association. Dewey's book *The School and Society* (1899) consists of lectures he gave at the Parents' Association and was originally published as a fundraiser for the school. It was an immediate sell out, and there have been countless reprints. The co-education of teachers, children and parents **by** one another, not just **with**

---

[6] Dewey defined an occupation as a child's activity that reproduced or ran parallel to work carried on in society (e.g. cooking, carpentry, etc.).

one another, reflected the active participation of all three groups. The Parents' Association was primarily a group with an educational focus. The teachers became the honorary but invited guests. Nellie O'Conner, a parent at the school, wrote an article describing the values from a parent's perspective:

> *"The main value, then, of the educational work of this Parents' Association was that of educating the parent in the principles of the school, thus bringing him necessarily into closer touch with the school, and, above all, by a greater sympathy between parents and teachers, making it possible to bring the school life of the child into the home, and the home life into the school, that the two might be welded into a compact and unified whole."*
>
> **— "The Educational Side of the Parents' Association of the Laboratory School"**

Topics for meetings included "Why Children Should or Should Not Learn to Read at an Early Age," "The Physical Life of the Child," "The Purpose of Outdoor Excursions," "How to Simplify the Lives of the Children," and "The Value of the Study of Literature." Such topics were timely in 1900, and would be timely today.

The practices at the Laboratory School were open to constant mockery. Children talking and moving about? Co-operation? Learning to read, write and spell through interests of the child? No marks or examinations? No textbooks? Extensive field trips? But the teachers were able to articulate the theories and the practice, and the Laboratory School became a beacon for early childhood professionals. The supervisor of instruction, Ella Flagg Young, later became the first woman superintendent of Chicago schools.

The school began with 12 children but grew quickly, eventually having 23 faculty, 20 graduate teaching assistants and 140 children. Finding adequate space and financial resources were constant problems. In 1898, one of Dewey's original aims was realized when children of ages four and five were added to the program. The weekly University newsletter, *The University Record,* kept parents, other teachers and University faculty aware of the school and its activities.

Play was basic to the program, and young children were the starting points for project-based programming:

> *"An expedition to a hardware store to see what tools a carpenter might use to build a house made one child want to build his own house to take home. Large boxes were used. The older children measured and cut all the paper for the walls. The little children tacked down the matting on the floors, made a table for the dining-room by fastening legs on a block. For chairs, they nailed a back to a cube and tacked on a leather seat. The older children made tables and chairs from uncut wood, which they measured and sawed by themselves. When finished, these were shellacked and the seats upholstered with leatherette and cotton. Some of the children painted the outside of the house so that its walls should be 'protected from the weather.' One of the results of this phase of the project was a gain in each child's ability to carry out his own ideas."*
>
> **— Mayhew and Edwards, *The Dewey School***

The school had supporting shops: a kitchen, a sewing room, and a carpentry room. Girls as well as boys took manual training (industrial arts). Children made real objects in cooperation with other children. A library helped the children gain perspectives other than their own on topics that they were investigating.

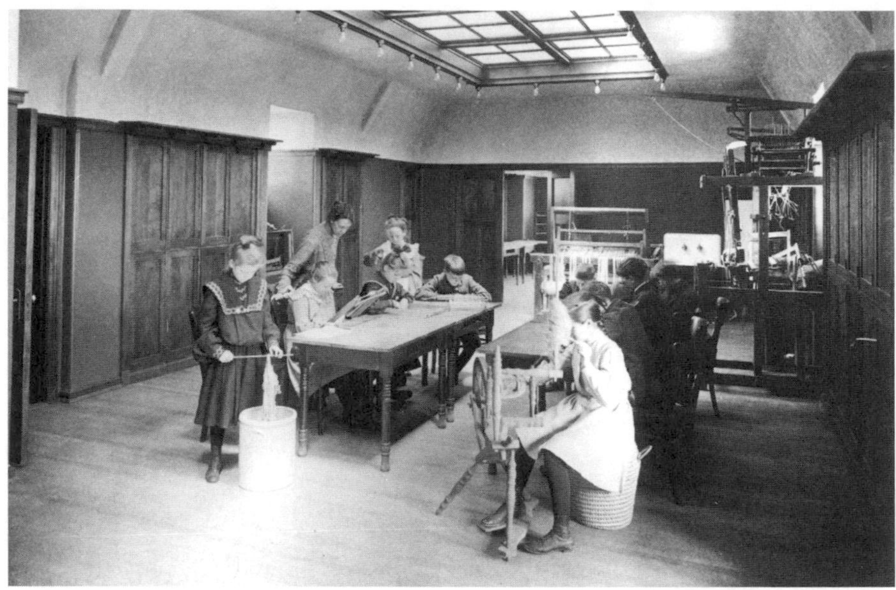

**Children spinning on a wheel, weaving and dyeing wool. (Used with permission of The University of Chicago, Department of Special Collections. IV Classes, Labs, Seminars, Lab School (old) #10.)**

**Two boys use drop spindles to spin wool while other children work with wool and skeins of yarn on the table. (Used with permission of The University of Chicago, Department of Special Collections. IV Classes, Labs, Seminars, Lab School (old) #20.)**

There was a sense of development in the occupations children engaged in as they moved through the school. Beginning in the early years with home and household occupations, occupations expanded to include immediate sources of such things as food and textiles. Children traced the sources of

**Children weaving on small handmade looms at the Dewey School. (Used with permission of The University of Chicago, Department of Special Collections. IV Classes, Labs, Seminars, Lab School (old) #3.)**

**Children are building houses and studying home construction, furnishings and types of homes. (Used with permission of The University of Chicago, Department of Special Collections. IV Classes, Labs, Seminars, Lab School (old) #11.)**

agricultural and manufacturing processes. Dewey saw occupations, the fundamental means of producing basic supplies and requirements of life, as key focal points for inquiry in the curriculum.

*What role do laboratory schools or demonstration early childhood programs play in a community?*

Older elementary-aged children looked at early cultures and re-created trade practices, and this often extended into discussions of and research into explorers. The next older group might study local history, settlers of Chicago and the American colonies.

A camera club made up of the oldest children had asked for a dark room, but there was no space in the school. The children then proceeded to build a clubhouse. Subcommittees were struck — architecture, building, sanitation, ways and means, interior design — and all had an educational focus. Except for the fireplace construction by a mason, children did all the construction. It became a community project involving children from a variety of groups. This project has been seen as a true example of the school as social enterprise.

**The Dewey School's location in 1898 was a large house at 5412 Ellis Ave. in Chicago. There were about 80 children at the school during this period. Previous locations had been on 57th Street, Kimbark, and Rosalie Court. (Used courtesy of Special Collections, Morris Library, Southern Illinois University, Carbondale, Illinois.)**

The school introduced foreign languages with a focus on conversation and activities, a radical departure from the language teaching of the day. A medical doctor was on faculty as part of the health program. Field trips both in the city and to quarries, clay bluffs, sand dunes and cotton mills were an integral component. Visitors were welcomed; they were free to move around the classrooms, and chairs were set out for them.

Throughout the history of the Laboratory School, teachers spent time discussing and reflecting on their practice, learning from one another and from the children.

Dewey succeeded in establishing the Department of Pedagogy (later Education) as a separate and independent department. In addition to teaching and researching, the members of the Department reached out to the community. Discussion groups for teachers were organized, educational organizations were brought to the campus for meetings and there was a celebration of the 150th anniversary of Pestalozzi's birth.

**Clubhouse at the Dewey School, 1901. Children planned and built this playhouse, learning about families and room functions. Under guidance they created the house and utilized many academic skills. *Used with permission of the Department of Special Collections, University of Chicago Library.***

## The Women Who Influenced Him

Jane Addams had an enduring influence on John Dewey's ideas about equality and democracy and continued to emphasize the importance of an educator's role as an advocate for the needs and rights of children and families. She encouraged Dewey to be more pragmatic and descend from the ivory academic tower.

**Alice Chipman Dewey collaborated with Dewey in the founding of the Dewey School and was an integral part of the program at all levels. This was taken in 1902. (Used with permission of The University of Chicago, Department of Special Collections. Schutze, Eva Watson Photographs.)**

Dewey's wife, Alice Dewey, formulated curriculum, taught at and was the principal of the School and was actively involved in all of the Dewey School's programs. She was equally instrumental in the School's original establishment, as Dewey often was more philosophical than practical in his approaches:

> *"Mrs. Dewey would grab Dewey's ideas — and grab him — and insist that something be done.... She was on fire to reform people as well as ideas."*
>
> — **Max Eastman, *Great Companions***

Dewey himself felt she put "guts and stuffing" into his intellectual conclusions. They made an imposing and effective couple. She forced Dewey to focus on the practical values and application of philosophical speculation.

Dewey expressed fundamental indebtedness to his wife in *How We Think*, writing that

> *"by [Alice] the ideas of this book were inspired, and through [her] work with the Laboratory School, existing in Chicago between 1896 and 1903, the ideas attained such concreteness as comes from embodiment and testing in practice."*

In *School and Society*, Dewey also stated his recognition of Alice:

> *"The clear and experienced intelligence of my wife is wrought everywhere in its [The Dewey School's] texture."*

Alice later collected and preserved many of the records of The Dewey School and started a written history of the project.

Alice Dewey wrote an article in 1903 called "The Place of the Kindergarten" in which she critiqued the Froebel kindergartens of the early 1900's. The material was originally prepared for an introduction to the topic of how kindergarten work fit in with the whole education of the child. The article focused on the strengths a child brings to school and the critical role of the teacher in planning curriculum while discovering what children already know:

> *"We place the child in the school to develop, not to isolate him socially. His intelligence is by no means a hothouse plant to be forced to a profusion of blooms too delicate for the winds of every day. His intelligence is experience, and we can enlarge it, give better means of enriching it, nothing more."*[7]

Alice Dewey was also active in many committees at the University of Chicago.

When Dewey first moved to Chicago, he became familiar with the work of Anna Bryan, a pioneer in kindergarten education. He worked with her in developing new types of kindergartens in Chicago and included a kindergarten in the Dewey School. He saw her as a "co-worker." In a conversation with Patty Smith Hill, Dewey said,

> *"Had she lived ten years longer, the education of young children would have progressed much more rapidly."*
>
> **— quoted in *Pioneers of the Kindergarten in America* by The Committee of Nineteen**

Another key person who helped shape his ideas was Ella Flagg Young, and Dewey credited the strong influence of both his wife and Young:

> *"It is due to these two that the laboratory school ran so much more systematically and definitely — free from a certain looseness of ends and edges."*
>
> **— quoted in McManis, *Ella Flagg Young and a Half-Century of the Chicago Public Schools***

Young had been a student of Dewey when she was 50 years old and brought years of teaching and administrative experience to her graduate studies at the University of Chicago. Young became supervisor of instruction at the Laboratory School at a period when the School did not yet have a secure place within the University, especially in terms of financial support. Her expertise created an effective forum for investigating theory and practice. Young also worked with the Parents' Association, reporting to parents about the School's activities and the impact on children.

**Ella Flagg Young in 1911. Ella Flagg Young (1845 – 1918) worked closely with Dewey as a graduate student and then a colleague. She strongly affected his ideas about education and democracy in education. In addition she was the first woman president of the National Education Association and author of many publications. She worked closely with Jane Addams. (Used with permission of the Chicago Historical Society. Ici=13109. Photographer: Mabel Sykes.)**

[7] Her use of the "gardening" metaphor is quite different from that of Rousseau or Froebel.

> *"It was from her that I learned that freedom and respect for freedom mean regard for the inquiring or reflective processes of individuals and that what ordinarily passes for freedom — freedom from external restraint, spontaneity in expression, etc. — are of significance only in their connection with thinking operations."*
>
> **— John Dewey, quoted in McManis, *Ella Flagg Young and a Half-Century of the Chicago Public Schools***

*From what you have read, how did Alice Dewey and Ella Flagg Young influence the ideas of John Dewey? Why are these women relatively unknown?*

> *"She was the wisest person about actual schools I ever saw. I would come over to her with these abstract ideas of mine and she would tell me what they meant."*
>
> **— John Dewey, quoted in Max Eastman, *Heroes I Have Known***

It was Young's idea to re-name the Dewey School the Laboratory School.

Young supported an environment for teachers identified by thinking, experimentation, exchange of ideas and respect. She believed in democracy in education. Her Ph.D. dissertation, later published as a book, *Isolation in the School*, looked at the conditions necessary for improvements in education. She advocated social equality for all involved in educational systems and was aware of the impact of gender, class, age and status on the educational process. Young focused on the importance of schools themselves being democratic while Dewey had a broader perspective. He came to believe that good education for citizens was necessary in order to ensure the continuation and strength of democracy.

---

Ella Flagg Young's life and contributions to education are discussed in McManis's *Ella Flagg Young and a Half-Century of the Chicago Public Schools*, Webb and McCarthy's "Ella Flagg Young: Tribute to a Pioneer Leader in Education," and Donatelli's *The Contributions of Ella Flagg Young to the Educational Enterprise*. Young (1845 – 1918) was a teacher, principal and superintendent of schools in Chicago, taught at the University of Chicago and was principal of the Chicago Normal School. Normal schools offered teacher-training programs; it was assumed that the teaching methods taught in these schools would become "normal" for all schools. Active in the women's suffrage movement, Flagg was also the first woman president of the National Education Association, edited *The Elementary School Teacher* and worked with Jane Addams on many social projects.

---

## Leaving Chicago

The productive relationship of Dewey and Young ended unexpectedly. During his last years at the University of Chicago, tensions developed between Dewey and William Harper, the president of the University. The Chicago Institute and the elementary school of Colonel Francis Parker had been merged under the auspices of the University of Chicago, leaving the Laboratory School without its unique position to continue its experimental work. Dewey disagreed with the differing theoretical orientation of the School and with one of the stipulations of the merger: that the daughter of Cyrus McCormick (Mrs. Emmons Blaine) would endow a grant of a million dollars to the Chicago Institute. Parker's school focused more on teacher training while Dewey's school continued to function as a laboratory for educational ideas. Dewey saw the child primarily as a part of society while Parker saw the child as part of nature. Dewey insisted that practice be based on sound theory and not empirical practice. Parker's school did not have this kind of theoretical basis but rather based instruction on the intuitive knowledge of what would help children learn.

**Francis Wayland Parker.** ***Used with permission of the Department of Special Collections, University of Chicago Library.***

---

Colonel Francis W. Parker (1837 – 1902) was born in New Hampshire and began teaching at 16. His career was interrupted to serve in the Union Army in the Civil War. After returning from the war, he headed a normal school in Dayton, Ohio. He went to Germany to study the progressive teaching methods of Pestalozzi, Froebel and others, returning to the U.S. to run schools in Quincy and Boston. His schools were known for more informal methods of teaching, elimination of rigid discipline and the introduction of science teaching. Academic subjects were taught through activities rather than through readers, spellers and copybooks. He later was the principal of the Cook County Normal School and of the Chicago Institute. Parker also supported public education and the mixing of all classes of society in schools. His 1894 book, *Talks on Pedagogics*, outlines many of his key ideas. Ida Cassa Heffron wrote an interpretive biography entitled *Francis Wayland Parker*, and Jack Campbell wrote another entitled *Colonel Francis W. Parker: The Children's Crusader*. Both give extensive descriptions of Parker's achievements and ideas. *"Schools of Tomorrow," Schools of Today,* edited by Semel and Sadovnik, devotes an entire chapter to the Francis Parker School from its inception until today. Dewey deeply respected Parker and called him the father of the progressive movement.

---

Under pressure from Colonel Parker's faculty, Harper gave Alice Dewey only a temporary position as principal. In 1904, Dewey resigned in response to what he saw as the indifference and hostility of the University administration. There is some evidence that Young supported the administration. In any case, Young did not have personal contact with the Deweys after they left Chicago.[8]

## New York and Columbia University

Dewey was not unemployed long. He had become well known in academic circles and had been named President of the American Psychological Association.

---

[8] The complex situation and his departure are analyzed in a series of three articles by Robert McCaul jointly titled "Dewey and the University of Chicago" as well as in Harms and DePencier's *Experiencing Education: 100 Years of Learning at The University of Chicago Laboratory Schools.*

In 1905, John Dewey moved to New York City to begin work at Columbia University where he remained for the next 47 years, including 25 years of active teaching. The Deweys lived at Broadway and Fifty-Sixth Street and later on a small farm on Long Island:

> *"He enjoyed telling how one day a hurry call came from a wealthy neighbor for a dozen eggs, and the children being in school, he himself took the eggs over in a basket. Going by force of habit to the front door, he was told brusquely that deliveries were made at the rear. He trotted obediently around back, amused and happy. Later he was giving a talk to the women's club of the neighborhood, and his wealthy customer, when he got up to speak, exclaimed in a loud whisper: 'Why, he looks exactly like our egg man!' "*
>
> **— Eastman, "America's Philosopher"**

*What do you think would have happened if Dewey had continued to be associated with a laboratory school?*

The unique working partnership with Alice was not possible in New York where Dewey did not run a laboratory school. After leaving Chicago, Dewey never again was directly involved in educational experimentation, and the essential aspects of his educational ideas did not change significantly. He no longer had a practical connection or testing ground for his theories. This points to the key importance of continuing contact with children and programs for children in order for theory to develop.

*What role do you think educators should play in social and political action?*

Dewey was always a man of action, not just of philosophical thought. He wanted to affect the current events of his time and to see ideas put into action. Dewey supported a variety of social causes and helped found the New School for Social Research in New York City, established to support academic freedom and expression of thought. Wesley Clair Mitchell, husband of Lucy Sprague Mitchell (see chapter 11) was another original supporter of the New School. Dewey worked tirelessly for the American Civil Liberties Union to confront violations of civil rights and was an active supporter of the women's suffragette movement. Unhappy with how both the Democrats and Republicans dealt with problems of the Depression, he helped organize a third political party. He was concerned that Franklin Delano Roosevelt's New Deal did not go far enough in a planned economy. He opposed violence as a solution to social change and worked with the poor at Lilian Wald's Henry Street Settlement. He defended the philosopher, mathematician and social reformer Bertrand Russell when conservatives tried to have him removed from his position at the College of the City of New York.

---

Bertrand Russell (1872 – 1970) was both a philosopher and mathematician and became active in social issues. He was a pacifist in World War I, lost his position at Cambridge University in England and was jailed. He and his wife Dora founded the experimental Beacon Hill School in England. The school encouraged creativity and independent thought. Self-discipline and freedom were emphasized though not with as much license as in A.S. Neill's Summerhill. The school's ideas also reflected those of Froebel, Montessori (but with less rigidity), Piaget, Freud, Pestalozzi and Margaret McMillan. Margaret McMillan with her sister Rachel founded an open-air nursery in Britain, and Margaret worked ceaselessly to improve the conditions of children through her nursery schools, teacher training, writing and speaking. Russell's ideas on education are found in *On Education: Especially in Early Childhood:* "My own belief is that education must be subversive if it is to be meaningful. By this I mean that it must challenge all the things we take for granted, examine all accepted assumptions, tamper with every sacred cow, and instill a desire to question and doubt. Without this, the mere instruction to memorise [sic] data is empty" (quoted in R. Clark's *The Life of Bertrand Russell).* Later he taught in the United States and received the Nobel Prize for Literature in 1950. He continued to work for nuclear disarmament and other issues until his death. He always saw education as an active process.

---

While in New York, Alice Dewey wrote a syllabus for an elementary education methods course and taught at the New York School of Liberal Arts and Sciences. Her teaching encouraged students to pose their own questions and find answers, think for themselves, and back up their ideas. The following are some guiding questions she posed in the course outline:

> *"Q1. (a) Describe in a general way your experience with children. (b) What training have you had? (c) Your nationality and that of the children among whom you work; the industrial and other conditions of your neighborhood; their amusements; religions and social ideals, and be sure to include all the conditions which are distinctly local.*
>
> *Q2. (a) Describe the teacher and methods you consider most successful in your own education.*
>
> *Q3. (a) Write...your ideal scheme of education for the children of your present neighborhood.*
>
> *Q4. Select some one 'method' with which you are already familiar which has had influence for a time and explain why you think it should or should not have passed out of use, such as 'object lessons,' 'phonetic reading.'"*
>
> **— quoted in Rose Spicola, *Alice Chipman Dewey***

John Dewey was invited to Japan, China, Turkey, Mexico, Russia and South Africa to lecture and consult on the educational systems in these countries. Many educators who were to have an influence on early childhood learned from him and his writings on education and social reform. While in Japan in 1919, he and Alice stayed at the Imperial Hotel designed by Frank Lloyd Wright after a Froebel block design. Alice described it as an

> *"... old barn of a place where we are paying as much as a Fifth Avenue hotel and get clear soup for dinner."*
>
> ***— Letters from China and Japan***

While in China, Alice Dewey inaugurated the position of Dean of Women at the National University of Nanking, emphasizing the possibilities of education for woman in any part of the world.

## Dewey's Teaching Style

**John Dewey was a prolific writer and thinker about education, philosophy, art, ethics and many other topics. He taught at Columbia University after his work with the Dewey School and the University of Chicago. (Used with permission of the Library of Congress, Washington, DC. LCUSZ62-51525.)**

Max Eastman, Dewey's student and assistant for four years at Columbia, described his mentor:

> *"I remember how he used frequently to come into class with his necktie out of contact with his collar, or a pants leg caught up on his garter. He would come in through a side door, very promptly and with a brisk step. The briskness would last until he reached his chair, and then he would sag. With an elbow on the desk he would rub his hand over his face, push back his hair, and begin to purse his mouth and look vaguely off over the heads of the class, as through he might find an idea up there along the crack between the wall and the ceiling. He would always find one."*
>
> **— Eastman, "America's Philosopher"**

Although Dewey was popular with students, his lectures were described as "boring" and "rambling," a philosopher contemplating ideas. He was unable to create in his lectures the focus on "interest" that dominated his writings. One of his students remembered his classroom:

> *"Seats were assigned by number, according to the alphabet. Since my name began with a B, I had to sit in a seat in the very first row. Then his assistants would walk up and down the aisle and take attendance which was compulsory. My problem was that he was so dull as a lecturer, and so dry, it was hard to keep awake. And there I was sitting right in front."*
>
> **— quoted in Dropkin and Tobier (Eds.),**
> ***Roots of Open Education in America***

Irwin Edman, a philosopher, recounts in *Philosopher's Holiday* that he was entranced by reading Dewey's books and looked forward to intellectual excitement from his lectures. However, he found that Dewey had "none of the usual tricks or gifts of the effective lecturer. He hardly seemed aware of the presence of a class." What Edman discovered was that he "had been listening to a man actually thinking in the presence of a class. Not every day or in every teacher does one overhear the palpable processes of thought."

Dewey initiated inquiry; he did not disseminate information. This approach was revealed most in seminar groups. Edman remembers Dewey's uncanny ability to see exactly what a student was trying to say and to express candidly his own ideas or prejudices:

> *"His instinctive deference, and unqualified giving-of-attention to whatever anybody, no matter how humble, might have to say, was one of the rarest gifts of genius. He would conduct long correspondences with obscure people — carpenters, plumbers, cigar-store keepers — from all over the world, discussing the problems of life with them as though they were heads of universities. Pecking away with two fingers on a worn old portable typewriter, he seemed to me to embody the very essence of democracy."*
>
> **— quoted in Eastman, "America's Philosopher"**

His wife remained active in the development of his educational ideas, stimulating his thinking. John and Alice hosted Maxim Gorky, the Russian writer, when he came to the United States to raise funds for the Russian Revolution. Attacked (even by Mark Twain) for his support of a man with socialist views who had an actress as a travelling companion, Dewey defended his hospitality to Gorky.

## Later Life

In 1927, Dewey suffered a personal and professional blow when his wife Alice died of arteriosclerosis and heart trouble at the age of 68. Her health had declined soon after arriving in New York though she continued to lecture and write. Alice Dewey had contributed to many of his ideas and publications. After Alice died, Dewey continued to lecture, research and write. He spent his summers at a lake southwest of Halifax, Nova Scotia. He impressed locals by swimming in all weather in Solar Lake and rescuing a woman from the water while in his 80's.

Dewey retired from active teaching in 1930 but continued to speak and write. Among his "retirement" books are *Logic: the Theory of Inquiry* (1938), *Freedom and Culture* (1939), and *Knowing and Known* (1949). The last was co-authored with Arthur Bentley and was an attempt at major revisions of philosophical terminology.

Dewey stayed single until 1946 when he married Roberta Lowitz Grant, a widow and daughter of an old family friend. Roberta was born in Oil City, Pennsylvania where Dewey first taught. Roberta is described as intelligent, outgoing and supportive of Dewey during her life with him. When they married, Dewey was 87 and Roberta was 42. They adopted two children, Adrienne and John Jr., in 1948.

John Dewey married Roberta Grant in 1946. This photo was taken just before their marriage. (Used with permission of the Chicago Historical Society. ICHI-30185. Photographer: Fred Must.)

John Dewey with his family in 1952, shortly before he died. From left to right: Roberta Grant Dewey, Adrienne and John, Jr. (children) and John Dewey. (Used with permission of the University of Vermont. Bailey-Howe Library. From the John Dewey Collection, Special Collections. Photo taken by T. O. Ruskin.)

## Ideas Communicated

Dewey was a voluminous writer. To list the more than 38 books and 815 articles and pamphlets he wrote would take over 153 pages of type. The titles of many of his books reflect his concern with balance and interaction between ideas, concepts and institutions:

*The School and Society* was one of more than 38 books that Dewey wrote. (From the personal collection of Jennifer Wolfe. Photo by Kitty Ng.)

| | |
|---|---|
| *The School and Society* | *How We Think* |
| *The Child and Curriculum* | *My Pedagogic Creed* |
| *Experience and Nature* | *Art as Experience* |
| *Democracy and Education* | *Experience and Education.* |

In addition to books and articles in professional journals, Dewey used all forms of public communication to disseminate his ideas — lectures, magazine articles, pamphlets, interviews, entries in encyclopedias, public letters, leaflets. He gave speeches to groups of students, academics, unions, political organizations, social agencies and scholars.

John Dewey at 90. (Used with permission of the University of Vermont. Bailey-Howe Library. From the John Dewey Collection, Special Collections.)

## The Elder Statesman

Dewey lived a long and healthy life. When he turned 90, 1,500 people attended a dinner party for him at the Hotel Commodore in New York City. The principal speaker was Supreme Court Justice Felix Frankfurter. So well known was Dewey that Jawaharlal Nehru, Prime Minister of India, and his daughter Indira came to pay their respects while they were attending a United Nations Conference. Nehru reflected back on times when he was not sure what to do and used the "ripe wisdom of Dewey" to coordinate theory and action.

President Truman sent a message with his regards:

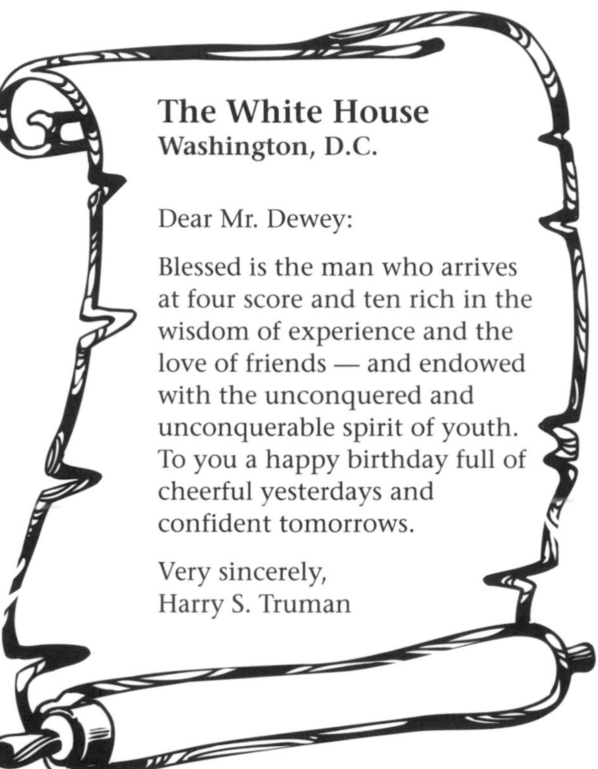

**The White House**
**Washington, D.C.**

Dear Mr. Dewey:

Blessed is the man who arrives at four score and ten rich in the wisdom of experience and the love of friends — and endowed with the unconquered and unconquerable spirit of youth. To you a happy birthday full of cheerful yesterdays and confident tomorrows.

Very sincerely,
Harry S. Truman

**— quoted in Laidler (Ed.), *John Dewey at Ninety***

During this celebration of his 90th birthday, Dewey looked not back to his past but to a "dedication to the work ahead" and to a "forward march."

A few days later, on October 26, 1949 a birthday celebration was held in Burlington, Vermont where he was honoured by the University of Vermont. He encouraged the audience to

> *"find the meaning, rather than be satisfied with the spectacle, of all that goes on around us."*
>
> **— "Try To Find Meaning of What Goes On Around," Says Philosopher John Dewey, *Burlington Free Press*, October 17, 1949**

The University of Vermont had a 90th birthday celebration for John Dewey on October 26,1949. Elias Lyman, Acting President, is shown shaking hands with Dewey. (Used with permission of the University of Vermont. Bailey-Howe Library. From the John Dewey Collection, Special Collections.)

**This photo was taken in 1949 at the Dewey family farm in Pennsylvania. (Used with permission of the University of Vermont. Bailey-Howe Library. Special Collections. Photo acquired through Mrs. Richard Gay, Dewey's daughter.)**

**John Dewey. (Used courtesy of Special Collections, Morris Library, Southern Illinois University, Carbondale, Illinois.)**

He remained active, vigorous and healthy most of the last two years of his life, writing, thinking and maintaining an interest in public affairs. In June 1951 he received, in person, an honorary degree from Yale University. He broke his hip in the autumn of 1951 and died of the complications of pneumonia on June 1, 1952.

## Enduring Educational Ideas

Though a philosopher in his academic background, Dewey's main concern was education, schools, children and, above all, learning. These key concepts are reflected in most of his writing:

- There should be a close relationship among school, home and community.
- Subject matter should be of real significance to the learner.
- Learning of symbols must be derived from the experience of the learner.
- Individual attention should be provided to each child.
- Children learn best not by memorizing extraneous information but when the material meets a recognized need.
- Children require contacts with people, places and things — not only books.
- School must be concerned with all areas of development in a child.
- Meaningful activity has more purpose than imposed routine.
- Curriculum becomes subject matter to the learner when it is used in purposeful activity.

One of the problems he saw was the lack of application of knowledge about children into the educational process:

> *"Incompetency is general not because people are not instructed enough as children, but because they cannot and do not make any use of what they learn."*
>
> — ***Schools of Tomorrow***

## Instrumental Theory of Knowledge

A central focus of Dewey's work was on the "theory of knowledge." Though most often called "epistemology," Dewey preferred the phrases "theory of inquiry" or "experimental logic."

*Describe an example of your work with children that would demonstrate Dewey's "instrumental theory of knowledge."*

With his instrumental theory of knowledge, Dewey saw both the mind and knowledge as instruments, or tools, for dealing with the situations of life. The organism (person) constantly interacts with the environment. This interaction was central to all of Dewey's educational thought. He saw knowledge as a direct by-product of action, inseparable from the activity that produced it. Acting upon the environment results in experience; therefore, the person learns the effect of the actions on the environment. This knowledge directs the course of further action. The person may or may not repeat the action depending on what has happened. Dewey saw this as a process of action and reaction. In this way the person learns about controlling (in a positive sense) the environment.

---

Imagine a young child who typically does not make inferences about science experiences. The teacher asks, "Why do you think the boat sank?" Then one day, the child makes a guess and says it sinks because it is heavy. The teacher does not say the child is wrong but sets up another experience with different weights and shapes of objects to see which float or sink. The child then gains the confidence to make another inference based on additional information.

For another example, consider a situation in which two young children are arguing over a truck that they both want. The first child hits the second child. Depending upon what happens in this situation, the first child may or may not hit another time; the child is learning and is using the mind as an "instrument" or "tool" to deal with the environment.

---

Dewey regarded environment as both physical and social in nature and believed that interactions with both were educative:

> *"The environment consists of those conditions that promote or hinder, stimulate or inhibit, the characteristic activities of a living being.*
>
> *The social environment consists of all the activities of fellow beings that are bound up in the carrying on of the activities of any one of its members."*
>
> ***— Democracy and Education***

## Definition of Education

Dewey defined education as the "reconstruction or reorganization of experience which adds to the meaning of experience and which increases the ability to direct the course of subsequent experience." Education is not automatic. For learning to occur, something has to change.

Dewey's sense of education was not necessarily formal education. It was any experience (short or long, informal or formal) that fit his definition. Education was therefore not divorced from living. A growing friendship with another person could be as rich in learning as a course in school. It was not the accumulation of knowledge for its own sake. Education began at birth and ended upon a person's death. Dewey saw education as living and learning in the moment, not as preparation for later life:

> *"education, therefore, is a process of living and not a preparation for future living."*
>
> — ***My Pedagogic Creed***

Learning should not be "fractionalized," as children do not see subjects as separate elements.

Subject matter would become meaningful as it connected to life's activities:

> *"If number is taught not as number, but as a means through which some activity undertaken on its own account may be rendered more orderly and effective, it assumes a different aspect, and affords insight into the ways in which man actually employs numerical relations in social life."*
>
> — ***University Record,*** **November 6, 1896**

> *"Nature — study, geography, and history are to be treated as extensions of the child's own activity; e.g., there is no sense (psychologically) in studying any geographical fact except as the child sees that fact entering into and modifying his own acts and relationships."*
>
> — ***Results of Child Study Applied To Education*****, 1895**

---

Think back to when you babysat before you studied in the field of early childhood. Now think about babysitting. You probably don't even call it babysitting anymore; in fact, the whole experience of caring for children has been transformed for you. In Dewey's scheme it would be considered to be **reconstructed or reorganized**, a reorganization that has allowed you to care for children more effectively. You may have cooked with children before, but now you see all the potential learning from something as simple as making pizzas or cookies or baking bread.

---

*Describe an "educational experience" you have had that was not in a formal educational setting. Use Dewey's definition of education as a basis.*

## Process of Learning

Dewey maintained that traditional education as preparation for examinations also fostered competitiveness and individual achievement without regard for others. He described the prevalent approach as

> *"a comparison of results in the recitation or in the examination to see which child has succeeded in getting ahead of others in storing up . . . the maximum of information. So thoroughly is this the prevalent atmosphere that for one child to help another in his task has become a school crime."*
>
> — ***The School and Society***

To counter this competitiveness, Dewey felt children must learn to work together on projects; children would learn that others could contribute to individual achievement as well as group goals. Once outside the school, success would depend on working with others, not in competition. Schools therefore needed to reflect this reality.

Motivation must always be internal, not focused on grade attainment or fear or desire to make an impression on a teacher.

Along with the sense that education was integral to the living process, Dewey felt that the aims of education must be within the process itself. He saw the goal of education as **the solution of an immediate problem that is significant to the learner.** As such there were no final goals. Education met its goal if the person could solve the next problem better than the last. Problems demanded inquiries, which in turn would reconstruct the problematic situations into resolved ones:

> *"Education has all the time an immediate end, and so far as activity is educative, it reaches that end — the direct transformation of the quality of experience.... What is really learned at any and every stage of experience constitutes the value of that experience."*

The goal of education was growth. The end of growth was more growth. Children's learning today would allow them to learn more and grow more tomorrow. Growth became the ideal of education and not preparation for some future life. Truth and knowledge were neither fixed nor existed on their own but were a set of beliefs and ideas to affect goals in life.

**Manila Paper House. Made by a 5-year-old child at the Dewey School. (From *The Elementary School Record,* June 1900, Volume 1, Number 5.)**

## Method — "something to do, not something to learn"

What was the method that Dewey saw for learning? How were children to learn? If learning was a by-product of action, then the method of learning must be constructed out of actions, experience and doing. He saw the key teacher's role as providing children with **something to do, not something to learn:**

> *"To realize what an experience . . . means we have to call to mind the sort of situation that presents itself outside of school; the sort of occupations that interest and engage activity in ordinary life. And careful inspection of*

**Manila Paper House. Made by a 4-year-old boy by folding and cutting. (From *The Elementary School Record,* June 1900, Volume 1, Number 5.)**

> *methods which are permanently successful in formal education . . . will reveal that they depend for their efficiency upon the fact that they go back to the type of situation which causes reflection out of school in ordinary life. They give the pupils something to do, not something to learn; and the doing is of such a nature as to demand thinking, or the intentional noting of connections; learning naturally results."*
>
> ***— Democracy and Education***

The life occupations provided the method for children to explore the more traditional academic subjects in the humanities, the arts and the sciences. This simple method had profound implications. If the teacher wanted a child to measure, the teacher would give the child some real project that required measuring, not a worksheet or drill on measuring. Dewey went further to insist that the **doing** be of a nature that required children to **think**. Worksheets or drills rarely necessitated real thinking. Projects such as sewing a quilt or making a wooden boat demanded that the child think and wonder and inquire. Through this process of doing and thinking, learning would naturally and inevitably occur:

> *"Experience is trying . . . undergoing. When we experience something we act upon it, we do something with it; then we suffer or undergo the consequences. We do something to the thing and then it does something to us in return.... Mere activity does not constitute experience."*
>
> ***— Democracy and Education***

*Dewey suggested that children have "something to do, not something to learn." How could you apply this to children learning to measure or learning to estimate?*

Learning from experience! Learning through active engagement. This meant doing real activities with real meaning. In contrast, rote learning was like learning to swim without going near the water.

Play was central to the process:

> *"The educational value of this play is obvious. It teaches the children about the world they live in. The more they play the more elaborate becomes their paraphernalia, the whole game being a fairly accurate picture of the daily life of their parents in its setting, clothes, in the language and bearing of the children. Through their games they learn about the work and play of the grown-up world. Besides noticing the elements which make up this world, they find out a good deal about the actions and processes that are necessary to keep it going."*
>
> ***— Schools of Tomorrow***

## Children's Interests

Programming needed to be built upon children's interests, but Dewey's sense of children's interests was complex:

> *"Interests … are but attitudes towards possible experiences; they are not achievements; their worth is in the leverage they afford."*
>
> — ***The Child and the Curriculum***

> *"No one has ever explained why children are so full of questions outside of the school [yet there is a] conspicuous absence of display of curiosity about the subject matter of school lessons."*
>
> — ***Democracy and Education***

*Dewey focused on children's interests that were absorbing. Describe a time when you observed a child demonstrating an absorbing interest.*

Children's activities did not need to be induced, drawn out or developed. The teacher's role was to ascertain the activities the children were interested in pursuing and furnish children with appropriate opportunities and conditions. Interests of the child were not ends but clues to the child's starting points and what Dewey called "universal capital." Ignoring children's interests would result in missed opportunities for growth:

> *"these native existing interests, impulses, and experiences are all the leverage that the teacher has to work with. He must connect with them or fail utterly."*
>
> — **"The Psychological Aspect of the School Curriculum"**

> *"[interest] is a name for the fact that a course of action, an occupation, or pursuit absorbs the powers of an individual in a thorough-going way."*
>
> — ***The Child and Curriculum***

**Absorbs** is a key word in Dewey's conception of interests. If teachers understood the value of a child's being absorbed in a task, the teachers could then build on children's interests to ensure coverage of the more traditional subject areas. The skills of the teacher were critical in being able to build projects with children that required in-depth study and thinking about a topic. The experiences needed to provide opportunities for growth of the individual. At the same time the child needed to be aware of the interdependence of all people in a society.

## Investigations in Action

Dewey described his vision of project work:

> *"What is needed, in a word, is to afford occasion by which the child is moved to educe and exchange with others his store of experiences, his range of information, to make new observations correcting and extending them in order to keep his images moving, in order to find mental rest and satisfaction in definite and vivid realization of what is new and enlarging."*
>
> — ***The Elementary School Record,*** **Vol.1 No.1**

> *"The problem of instruction is thus that of finding material which will engage a person in specific activities having an aim or purpose of moment or interest to him."*
>
> — ***Democracy and Education***

The entire Volume 1 of *The Elementary School Record* describes projects from the Laboratory School at the University of Chicago.

Dewey laid out four criteria for projects (called occupations), which are as relevant today as they were 100 years ago. Projects must

- be of interest to the children,
- involve thought,
- evoke curiosity and lead children to new areas,
- entail an extended period of time for investigation.

**Poplar wood fence made by children in The Dewey School. The posts were 6 inches (15 cm) tall and 1/2 inch (1 cm) wide. Children used a plane, saw, chisel and file to prepare the posts and rails. Holes in the posts were bored with a gimlet (hand-held boring tool). (From *The Elementary School Record,* February 1900, Volume 1, Number 1.)**

For example, the younger group might investigate a grain farm after talking about foods and how they were obtained. Typically the urban children would not realize the sources of the foods or the processes utilized in their production, only that the food came from "the store." The children planted a small window box garden with winter wheat and made post/rail fences, wagons and carts.

Since the wheat would take a long time to grow, they visited a farm, bringing back wheat stalks that were threshed with flails made in the shop. The wheat was ground and sifted. The flour was then used to bake various items.

In their sociodramatic play the children would act out the roles of farmers, millers and those involved with grain transport. Producers and consumers were seen as interconnected elements.

The grain farm led to studies of dairy farms and sheep farms. At other times the children studied the home — work in the home and outside the home, different types of homes, construction, home furnishings.

Investigation by the children, problem solving, and inquiry were hallmarks of the entire process.

**The materials below were used by children in the Dewey School to explore the processes involved in spinning and weaving. (From *The Elementary School Record,* April 1900, Volume 1, Number 3.)**

Another focus for many ages was exploring the textile industry with the following activities:

- carding, spinning, dyeing and weaving wool,
- growing flax and making it into cloth,
- making looms, shuttles, and carders in the shop,
- weaving baskets from reeds,
- sewing,
- studying silk cocoon and silk.

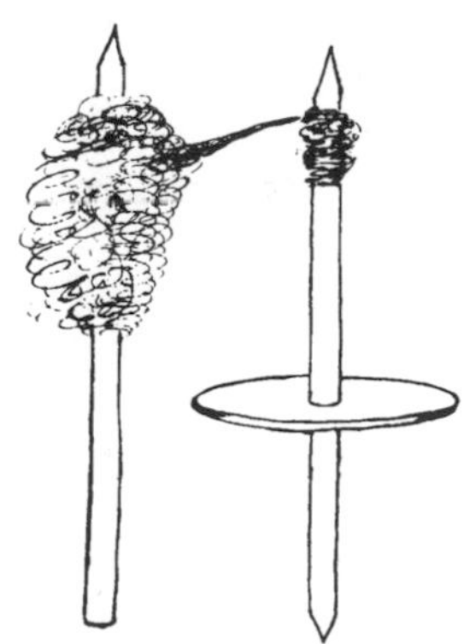

**Distaff and Spindle for spinning wool.**

**Shuttle for putting the thread (weft) through the loom's warp threads.**

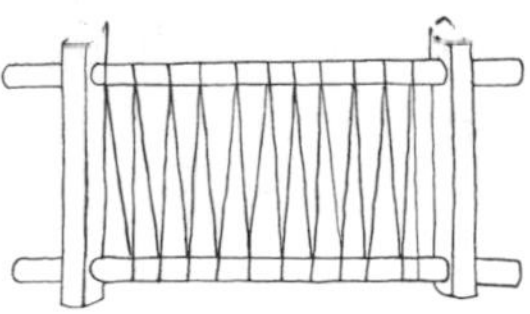

**Loom for weaving. Warp has been strung on the loom made by the children themselves. The loom was 8 x 10 inches (20.5 cm x 25.5 cm).**

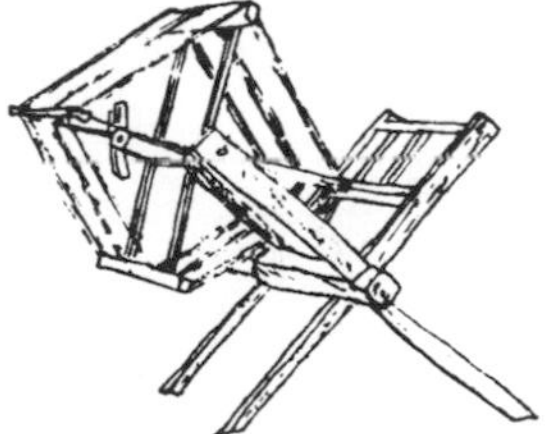

**Triple Reel for winding yarn.**

Children explored cooking different types of cereal grains (flaked corn, flaked wheat, cracked wheat) in the kitchen and found by experimentation the different amounts of water needed. They soon learned that records needed to be kept to avoid re-calculation each time.

**[See end of chapter for a detailed description of the program (Program of Group III) for six year olds as recorded by two sisters, Mayhew and Edwards, former teachers at the school.]**

## Schools of Tomorrow

Dewey and his eldest daughter, Evelyn, wrote *Schools of Tomorrow* in 1915. The book refers extensively to Rousseau, Pestalozzi and Froebel. In the preface John Dewey said,

> *"We have tried to show what actually happens when schools start out to put into practice, each in its own way, some of the theories that have been pointed to as the soundest and best ever since Plato."*

*"Schools of Tomorrow," Schools of Today* edited by Susan Semel and Alan Sadovnik is a 1999 book which discusses schools that the Deweys highlighted and that still exist today as well as other contemporary progressive schools.

The book highlighted many progressive schools of the day, including the Play School of Caroline Pratt (see chapter 10) and the Marietta Johnson School of Organic Education. Evelyn Dewey made all the visits to the schools except to Marietta Johnson's school which Dewey himself visited. Underlying her school's programming was a respect for the dignity of the children. Children were given responsibilities within the school. Teachers were seen as "students of teaching," needing to be open to continual learning about their profession.

Burges Johnson describes an amusing incident when he worked at Dutton's publishing company and received a manuscript of *Schools of Tomorrow*. He went to see Dewey at Columbia University with his concerns about the obtuse and dry style in the first chapter as compared to the well-expressed and clear second chapter. He asked Dewey if those two chapters could be reversed. Dewey listened quietly and then said,

> *"What you say interests me greatly. I wrote the first chapter, and my daughter Evelyn wrote the second."*
>
> — **from B. Johnson, *As Much As I Dare***

In 1919 his daughter Evelyn wrote *New Schools For Old,* describing the Porter School in northern Missouri which stimulated the rural community to new life by giving children the kind of education they needed. It showed a school that was built on common interests of all people in the community, helping people to work together on common problems and creating a renewed sense of democracy.

**Marietta Johnson (1864 – 1938), though relatively unknown in the annals of education, developed a school in Fairhope, Alabama. Her school focused on "education as life." Her ideas developed from Rousseau, Froebel, Dewey, William James, C. Hanford Henderson and Nathan Oppenheim. In turn, her unique program influenced Caroline Pratt (see chapter 10) as well as many other educators of the time. (Courtesy of the Marietta Johnson Museum in Fairhope, Alabama.)**

**Archery Class. This photo taken in the early 1920's shows children in the gully near the school buildings of the Marietta School of Organic Education. Field trips and outdoor experiences were a key part of the program. John Dewey commented on this in *Schools of Tomorrow:* "A gully near the school building not only furnishes a splendid place for play but serves as a textbook in mountain ranges, valleys, and soil and rock formation." (Courtesy of the Marietta Johnson Museum in Fairhope, Alabama.)**

## The Marietta Johnson School of Organic Education

Marietta Pierce Johnson (1864 – 1938) translated into practice the educational theory and knowledge of her day. Her school in Fairhope, Alabama on the eastern shores of Mobile Bay was a pioneer in progressive education. Though influenced by people like Rousseau, Froebel, Dewey, William James, C. Hanford Henderson *(Education and the Larger Life)* and Nathan Oppenheim, Johnson created her own unique combination of ideas for her work with children. In many ways she developed her ideas independently of others far more "famous."

Born in Minnesota, Marietta Pierce married Frank Johnson, a farmer. A skilled teacher, she worked with normal schools in training other teachers. She read *The Development of the Child* (1898) by Nathan Oppenheim, a pediatrician in New York City, and was impressed with his ideas on the importance of childhood and the special environment needed to nurture a child's development. After reading his book she would say that "the scales are off" in terms of current educational practice.

> *"Childhood is not a preparation for adult life. It is important for itself. The school must satisfy the interests of childhood."*
>
> — **"Standards and the Child"**

Marietta and her husband were attracted to a community in Alabama called Fairhope. A model town, originally settled by social reformers from the Midwest, the name Fairhope reflected their vision of a new order that did not see the huge gap between rich and poor. The group subscribed to the ideas of Henry George in *Progress and Poverty* (1879) and advocated a single tax on land. The colony of Fairhope owned the land, and the people had long term leases. The rent paid was the "single tax"; it generated funds for public projects. The community was well known and visited by Upton Sinclair (novelist and author of *The Jungle*) and Clarence Darrow (lawyer involved with the Pullman strike and the Scopes trial).

**Likely taken by John Dewey on his visit in 1913, this photo shows Marietta Johnson talking with the children in an outdoor lesson. (Courtesy of the Marietta Johnson Museum in Fairhope, Alabama.)**

**These ten- and eleven-year-old children made their stilts in a woodworking class. (Courtesy of the Marietta Johnson Museum in Fairhope, Alabama.)**

**Children learned arithmetic and social skills while playing store. In the Marietta Johnson School of Organic Education, practical needs prompted the study of academic subjects. (Courtesy of the Marietta Johnson Museum in Fairhope, Alabama.)**

The Johnsons and their two children visited and stayed briefly at Fairhope in 1903 but then moved to Mississippi where Frank Johnson ran a pecan farm. After their farm was destroyed by fire, the Johnsons returned to Fairhope in 1907. Marietta began her visionary school and Frank helped raise the children and taught manual arts in the school.

Fairhope was the chance for Johnson to try out the changes she saw necessary in education. The Marietta Johnson School of Organic Education, as it became known, focused on the idea that education was life:

> *"Education is life, growth; it has no ends beyond itself. It is dynamic, not static; the ends are immediate; the process and the end are one. Progressive education has set itself the task of ministering to the growing child. Its job is, therefore, to study, to know, and to meet the needs of the unfolding organism. The institution [the school] may not make demands; it must meet demands, and these demands are indicated by the nature of childhood and youth."*
>
> *"The best preparation for the future is a well-spent to-day."*
>
> **— "Standards and the Child"**

Organic implied that the needs of the child's organism were followed. The school began in 1907 with a kindergarten program. The colony supported the school, so local children attended without having to pay tuition.

Children could learn through play and needed experiences with working together if they were to develop essential skills of living. The teacher's role was to assist the learning. The school had no grades, no report cards, no homework and no tests and no fixed seating. Children's academic learning developed out of the desire to learn:

> *"The only real reward any one ever needs for working or for study is the resulting inner satisfaction and consciousness of power! All external standards — grades, marks, promotions and the like tend to make the child dependent upon outer suggestion and thus to weaken the inner creative power."*
>
> **— "If Education is Life"**

**Taken about 1910 – 1911, this photo shows children involved in outdoor dramatization. Storytelling and dramatization took the place of what Johnson saw as premature introduction of reading. (Courtesy of the Marietta Johnson Museum in Fairhope, Alabama.)**

**John Dewey took this photo in 1913 when he visited the Organic School of Marietta Johnson. Left to right in the photo are: Herbert Foster, unidentified girls on the ground, Esther Gilmore, Marietta Johnson (talking), Eleanor Coutant, Ruth Glenn, Estelle Larson, Ralph Brown, Camilla Roberts, Clifford Earnest Johnson (Marietta Johnson's son). (Courtesy of the Marietta Johnson Museum in Fairhope, Alabama. Photo taken by John Dewey.)**

Children were divided into "life classes" which were groupings of mixed ages of children. Thus the school was flexible in meeting a wide range of developmental abilities, and failure was not permitted:

> *"All children must succeed. None must fail. The child of slow development has as sacred a right to that slowness as the quick developer has to his rate of growth."*
>
> **— quoted in Bennett, "Adjusting the Education to the Child"**

Discipline issues were minimized as children were engaged in meaningful experiences. The soil around Fairhope was primarily clay, and rains created deep gullies. The gully became the "textbook" for learning about rivers, soil, rock formation, erosion, flooding and mountains.

The program also involved handwork (where boys and girls would get equal experience with cooking and carpentry), dramatization, storytelling, music, folk dancing, arts and crafts, nature study and long term projects. Marietta Johnson believed in the value and joy of learning in these projects and was not focused on the potential academic connections:

> *"The 'project,' however, is not obliged to furnish the means of acquiring subject matter or skill, though these often do result."*
>
> **— *Teaching Without Failure***

Reading was postponed until children were at least eight years of age, when the children had a good grounding in the world around them. Reading was not an isolated process but something children wanted because it would open new doors to learning.

Impressed with Johnson's ideas, John Dewey arrived in December of 1913 to critique the school. It was Christmas holidays and Johnson asked the children if they wanted to hold classes during the holidays. They unanimously voted in favour of the extended school term, and Dewey arrived with his 14-year-old son Sabino. His son attended the school for a week and wanted to stay! And Dewey, the New York academic philosopher, played Santa Claus. Dewey's expectations were exceeded in his visit to the school. A detailed description is included in John and Evelyn Dewey's book *Schools of Tomorrow*. A photo taken by John Dewey of Johnson and a group of students was the frontispiece for the book.

After Dewey visited the school, he wrote a positive report praising the program in *Survey* (May 1931):

> *"In my judgment the school has demonstrated that it is possible for children to lead the same natural lives in school that they lead in homes ... outside of school; to progress bodily, mentally, and morally in school without factitious pressure, rewards, examinations, grades, or promotions; while they acquire sufficient control of the conventional tools of learning and of the study of books — reading, writing, and figuring — to be able to use them independently. There are no tricks of the trade, no patent devices, no unique nor even peculiar appliances, no methods in one sense of that term.... What impressed me most on the side of educational procedure was negative; namely, the absence of all special devices calculated to make up for the lack of the various forms of pressure usually brought to bear upon children. What has been done is simply to provide the conditions for wholesome, natural growth in small enough groups for the teacher (as a leader rather than as an instructor) to become acquainted with the weaknesses and powers of each child individually, and then to adapt the work to the individual needs."*

Johnson traveled widely, lecturing and raising funds for the school. Other schools based on her ideas were started in various parts of the United States. The wife of Alexander Graham Bell, Mabel, sponsored one of the lecture tours, and Johnson's fame spread. Johnson wrote two books, *Youth in the World of Men* and *Thirty Years with an Idea,* which were later combined into one volume, *Teaching Without Failure.* She was one of the founders of the Progressive Education Association. To the town of Fairhope, she was known as "Aunt Mettie," trusted by adults and children.

The school grew and reached its peak in the 1920's. Beset with financial problems in the Depression, Johnson never gave up her vision. Even after a heart attack in 1936, she continued to be active. She died in 1938.

Despite problems and changes from the original vision, The Organic School still exists in Fairhope, Alabama. Johnson's *Teaching Without Failure* can be obtained from:

***The Marietta Johnson Museum***
(http://www.mariettajohnson.org)
or by mail at: 10 South Street, Fairhope, Alabama, 36532, U.S.A.

The school's address is:

8 Marietta Drive
Fairhope, Alabama 36532
U.S.A.

Website: http://schooloforganiceducation.org

## An Inspiration to Others

*The School in Rose Valley* by Grace Rotzel and *My Country School Diary* by Julia Weber Gordon were written in Dewey's time and reflect his ideas in practice in other parts of the United States. Both books looked at local individual schools that engaged children's interests and were tied directly to the life of the local community and families.

Julia Weber Gordon wrote T*he School in Rose Valley* about her one-room school in 1930, but it was not published until 1946. It describes an experiment in democratic living, projects, multiage grouping and reflective teaching. The children, teacher, and parents all grew together as they built a sense of community within their school. Learning was seen as a by-product of experience within a social context.

Grace Rotzel, the founding principal of The School in Rose Valley, had also been a teacher/intern for five years with Marietta Johnson in Fairhope. The School in Rose Valley began in 1929 and reflected the ideas of Johnson, Dewey and other progressive educators of the time. It was a school based on freedom but not with an "anything goes" philosophy: it was understood that children needed supports for their growth within a democratic school environment. Rotzel envisioned "freedom with a fence around it." Children had reports on their growth, not grades. The school avoided accelerating children into higher grades before they were ready. The wood shop was the first space created, and it embodied the school's focus on learning through direct experience:

> *"We were always holding off parents who wanted us to teach more, 'to cultivate the mind,' as if the mind wasn't working unless it was being force fed. Our answer was, 'Take the child on a bug-collecting tour and watch him use his mind. Watch him make a dump-truck in shop. Don't minimize the learning going on. Give him time to BE'."*
>
> **— Rotzel, *The School in Rose Valley***

The School in Rose Valley continues its traditions of progressive education and learning through direct experiences. Preschool through school-aged children are actively involved in their learning through discovery, experimentation, challenge, risk, choice and planning. The joy in learning is always a goal as well as the development of inner discipline and self-esteem. Learning needs of individuals balance with the needs of the group. Seasonal community events and traditions frame the year with such events as apple day, May Fair, Winter Festival, and the end-of-year Bead Ceremony. All children from preschool onward keep journals. Academic content is embedded in a rich variety of experiential learning.

***The School in Rose Valley***
20 School Lane
Rose Valley, Pennsylvania 19063
U.S.A.

Website: http://schoolinrosevalley.org

Another educator who was influenced by Dewey was Mary Hammett Lewis, a teacher at the Horace Mann School of Columbia University who sought new ways to try out her developing educational ideas on meeting the needs of children:

> *"there had been growing upon me a firm conviction that something was radically wrong with schools everywhere. All my life I had played with children and found them inventive, imaginative, full of ideas, with never quite time enough to carry them out. Yet here in this school, a leader in schools in this country, we felt stifled, suffocated, when we tried to play."*
>
> **— Lewis, *An Adventure With Children***

She ordered a "big, friendly rug," and it became a "magic carpet" for adventures with the children. Soon the carpet moved to the roof top of one of the college buildings. A tent was raised and the school now had an open-air classroom.[9] There were animals, gardens and home-made furniture. She found children "learned to love work because they could see its real significance." She wanted to create a "children's school."

Parents in Buffalo, New York approached Dewey for assistance in setting up a progressive school. He sent them to observe Lewis. They saw children's work that fascinated them, and they were convinced:

> *"Six or eight children were measuring the open part of the roof to see if they could afford the space to have another class up there next year and, if so, how much space would be left for a playground. A small boy was feeding a mother hen whose chicks were almost ready to hatch; a little girl had chosen a shady corner of the roof and was reading aloud to some of their mates who were making sunbonnets; a small boy was building the day's list of spelling words; other children were making the morning cocoa."*
>
> **— Lewis, *An Adventure With Children***

The Park School
of Buffalo
4625 Harlem Road
Buffalo, New York
14226-3846
U.S.A.

Website: http://www.theparkschool.org/

Lewis moved to Buffalo and organized the Park School, which opened in 1912.[10]

Learning revolved around projects meaningful to children:

> *"I found the kindergartners one morning clearing up a neglected piece of ground near their house, carrying to a bonfire everything which could be burned and to another pile everything which could not, making the ground ready for sunflower seeds. When the plants came up, they weeded them and cared for them, and on the opening day of school in the fall gorgeous blossoms nodded their welcome to the new kindergartners. The seeds were fed to the third-grade chickens."*
>
> **— Lewis, *An Adventure With Children***

---

[9] Open-air schools began in Germany in 1904 to both teach and cure children who had been ill, or were mentally or physically disabled. The idea spread in Europe and North America, and they became schools for "ordinary" pupils. *Open-Air Schools (1910)* by Leonard Ayres is an extensive book about the development and practices of these schools.

[10] See *"Schools of Tomorrow," Schools of Today*, edited by Semel and Sadovnik, for an extensive chapter on the Park School's beginning and more recent history.

Visitors came from afar to view the new methods Lewis initiated. She believed strongly that educational theories were ignored because

> *"We talk too much, all of us, and observe and live with children far too little."*
>
> — **Lewis, *An Adventure With Children***

Visits to other schools and teacher meetings discussing programming that would meet the real needs of children helped keep the teachers growing professionally and helped ensure that theory and practice were interacting.

John Dewey visited and was "adopted" by the children as their guest of the day. Lewis told the story of a five-year-old boy who was watching a girl wash doll clothes and wanted to participate. The little girl ignored him but Dewey spoke for the child, asking if the girl could find something for the boy to do. The girl was impatient with the interruption and said,

> *"If you want something to do, just go inside there and ask the teacher. I'm busy."*
>
> — **Lewis, *An Adventure With Children***

Later in the day Dewey involved himself with children planning a tour around the world with maps, atlases, and ship and railroad posters. They were writing advertisements for their own routes, and each tried to get Dewey to come with him or her.

---

Shady Hill School — established in 1915 in Cambridge, Massachusetts — reflected the project ideas of John Dewey, Francis Parker and Marietta Johnson. It was founded by William and Agnes Hocking, who hired Katharine Taylor, one of the Francis W. Parker School's first teacher graduates, as principal. Children here, for example, created an entire village in an outdoor area. Houses, stores, service buildings were planned and built by the children as a full-year project.

Shady Hill School continues to operate with a project focus.

Shady Hill School
178 Coolidge Hill
Cambridge, Massachusetts 10238
U.S.A.

Their website describes the school and gives many detailed examples of children's projects.

Website: http://www.shs.org/

---

**The Shady Hill School of Cambridge, Massachusetts was founded in 1916 by the Hockings and was directly influenced by the ideas of John Dewey, Marietta Johnson and Francis Parker. These two photos (taken in 1928 and 1930) show the village project. The children planned and built these houses, stores and service buildings as a full-year project. (Used courtesy of The Shady Hill School, Cambridge, Massachusetts.)**

A younger contemporary of John Dewey was Earl Kelley. Far less known than Dewey, he thought about, wrote about and created schools that would be more democratic for children and adults. Dewey wrote an introduction to Kelly's book *Education for What is Real* in which he stated that the book's "significance will prove virtually inexhaustible." Kelley, along with Dewey, suggested fundamental changes in the educational system. Kelley's books also included *The Workshop Way of Learning* and *Education and the Nature of Man* (written with Marie Rasey).

## Dual Grounded Curriculum

Dewey believed in building learning from the child's experience but did not advocate "child centred education" or "child centred schools" — children were not left to their own devices. Teachers and their knowledge of curriculum played a central role. Dewey was often associated with child centred education, but connecting his ideas with a sole focus on child centred practice and permissiveness is a misinterpretation of his theory. Just because schools called themselves "progressive" did not mean they understood or followed the critical components he had articulated.

Dewey's view of curriculum had two equally important pillars — the children's base of activities and the teacher's base in subject matter. Both needed to be considered as curriculum emerged. Dewey felt that activities and subject matter needed to be considered equally; without a real connection between these two pillars, a false dualism would result. Such a false dualism between the mental operations of the child and intellectual content from the teachers would destroy learning:

> *"It is not a question of how to teach the child geography but first of all the question of what geography is for the child."*
>
> *"But when this adult material is handed over ready-made to the child, the perspective is ignored, the subject is forced into false and arbitrary relations, the intrinsic interest is not appealed to, and the experience which the child already has, which might be made a vital instrument of learning, is left unutilized and to degenerate."*
>
> — **"The Psychological Aspect of the School Curriculum"**

Subject matter was not a static entity:

> *"Abandon the notion of subject-matter as something fixed and ready-made in itself, outside the child's experience; cease thinking of the child's experience as also something hard and fast; see it as something fluent, embryonic, vital; and we realize that the child and the curriculum are simply two limits which define a single process."*
>
> ***— The Child and The Curriculum***

*How do current "project approach" programs differ from Dewey's sense of project-based learning? How are they similar?*

Dewey's sense of projects based on his model of thinking was modified and developed by William Heard Kilpatrick, one of his former students, who popularized the "project approach" with purposeful activity.[11] Dewey's concept involved purpose and intent but also the previously mentioned elements: thought, curiosity and extended time focus. Curriculum for Dewey was never a series of unrelated projects but would entail a logical, progressive development.

---

Today's model of the project approach is best exemplified by writers such as Lilian Katz and Sylvia Chard. See Katz and Chard's *Engaging Children's Minds: The Project Approach* and Chard's *The Project Approach: Making Curriculum Come Alive* and *The Project Approach: Managing Successful Projects.*

There are several informative websites and both have links to others.

http://www.project-approach.com/

http://ericeece.org/project.html

---

## Role of the Teacher

The role of a teacher was as an active guide and organizer in integrating subject matter with the child's life experiences:

> *"It is the business of the school to set up an environment in which play and work shall be conducted with reference to facilitating desirable mental and moral growth."*
>
> ***— Democracy and Education***

The educator's job was to

> *"survey the capacities and needs of the particular set of individuals with whom he is dealing and . . . at the same time arrange the conditions which provide the subject-matter or content for experiences that satisfy these needs and develop these capacities. The planning must be flexible enough to permit free play for individuality and yet firm enough to give direction towards continuous development of power."*
>
> ***— Experience and Education***

---

[11] See Kilpatrick's "The Project Method" and *Remaking the Curriculum* as well as Samuel Tenebaum's biography *William Heard Kilpatrick.* A biography of Kilpatrick is included in the ACEI Later Leaders Committee's *Profiles in Childhood Education 1931 – 1960.*

Learning needed to be grounded in real life experiences:

> *"If language is abstracted from social activity, and made an end in itself, it will not give its whole value as a means of development.*
>
> *If number is taught not as number, but as a means through which some activity undertaken on its own account may be rendered more orderly and effective, it assumes a different aspect. The children who have been taught abstract relations only cannot translate them into the concrete form required by practical life."*
>
> **— "The University School," November 6, 1896**

> *"There is no ground for holding that the teacher should not suggest anything to the child until he consciously expressed a want in that direction… the suggestion must fit in with the dominant mode of growth in the child."*
>
> ***— The School and the Child***

The teacher's challenge would be finding ways to integrate traditional curriculum into topics of interest to the children. Teachers at the Dewey School met weekly to refine and process the work they did, and Dewey's theory developed along with the practice. He saw his principles and ideas as working hypotheses:

> *"The teacher's business is to see that the occasion is taken advantage of. Since freedom resides in the operations of intelligent observation and judgment by which a purpose is developed, guidance given by the teacher to the exercise of the pupils' intelligence is an aid to freedom, not a restriction upon it."*
>
> ***— Experience and Education***

## Thinking and Education

Dewey believed that a democracy needed thinking citizens and that producing them was the responsibility of the educational system:

> *"The accumulation and acquisition of information for purposes of reproduction in recitation and examination is made too much of. 'Knowledge', in the sense of information, means the working capital, the indispensable resources of further inquiry; of finding out, or learning, more things. Frequently it is treated as an end itself, and then the goal becomes to heap it up and display it when called for. This static, cold-storage ideal of knowledge is inimical to educative development. It not only lets occasions for thinking go unused, but it swamps thinking. No one could construct a house on ground cluttered with miscellaneous junk. Pupils who have stored their 'minds' with all kinds of material which they have never put to intellectual uses are sure to be hampered when they try to think. They have no practice in selecting what is appropriate and no criterion to go by; everything is on the same dead static level."*
>
> ***— Democracy and Education***

*Dewey and many other historians advocated "thinking" as a key goal for children in schools. Is this a primary goal in programs you have observed? How do you see it in practice? Do elementary schools use this as a key goal? How?*

Children (and adults) needed a desired end and the freedom to work towards it themselves. Thinking and learning would dissipate if

- *Time was frittered away.* This would be a waste of intellectual energy. Learning that was important to the teacher was not necessarily meaningful to the child.
- *Work was dictated.* This eliminated searching, reaching out and investigating. It was fine for horse or dog training where you would assign a specific thing to do, dictate how it is done and then reward the accomplished task.
- *Formulas were ready made.* This removed experimentation as teachers tried to eliminate error or failure with children.

> *"It is quite safe to say that no two grown persons get the same result by the same method unless the situation is an exceedingly simple one."*
>
> — **"Reasoning in Early Childhood"**

The current strong emphasis on testing, measurable accountability and some computer learning counters Dewey's goals for knowledge and thinking.

Dewey also felt that conclusions needed to be established enough to empower action but broad and open enough to encourage further inquiry and investigation. Right answers alone could never be the goal. For example, a study of the ancient Phoenicians focused on their problems, but the *real* issue was developing problem-solving skills that the children could use in their own problem situations. The problems chosen for the child must be the child's, not the teacher's, and must contain obstacles to the child's own ends:

> *"The better way of thinking is reflective thinking."*
>
> — ***How We Think***

Dewey had a five-step method for solving problems:

1. definition of the problem,
2. observation of the problem's surroundings,
3. formulation of hypotheses to solve the problem,
4. detailing of the consequences of acting upon each of the hypotheses,
5. active testing of the ideas to see which best solves the problem.

Though listed in steps, Dewey emphasized that these were not discrete or always in the exact order. Along with the steps, learners needed attitudes of intellectual curiosity and perseverance, always with the desire to continue learning.

## Discipline

Dewey felt that children who were absorbed in an activity not imposed on them by someone else developed self-discipline. He defined discipline as

> *"the deliberate or conscious disposition to persist and endure in a planned course of action in spite of difficulties and contrary solicitations,"*

and the

> *"power to endure in an intelligently chosen course in the face of distraction, confusion, and difficulty."*
>
> — ***Democracy and Education***

This concept of self-direction developed out of his experiences at the Laboratory School, which did have small classes, individual attention for each child, and engaging projects. Focusing on children's interests within a subject matter curriculum allowed discipline to develop naturally. Teachers dealt with behaviour "problems" by redirecting children into other comparable activities. Knowing the individual children and re-channeling energy toward growth were essential to the process. Their success in this area was likely aided by the small class sizes and low child-teacher ratio.

## Education and Society

Did schools provide a service in Dewey's mind? Yes! He did not question the existence of schools but criticized their isolation from the community and from the lives of children. Dewey believed that schools needed to be a specialized kind of environment to assist the learning process for children or adults. He described the school as an "embryonic society" and a "form of community life." Schools had libraries, trained teachers, other children, and organized experiences such as field trips. But all the while, schools must help children derive meaning from life experiences and should never be set apart from children's ongoing lives. Educational goals must remain in the present to be effective in the future.

Dewey saw the individual and society as two key factors that are in constant interplay and interaction. The child is born into the society of the home with parents. Later, the child brings what he or she learned in this miniature society to the widening community of the school. The school must continue this process of learning by

> *"functioning as that form of community life in which all those agencies are concentrated that will be most effective in bringing the child to share in the inherited resources of [humans] and to use his own powers for social ends."*
>
> — ***The School and Society***

For Dewey, a learner's motivation must be internal, for external motivation meant the activity would cease as soon as the motivation was withdrawn. Dewey was concerned that children's learning continue after leaving school, as children and as adults.

Dewey believed that since the school was a microcosm of society, it should reflect the wider community and society as a whole. Schools should not be isolated from the worlds in which the children lived; relevance was absolutely critical. Schools needed to be

> *"a genuine form of active community life, instead of a place set apart in which to learn lessons."*
>
> *"a miniature community, an embryonic society."*
>
> — ***The School and Society***

Dewey believed schools had a key role in building a new social order. He saw current schools as reproducing rather than influencing society's functioning and knew that if schools were to be part of social reform, they needed to be "reconstructed."

> *"Laying the basis, intellectual and moral, for a new social order is a sufficiently novel and inspiring ideal to arouse a new spirit in the teaching profession."*
>
> — **"Can Education Share in Social Reconstruction?"**

In many ways, Dewey also laid the philosophical and educational foundations for "community schools" in his statements about the social as well as intellectual functions of schools to create a better future society. In 1939 Dewey wrote an introduction to a book on community schools indicating his conception of the evolving school:

> *"A community school is not provided, it grows, by joint concurrence and consent. It is a function, never a system. It is a joint production, the result of living and learning, shaped and guided by many events and purposes, and by the feelings and responses of a large number of people, above all by the desires and needs of the people whose school it was."*
>
> — **Introduction to *Community Schools in Action* by Clapp**

## Schools and the Political Process

Dewey, like Plato, believed that any theory of education must be connected to a political system and its ideals. Political systems set goals for education, and educators must keep in mind the kind of society they envision. For Dewey, that meant a democracy for all citizens. It was a society of equality, participation, and voices that were heard:

> *"The conception of education as a social process and function has no definite meaning until we define the kind of society we have in mind."*
>
> — ***John Dewey: The Middle Works 1899 – 1924***

> *"I believe that education is the fundamental method of social progress and reform."*
>
> — ***My Pedagogic Creed***

Dewey fought against education that would look at vocational training, moulding students for the job ahead. He felt that vocational training would accentuate class differences by sorting students into different career routes.

Dewey always saw education as a reflection of the social, political and cultural environment of the time. Late in his life, when he saw continued attacks on the achievements of progressive education, Dewey said,

> *"The current effort to turn the clock back in education is real cause for alarm but not for surprise. The educational system is part of a common life and cannot escape suffering the consequences that flow from the conditions prevailing outside of the schools. The repressive and reactionary forces are in such entrenched strength in all our other institutions that it would be folly to expect the schools to get off free."*
>
> **—quoted in Dropkin and Tobier (Eds.), *Roots of Open Education in America***

This was the period when in the United States Joseph McCarthy and others were viciously attacking, without evidence, members of the government, the arts, television and films, accusing them of being communists. Education never exists in a vacuum. Dewey saw the integral position that education played in society.

*Dewey suggested equal salaries for teachers in public schools and for university professors. Assuming equal education and experience, what is your opinion of this recommendation? Why are day care workers' salaries substantially lower than salaries for elementary and secondary school teachers?*

Dewey promoted establishing equal salary levels for public school teachers and university professors, both equally important jobs, both equally needed by society.

## Theory and Practice

Dewey also addressed the reasons schools and teaching did not reflect the theories known about children and learning. If teachers themselves had not experienced a different type of learning, then they would have a difficult time actualizing the theory they had learned. It would not be fully understood or able to be applied. This realization has strong implications for teacher education and the kind of learning that college and university students receive:

> *"Why is it, in spite of the fact that teaching by pouring in, learning by a passive absorption, are universally condemned, that they are still so entrenched in practice? ... Is not this deplorable situation due to the fact that the doctrine is itself merely told? It is preached; it is lectured; it is written about."*
>
> ***— Democracy and Education***

One of his Ph.D. students, Edward Scribner Ames, remembered Dewey's questioning and reflective demeanour: "Even when he was lecturing, he was still inquiring." He saw Dewey's philosophy as never an exercise in abstractions or a pursuit of intellectual luxury but

> *"a method of analysis and criticism for the understanding of real problems and of guidance with their solution."*
>
> **— Ames (Ed.), *Beyond Theology***

Educational practice would test theory, and Dewey believed much of school practice was based more on habit than theory. Good theory *was* practical.

*How did Dewey's early-life experiences affect his later thinking as a philosopher and educator?*

Philosophically and educationally, Dewey believed that there was a critical connection between schools and society. He felt that a society would not survive unless it provided equal opportunity for all children to work to their full potential in cooperative endeavours. Dewey strove to transform schools into interesting places for children, reflective of the real world. These are still dreams today!

Why is there such resistance to change in education? Underlying the educational system is society's beliefs that the purposes of education are primarily to

- prepare children for later life,
- make children adept in relation to existing institutions,
- conform children to societal norms.

Basic skills (though these may be variously described) have frequently become the organizing units for schools. Group norms that are tested revolve around subject matter and content-focused teaching. These are the kinds of school programs that Dewey believed undermined democracy and the individual within a group context.

Growth as a continuous progress, self-direction and an individual's capacity to deal with problem situations were at the heart of Dewey's pragmatic approach to education. Small class sizes allowed the individualization of teaching.

At Dewey's 90th birthday celebration, Lady Allen of Hurtwood, world-renowned early childhood specialist and advocate of adventure playgrounds, summed up the tremendous contributions of John Dewey:

> *"Dear Professor Dewey:*
>
> *I am proud to send you this message of greeting on the occasion of your 90th birthday.*
>
> *By thinking of the school as part of society and by appreciating that we do not know what will be the major problems of the future, you have taught us that we must help children to develop their powers of adaptability and be taught how to think, if they are to grow up as free and independent citizens.*
>
> *You have exposed the fallacies of the cut-throat competition that is so common in formal teaching, and have shown us instead the richness of democratic cooperation between children who work together for a common purpose, and in so doing achieve their own discipline and self-control. Above all, you have brought us back to the great principle of studying children's play and have made us conscious of the processes of thought."*
>
> **— quoted in Laidler (Ed.), *John Dewey at Ninety***

## Current University of Chicago Laboratory Schools

The University of Chicago Laboratory Schools still exist and are located at:

1362 East 59th St.
Chicago, Illinois 60637
U.S.A.

There are actually four schools — Nursery/Kindergarten, Lower, Middle and High Schools — with a total enrollment of over 1,600 students.

> *"Our method — unregimented but demanding — focuses on teaching students to analyze and critically solve problems, rather than simply absorb facts."*
>
> *[At the nursery level] "our children enjoy opportunities to nurture individual initiative, build a sense of community, expand language and logical thinking, and develop social awareness."*
>
> **— quoted in the admissions brochure *Learning For Life***

The Laboratory Schools also run afterschool programs, summer camps and summer specialty schools.

Their website is:

http://www.ucls.uchicago.edu/

*A video on math —* There's Math in Deviled Eggs: Strategies for Teaching Young Children — *for preschool and kindergarten children was produced at the University of Chicago Laboratory Schools in collaboration with the Erikson Institute for Advanced Study in Child Development. It is available from:*

*Agency for Instructional Technology,*
*Box A,*
*Bloomington, Indiana*
*47402-0120*
*U.S.A.*

*The Center for Dewey Studies*
*Southern Illinois University*
*Carbondale, Illinois*
*62901*
*U.S.A.*

*The Center for Dewey Studies is a library, research and publications centre for materials related to John Dewey and his ideas.*
*Website:*
*http://www.siu.edu/~deweyctr/index2.html*

*Special Library Collection*
*University of Vermont*
*Bailey-Howe Library*
*John Dewey Collection*
*Special Collections*
*Burlington, Vermont*
*05405*
*U.S.A.*

The Progressives *looks at the ideas of Dewey, Francis Parker, Ella Flagg Young and G. Stanley Hall.*
*It is available from:*
*Insight Media*
*2162 Broadway*
*New York, New York*
*10024-0621*
*U.S.A.*

# Program Of Group III (Age Six)

**— from *The Dewey School* by Katherine Camp Mayhew and Anna Camp Edwards**

The group went outdoors every day and noted the changes taking place in the woods, fields, and parks. Insects were found going into winter quarters, and many kinds of seeds were collected. The question of seed distribution came up, and the children thought of various agents — the wind, people, and various sorts of animals. Talk and interest centered for some time on seeds, and excursions were taken to the park and the woods twenty blocks away, where several seeds that were good to eat were found. This suggested others also good for food, and finally, each child made a list of such seeds and with help, classified them as (1) those where the seed house was good to eat, (2) where the seed house was not good, (3) those fruits such as the tomato, the bean, and the cucumber where both the seed and seed house were good for food. The next point developed was that certain seeds are cultivated for their food value by people who are called farmers. This took the children's thoughts into the country and back to their previous year's experience and the various farms they had visited. Some one suggested, "let's make a farm," and they were then started on a project similar to that of the previous years. There are, however, several points of difference worthy of notice. Although the same use of materials continued with these children, more definite forms of control were established. Desirable means were considered with relation to desired ends. This is well illustrated by the way in which the seeds that are good for food, the cereals, were studied in cooking. The preparation and cooking of the cereals brought out their constituents. This led to an additional classification of foods with relation to their source, whether the seeds, the stalks, or the roots of plants.

## General Program of a Typical Group

The first project of the year started off with the building of a farm-house and barn out of large blocks varying in size up to six inches. In order to find the dimensions of their square houses, the children added the lengths of the blocks on one side and found the sum to be twelve inches or one foot. A plan for a chicken coop of manilla paper was then discussed and was finally marked off in two-and three-inch lengths, a rough approximation to keep in scale with the house. In the meantime, attention was centered on the farm itself, and the decision was made to raise corn and wheat and to have sheep and a dairy. The land was divided into fields and pastures, which were then fenced. For this they gathered twigs (to take the place of logs in making a rail fence), cut them into six-inch lengths, and built the fence three rails high. Around their pastures, however, they decided to have a stone fence, as they thought this was stronger. Work continued to some extent on the farmhouse. Boards were cut to proper lengths, with spaces for the door and windows. A chicken coop was started. In planning the back part of this, when laying off spaces for the windows and doors, it suddenly struck the children that the door was wider than it was high. One of the children went to another table and measured the door already laid off for the front of the farmhouse, and came back with the correct dimensions. This was an encouraging indication of a developing power of initiative and judgment. The square, the triangle, and the ruler were used freely. Although they had used the latter only a short time, they were very apt in its use. They knew the inch and half-inch, but hesitated on the quarter-inch. In general, it was found that they all took manual directions very well and showed great ability to plan and a high degree of independence in the execution of their plans, doing all the measuring and sawing themselves. As the project developed they suggested many of the things necessary in the making of a suitable house. The interest was well-sustained. In the kindergarten these children had been accustomed to making things that could be finished in one day, but they worked on this for almost two weeks without any loss of interest.

Early in the fall the group measured off and cleaned a space in the school yard five by ten feet for planting their winter wheat. A method of plowing was discussed and at one child's suggestion, a sharp stick was used and the field prepared in which the wheat was sown. In their sand-box farm their imaginary crop had come to fruition and, like the sheaf brought in from the farm, was ready for threshing. The various parts of the whole plant and their uses were discussed with the conclusion that the seed was of most value to people. A list was made of the wheat foods they had eaten — breakfast foods of coarsely ground wheat, and bread and cake from the finely ground flour. They played that they were farmers and discussed the best means of getting the seeds from the hulls, as they called the process of threshing. At first they picked it out by hand. This was too slow, so they suggested beating it with a stick and found that only the edge of the stick struck the ground. The problem was taken to the shop director, and with the help of some questioning, the children decided that if the farmer had two sticks joined together, more of the stick would hit the grain and thus the work would be done more quickly. The handle of the flail was made twice as long as the part that hits the grain. The next stop was to experiment with the wheat they had threshed and winnowed. Accordingly, it was pounded in a mortar and compared to some fine, white flour. They saw that the inside of the grain was soft and white like the fine flour, but that it was mixed with coarse, yellow particles. A child suggested putting this meal through a sieve to separate the coarse from the fine. This was done, but although the meal was a good deal finer, some of the yellow particles still remained. They then wanted to put it through a still finer sieve, but as there was none convenient, the process of bolting was explained to them, and the flour was sifted through some cheese cloth. This took out all the yellow particles and left the flour fine and white. They had in the end about three tablespoonsful of it, which was used in making a cake.

When they talked about grains in the classroom, they cooked cereals in the kitchen. For this they needed to learn to measure, to know how many teaspoons equal one tablespoon, how many tablespoons equal one cup, and so on. They discovered that two halves make a cupful, just the same as three thirds, or four quarters, and they came to talk about 1/2, 1/3 or 1/4 of a cupful, with ease and certainty. It was easy for them to see that 5/3 of a cup of water is 1 and 2/3 of a cup.

Much also of the number work was related to the construction work done on their farm or in connection with it. When their sand-table farm had to be divided into several fields for wheat, corn, oats, and also for the house and the barn, the children used a one-foot ruler as a unit of measurement and came to understand what was meant by "fourths and halves" — the divisions made, though not accurate, were near enough to allow them to mark off their farm. As they became more familiar with the ruler and learned the half-foot, and the quarter-foot and inch, finer work was naturally expected of them and obtained. Their use of this tool made it easy to distinguish those children who had had a kindergarten education from those who had just entered the group. When building the farm-house, four posts were needed for the corners and six or seven slats, all of the same height. In measuring the latter, the children frequently forgot to keep the left-hand edge of the ruler on the left-hand side of the slat, so the measurements had to be repeated two or three times before they were correct. What they did to one side of the house, they also did to the other and naturally worked more rapidly and more accurately as the work was repeated.

## Details of Early Dramatic Play

Dramatic play frequently helped initiate a new phase of the activity and frequently was the means of summarizing the result of a period's work. The distribution of the threshed or milled wheat started off with such a play. The setting for the play, the farm and the mill, was constructed of large blocks; some children played they were farmers; others were millers. The farmers carried wheat to the mill; the millers ground it. The farmer paid the miller by letting him keep some of the flour and carried home the rest for bread in sacks already prepared for this purpose by the children. Wagons were needed, and in a day or two these outnumbered their horses. Day by day the idea grew, helped on by timely hint or suggestion.

It was explained that times had changed, that now there was no small near-by mill where a farmer could take his grain. It must be sent many miles away to a large mill, which ground the wheat of many farms, and when each farmer wanted flour, he bought it at a grocery store in the nearest town. It took some time for them to get a clear idea of the modern transportation of wheat from the farm to the big mill and the distribution of the flour from the mill. Here again, their first ideas were worked out through dramatic play. Some of them were to be farmers, some trainmen, some mill hands, and some grocers in different towns. The farmers were to take the wheat to the nearest small town where it could be put on the train and sent to a large city mill many miles away. Here the millers would receive it and, after making it into flour, would put it on another train and send it to the grocers in the different towns where it would be sold to the farmers when they might want it. In order that the play should be a success, much preparation was required, and the little farmers were again busy in the shop, making miniature bushel, peck, and other necessary measures. These, through the careful planning of the teacher, were circular; all had bottoms of the same size and varied only in height. Incidentally, but logically, they then saw that to be good actors, they must learn how to use these tools in order to measure out their grain.

The winter quarter was begun with talk of the sheep-raising business on a farm. The kind of land was considered that a farmer would use for the pasture for sheep. After much discussion supplemented at the right moment by bits of information and timely reference to maps on the part of the teacher, the group finally decided that a temperate climate would be the best. The cold winters would make the wool grow well, and the sheep would not miss their warm coats in the summer. On the globe, they found the principal sheep-raising districts, which were located midway between the equator and the poles. The raw wool was examined and its agency in seed distribution was noted. The natural oil in the wool of the sheep was discovered by dipping the wool into water and noticing how it shed the water. Wool was compared with duck feathers that also shed water; wool was burned to get the odor, which the children compared with burning fat and burning hair. They then tested different kinds of cloth to see if they could tell those made of wool, first by feeling of it, then by noticing its absorbent qualities, and then by burning. As a next step, the wool was pulled out and twisted to show how easily it could be made into thread. The manner of shearing, of washing, and of transporting the fleece to the factory was discussed. Through picture, song, and story this age-old occupation was surrounded by and linked to some of its many esthetic connotations.

## John Dewey—References for Further Study

ACEI Later Leaders Committee. (1992). *Profiles in Childhood Education 1931 – 1960.* Wheaton, MD: Association for Education International.

Adams, A. (1981). The long conversation: Tracing the roots of the past. *Journal of Experiential Education, 4,* 21 – 28.

Addams, J. (1910). *Twenty years at Hull-House, with autobiographical notes.* New York: Macmillan.

Addams, J. (1912). *A new conscience and an ancient evil.* New York: Macmillan.

Addams, J. (1930). *The second twenty years at Hull-House.* New York: Macmillan.

Addams, J. (1937). *The spirit of youth and the city streets.* New York: Macmillan.

Ames, V. M. (Ed.). (1959). *Beyond theology: The autobiography of Edward Scribner Ames.* Chicago: The University of Chicago Press.

Apelman, M. (1975, Autumn). On reading John Dewey today. *Outlook, 17,* 18 – 28.

Archambault, R. (Ed. and Introduction). (1964). *John Dewey on education: Selected writings.* New York: Random House.

Ayres, L. (1910). *Open-air schools.* New York: Doubleday, Page & Company.

Baker, M. (1966). *Foundations of John Dewey's educational theory.* New York: Atherton Press.

Bauner, R. (1978). The Dewey School photographs. *Icarbs, 4,* 24 – 40.

Beck, R. (1958 – 59). Progressive education and American progressivism: Caroline Pratt. *Teachers College Record, 50,* 129 – 137.

Bennett, H. C. (1914, May). Adjusting the education to the child. *McCall's Magazine,* 11 – 13.

Berger, M. I. (1959, March 28). John Dewey and progressive education today. *School and Society,* 140 – 142.

Biesta, G., & Miedema, S. (1996). Dewey in Europe: A case study on the international dimensions of the turn-of-the-century educational reform. *American Journal of Education, 105* (1), 1 – 26.

Boisvert, R. (1998). *John Dewey: Rethinking our time.* Albany, NY: State University of New York.

Borup-Nielson, G. (1995). *A study of the two experimental schools of C.N. Starcke and John Dewey.* Lewiston, NY: The Edwin Mellen Press.

Boydston, J. A. (General Ed.). (1967). *John Dewey: The Early Works, 1882 – 1898. 2:1887.* Carbondale: IL: Southern Illinois University.

Boydston, J. A. (General Ed.). (1969). *John Dewey: The Early Works, 1882 – 1898. 1:1882 – 1882.* Carbondale: IL: Southern Illinois University.

Boydston, J. A. (General Ed.). (1969). *John Dewey: The Early Works, 1882 – 1898. 3:1889 – 1892.* Carbondale: IL: Southern Illinois University.

Boydston, J. A. (General Ed.). (1971). *John Dewey: The Early Works, 1882 – 1898. 4:1893 – 1894.* Carbondale: IL: Southern Illinois University.

Boydston, J. A. (Ed.). (1976). *John Dewey: The middle works 1899 – 1924.* Carbondale, IL: Southern Illinois University Press.

Brickman, W., & Lehrer, S. (Eds.). (1961). *John Dewey: Master educator.* New York: Society for the Advancement of Education.

Brown, G. (1987). Dr. John Dewey's educational experiment. *The Public School Journal, 16,* 533 – 537.

Brown, S., & Finn, M. (Eds.). (1988). *Readings from progressive education: A movement and its professional journal Volume I.* Lanham, MD: University Press of America.

Cahan, E. (1992). John Dewey and human development. *Child Development, 28* (2), 205 – 214.

Camp, K. (1903). Elementary science and the laboratory school. *Elementary School Teacher, 4* (1), 1 – 8.

Campbell, J. (1967). *Colonel Francis W. Parker: The children's crusader.* New York: Teachers College Press.

Chard, S. C. (1998). *The project approach: Making curriculum come alive.* New York: Scholastic.

Chard, S. C. (1998). *The project approach: Managing successful projects.* New York: Scholastic.

Chase, F. (1980, Winter). The Chicago laboratory schools: Retrospect and prospect. *UCLA Educator, 21,* 38 – 44.

Clapp, E. R. (1939). *Community schools in action.* New York: Viking Press.

Clark, R. (1975). *The Life of Bertrand Russell.* London: Jonathan Cape and Weidenfeld & Nicolson.

Clayton, S. (1959). The educational philosophy of John Dewey. *Phi Delta Kappan, 12* (1), 10 – 13.

Cohen, B. (1969). *Educational thought.* London: Macmillan.

Cohen, D. (1998). Dewey's problem. *The Elementary School Journal, 98* (5), 427 – 446.

Committee of Nineteen. (1924). *Pioneers of the kindergarten in America.* New York: The Century Co.

Coughlan, N. (1975). *Young John Dewey.* Chicago: The University of Chicago Press.

Cremin, L. (1961). *The transformation of the school: Progressivism in American education.* New York: Alfred Knopf.

Cuffara, H. (1995). *Experimenting with the world: John Dewey and the early childhood classroom.* New York: Teachers College Press.

Dennis, L. (1970). Play in Dewey's theory of education. *Young Children, 25* (4), 230 – 235.

DePencier, I. (1967). *The history of the laboratory schools.* Chicago: Quadrangle Books.

Dewey, A. (1903). The place of the kindergarten. *The Elementary School Teacher, III* (5), 273 – 288.

Dewey, E. (1972 reprinted from 1935). *Behavior development in infants: A survey of the literature on prenatal and postnatal activity, 1920 – 1934.* New York: Arno Press.

Dewey, J. (1887). *Psychology.* New York: Harper.

Dewey, J. (1895). Results of child study applied to education. *Transactions of the Illinois Society for Child Study, 4,* 18 – 19.

Dewey, J. (1896, November 6). The University School. *University Record, 1* (32), 417 – 419.

Dewey, J. (1896, September 18). Pedagogy as a university discipline. *University Record, 1* (25) 353 – 355.

Dewey, J. (1897). My pedagogic creed. *The School Journal, LIV* (3), 77 – 80.

Dewey, J. (1897, April). The psychological aspect of the school curriculum. *Educational Review, 13,* 356 – 369.

Dewey, J. (1900). General introduction to groups V and VI. *Elementary School Record, 2,* 49 – 52.

Dewey, J. (1900). *The school and society.* Chicago: The University of Chicago Press.

Dewey, J. (1900, February). Froebel's educational principles. *Elementary School Record, 1* (1), 143 – 151.

Dewey, J. (1910). *How we think.* Boston: D.C. Heath.

Dewey, J. (1914). Reasoning in early childhood. *Teachers College Record, XV* (1), 9 – 15.

Dewey, J. (1915). Reasoning in early childhood. In P. S. Hill (Ed.), *Experimental studies in kindergarten theory and practice.* New York: Teachers College, Columbia Universities.

Dewey, J. (1916). *Democracy and education: An introduction to the philosophy of education.* New York: Macmillan.

Dewey, J. (1929). *My pedagogic creed.* Washington, DC: The Progressive Education Association.

Dewey, J. (1933, revised edition). *How we think.* Boston: D.C. Heath & Company.

Dewey, J. (1934). *Art as experience.* New York: Capricorn Books.

Dewey, J. (1934, October). Can education share in social reconstruction? *The Social Frontier,* 1, 11 – 12.

Dewey, J. (1938). *Experience and education.* New York: Macmillan.

Dewey, J. (1939). *Freedom and culture.* New York: Putnam's Sons.

Dewey, J. (1956). *The child and the curriculum and the school and society.* Chicago: the University of Chicago Press. (Original works published 1899 and 1902)

Dewey, J. (1957). *Reconstruction in philosophy.* Boston: Beacon Press.

Dewey, J. (1959). *Dewey on education.* New York: Bureau of Publications, Teachers College, Columbia University.

Dewey, J. (1959). *Moral principles in education.* New York: Greenwood Press, Publishers. (Original work published 1909)

Dewey, J. (1974). (R. Archambault, Ed.). *John Dewey on education.* Chicago: University of Chicago Press.

Dewey, J. (1990 edition, with introduction by P. Jackson). *The school and society and the child and the curriculum.* Chicago: The University of Chicago Press.

Dewey, J., & Dewey, A. C. (1920). *Letters from China and Japan* (E. Dewey, Ed.). New York: E. P. Dutton.

Dewey, J., & Dewey, E. (1915). *Schools of tomorrow.* New York: E. P. Dutton.

Dewey's entire life an inquiry says Dr. Schneider. (1949, October 27). *Burlington Free Press.*

Diffily, D. (1995). The project approach: A museum exhibit created by kindergartens. *Young Children, 51* (2), 72 – 75.

Donatellis, R. (1971). *The contributions of Ella Flagg young to the educational enterprise.* Unpublished doctoral dissertation, University of Chicago, Chicago, IL.

Dropkin, R., & Tobier, A. (Eds.). (1976). *Roots of open education.* New York: Workshop Centre for Open Education.

Dworkin, M. (1959). Introduction and Notes to *Dewey on education.* New York: Teachers College Press.

Dworkin, M. (1959). John Dewey: A centennial review. *The School Executive, 79* (2). 52 – 55.

Dykhuizen, G. (1959, October – December). John Dewey: The Vermont Years. *Journal of the History of Ideas, 20,* 515 – 544.

Dykhuizen, G. (1960, October – December). John Dewey and the University of Michigan. *Journal of the History of Ideas, 23,* 512 – 544.

Dykhuizen, G. (1973). *The life and mind of John Dewey.* Carbondale, IL: Southern Illinois University Press.

Eastman, M. (1941, December). John Dewey. *Atlantic Monthly, 168,* 671 – 685.

Eastman, M. (1942). *Great companions.* New York: Farrar, Strauss & Giroux.

Eastman, M. (1942). *Heroes I have known.* New York: Simon and Schuster.

Eastman, M. (1953, January 17). America's philosopher. *Saturday Review 36,* 23 – 24, 38.

Eastman, M. (1959). *Great companions.* London: Museum Press Ltd.

Edman, I. (1938). *Philosopher's holiday.* New York: Viking Press.

Edman, I. (1949, October 16). America's philosopher attains an alert 90. *New York Times Magazine,* 17, 74 – 75.

Ehrlich, T. (1998). Reinventing John Dewey's "Pedagogy as university discipline." *The Elementary School Journal, 98* (5), 489 – 509.

*Elementary School Record, 1* (1), 1 – 9. (February 1900).

Gallant, T. (1972). Dewey then — experiential education now. *School and Society, 100,* 303 – 308.

Gallant, T. (1973). Dewey's child centered education in contemporary academe. *Educational Forum, 37* (4), 411 – 419.

Ginger, R. (1958). *Altgeld's America.* Chicago: Quandrangle Books.

Gordon, J. W. (1970). *My country school diary: An adventure in creative teaching.* New York: Delta Books. (Original work published in 1946)

Greenberg, P. (1992). Why not academic preschool? Part 2, autocracy or democracy in the classroom? *Young Children, 47* (3), 54 – 64.

Greene, M. (1959, October 10). Dewey and American education, 1894 – 1920. *School and Society, 87,* 381 – 386.

Hall, G. S. (1900). Child-study and its relation to education. *Forum, 29,* 688 – 702.

Hall, G. S. (1901). The ideal school as based on child study. *Forum, 32,* 24 – 39.

Harding, H. H. (1903). Social needs of children. *Elementary School Teacher, 4* (4), 205 – 209.

Harmer, A. (1900, April). Textile industries. *Elementary School Record, 1* (3), 71 – 81.

Harms, W., & DePencier, I. (1996). *Experiencing education: 100 years of learning at the University of Chicago Laboratory schools.* Chicago: University of Chicago Laboratory Schools.

Heffron, I. C. (1934). *Francis Wayland Parker: An interpretive biography.* Los Angeles: Ivan Deach, Jr.

Heise, K. (1990). *The Chicagoization of America 1893 – 1917.* Evanston, IL: Chicago Historical Bookworks.

Henderson, C. H. (1902). *Education and the larger life.* Boston: Houghton Mifflin.

Henderson, C. H. (1914). *What is it to be educated?* Boston: Houghton & Mifflin.

Hermanowicz, H. (1961). Problem solving as a teaching method. *Educational Leadership, 18* (5), 299 – 306.

Hocking, E., & Hocking, A. (1955, December). Creating a school. *Atlantic Monthly, 96*, 63 – 66.

Hogan, D. J. (1985). *Class and reform: School and society in Chicago 1880 – 1930.* Philadelphia, PA: University of Pennsylvania Press.

Hook, S. (1939). *John Dewey: An intellectual portrait.* New York: The John Day Co.

Jackman, W. S. (1904). A brief history of the school of education. *University Record, 1* (25), 353 – 355.

Jackman, W. S. (1904). A brief history of the school of education. *University Record, 9*, 2 – 7.

Jackson, P. (1998). *John Dewey and the lessons of art.* New Haven, CT: Yale University Press.

Jackson, P. (1998). John Dewey's *School and Society* revisited. *The Elementary School Journal, 98* (5), 415 – 426.

Jervis, K., & Montag, C. (Eds.). (1991). *Progressive education for the 1990's.* New York: Teachers College Press.

John Dewey's birthday (1949, October 20). *Burlington Free Press.*

Johnson, B. (1944). *As much as I dare.* New York: Ives Washburn, Inc.

Johnson, M. (1988). Problems of the progressive secondary school — a symposium. In Brown, S. & Finn, M. (Eds.), *Readings from Progressive Education: A movement and its professional journal Volume I.* Lanham, MD: University Press of America.

Johnson, M. (1929). *Youth in a world of men.* New York: The John Day Co.

Johnson, M. (1931). Standards and the child. *Progressive Education Magazine, 8,* 692-694.

Johnson, M. (n.d.) If education is life. [one page handout]. *Alabama School Journal.* The Marietta Johnson Museum in Fairhope, Alabama.

Katz, L. G., & Chard, S. C. (1989). *Engaging children's minds: The project approach.* Norwood, NJ: Ablex.

Keehane, M. (1970). A. S. Neill: Latter day Dewey? *Elementary School Journal, 70*, 401 – 410.

Kilpatrick, W. H. (1918). The project method. *Teachers College Record, 19* (4), 314 – 335.

Kilpatrick, W. H. (1936). *Remaking the curriculum.* New York: Newson and Company.

Kilpatrick, W. H. (1961). Reminiscences of Dewey and his influence. In Brickman, W. & Lehrer, S. (Eds.), *John Dewey: Master educator.* New York: Society for the Advancement of Education.

Kliebard, H. (1986). *The struggle for the American curriculum.* Boston: Routledge & Kegan Paul.

Lagemann, E. C. (1996). Experimenting with education: John Dewey and Ella Flagg Young at the University of Chicago. *American Journal of Education, 104*, 3, 171 – 185.

Laidler, H. (Ed.). (1950). *John Dewey at ninety.* New York: League for Industrial Democracy.

Landsmann, L. T. (1991). *Culture, schooling and psychological development.* Norwood, NJ: Ablex.

Lascarides, V.C. & Hinitz, B. (2000). *History of Early Childhood Education.* New York: Falmer Press.

Lasch, C. (Ed.). (1965). *The social thought of Jane Addams.* Indianapolis, IN: The Bobbs-Merrill Company, Inc.

Lauderdale, W. B. (1981). *Progressive education: Lessons from three schools.* Bloomington, IN: Phi Delta Kappa Educational Foundation.

Levine, D. (1971). *Jane Addams and the liberal tradition.* Madison, WI: State Historical Society of Wisconsin.

Lewis, M. H. (1928). *An adventure with children.* New York: Macmillan.

Lewis, M. H. (1985). *An adventure with children.* Lanham, NY: University Press of America.

Lu, H. (1968). Dewey's logical theory and his conception of education. *Educational Theory, 18* (4), 388 – 395.

Maxson, M. (1976). Dewey's School: No playground but a structured laboratory. In O.L. Davis (Ed.), *Perspectives on curriculum development 1776 – 1976.* Washington, DC: Association for Supervision and Curriculum Development.

Mayhew, K. C., & Edwards, A. C. (1966). *The Dewey School.* New York: Atherton Press. (Original work published in 1936)

McCaul, R. (1959). Dewey's Chicago. *School Review, 67* (2). 258 – 280.

McCaul, R. (1961, March 25). Dewey and the University of Chicago, Part I: July, 1894 – March, 1902. *School and Society*, 152 – 157.

McCaul, R. (1961, April 8). Dewey and the University of Chicago, Part II: April, 1902 – May, 1903. *School and Society*, 179 – 183.

McCaul, R. (1961, April 22). Dewey and the University of Chicago, Part III: September, 1903 – June, 1904. *School and Society*, 202 – 206.

McCormack, T. J. (1900, September). The school and society. *Open Court, 14,* 564 – 69.

McManis, J. (1916). *Ella Flagg Young and a half-century of the Chicago public schools.* Chicago: A.C. McClurg & Co.

Misner, P. (1959, December). What did Dewey do for education? *National Parent-Teacher, 54* (4), 9.

Mooney, C. (2000).*Theories of childhood: An introduction to Dewey, Montessori, Erikson, Piaget & Vygotsky.* St. Paul, MN: Redleaf Press.

Newman, J. (1997, October 7). Experimental school, experimental community: The Marietta Johnson School of Organic Education in Fairhope, Alabama. *The*

*Harbinger*, n.p. Retrieved March 25, 1999 from the World Wide Web: *http://entropy.me.usouthal.edu/harbinger/xvi/971007/newman.html*

Newman, J. (1997, October 28). The Organic School after Marietta Johnson. *The Harbinger*, n.p. Retrieved March 25,1999 from the World Wide Web: *http://entropy.me.usouthal.edu/harbinger/xvi/971028/newman.html*

Nolan, J. (1982). Professional laboratory experiences: The missing link in teacher education. *Journal of Teacher Education, XXXIII* (4), 49 – 53.

O'Connor, N. (1904, March). The educational side of the Parents' Association of the Laboratory School: From a parent's point of view. *The Elementary School Teacher,* V, 532 – 535.

Oppenheim, N. (1910). *The development of the child.* New York: Macmillan. (Original work published 1898)

Parker, F. (1961). Chicago in the 1890's. In Brickman, W., & Lehrer, S. (Eds.), *John Dewey: Master educator.* New York: Society for the Advancement of Education.

Parker, F. W. (1894). *Talks on pedagogics.* New York: E. L. Kellogg.

Pelaghi, C. (1965, January 28). Oil city fails to acclaim the famous ex-president. *The Derrick,* 17.

Peltzman, B. R. (1998). *Pioneers of early childhood education: A bio-bibliographical guide.* Westport, CT: Greenwood Press.

Perkinson, H. (1976). *Two hundred years of American educational thought.* New York: David McKay Company, Inc.

Perkinson, H. (1977). *The imperfect panacea: American faith in education, 1865 – 1976.* New York: Random House.

Phillips, D. C. (1998). John Dewey's *The child and the curriculum*: A century later. *The Elementary School Journal, 98* (5), 403 – 414.

Prochner, L. & Howe, N. (2000). *Early childhood education and care in Canada.* Vancouver: UBC Press.

Professor Dewey's report on the Fairhope experiment in organic education. (1914, May). *Survey, 16,*199.

Provenzo, E. (1979). History as experiment: The role of the Laboratory School in the development of John Dewey's philosophy of history. *History Teacher, 12,* 373 – 382.

Ravitch, D. (1983). *The troubled crusade: American education, 1945 – 1980.* New York: Basic Books.

Rotzel, G. (1971). *The school in Rose Valley: A parent venture in education.* Baltimore, MD: Johns Hopkins Press.

Ruenzel, D. (1995, February 1). In search of John Dewey. *Education Week,* 7, 23 – 29.

Ruenzel, D. (1995, February). Looking for John Dewey. *Teacher, 6,* 32 – 37.

Rugg, H., & Shumaker, A. (1928). *The child-centred school.* New York: World Book Co.

Russell, D. (1998). Cultivating the imagination in music education: John Dewey's theory of imagination and its relation to the Chicago Laboratory School. *Educational Theory, 48* (2), 193 – 210.

Ryan, A. (1995). *John Dewey and the high tide of American liberalism.* New York: W. W. Norton & Co.

Ryan, A. (1998). *Liberal anxieties and liberal education.* New York: Hill and Wang.

Sadovnik, A. & Semel, S. (Eds.). (2002). *Founding mothers and others: Women educational leaders during the progressive era.* New York: Palgrave.

Salute to John Dewey. (1949, October 22). *The New Leader,* 51 – 58.

Sarason, S. (1971). *The culture of the school and the problem of change.* Boston: Allyn and Bacon, Inc.

Scates, G. (1900, June). School reports: the subprimary (kindergarten) department. *Elementary School Record, 1* (5), 129 – 142.

Schilpp, P. A. (Ed.). (1939). *The philosophy of John Dewey.* Evanston, IL: Northwestern University.

Schilpp, P. (1951). *The philosophy of John Dewey*. New York: Tudor Publishing Co.

School record, notes and plan: The University of Chicago School. (1896, November 6). *University Record, 1,* 419 – 422.

School record, notes and plan: VI: The University of Chicago School. (1896, December 4). *University Record, 1,* 460 – 461.

Seguel, M. L. (1966). *The curriculum field: Its formative years.* New York: Teachers College Press.

Seller, M. (1994). *Women educators in the United States, 1820 – 1993.* Westport, CT: Greenwood Press.

Semel, S., & Sadovnik, A. (Eds.). (1999). *"Schools of Tomorrow," Schools of Today: What happened to progressive education.* New York: Peter Lang.

Shapiro, M. S. (1983). *Child's Garden: The kindergarten movement from Froebel to Dewey.* University Park, PA: The Pennsylvania State University Press.

Shulman, L. (1998). Theory, practice, and the education of professionals. *The Elementary School Journal, 98* (5), 513 – 526.

Smith, J. (1979). *Ella Flagg Young: Portrait of a leader.* Ames, IA: Educational Studies Press and the Iowa State University Research Foundation.

Smith, T. (Ed.). (1907). *Aspects of child life and education by G. Stanley Hall and some of his pupils.* Boston: Ginn & Company.

Spicola, R. (n.d.). *Alice Chipman Dewey.* Denton, TX: Texas Women's University.

Spring, J. (1971). *Education and the rise of the corporate stage.* Cuernavaca, Mexico: Centro Intercultural de Documentacion.

Spring, J. (1990). *The American school: 1642 – 1990.* New York: Longman.

Tanner, L. (1991). The meaning of curriculum in Dewey's Laboratory School (1896 – 1904). *Journal of Curriculum Studies, 23* (2), 101 – 117.

Tanner, L. (1997). *Dewey's laboratory school: Lessons for today.* New York: Teachers College Press.

Tenenbaum, S. (1951). *William Heard Kilpatrick: Trail blazer in education.* New York: Harper & Brothers.

The University Elementary School, history and character. (1897). *University Record, 3,* 72 – 75.

The University Elementary School. (1898, November 25). *University Record, 3,* 220 – 221.

The University of Chicago Laboratory Schools. (1998). *Learning for life* [admissions brochure]. Chicago: University of Chicago.

Try to find meaning of what goes on around, says philosopher John Dewey (1949, October 27). *Burlington Free Press.*

Tsuin-Chen, O. (1961). A re-evaluation of the educational theory and practice of John Dewey. *Educational Forum, 25,* 277 – 300.

Walker, L. R. (1997, Summer). John Dewey at Michigan. Part 1. *Michigan Today.* Retrieved October 8, 1999 from the World Wide Web:*http://www.umich.edu/~newsinfo/MT/97/Sum97/mta1j97.html*

Walker, L. R. (1997, Fall). John Dewey at Michigan Part 2. *Michigan Today.* Retrieved October 8,1999 from the World Wide Web: *http://www.umich.edu/!newsinfor/MT/97/Fal97/mt13f97.html*

Webb, L., & McCarthy, M. (1996). Ella Flagg Young: Tribute to a pioneer leader in education. *Initiatives, 58,* 11 – 19.

Weber, E. (1969). *The kindergarten: Its encounter with educational thought in America.* New York: Teachers College Press.

Westbrook, R. (1991). *John Dewey and American democracy.* Ithaca, NY: Cornell University Press.

Westbrook, R. (1992, August). Schools for industrial democrats. *American Journal of Education, 100,* 401 – 419.

Westbrook, R. (1993 – 94). Dewey. In Z. Morsy (Ed.), *Thinkers on education.* Paris, France: United Nations Educational, Scientific and Cultural Organization (UNESCO).

Wingo, G. M. (1965). *The philosophy of American education.* Lexington, MA: D.C. Heath and Company.

Wingo, G. M. (1974). *Philosophies of educaton: An introduction.* Lexington, MA: D.C. Heath and Company.

Wirth, A. (1964). John Dewey's design for American education: An analysis of aspects of his work at the University of Chicago, 1894 – 1904. *History of Education Quarterly, 4,* 83 – 105.

Wirth, A. (1968). The Deweyan tradition revisited. *Washington University Magazine, 38* (2), 47 – 51.

Wood, J. (1981). The Dewey School revisited. *Childhood Education, 58* (2), 99 – 101.

Yeomans, E. (1979). *The Shady Hill School: The first fifty years.* Cambridge, MA: Windflower Press.

Young, E. F. (1901). *Isolation in the school.* Chicago: The University of Chicago Press.

Young, E. F. (1916). Democracy and education. *Journal of Education, 84* (1), 5 – 6.

# Chapter 8 — *Maria Montessori*

**1870 – 1952**

*"To stimulate life — leaving it free to develop, to unfold — herein lies the first task of an educator."*

*"From the child he will learn how to perfect himself as an educator."*

*"Our educational aim with very young children must be to aid the spontaneous development of the mental, spiritual, and physical personality."*

— ***The Montessori Method***

Everyone in the field of early childhood has heard of Maria Montessori and some of her contributions and ideas. But who was this woman? What motivated her? What events shaped her life? Why did her ideas flourish in Europe but languish in North America for such a long time? What caused the resurgence of her ideas in North America after her death?

## Early Life

She was born in Chiaravelle in the province of Ancona, Italy on the Adriatic Sea in 1870, the year of Italy's unification. It was a time of hope in Italy but also a time of fragmentation between classes and rifts between the church and secular powers.

Her father, Alessandro, had been a soldier but then became a civil servant in the state-run tobacco industry. Her mother, Renilde Stoppani, was well educated for a woman of that time. Maria's grandfather was a geology professor and liberal lay member of the church. Early in Maria's life, her father became an accountant and was transferred to a government position in Rome, where the family believed better educational opportunities awaited their daughter.

There is contradictory information about Maria's childhood though it is clear that her mother was strict with her; she was raised as a devout Roman Catholic and was required to knit for the poor. The family lived in an apartment in Rome, and Maria had a lot of contact with other children.

In her early years in school, she did not excel but was known for standing up for her own ideas to both children and teachers. She was confident and self-assured. Most girls stopped their education at the age of 12, but Maria continued on. Her parents wanted her to have a classical education, but Maria went against their wishes and, building on her strong mathematical skills, attended a technical school, planning a career in engineering, a choice unheard of for a woman at the time.

Montessori recognized that the prevalent educational methods of the day, with lock step learning, everyone being kept to the same pace, and predetermined skills and facts, created a system that suppressed individuality. Girls were separated from boys at recess, so the girls stayed in a room by themselves while the boys played outside. Maria graduated in 1886 with high academic marks but critical views on education. She once described education as a system where

**Montessori was born in Chiaravelle, Italy in the circled area of the map. Her family moved to Rome where she later graduated as the first female doctor in Italy.**

**Maria Montessori in 1886. (Used with permission of the Association Montessori Internationale.)**

> *"the children, like butterflies mounted on pins, are fastened each to his place, the desk, spreading the useless wings of barren and meaningless knowledge which they have acquired."*
>
> — ***The Montessori Method***

She abandoned her engineering goal as she became interested in the biological sciences and entertained the idea of becoming a medical doctor. A woman studying medicine in Italy in the 1800's! It had never been done before. Her friends and family were shocked with this new direction, but Maria persevered and entered the University of Rome in 1890.

## Medical School and Early Projects

After two years of pre-medicine, she was accepted into medicine. Though she won numerous scholarships for academic achievement, she was not allowed to interact freely with the men of the program. She had to wait for all the men to be seated in the lecture hall before she was able to take her seat. Unable to do dissections in the same laboratory as the men, she had separate private sessions. At the beginning of the program, the men taunted and shunned her. Despite incredible obstacles and lack of support from her father, she had the inner strength to persevere. When a major weather storm in Rome kept all other students away, she was the only student to appear at a lecture. The astonished professor delivered the lecture to his sole student that day. She studied pediatrics in the last two years and graduated with high honours. In 1896 Montessori became the first woman in Italy to obtain a Doctor of Medicine. The language of her diploma had to be altered from the regular masculine form to indicate that the graduate was a female.

Montessori immediately got a job as a surgical assistant. She did research at psychiatric clinics and encountered children in Rome's asylums for the insane who were simply unable to function in their families or community. They were labelled "insane" or "idiot children." Montessori was convinced they were neither and began reading more on "mentally defective children." She was appalled at their care and the sparse, non-stimulating conditions of the asylums. She encountered the writings of Jean-Marc Itard and Edouard Seguin,[1] 19th-century French doctors who had found effective methods and materials to work with "mentally deficient" children. Montessori found the validation she needed and came to believe that children were "mentally defective" primarily because they had not been taught properly:

> *"I felt that mental deficiency presented chiefly a pedagogical, rather than a medical problem."*
>
> — ***The Montessori Method***

---

[1] Jean Itard (1775 – 1838) had worked with the "Wild Boy of Aveyron," raised by wolves and then "re-educated" as a boy. Edouard Seguin (1812 – 1880), a student of Itard, was a social reformer and developed didactic materials for "severely retarded" children. The direct usage of Seguin's materials by Montessori was documented by Katrina Myers in 1913 in "Seguin's Principles of Education as Related to the Montessori Method."

Our current surge of research on the long-term economic cost benefits of quality preschool programs reflects the same view as Montessori encountered. The value of these programs for the development of children is apparently not enough. Society wants cost savings! And even then it is hard to convince politicians to fund quality early childhood programs when other agendas are pressing. Savings created from quality early childhood programs are often seen years later, and most politicians deal with the present and immediate needs.

See W.S. Barnett's (1985) *The Perry Preschool Program and Its Long-Term Effects: A Benefit-Cost Analysis* and Gordon Cleveland and Michael Krashinsky's 1998 Canadian study *The Benefits and Costs of Good Child Care: The Economic Rationale for Public Investment in Young Children.*

In 1897 Montessori began a concentrated study of education and read all she could about education — John Locke, Jean-Jacques Rousseau, Friedrich Froebel, Johann Pestalozzi, Robert Owen. She did not agree with Rousseau's idea of the corrupt environment and the need to isolate the child; rather, she wanted to use the world to help the child and planned to use sensory education.

Montessori became convinced of the need for special schools for children who were labelled "mentally retarded" or emotionally disturbed. Working jointly with her physician colleague Dr. Giuseppe Montesano, she studied and wrote about her emerging educational ideas. These were not of interest to a society which viewed such children as dispensable. Appealing to people's concern or compassion did not work, but an appeal to their pocketbooks did have an influence — Montessori lobbied that these children would be less of a financial drain on society if they became productive citizens:

> *"Our efforts will have to go into gaining an understanding of those children who have the most difficulty adapting to society and helping them before they get into trouble."*

Montessori organized multi-disciplinary teams of teachers and doctors to work with the children. Sense education was to be the foundation for all later cognitive education. Finally people began to listen to her and see her as an expert in the field of special education.

Montessori was also an outspoken proponent of equality for women; she represented Italy at a feminist congress in Berlin in 1896 and in London in 1900. She spoke out against child labour and for the rights of working women.

In 1899 she began to lecture at the Regio Instituto Superior di Magistero Femminile, one of two teacher training colleges for women in Italy. The next year a school opened in Rome to train teachers for the care and education of children with special needs. It included a practice demonstration school, named the Orthophrenic School, with Montessori as the director and Dr. Montesano as co-director. The results were impressive: children learned to read and write and passed the same examinations as the "normal" children.

Montessori stayed two years at the Orthophrenic School and developed both her materials and methods. The approach was so successful that she began to wonder how it would work with normal children if it worked so well with "idiots" and "defective children" from asylums. She was convinced that the methods would free children's personalities in marvelous and surprising ways.

## Motherhood or Career?

*If you had been in Montessori's position of choosing motherhood or a career at that time in Italy, what do you think you would have chosen?*

Although she left the school ostensibly to study normal children, Montessori had personal reasons for leaving. She had developed an intimate relationship with Dr. Montesano, and they had a child who was sent to a wet nurse. Both parents agreed to keep it a secret that the child was Montessori's. They also had agreed not to marry each other or anyone else, but Montesano soon broke the promise when he married. It was at this point that Montessori left the school. There are conflicting reports about this part of her life. Some of the literature says she left the school when the child was born, while others report her resignation came later.

In this era, if Montessori had acknowledged the birth of a child outside of a marriage, her career as a female doctor would have been over. Mario, her son, would not know his mother or re-enter her life until he was 15, and even then his true relationship to Montessori was not revealed for a long time. Eventually Mario adopted Montessori as his last name and became an integral part of his mother's life and career. After his mother's death, he continued the Montessori program leadership.

## Educational Studies

Montessori enrolled at the University of Rome in 1901 as a student in the philosophy department, which also housed the department of psychology. Montessori was very successful in her studies and began teaching the applications of anthropology to education at the University. She continued to lecture on the need for educational methods to follow a sound knowledge of children:

> *"we cannot educate anyone until we know him thoroughly."*
>
> — ***Pedagogical Anthropology***

*Montessori used two skeletons to demonstrate the difference between children and adults. How do you use visuals with young children in songs, with stories and in other programming elements? What are some of the advantages and challenges?*

Montessori became known as well for her use of "visual aids" — using charts, graphs, photos, and diagrams in her lectures. She wanted to ensure that lectures came alive for students. In later talks on children, she used two skeletons, one of a child and one of an adult, to point out that the differences between the two went far beyond the physical to the psychological.

Montessori was also concerned that teacher education respond to the changes in society. Schools needed to adapt to the rapidly changing industrial, urban life of many people. Women were in the work force in unprecedented numbers. Montessori encouraged free lunches for children who were coming to school hungry; this step addressed social needs within an educational context.

In 1904 Montessori was named Professor at the University of Rome where she taught anthropology; her first major publication was called *Pedagogical Anthropology*.

Montessori saw teachers as having a mission to improve society. Her chance to put many of her ideas into a larger practical context came in 1907. Rome had experienced a period of rapid growth with associated societal problems. New housing was desperately needed. A new housing project that would include child care for working parents was planned for the overcrowded slum district of San Lorenzo.

## Casa dei Bambini

Montessori was hired by Edoardo Talamo, director-general of the Roman Association of Good Building, to set up the child care program. She was given a room with one adult and 50 children from three to seven years of age. In January 1907 in San Lorenza's tenement, the first Casa dei Bambini (Children's House) opened.

**Child at the Casa dei Bambini learning to write at the age of four years. (From J. Tozier's 1911 article "Educational Wonder-Worker: The Methods of Maria Montessori in *McClure's Magazine*.)**

> In the House of Childhood attention will be paid to the education, the health, and the physical and moral development of the children, by means of lessons and exercises adapted to their age.
>
> All children of the block between the ages of three and seven have the right of admission to the House of Childhood.
>
> The parents of children attending the House of Childhood pay no contribution whatever; but they assume the following imperative obligations:
>
> a) To send their children to the school-room at the specified hours, clean in person and clothes, and wearing a suitable pinafore;
>
> b) To show the greatest respect and deference toward the directress and staff of the House of Childhood, and to cooperate with the directress in promoting the education of the children. At least once a week mothers can speak to the directress, reporting their observations of their children at home, and receiving from the directress notes and suggestions for the good of the children.
>
> Pupils will be expelled from the House of Childhood
>
> a) Who present themselves in an unwashed and slovenly condition;
>
> b) Who are not amenable to discipline;
>
> c) Whose parents fail in respect to the persons in charge of the House of Childhood, or in any way threaten to counteract by bad conduct the aims and the educative work of the institution.
>
> In the assignment of annual prizes for the best-kept house, account will be taken of the way in which the parents have cooperated with the directress in the education of their children.
>
> **— Posted on each tenement block, included in J. Tozier's article "Educational Wonder Worker"**

The plan was to hire a person from the tenement to provide a better linkage for families. The school was owned communally by the parents and open from 9:00 a.m. – 5:00 p.m. in winter and 8:00 a.m. – 6:00 p.m. in summer to accommodate parents' working schedules:

> *"The idea of collective ownership is new and very beautiful and profoundly educational."*
>
> ***— The Montessori Method***

**At the Casa dei Bambini, the children are using various blocks and materials to learn mathematical concepts.***

**The child at the left is learning letters by tracing her hand over sandpaper letters. The middle two children are constructing words from cardboard letters, and the girl on the right is writing letters on paper.***

*** These photos are all taken from J. Tozier's 1911 article "Educational Wonder-Worker: The Methods of Maria Montessori: in *McClure's Magazine.***

**The children are learning shapes by feeling with their forefingers the edges of the figures and then the empty inset. The shapes would then be placed in the inset.***

**The children are learning shades of colour by seriating 8 colours in 8 shades from lightest to darkest. Coloured silk was fastened to wooden tablets.***

She wanted parents to leave their children with "easy minds" and believed that poor families deserved the same care for their children as rich families. A doctor at the school provided medical services to children who would otherwise have none.

Montessori brought materials she had previously developed for "defective" children, adapted them and continued to develop methods for their use. She was a researcher in the classroom, watching the children's reactions and modifying the approaches.

When the program began, the directress (teacher) handed out materials and collected them after the children were finished with them. Later, the children were allowed to select their own activities and put them away when they were done. Low open shelves allowed the children to easily access materials. Montessori also introduced child-sized tables and chairs.

Montessori found that the children wanted to help clean up and order their environment and that they were interested in the activities, not in rewards or external motivation. Children gained a sense of mastery through their work with the materials. A sense of order and quiet prevailed in the classroom as children worked on activities by themselves.

Montessori's sensory materials isolated one attribute (colour, size, shape, etc.) to assist children's learning about properties of materials and more abstract concepts. For example, a series of colour tablets or palettes varying only in shade would encourage seriation (ordering).

Practical life experiences such as buttoning, dusting, and so on were added to the program along with the didactic (self-correcting) materials. Personal hygiene, cleanliness and manners were integral parts of the day.

## Freedom

*How did Montessori see freedom in her program? How would you express the inclusion of freedom in your work with children?*

Freedom for Montessori had a meaning very different from the way it was understood by Rousseau or by A.S. Neill in his Summerhill School in England. Freedom meant making certain choices within clearly prescribed limits and in the collective interest. Her program was somewhat child-centred because children's nature and needs were starting points. But ultimately the teacher knew best and materials had to be used in prescribed ways. Montessori believed that children wasted their efforts and failed to achieve their potential if their environment was not highly organized.

Although she believed in an organized environment, Montessori also believed that the school must allow children to develop their knowledge and skills naturally; this was in stark contrast to the rigidity she saw in schools at that time. She did not look toward what children might need in the future or toward what wealthier children had. She focused on what children needed to fulfill their potential.

Punishment was not a part of the program except that the child could be denied an activity to do. In addition, in the Children's House pupils were expelled if they were not "amenable to discipline" (see full quote from the poster cited earlier):

> *"As for punishments, the soul of the normal man grows perfect through expanding, and punishment as commonly understood is always a form of repression."*
>
> — ***The Montessori Method***

Rewards were intrinsic to doing a task, and prizes were not given to children:

> *"He who accomplishes a truly human work, he who does something really great and victorious, is never spurred to his task by those trifling attractions called by the name of 'prizes', nor by the fear of those petty ills which we call 'punishments.' "*
>
> — ***The Montessori Method***

## Role of the Directress (Teacher)

The role of the directress was to

- prepare the environment ("keeper and custodian"),
- observe the child (Montessori once compared the directress to an astronomer gazing at the heavens, recording observations),
- show the child how to use the materials correctly through specific one-to-one demonstrations (fundamental lessons),
- leave the child to use the materials without interference.

The materials and things in the school, rather than the directress, would become the **real** teachers:

> *"We may liken the child to a clock, and may say that with the old time way it is very much as if we were to hold the wheels of the clock quiet and move the hands about the clock face with our fingers. The hands will continue to circle the dial just so long as we apply, through our fingers, the necessary motor force. Even so it is with that sort of culture which is limited to the work which the teacher does with the child. The new method, instead, may be compared to the process of winding, which sets the entire mechanism in motion. . . .*
>
> *Our educational aim with very young children must be to aid the spontaneous development of the mental, spiritual, and physical personality."*
>
> — ***The Montessori Method***

*What influence do Montessori programs have on the common current perception that childhood play does not have educational value?*

Montessori saw play as a poor substitute for work and believed that it undermined the dignity of childhood. She once described the Children's House as a "hive of bees humming as they work."

## The Program Evolves

Montessori's original program in the tenement was intended for young poor children but was later extended into programs for older children and children from middle and upper incomes. Reading and writing were taught with the same sensorial base used in the earlier experiences. For example, sandpaper letters to feel were part of learning the alphabet and reading. She wanted the learning to be easy and natural for the child.

Early in her career, Montessori had devoted followers who shared her mission. Visitors converged on the Casa dei Bambini. Soon similar schools were set up outside Rome, and in 1909 expanded outside Italy to Switzerland. Previously the orphanages and kindergartens in Switzerland had been modelled on Froebel's ideas but they converted to Montessori's methods.

Montessori wrote her ideas down in her book *The Montessori Method* in which she gave a full description of the method, materials and organization of the classroom. She believed the goal of education was to be in control of oneself, and this goal would be achieved through independence, self-discipline, concentration and motivation. The materials were developed to meet this goal.

The method was in strong contrast to the prevailing method of education full of group lessons and rote memorization. In Montessori programs, children were free to choose which activity they wanted to do. Boys and girls were treated the same, sharing equally in classroom tasks.

Many leaders in psychology, education and social services visited Montessori at the Casa dei Bambini including Arnold Gesell (child psychologist), William Heard Kilpatrick (educator/philosopher), G. Stanley Hall (psychologist) and Jane Addams (social work pioneer and founder of Hull House in Chicago). Articles by Montessori began to trickle into the United States. The first Montessori school in the U.S. was in Tarrytown, New York in 1911. Wealthy and cultured children attended it, their families pursuing what they believed to be the best education possible for their children.

## Promotion of Ideas and U.S. Tour

In 1910 Montessori began to devote her life to setting up schools, Montessori societies and teacher training programs. She saw herself as an apostle on a mission. She had given up both her academic and medical careers. The Montessori movement began to become big business with the use of her name and the development of the materials. Montessori surrounded herself with devotees who were more like disciples, working tirelessly under her inspiration.

McCLURE'S MAGAZINE

VOL. XXXVII MAY, 1911 No. 1

AN EDUCATIONAL WONDER-WORKER

THE METHODS OF MARIA MONTESSORI

BY

JOSEPHINE TOZIER

Many journals wrote of Montessori schools and her ideas but it wasn't until *McClure's Magazine* published a series of articles that the approach got wide coverage.[2] An influential journalist, S.S. McClure[3] commissioned writers to report on Montessori's methods. Josephine Tozier wrote one of the most descriptive articles in 1911 entitled "An Educational Wonder-Worker." McClure knew the articles would be controversial and would therefore sell well.

---

[2] *McClure's Magazine* was one of the muckraking magazines of the times, doing articles on real or alleged corruption on the part of business or politicians. Teddy Roosevelt used the word "muckraker" as he cited from *Pilgrim's Progress*, where a man stands with a hoe raking the muck and not looking up. Later people like Lincoln Steffens *(Shame of the Cities)* used the word with a more positive connotation.

[3] See Peter Lyon's biography *The Life and Times of S.S. McClure.*

**In 1911 *McClure's Magazine* published an article on Montessori's work which was subtitled, "The Italian Educator Who Has Originated A New and Remarkably Successful Method of Teaching Young Children." The article got wide coverage in North America and precipitated her lecture tour two years later. (From J. Tozier's 1911 article "Educational Wonder Worker: The Methods of Maria Montessori" *in McClure's Magazine.* )**

At the urging of McClure, who had a vision of a transformed U.S. primary educational system using Montessori's ideas, Maria Montessori came to the U.S. in 1913 for a speaking tour. The lecture tour was co-sponsored by McClure who retained rights for the use of her films in the lectures. McClure saw the tour and dissemination of her ideas and materials as moneymakers.

Montessori's first lecture on this tour was at Carnegie Hall in New York; the lecture was sold out and Montessori was introduced by John Dewey.

On her U.S. tour, Montessori gave many speeches on many topics. In one interview, she was asked whether women should work. She answered,

> *"In the continual social progress of the world women are more and more taking up different lines of work. Anything that tends to broaden the mother is of advantage to the child."*
>
> **— cited in Kramer, *Maria Montessori***

Montessori condemned the use of wet nurses for young children and declared a baby's right to his mother's milk as sacred. Her disapproval of wet nurses seems ironic as she had herself used one for her son.

Children's rights were a theme she championed strongly:

> *"What cowardliness to recognize the adult's rights and not those of the child! Shall we give justice only to those who can defend and protect themselves and in all else remain barbarians?"*
>
> **— "The Mother and the Child"**

Montessori was eloquent in her interviews and enunciated her lofty vision for education:

> *"My larger aim is the eventual perfection of the human race."*
>
> **— "Dr. Montessori's Aim," *The New York Times*, 1913**

*Should women work outside the home? Should they work only if it is an economic necessity for the family? Are there other motivations for women to work in terms of careers? Personal goals? This continues to be an issue that stirs emotion and controversy.*

Her first tour led her to Washington, D.C.; New York; Boston; Chicago and Philadelphia, where she met with Helen Keller. Keller, blind and deaf from the age of two, was taught by Anne Sullivan, under whose tutelage Keller rapidly learned and was eventually able to graduate from Radcliffe College with honours. Sullivan and Montessori had heard of each other, and during their emotional meeting they discussed the issue of change and whether the environment or the child was the start. Montessori's next book on her didactic materials, *A Montessori Handbook,* was dedicated to Helen Keller.

This U.S. tour represented the height of American interest in Montessori while she was alive.

After Montessori returned to Europe, McClure continued to promote her ideas through lectures and through showing her films. McClure exploited Montessori's work all for his own profit. She was appalled and rejected any further collaboration with McClure including his offer to build a Montessori Institute in America. But even with Montessori herself, the work had become more like a "commercial franchise" than a theory of education. Most educational theory was now developed within an academic context with refinement of ideas, testing, researching. The Montessori method had become more of a business with Montessori as the sole director and in total control. The mass media had assisted in the spread of her ideas.

In Montessori's mind, her ideas, methods and materials were more than a theory. They represented an approach to education and to the improvement of society and had to be maintained as she alone intended. She condemned the unauthorized use of her ideas, methods and materials.

Alexander Graham Bell, inventor of the first telephone and teacher of the deaf, and his wife, Mabel, became interested in the Montessori method. Bell became president of the American Montessori Association, the only recognized U.S. association among many non-sanctioned Montessori groups. Other early supporters of the Montessori approach were Dean Henry Holmes of Harvard's School of Education; the inventor Thomas Edison; Margaret Wilson, daughter of President Woodrow Wilson; and Dorothy Canfield Fisher, author of *The Squirrel Cage*, *Hillsboro People*, and *The Bent Twig*. Fisher had observed Montessori's classes at the Casa dei Bambini and wrote *A Montessori Mother* to help parents understand the Montessori method.

Montessori did return to the U.S. but not with any association with the Bells or McClure. Her next visit was under the sponsorship of the National Education Association and took her to the West Coast. This visit was more of a troubled time for her with monetary worries as well as concerns for finding new supporters for her theories. She returned for a few more visits but made her last U.S. journey in 1918.

## The Decline of Montessori in the U.S.

While she was alive, her U.S. following diminished with the concurrent rise of American educators including John Dewey and William Heard Kilpatrick and the rise of what became known as the progressive movement in education (see Chapter 7 for a discussion of the progressive movement). Montessori associations continued to splinter, a characteristic of the Montessori movement throughout its history. Part of the continuing problem seems to have been her unwillingness to see modifications to the method except as she would deem them necessary. As a "movement" her ideas were always directly associated with her. With John Dewey and others, their ideas fit into a larger framework of the progressive movement or progressive education. There was never a "Dewey Movement" or a "Dewey Method."

Why did the Montessori movement flounder in the U.S. after such initial enthusiasm? The reasons seem varied but relate to

- Montessori's autocratic hold on the purity of her method; Montessori did not trust others to carry on and interpret her work,
- dissension among Montessori associations,
- the fact that Montessori was a woman, foreigner and Catholic,
- lack of U.S. Montessori training facilities,

**Montessori in 1913. Montessori is working with a child and the "pink tower" to isolate the variable of size and learn seriation. (Photo used with permission of the Association Montessori Internationale.)**

- Montessori's unwillingness to incorporate new knowledge about child development from other theorists,
- the rise of the progressive movement in the U.S.

The voices of the dissenters in the progressive movement were powerful. William Heard Kilpatrick, from his post as a professor at Columbia University, denounced the Montessori approach in a book entitled *The Montessori System Examined*. He had visited her programs in Italy and criticized them soundly for their lack of opportunity for free play, social interaction, imagination, real life experience and sociodramatic play:

> *"The Montessori curriculum affords very inadequate expression to a very large portion of child nature."*
>
> *"In her scheme [autoeducation] is too intimately bound up with the manipulation of the didactic apparatus."*
>
> *"Madam Montessori's doctrine of sense-training is based on an outworn and cast-off psychological theory."*
>
> *"On the whole, the imagination, whether of constructive play or of the aesthetic sort, is but little utilized."*
>
> *"Her doctrine of education as unfolding is neither novel nor correct."*
>
> **— Kilpatrick, *The Montessori System Examined***

Patty Smith Hill (see chapter 9) was impressed with Montessori's work but was concerned that Montessori was

> *"wandering still farther afield from play and the nature and needs of young children. In the Montessori system imaginative play is not only not provided for, but frowned upon as a somewhat unfortunate pathological tendency of early childhood.*
>
> *Montessori underestimated the ability and desire of young children to work together, as well as separately."*
>
> **— quoted in Hill's Introduction to *Permanent Play Materials For Young Children* by Garrison**

*Do you think the criticisms of the Montessori program are valid?*

Since many Montessori programs still follow her ideas exactly today, these criticisms remain as relevant as when Kilpatrick and Hill wrote them in the early 1900's. Her personal magnetism seemed to create a closed system that ignored criticism and other ideas on education and child development.

The movement had a resurgence in the late 1950's when Nancy Rambusch opened a school in Connecticut and began promoting Montessori's ideas. The timing was right, as there was dissatisfaction with existing public education as well as Catholic parochial education. Rambusch's personal energy and commitment, the ability of European Montessori specialists to travel to the U.S. and the rise of television, which helped disseminate information, contributed to the revival. Maria Montessori appointed Rambusch as the U.S. representative of the Association Montessori Internationale. Montessori schools, training programs and associations remain strong as we enter the 21st century.

## Her Ideas Spread

Meanwhile in other parts of the world, Montessori schools spread and flourished. In Italy the school gained the support of Mussolini, Premier and the new head of government. Montessori's emphasis on order, control and creating a new social order from infancy seemed to appeal to the Fascist dictator. Mussolini saw the method as a means of mass education starting with infants. He had even been President of the Montessori Society in Italy in 1929.

During this period, concern was expressed about the use of her name in programs where people did not necessarily understand or use her ideas. George Bernard Shaw, Irish playwright and critic, foresaw a problem that exists today:

> *"If you are a distressed gentlewoman, starting to make a living, you can still open a little school; and you can easily buy a secondhand brass plate, inscribed Pestalozzian Institute, and nail it to your door, though you have no more idea who Pestalozzi was and what he advocated… . Or you can buy a cheaper plate, inscribed Kindergarten, and imagine, or leave others to imagine, that Froebel is the governing genius of your creche. No doubt the new brass plates are being inscribed Montessori Institute, and will be used when the Dottoressa [Montessori] is no longer with us."*
>
> **— written in *John O'London's Weekly* in 1928**
> **— cited in Kramer, *Maria Montessori***

As an adult, Montessori's son Mario became her constant companion and colleague. Maria and Mario co-founded the Association Montessori Internationale (AMI) to coordinate all official Montessori activities. Mario increasingly took over responsibility for the AMI. The AMI exists today as the official "pure" Montessori association. Mario soon became the prime spokesperson for his mother's ideas, though Maria continued to be active in lecturing and in training.

*Why do you think Montessori was so rigid in her approach? Why did she want to maintain total control? Do you see any dangers in this attitude?*

Anna Freud, daughter of Sigmund Freud and a pioneer in psychotherapy with children, met Montessori and was interested in many of her ideas. Montessori later received a letter from Sigmund Freud indicating his support for her initiatives:

> *"Since I have been preoccupied for years with the study of the child's psyche, I am in deep sympathy with your humanitarian and understanding endeavors, and my daughter who is an analytical pedagogue, considers herself one of your disciples."*
>
> ***— Letters of Sigmund Freud***

Jean Piaget was also interested in Montessori's ideas and was head of the Swiss Montessori Society. He had done many of his child observations in a Montessori school and was impressed with her ideas on "sensitive periods" and the need for a stimulating environment for children.

Montessori's ideas were ahead of her time, but she failed to keep up with other thinkers in the field of psychology and education. Not only were the sense and the intellect important but so were feelings, the unconscious and fantasy, all of which had no part in Montessori's programs. She maintained a closed system: others learned from her but she remained static in her own sphere of learning.

Politics began to affect the Montessori movement as Hitler gained increasing power in Europe. When Austria was annexed in 1938, all Montessori schools were closed. In Italy the Fascist movement began to penetrate the schools with youth required to wear their army uniforms in

**Montessori 1933. This was taken in Amsterdam which became the headquarters of the Association Montessori Internationale. (Photo used with permission of the Association Montessori Internationale.)**

school. Teachers had to take an oath of allegiance to the Fascists. Montessori saw herself as an apolitical person but reacted when her work as a teacher and teacher educator was affected.

## World War II and Beyond

Montessori temporarily moved to England in 1936. She had become an exile from both Spain and Italy because of the widening influence of the Fascists. Amsterdam had become the headquarters of the AMI, and from there Montessori continued to lecture on the importance of the early years in the formation of character.

In 1939, at the age of 69 years, Montessori went to India to organize a training program in Madras. She was welcomed with a flood of positive reactions. But when the Italians joined forces with the Germans in 1940, the British interned any Italians who were in British colonies, seeing them as alien enemies. Both Maria and her son Mario were interned in India, though Maria for a much briefer period. However the Viceroy, the governor of India, gave her son's freedom as a birthday present to Maria. When Mario was released, Montessori was 70 years of age, and it was the first public written acknowledgement that he was her son.

The two continued to lecture and train teachers in India for the rest of the war. Montessori was known personally by Indian leaders such as Mahatma Gandhi and Jawaharlal Nehru. During this period, Montessori began to study infants, as babies in extended families surrounded her. *The Absorbent Mind* was produced in this period. She was extremely critical of the western practice of separating infants at birth for medical procedures rather than giving them immediately to their mothers to breast-feed.

*Montessori saw herself as non-political. Do you think you can be non-political in the field of early childhood? What impact does politics have on your work with children and families?*

After the war, Montessori returned with Mario to Holland and they were reunited with Mario's children who had spent the war there. Maria continued to travel, lecturing and training. A plan was formulated to set up a Montessori university in Madras, but the partition of India and Pakistan prevented this. Mario remarried, and his wife Ada joined the Montessori family team. From 1947 – 1949 Maria Montessori trained teachers in both India and Pakistan and was nominated for the Nobel Peace Prize three years in a row (1949 – 51). She continued to believe that the solution to world problems would be found in her method and materials. Montessori died of a cerebral hemorrhage in 1952, just before her 82nd birthday. She was buried in a cemetery near the Hague. Mario inherited not only her possessions but the rights to the continuation of the Montessori Method.

## Enduring Montessori Program Elements

### Respect for the Child

Above all, Montessori believed childhood must be respected and that each child must be treated as an individual. Children must be seen as distinctly different from adults. Her demonstration with the adult and child skeletons was an example of how she tried to convince others of this principle. She believed that adults often could not separate their needs and goals from those that were appropriate to a specific child. If children were respected, they would grow into adults who would respect others.

Montessori had a deep respect for childhood. In 1951 she presented a chart showing stages (planes) of development and society's educational system to support these stages. In between the two streams, she drew an X which means "the unknown." She felt that much of childhood still remained unknown and must be honoured.

### Sensitive Periods and Absorbent Mind

*How do the ideas of "sensitive periods" and the "absorbent mind" concur with current beliefs about children's development?*

Montessori saw children as having "sensitive periods," windows of opportunity for growth. Education must respond to these sensitive periods if learning was to proceed easily. These sensitive periods involved sensitivity to language, to order, and to moving in the environment. The teacher's role in knowing the stage was critical here, and observation would be the key skill used to identify these periods. Montessori felt that once the period passed, the child would never again have that stage with such intensity. We might now call this concept readiness.

The sensitive period for language was from birth through three years in which children rapidly absorbed, comprehended, reproduced and understood the language (or languages) of their environment.

Montessori felt that the sensitive period for imagination was between six and 12 years of age. This may explain in part why fantasy and sociodramatic role-play are not seen in Montessori practice with young children. She felt children could learn "grown up" skills in the practical life area and would be involved in some role-play. The children would also dress up in clothes from different geographic locations to imagine living in these climates. Imagination would develop in these more realistic ways. In her staunch adherence to these beliefs, Montessori overlooked the fantasy capabilities of young children.

The greatest potential for learning was in early childhood, from birth to six years of age. It was when the child had an "absorbent mind," ready to acquire a tremendous amount of learning.

## Prepared Environment

The "prepared environment" was critical for responding to the sensitive periods and absorbent mind. The goal of the prepared environment was to make the child independent from the adult in whatever setting, whether it was in the home or classroom. The atmosphere created would enable the child to learn in a peaceful and orderly fashion with surroundings adapted to the child's size and interests. Materials were carefully selected and organized for the children. Child-sized furniture, materials stored in specific and organized ways, low chalkboards, small individual floor rugs allowed the child to work independently. Clutter was seen as a distraction for both children and adults. Children could choose which activity they wanted to do as long as the teacher demonstrated the correct way to use the materials. The child took out the activity and had to put it back in exactly the same way it was found. Typically each classroom had only one of each kind of material. A child had to learn to wait for the activity if another child was using it.

## Didactic Materials/Auto-Education — Children Working on Their Own

**Sensory Learning. The child on the left is learning the words "smooth" and "rough" by feeling cardboard and sandpaper. The boy in the middle is learning shapes by putting them into pre-cut inserts without his sense of sight. The girl on the right is also blindfolded as she distinguishes different textures. (From J. Tozier's 1911 article "Educational Wonder-Worker: The Methods of Maria Montessori" in *McClure's Magazine*.)**

Montessori believed that children learned best from the materials and activities they chose. Each of these was self-correcting and graded according to difficulty. The teacher did not need to be present to tell the child if the answer or solution was correct. The materials would "tell" the child as the child interacted with the materials. The materials were labeled "didactic" as they were designed to teach. Montessori called this a "control of error" which allowed the child to increasingly become an independent worker.

The cylinder block used in Montessori classrooms is an example of a self-correcting material. In it there are holes of varying depths, and each hole has a corresponding cylinder that fits it exactly. When all the cylinders are removed, the child must find the correct hole for each cylinder:

> *"If he mistakes, placing one of the objects in an opening that is too small for it, he takes it away, and proceeds to make trial, seeking the proper opening. If he makes a contrary error, letting the cylinder fall into an opening that is a little too large for it, and then collects all the successive cylinders in openings just a little too large, he will find himself at the last with the big cylinder in his hand while only the smallest opening is empty. The didactic material controls every error. The child proceeds to correct himself."*
>
> — ***The Montessori Method***

Later the child would be introduced to a set of ten red cylinders of varying thickness but without the pre-set holes.

*What is your opinion of didactic materials such as the "pink tower"?*

Another example of self-correcting materials is the pink tower of graduated cubes, which could be built upright or laid flat, but worked only if the cubes were in the correct sequence. The goal was to put the ten cubes from 1 $cm^3$ to 10 $cm^3$ in a sequence from smallest to biggest.

Montessori recognized the power of repetitive behaviour in emerging mental ability and intelligence.

> *"I watched the child intently without disturbing her at first, and began to count how many times she repeated the exercise; then, seeing that she was continuing for a long time, I picked up the little arm chair in which she was seated and placed chair and child upon table; the little creature hastily caught up her case of insets, laid it across the arms of the chair and gathering the cylinders into her lap, set to work again. Then I called upon the children to sing; they sang, but the little girl continued undisturbed, repeating her exercise even after the short song had come to an end. I counted forty-four repetitions; when at last she ceased, it was quite independently of any surrounding stimuli which might have distracted her, and she looked around with a satisfied air, almost as if awakening from a refreshing nap."*
>
> — ***Spontaneous Activity in Education***

### Mixed Aged Grouping

Children were not age separated, because Montessori believed that children learned from each other and could help each other. The older children acted as role models for the younger children. Mixed aged grouping also allowed for the breadth of development within any age grouping and developmental area. Often the teacher stayed with the children for several years providing consistency, continuity and improved learning.

### Self-Paced Activities

Children could learn at their own rates. They would not be held back from reading if they were ready to acquire the needed skills. The teacher would observe each child to determine whether the child needed more practice with skills or was ready to move on to a higher level.

## The Three Areas of Child Involvement

### 1. Practical Life

Montessori developed activities of daily living which involved simple practical life activities with long-term, complex goals. These were experiences to help a child become a member of the human society. Learning about the different order in their own lives, self control, independent work habits, coordination of movement, responsibility, and so on would assist with domestic life. The teacher would develop most of these materials but there were some manufactured products such as child-sized brooms, brass to polish, and dressing frames.

These activities had precise and exact methods of execution. For example, dusting would begin with a close look, at eye level, on the surface of the table. The front half of the table would be the first area dusted and then the back half. The dust would be wiped away from the body, using circular movements and going from one side to the other. The edges of the table would be done next and then the legs and finally the table's underside. After finishing, the duster would be shaken out into a waste basket (or outside in good weather).

The practical life activities were divided into four areas:

- **care of the environment**

  *pouring* such things as water and beans

  *transferring* — sequence of spooning activities, use of tongs, basters, tweezers, eyedroppers

  *cleaning and polishing* — wood and metal, from dishes to tables, dusting; clothes washing would be a more complex task

  *raking leaves; shining leaves on plants*

- **care of self or the person**

  *dressing frames* — hardwood frames with cloth attached on the sides; various attachments allow the child to practice buttoning, bow tying, lacing, hook and eye joining, safety pinning, snapping, zipping, buckling, shoe buttoning, shoe lacing

  *grooming and cleanliness* — from hand washing to tooth brushing and nose blowing

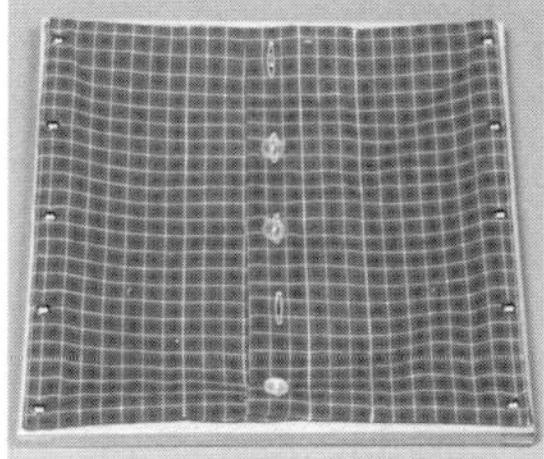

**Buttoning Frame. As part of practical life experiences, children practiced buttoning, lacing, zipping, etc. on dressing frames. (From the personal collection of Jennifer Wolfe. Photo by Kitty Ng.)**

- **life skills**

  *fastening* (jars with lids, nuts and bolts, lock and keys)

  *cooking*

  *sorting*

  *bead stringing*

  *sewing*

- **grace and courtesy**

  *laying out* tablecloth and setting table

  *walking* on a line

  *offering* a cup of juice

  *opening* a door quietly

  *knowing* what to say if you bump into someone.

## 2. Sensorial Materials

(also called Materialized Abstractions, Keys to the Universe, Paths to Culture)

*Montessori used pre-cut shapes and inserts to teach the concept of shape. How do you help children learn about shapes?*

These materials built on children's own spontaneous activities to sort and to order objects, allowing children to do these tasks in an organized fashion. These materials isolated one quality or attribute at a time, provided sensory stimulation to sharpen skills of perception and progressed from simple to complex. They allowed children to learn abstract concepts from concrete materials and to work independently and learn from their mistakes. Materials were consistent in appearance, attractive and manufactured according to Montessori's specifications. The child's errors were controlled as the materials "showed" the mistakes; a tower, for example, would not stand solidly if it were not assembled properly. Some examples include:

**Pink Tower. Sensorial materials isolate one attribute at a time. The pink tower has graduated sizes of pink cubes to help children learn to seriate. (From the personal collection of Jennifer Wolfe. Photo by Kitty Ng.)**

- cylinder blocks — knobbed wood cylinders in graduated sizes that fit into a frame,
- pink tower — pink cubes in graduated sizes from 1 $cm^3$ to 10 $cm^3$ that were stacked from biggest to smallest,
- colour tablets — painted wood rectangles with plastic handles for sorting and seriation,
- fabric box — fabrics of different textures to match,
- pressure cylinders — spring loaded plungers in wood cylinders for the child to sense the differing resistance.

## 3. Academic (language, writing, reading, mathematics) Materials

Montessori identified four stages of language work in early childhood:

- *oral/auditory level* — stories, fingerplays, songs, poems, naming activities
- *mechanical level* — equipment like sandpaper letters and metal insets of shapes, double sandpaper letters for phonics, movable alphabet letters
- *word reading level* — object boxes with common phonetic sounds, dictation games
- *sentence reading level* — definitions, small books, interpretive reading like charades, early grammar, dictionary work.

The mathematics materials focused on addition, subtraction, multiplication and division. Activities were based on materials such as number rods, sandpaper numerals, golden beads (small beads representing single, ten, hundred and thousand units), bead frames, cubes for learning powers, and so on.

All the academic materials were based on skills learned with Practical Life and Sensorial Materials.

## 4. Cultural Materials

This area included the arts, sciences and social sciences.

## Montessori Resources

There are many associations, training programs, periodicals, and societies related to Montessori's ideas, but the Montessori name is sometimes used without regulation or accreditation. The name itself does not specify the nature of the program or its association with Montessori's ideas.

### Professional Associations

Two main Montessori professional associations are:

The Montessori name is used without restriction; a close scrutiny of any program is necessary to assess how close it is to a pure Montessori model. The array of fragmented Montessori program models has also hindered standardized research.

***Association Montessori Internationale (AMI)*** — This association was established in 1929 by Maria and Mario. It represents the pure, orthodox interpretation of Montessori's ideas, and programs are identical the world around.

Association Montessori Internationale
Koninginneweg 161
1075 CN Amsterdam
The Netherlands

***Association Montessori Internationale — U.S. Branch***
410 Alexander Street
Rochester, New York 14607
U.S.A.
http://www.montessori-ami.org

*The Montessori Promise* is a video available from the AMI/USA and is a clear portrayal of the Montessori Method, including archival footage.

***American Montessori Society (AMS)*** — This society, founded by Nancy Rambusch in 1960, acknowledges some of the new developments in psychology and integrates them into Montessori programs within an American cultural context.

American Montessori Society
281 Park Ave. South, 6th Floor
New York, New York 10010-6102
U.S.A.
www.amshq.org

The AMS produces an informational video entitled *Nurturing the Love of Learning: The Montessori Method,* available from:

Educational Video Publishing
401 South High Street
Yellow Springs, Ohio 45387
U.S.A.

Website: http://www.edvid.com

## Teacher Training

Montessori training programs exist around the world, and information can be obtained from both Montessori Associations. For most types of training a four-year bachelor's degree is a prerequisite for entrance.

Information on training, videos and books can also be obtained from:

**North American Montessori Teachers Association (NAMTA)**
13693 Butternut Road
Burton, Ohio 44021
U.S.A.
Website: http://www.montessori-namta.org/

*How have Montessori materials influenced early childhood programs that you are familiar with?*

NAMTA produces an introductory video on the Montessori method called *Is Montessori For Me?*

## Montessori Equipment

Nienhuis Montessori Canada
75 Watline Ave. Unit 101
Mississauga, Ontario L4Z 3E5
Canada

Nienhuis Montessori USA
320 Pioneer Way
Mountain View, California 94041-1576
U.S.A.

Website: http://nienhuis.com

*Special Collection*
*J. Robert Charette Montessori Memorial Collection*
*Leddy Library*
*University of Windsor*
*Windsor, Ontario*
*N9B 3P4*
*Canada*

## Maria Montessori — References for Further Study


Appelbaum, P. (1971). *The growth of the Montessori movement.* Unpublished doctoral dissertation, New York University, New York.

Barnett, W. S. (1985). *The Perry Preschool Program and its long-term effects: A benefit-cost analysis.* High/Scope Early Childhood Policy Papers (No. 2). Ypsilanti, MI: High/Scope Press.

Barnett, W. S. (1992). Benefits of compensatory preschool education. *Journal of Human Resources, 27* (2), 279-312.

Beyer, E. (1962, November). Let's look at Montessori. *Journal of Nursery Education,* 4-9.

Chattin-McNichols, J. (1992). *The Montessori controversy.* Albany, NY: Delmar.

Cleveland, G., & Krashinsky, M. (1998). *The benefits and costs of good child care: The economic rationale for public investment in young children.* Toronto, Canada: University of Toronto.

Cohen, S. (1968). Educating the children of urban poor. *Education and Urban Society, 1,* 61-79.

Cohen, S. (1969). Maria Montessori: Priestess or Pedagogue? *Teachers College Record, 71* (2), 313-326.

Dr. Montessori's aim. (1913, December 9). *New York Times.*

Fisher, D. C. (1917). *A Montessori mother.* New York: Holt, Rinehart & Winston, Inc.

Freud, E. (Ed.). (1960). *Letters of Sigmund Freud.* New York: Basic Books.

Grazzini, C. (1996). Four planes of development. *NAMTA Journal, 21* (2), 208-241.

Hainstock, E. (1968). *Teaching Montessori in the home.* New York: Random House.

Hainstock, E. (1986). *The essential Montessori.* New York: New American Library.

Hill, P. S. (1926). Introduction to *Permanent play materials for young children* by C. Garrison. New York: Charles Scribners & Sons.

Humphryes, J. (1998, July). The developmental appropriateness of high quality Montessori programs. *Young Children, 53* (4), 4-16.

Johnson, R. (1987). *Approaches to early childhood education.* Columbus, OH: Merrill.

Kilpatrick, W. H. (1913, Autumn). Montessori and Froebel. *Kindergarten Review, 2,* 491-496.

Kilpatrick, W. H. (1914). *The Montessori system examined.* Boston: Houghton Mifflin.

Kramer, R. (1988). *Maria Montessori: A biography.* Reading, MA: Addison-Wesley Pub. Co.

Lascarides, V.C. & Hinitz, B. (2000). *History of Early Childhood Education.* New York: Falmer Press.

Lillard, P. P. (1996). *Montessori today: A comprehensive approach to education from birth to adulthood.* New York: Schocken Books.

Lyon, P. (1963). *The life and times of S. S. McClure.* New York: Charles Scribner's Sons.

Merz, C. (1916, August 26). Montessori for president. *New Republic, VIII* (95), 89-91.

Montessori, M. (1913). *Pedagogical Anthropology.* (F. T. Cooper, Trans.) New York: FA Stokes.

Montessori, M. (1917). *The advanced Montessori method. V. 1 Spontaneous activity in education* (F. Simmonds, Trans.) *V.2 The Montessori elementary material* ( A. Livingston, Trans.). New York: Frederick A. Stokes Co.

Montessori, M. (1964). *Spontaneous activity in education.* Cambridge, MA: Robert Bentley Inc.

Montessori, M. (1964). *The Montessori method.* New York: Schocken Books.

Montessori, M. (1965). *A Montessori handbook: Dr. Montessori's own handbook.* New York: Putnam.

Montessori, M. (1965). *Spontaneous activity in education.* New York: Schocken Books.

Montessori, M. (1966). *The secret of childhood.* Notre Dame, IN: Fides Publishers.

Montessori, M. (1967). *The discovery of the child.* Mattituck, NY: Amereon House.

Montessori, M. (1995). *The absorbent mind.* New York: Henry Holt.

Montessori, M. (1995). The mother and the child. *NAMTA Journal, 20* (3), 29-41. (Original work published 1915)

Montessori, Mario (1966). *The human tendencies and Montessori education.* Amsterdam, Netherlands: Association Montessori Internationale.

Montessori, Mario. (1976). *Education for human development.* (P. P. Lillard Ed). New York: Schocken Books

Mooney, C. (2000).*Theories of childhood: An introduction to Dewey, Montessori, Erikson, Piaget & Vygotsky.* St. Paul, MN: Redleaf Press.

Murray, E. R. (n.d.). *A story of infant schools and kindergartens.* London: Sir Isaac Pitman & Sons.

Myers, K. (1913, May 15). Seguin's principles of education as related to the Montessori method. *Journal of Education, 77,* 538-541.

Orem, R. C. (Ed). (1971). *Montessori today.* New York: Putnam.

Peltzman, B. R. (1998). *Pioneers of early childhood education: A bio-bibliographical guide.* Westport, CT: Greenwood Press.

Pitcher, E. (1966). An evaluation of the Montessori method. *Childhood Education, 42* (8), 189-192.

Prochner, L. & Howe, N. (2000). *Early childhood education and care in Canada.* Vancouver: UBC Press.

Publications Committee of the National Association for the Education of Young Children. (1966). *Montessori in perspective.* Washington, DC: National Association for the Education of Young Children.

Sheehan, J. E. (Sister Marie Chaminade Sheehan). (1969). *A comparison of the theories of Maria Montessori and Jean Piaget in relation to the bases of curriculum, methodology, and the role of the teacher.* Doctoral Dissertation, St. John's University, New York.

Standing, E. M. (1957). *Maria Montessori: Her life and work.* Fresno, CA: Academy Library Guild.

Tenenbaum, S. (1951). *William Heard Kilpatrick.* New York: Harper & Brothers.

Tozier, J. (1911). Educational wonder-worker: The methods of Maria Montessori. *McClure's Magazine, 37* (1), 3-19.

Weber, E. (1969). *The kindergarten: Its encounter with educational thought in America.* New York: Teachers College Press.

# Chapter 9 — *Patty Smith Hill*

**1868 – 1946**

*"In a true democracy the rights of all levels of maturity should be equally respected and protected, irrespective of sex, race, creed, or class, with no favoritism or prejudice. The right to grow is a righteous demand whether made for the child four to six, six to twelve or eighteen to twenty."*

*"There should be a national convocation of nursery school, kindergarten, and primary teachers, leaders in the fields of household economics, child welfare, nutrition, pediatrics and parent education to draw up a five-year plan for an annual increase in the care of young children."*

**— "The Kindergarten Child in the New Deal"**

*"There are two great divisions of teachers, you know: cookbook teachers and checkerboard teachers. A cookbook teacher sits down in the evening, measures out so much arithmetic, so much spelling, so much music, according to a pedagogical recipe and next day spoonfeeds it into his pupils. He calls the process education. But suppose he were getting ready for a game of chess or checkers. Would it do any good to take the board the evening before and figure out the campaign — first this move, then that move? When he sat down with his opponents he would find that the vital factor had been entirely omitted from his calculations: the reaction of the other mind. Of course cookbook teaching is easier. But the other kind — well, from the child's point of view the other kind offers possibilities of real adventure."*

**— from an interview with Hill in Amidon, "Forty Years in Kindergarten"**

*"... those who have the care and training of the preschool period must have the best professional preparation possible to secure."*

*" Growth, then, is the birthright of all levels, and arrested development a crime at any period, for it not only mars the particular period but all later periods."*

**— "Preschool Education as a Career"**

## Early Life in "The Gateway City to the South"

As with all the historical figures discussed in this book, Patty Smith Hill's ideas developed from her own life experiences:

> *"If I am to talk to you about my work and the changes in education with which I have been associated, I must start by talking to you about my mother and father and the wonderful home in which I grew up. My wish to work and my ability to work I trace back to the childhood."*
>
> **— from an interview with Hill in Amidon, "Forty Years in Kindergarten"**

Hill reflected that her vision of education expanded throughout her life from being child-centred to family-centred and finally community-centred. The ideal would encompass all three interacting with each other.

Patty Smith Hill began her journey near Louisville, Kentucky. She was born on March 27, 1868 in what came to be known as the Reconstruction South after the Civil War. She had two unique parents who both influenced her childhood and later life. Her father, William, was a minister who had obtained a doctorate in theology from Princeton University in 1838. During the time of his early ministry he endured multiple tragedies when his infant twins and then his wife died. After his second marriage to Martha Jane Smith in 1858, he edited a journal called *The Presbyterian Herald*. Its distribution became impossible when the Civil War disrupted the mail service, and it ceased publication.

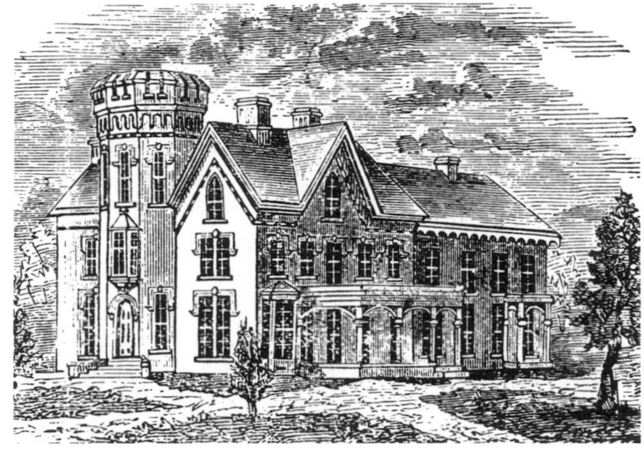

**Patty Smith Hill's father, William, established and ran the Bellewood Female Seminary. He wanted to provide a strong education for girls and young women in the southern United States. Patty spent the first six years of her life here. (Used with permission of The Filson Club Historical Society, Louisville, Kentucky.)**

Using his own finances, he then began a school for girls called Bellewood Female Seminary in Anchorage, Kentucky, a half-hour train ride from Louisville. Hill believed strongly in the education of girls and women. He offered students courses that others at the time considered unsuitable for "young ladies" — geology, logic, mathematics, astronomy, and philosophy. The school flourished as an education advantage for girls from the South.

Patty Smith Hill later described him as a man who understood young people, giving them "wise freedom."

Patty Smith Hill remembered that her father

> *"believed that every girl should grow up with a profession. This was a radical idea everywhere [in the 1880's] particularly in the South. My father had a horror of girls 'marrying for a home,' and he felt that the only way to avoid this catastrophe was to prepare every young woman to 'stand on her own feet' economically. For this reason from our earliest years sisters and brothers alike discussed together and with our parents the type of work we wished to pursue when we were grown."*
>
> **— from an interview with Hill in Amidon, "Forty Years in Kindergarten"**

Patty Smith Hill's mother, Martha Jane Smith, wanted her children to grow up with all the advantages she had not had, but she did not mean monetary benefits. She wanted her children to be both happy and responsible without the cloud of discipline ruling their lives. Martha's own parents had died very early in her life, and an extremely rigid and authoritarian aunt and uncle had raised her. Growing up on a plantation in Danville, Kentucky, she demonstrated her already progressive ideas in secretly teaching the slaves to read, write and calculate. The laws in the South prohibited teaching slaves. Martha had tried to attend Centre

College but had been refused admission because she was female. She, along with the two daughters of the College president, did obtain private tutoring from some professors, but she was denied a formal degree.

*Hill's early upbringing had a strong impact on her views of women, play and other issues in the field of early childhood education. How have your early childhood experiences affected your career, views of children, etc?*

Play was central to the upbringing of Martha's own six children (Mildred, Mary, Wallace, Patty, Archibald, and Jessica). She encouraged them to think independently, to play outdoors as much as possible and to enjoy their childhood. Blocks, empty barrels and bricks were all provided as play objects. She created a "knock shop" (carpentry shop), and the children had a well-equipped playroom to encourage their creativity and imagination without the constraints of adult interference. The children had farm animals (a "peck house"[1] with chickens) and gardens and spent long hours in the woods and fields. Martha had a musical and literary flare and created songs for even the most mundane tasks and chores. A red flag was raised to tell the children when it was time to come in from play. Hill had vivid memories of these "play spaces" and the uninterrupted time she had to explore. Martha and William discussed the pros and cons of using fairy tales with their children and decided that they would use fairy tales but would ensure the children knew they were make believe in the same way that Santa Claus was make believe.

**Patty Smith Hill recorded her childhood memories in handwriting. (Used with permission of the Filson Club in Louisville.)**

Hill's Memories of Her Childhood

"Mother playful with children — made rhymes for disagreeable tasks — Down in the water, down, down, down."

"[Mother] highly approved of play when the world around her called it a dangerous evidence of original sin."

"Boards, empty barrels, bricks provided for building playhouses, brick stoves to cook, roast apples, etc."

"An unhappy childhood of her own [speaking of her mother] made her a great believer in happiness for children."

"Early memories of his [her father's] questions of daughters and sons — What do you want to do for the world when grownup?"

**— from handwritten notes of Patty Smith Hill, in the Filson Club Archives, Louisville, Kentucky**

[1] Both the "peck house" and "knock shop" were name creations of Patty Smith Hill who used words creatively to represent her sense impressions.

**Off to School. Patty Smith Hill (on right) at about age 12 with her younger sister (likely Jessica) at age 6 starting school. (Used with permission of the ACEI and the ACEI Archives, Special Collections, University of Maryland.)**

Early in her life Patty Smith Hill knew that she wanted to work with children who had less happy lives than she had. Her original aim from age eight was to work with orphans. She knew that her childhood was unusual for the time. Around her, children were being shaped into what adults wanted them to be. She saw severe discipline, rote learning and inactivity as the "slogans" of schools. Child labour, malnutrition, and high child poverty and death rates surrounded and profoundly affected her.
When she was 14, she spent the summer providing baby care for a family with a large number of children.

In 1874, when Patty was six, her father became president of Fulton Synodical Female College. The family settled into a new home in Missouri, and Martha created new play spaces for the children. Mary edited a family newsletter called "The Morning Dewdrop," and Patty became the poet. William planned to make Fulton Synodical Female College a leader in women's education and a cultural centre for the area. However, William became seriously ill with eye and heart problems, and the family moved to Sherman, Texas for his health. Here he planned to set up a new college for young men, but he suffered a minor stroke and could not continue working. He died soon afterwards in 1878, and most of the family contracted typhoid. Patty remained bedridden for six months and also sustained an attack of spinal meningitis. The family returned to Louisville extremely ill and in dire poverty. Even the family cow, "Thanky," was sold to pay off debts, and Martha took in lodgers.

*Patty Smith Hill knew very early in her life that she wanted to work with children. How did you choose this career?*

Receiving a small legacy from her grandfather, Patty Smith Hill was able to go to the newly opened Louisville Collegiate Institute (high school) where she received a solid classical education and graduated at the age of 18.

**Patty Smith Hill in 1886 at the age of 18 with her friend Mary Weller (on the right). (Used with permission of the ACEI and the ACEI Archives, Special Collections, University of Maryland.)**

## Kindergarten Training

At that time, the kindergarten movement was developing in the United States. The child was seen as a symbol of hope for the future, and the kindergarten was central to this hope. Louisville had become a big city and was experiencing all the problems of rapid urban growth.

Kindergartens were seen as a way to change the future. It was believed that kindergarten would be an educational remedy for urban poverty and a source of positive family changes through parent education. Anna E. Bryan, a proponent of kindergartens, had gone to the Chicago Free Kindergarten Association to learn how to train kindergarten teachers. Modifying some of Froebel's more rigid ideas, Bryan started a training program in Louisville. The program, a two-year course combining theory and practice, opened in September 1887 in the Holcombe Mission. On August 11, 1887 *The Louisville Courier-Journal* announced the following:

### A Free Kindergarten

Miss Bryan returns to her Kentucky Home to Instruct Poor Children

She Will Also Train Young Ladies for Teaching Methods of the Celebrated System

The article went on to describe the nature of Bryan's program:

> *"Connected with the kindergarten will be a training class for young ladies who wish to prepare themselves for this work. There will be two lessons each week for the training class, which will also be free, the members of the class giving their services during a portion of the day as teachers. The kindergarten is evolved from the principle that an ounce of prevention is better than a pound of cure. An impression prevails among those who do not understand the work, that it does not require much training to play with children, but experience shows that it requires infinite tact and more training than is necessary for children who are old enough to go into school."*

In a later essay on Anna Bryan in *Pioneers of the Kindergarten in America* by the Committee of Nineteen of the International Kindergarten Union,[2] Hill describes a visit she and her mother made to Anna Bryan after reading the article in the paper. Both were impressed with Bryan and invited her to their house for dinner:

> *"… an invitation was given to dinner in my home, as no move was made in the life-work of any one member of the family without appealing to the judgment of the whole. Before the end of the evening there was no question in the minds of all those who had had the opportunity of meeting*

---

[2] The Committee of Nineteen was formed in 1904 to develop contemporary kindergarten thought and consisted of people from varying kindergarten orientations. The nature of play was one of the key issues in dispute. It is noteworthy that the Committee of Nineteen unanimously disagreed with Montessori's stress on pre-writing and pre-reading in place of play and imagination.

> *Miss Bryan that it was going to be a rare opportunity to place a member of the family in her care and training."*

Patty Smith Hill became one of Bryan's first five students and the youngest at the Louisville Training School. Bryan encouraged her students to question instead of blindly following the ideas of Froebel. Hill recalled that she "set a standard for liberty of thought." Bryan inspired Hill in her own quest to encourage children's growth.

At her graduation ceremony, Hill read a paper she had written on her philosophy of play that included the following thoughts:

> *"Play is universal."*
>
> *"In order to develop itself, childhood is given this instinct to almost ceaseless activity...life seeking activity through action...is the law of growth."*
>
> **— quoted in Fowlkes, "Gifts from Childhood: Godmother Patty Smith Hill."**

**Patty Smith Hill in about 1890. (Used with permission of the *Louisville Courier-Journal*, Louisville, Kentucky.)**

The paper also included a quotation from the poet Johann Schiller: "Deep meaning lies in childish play." These words were to hallmark Hill's future career.

Hill finished the program at the Louisville Training School for Kindergartners in 1889 at the age of 21. She immediately began a demonstration kindergarten for the training program. Hill soon surpassed the experimentation of her own teacher, taking the Froebel blocks and creating projects with them. She encouraged children to use other constructive materials (blocks, clay, coloured pencils and paper) to express themselves. Children were to be trusted with their own purposes in play. Hill's own strong sense of play as a way to learn was embedded in her from her own childhood and the influence of her parents.

In 1890, Bryan and Hill travelled together to the annual meeting of the National Education Association, where they presented a talk called "The Letter Killeth," condemning the prevalent rigid approach to teaching drawing as well as the rigid usage of Froebel materials. While Bryan lectured, Hill showed charts of children's creative work based on their interests and purposes.

**Hill's first kindergarten was in the Holcombe Mission, Jefferson Street, Louisville, Kentucky. This photo was taken sometime between 1890 – 1893. Hill is likely the person on the right. Note the use of the piano in circle time. (Used with permission of the ACEI and the ACEI Archives, Special Collections, University of Maryland.)**

John Dewey was impressed with her work and encouraged Patty and one of her sisters, Mary Hill, to write a series of monthly articles in the *Kindergarten Magazine*. The series was entitled "Typical Lessons for Mothers and Kindergartners" and ran from September 1890 to June 1891. These lessons show a basis in Froebel methodology and materials but are far broader and diverge from his approaches. One article looks at "fruit," starting with literal fruits (apples, oranges) and moving into the more biological definition of fruit for reproduction of plants. Songs and activities develop the concepts as the children explore the more abstract "fruit" of labour (wool, butter, honey, etc.).

In the summer of 1890 Hill also studied with Francis Parker at the Cook County Normal School in Chicago, one of the leading centres for change in education. Parker later visited Hill and her kindergarten programs in Louisville. He was among the 30,000 visitors in one year.

Hill became the director of the Louisville Free Kindergarten Association and continued her studies to learn more about development and play. Hill supervised nine kindergartens and oversaw teacher training, a program for Sunday school teachers, a nursing department, as well as parent and community programs. She was a leader developing emerging leaders. School directors were given ideas to consider but were also encouraged to try strategies in their own schools. Later sessions would review their efforts and results. She encouraged prospective teachers to be independent so they would not rely on the ideas and methods of others. In 1893 John Dewey visited Hill in Louisville, which had become a mecca for the training of kindergarten teachers and a centre of the new kindergarten movement. Hill also gave a workshop at the 1893 Chicago World's Fair, and 3,000 teachers attended.

**A Meeting of Minds. In 1909 G.S. Hall, President of Clark University, brought the leading thinkers of psychology to the United States for a series of lectures. G.S. Hall is in the front middle. To the left of him is Sigmund Freud (founder of psychoanalysis) and to the right is Carl Jung (founder of the analytical school of psychiatry). In the back row from left to right are: A. A. Brill (American psychiatrist and translator of Freud's and Jung's works), Ernest Jones (British psychoanalyst who taught at the University of Toronto) and Sandor Ferenczi (Hungarian psychoanalyst who experimented with new therapy techniques). (From the personal collection of Jennifer Wolfe.)**

## G. Stanley Hall

In 1896, Anna Bryan and Patty Smith Hill journeyed north for a summer session organized by G. Stanley Hall, then President of Clark University in Worcester, Massachusetts. Hall's lecture focused on his increasing knowledge and insights about child development. He was, by this time, a well-known psychologist and educator who inaugurated the child study movement. Hall was also the first person to take a Ph.D. in psychology at Harvard University.

Hill and Bryan were part of a group of 35 leading kindergarten educators invited to the special session. Outraged by Hall's statements on the unsoundness of rigid Froebel methodology, all but two of the educators left after the first lecture; only Bryan and Hill remained with Hall in the large lecture hall. Staying the rest of the summer, they worked with Hall to develop new curricula for young children. Hill and Bryan learned the key values of a multidisciplinary approach to early childhood as well as the need for scientific studies of children.

Mary Sheldon Barnes was married to Earl Barnes. Her father, E.A. Sheldon, had been a leader in the Pestalozzian movement (see chapter 4) and founded the Oswego Normal School. Mary attended this program and then entered the University of Michigan where she was in the first class to which women were admitted. One of her classmates was Alice Freeman Palmer, who became president of Wellesley College and mentor of Lucy Sprague Mitchell (see chapter 11). Mary became the chair of history at Wellesley and the first woman faculty member at Stanford University. She was an eminent scholar, revered historian and teacher and multilingual in both ancient and modern languages.

Hill was also influenced by other thinkers and writers of the day and based her work with children on the best known knowledge of her time. The thinkers she learned from included:

- William James (1842 – 1910) and his work on habit formation. James was a philosopher and psychologist who believed that the meaning of ideas is embedded in their possible consequences. Brother of novelist Henry James, he wrote *The Principles of Psychology*. Hill first encountered his ideas when his articles were given out by Anna Bryan in her training program.
- Earl Barnes (1861 – 1935) and his work on psychology and the teaching of play. Barnes wrote *The Psychology of Childhood and Youth: Outlines of Thirty Lectures*. Hill studied with him in 1895.
- E.L. Thorndike (1874 – 1949) and his work on the importance of testing. Thorndike taught at Columbia University and wrote extensively in the area of educational psychology. He also helped Hill understand the value of knowledge gained by others as well as from her own work with children.
- Luther Gulick (1865 – 1918) on the psychology of play and play materials. Gulick was a playground and physical education pioneer who wrote *A Philosophy of Play*. Hill studied with Gulick in 1898 and began to devise new games for children that were more suitable to their ages.

Hill was thoroughly familiar with Comenius, Pestalozzi, Froebel, and Dewey, and she always saw early childhood development within its historical and evolving conceptual framework.

## Kindergarten Changes

Returning to Louisville, Hill changed her kindergarten practice even more and began to extend her ideas. She came to believe that parents and teachers alone could not, in themselves, address the needs of the developing child. Referring to the "whole child," she said children needed the care and attention of physicians, dieticians, social workers, psychologists, artists and other professionals. This sense of children's needs and the community involvement was unheard of in Froebel's kindergarten movement. She saw the Froebel gifts as toys, not as a sacrosanct assortment of symbols. Hill allowed children to create doll beds from combinations of Froebel gifts and make their own paper dolls to use in their play.

Hill had already articulated her belief in helping children grow, as opposed to helping educational systems grow:

> *"If one is not absorbed in 'administering a system' one can learn much from both children and teachers."*
>
> **— from an interview with Hill in Amidon, "Forty Years in the Kindergarten"**

Seeing a need for a more integrated approach to teaching children from ages two through eight, Hill advocated a continuity of teaching practices and methodology. She wanted to help teachers

> *"see that creative play when analyzed into its constituent elements revealed the beginnings of all the later subject matter of the school in its content. This paved the way for unifying the kindergarten and the primary grades, making it possible for the child to pass from one into the other without experiencing the sense of shock which the formality of the primary grades often forced upon him."*
>
> **— from Gwinn, *Patty Smith Hill in Louisville***

Of course there was opposition to the new kindergarten ideas, and many saw these kindergarten leaders as a

> *"group of deluded women, who believed it possible to teach anything of importance through so insignificant a medium as play."*
>
> **— quoted by Gwinn in "Patty Smith Hill: Louisville's Contribution to Education"**

The Louisville kindergartens under Hill and others became renowned for innovative kindergarten practice. Hill worked to improve sanitation and health in the school, introducing separate drinking cups or drinking fountains, baths for children, paper handkerchiefs and medical supervision of children.

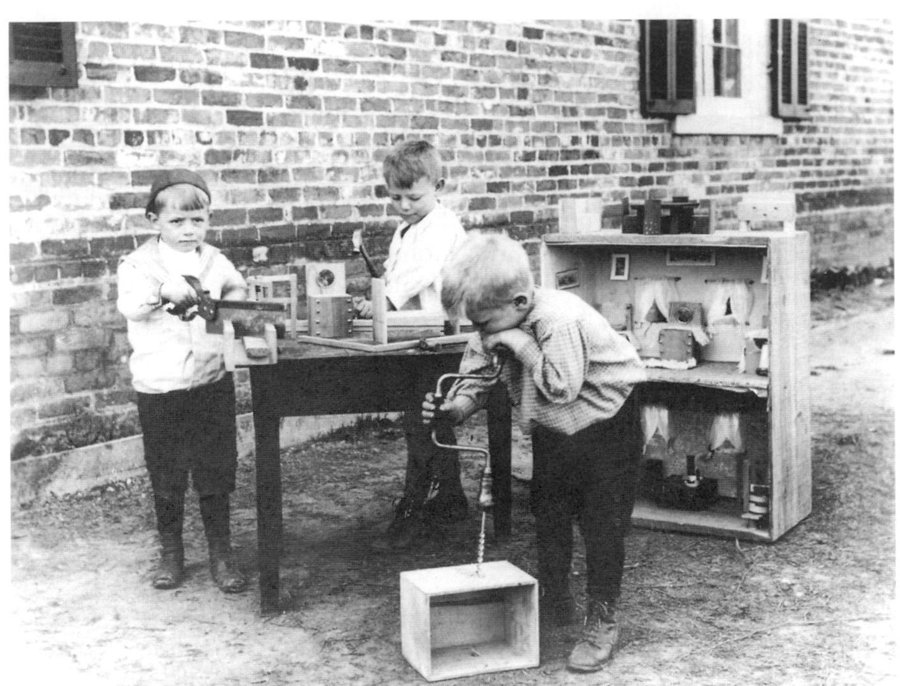

With real tools, these children in one of Hill's kindergartens are creating furniture for the large dollhouse on the right. (Used with permission of Special Collections, Milbank Memorial Library, Teachers College, Columbia University.)

In one of the Hill kindergartens in Louisville in 1900, boys and girls iron clothes. (Used with permission of Special Collections, Milbank Memorial Library, Teachers College, Columbia University.)

This photo, taken in 1900, shows the inside carpentry class in one of the Hill kindergartens in Louisville. The frame for the playhouse and the wagon with blocks can also be seen. Platforms allowed shorter children to reach the carpentry bench and its tools. (Used with permission of Special Collections, Milbank Memorial Library, Teachers College, Columbia University.)

## Origins of a Famous Song

Mildred Hill, who was a musician, and Patty Smith Hill wrote many songs together for the children. A good morning song "Good Morning To All" or "Good Morning" was created in 1893 and included in books called *Songs of Nature and Childlife, Song Stories for the Sunday School, Song Stories for the Kindergarten,* and *Songs Children Like — Folk Songs From Many Lands:*

***Good morning to you***
***Good morning to you***
***Good morning dear children***
***Good morning to all***

Another variation was "Good Morning Dear Teacher."

**Mildred Hill composed the music to "Happy Birthday To You" ("Good Morning to You") and many other songs for children. (Used with permission of the *Louisville Courier-Journal* in Louisville, Kentucky.)**

**Good Morning To All. The words to "Good Morning To All" were written by P.S. Hill with music by Mildred Hill. (From P.S. Hill and Mildred Hill's *Song Stories for the Kindergarten* published originally in 1896, republished in 1921 by Clayton F. Summy Co. of Chicago.)**

**Good Morning. "Happy Birthday to You" developed from classroom greeting songs "Good Morning" and "Good Morning To All." (From A. Moore and M. Hill's *Songs of Nature and Childlife* published in 1898 by Clayton F. Summy Co. of Chicago.)**

1935 marked the debut of the version called "Happy Birthday To You." Patty and Mildred felt that children needed a special song to commemorate their birthday celebrations. Patty wrote the lyrics, and Mildred wrote the melody.

Only six words! It was to become one of the most famous songs of all time.

The Hill sisters apparently obtained copyright in 1935 only as a "joke," but the story is told that Patty Smith Hill and Jessica Hill (Mildred had passed away, and Jessica was teaching English at Columbia) later heard this song sung in a Broadway play and filed suit for copyright infringement. It was being used in Irving Berlin and Moss Hart's "As Thousands Cheer." Patty Smith Hill won the lawsuit and gave a large sum of money to inner-city programs in New York.

The only stipulation that Patty put on the song was that it could not be sung to "swing" music!

Later Patty and her younger sister, Jessica, used the royalties of the song to set up a trust fund called the Hill Foundation to further the interests of children. The Association for Childhood Education International (ACEI) later received some of the royalties for the song. In a letter of May 21, 1945 Patty Smith Hill wrote to the ACEI:

> *"If 'Happy Birthday' turns out as well as it now promises, in a year or two more, or after our deaths, it may bring you [the Association] a steady income of royalties."*
>
> **— quoted in "The Gift of Music" by Odland (*Childhood Education*, Fall 1996)**

A recent *New York Times* newspaper article on the song ("Happy Returns of 'Happy Birthday'") refers to Patty and Mildred as "two schoolteaching sisters." It is interesting to remember this phrase as we regard Patty's later distinguished career. Why did the *New York Times* ignore her full professorship at Columbia University and her founding of professional associations that still exist today?

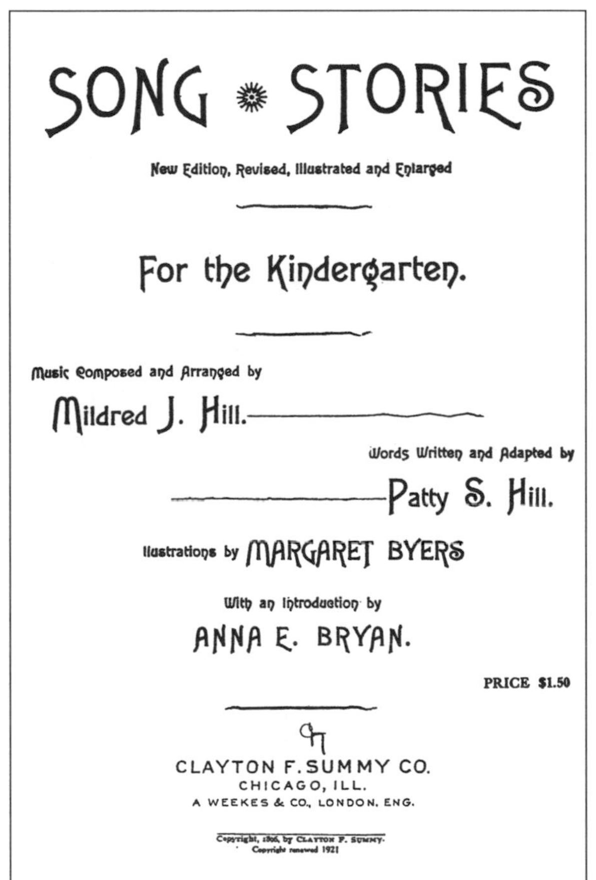


**Title page of P.S. Hill and Mildred Hill's *Song Stories for the Kindergarten* published originally in 1896, republished in 1921 by Clayton F. Summy Co. of Chicago.**

## Other Musical Notes

Mildred and Patty wrote and developed many songs and published these for teachers. They fought against formal concert singing for children, encouraging more informal usage of songs in the daily program. *Song Stories for the Kindergarten* was first released in 1896. Anna Bryan provided the introduction to the book and stressed the importance of the songs to help children experience the unity of life. Songs could supply more than facts; they could portray inner meanings while utilizing the poetic sounds of words. Patty Smith Hill wrote the words to "Nature's Good Night" which showed this imagery and representation:

**Nature's Good Night**

***Clouds of gray are in the sky,***
***Flocks of birds are passing by***

***Trees now dress'd in faded brown,***
***Send their leaves all rustling down,***

***Little flow-rets downward creep,***
***Nod their drowsy heads and sleep.***

***All the world must say 'good night',***

***Till spring comes back with sunshine bright.***

**Nature's Goodnight was created by P.S. Hill and Mildred Hill to teach children the meaning of nature with poetic words and music. (From P.S. Hill and Mildred Hill's *Song Stories for the Kindergarten.)***

"The Story of Bread" helped children understand the transformation of wheat to bread and see the interconnections of rain, wheat, harvest, milling, mixing, baking and finally eating bread:

**The Story of the Bread**

***Way down in the field where the wheat seeds lie,***
***The raindrops have fallen from clouds on high,***
***Then the wheat grows up and the reapers sing,***
***As they cut it all down with a steady swing***

***Way down on the stream there stands an old mill,***
***And never till night does its wheel stand still,***
***As it grinds all the wheat into flour so white,***
***The miller sings out to his great delight.***

A current curriculum guide from Bank Street College of Education, *Explorations with Young Children* edited by Anne Mitchell and Judy David, devotes a full chapter to an integrated curriculum study of bread and bakeries. Unity may be an "old" concept, but seeing the interconnections in our lives is a recurring approach to helping children understand their world.

Mildred Hill also included music that was integrated in meaning with the text. In the song "The Caterpillar and Moth," a constantly repeated **D** note with the piano pedal suggested the caterpillar walking and a later waltz-like tempo portrayed the moth flying.

Froebel's ideas on unity and interconnected elements[3] had taken on new meanings.

Patty Smith Hill later wrote an article in 1910 on "The History of the Kindergarten Song in America" that reflects her strong sense of knowing not just songs but the musical needs of children. The article was based on a talk she gave at the International Kindergarten Union Convention (conference) and shows her deep knowledge of the history of the field of early childhood music education and her commitment to research through interviewing kindergarten leaders on the topic.

[3] There were a number of articles written about the "unity" or "connectedness" in songs for children, encouraging this in programs above the kindergarten. "Connectedness and Continuity in Musical Education" by Annie Curwin in 1899 contains the following quotation: "... let us try to create a musical 'circle of thought' which shall be complete in itself, and which, as it widens, will be found to touch other circles at different points of its circumference."

**"The Story of Bread" by P.S. Hill and Mildred Hill helped children understand the transformation of wheat to bread and showed some of the same "unity" and interconnected themes of Froebel. (From P.S. Hill and Mildred Hill's *Song Stories for the Kindergarten.*)**

**"The Caterpillar and Moth." This song by P.S. Hill and Mildred Hill integrated music that accented the words. (From P.S. Hill and Mildred Hill's *Song Stories for the Kindergarten.*)**

**The Rainbow**

Rainbow, rainbow,
Bridging o'er the sky,
Who can cross that lovely bridge?
Neither you nor I.
A rainbow bridge with colors bright,
Of violet, blue and green
Is gold enough for you and me,
Enough just to be seen!

**Taking Care of My Brand New Shoes**

Does no one see my shoes-
My shiny, squeaky shoes
My brand-new, shiny, squeaky shoes?
I love to see them twinkle
In the sun
As I run!
Yes, it's fun, fun, fun,
To twinkle, squeak and run
In my brand-new — shiny,
squeaky shoes

**My Hobby Horse**

Whoopee! Yippee!
Hi-ho! Whee!
Jump up on a hobby horse
To gallop far and free;
Some like a motor car,
Some like a train,
While others like to fly up high,
In a zooming aeroplane;
But I like my hobby horse
The very best of all,
As he stands ever ready,
While resting in his stall.

## Learning Poems

Hill also wrote numerous learning poems to use with children in programs. The poems at the left are some samples that are in the archives of The Filson Club Historical Society, Louisville, Kentucky.

Hill loved poetry and saw the value of exposing children to many different types of verses. In an introduction to Alice Hubbard and Adeline Babbitt's *The Golden Flute*, an anthology of poetry for young children, Hill stated,

> *"Poetry of excellence on the child's level of maturity will stimulate his natural tendencies to voice his own experiences and feelings in rhythmic form at a stage in his development when he tends to chant as naturally as he sings or speaks."*

She felt poetry was a frequently neglected part of early childhood programs. Hill felt that poetic feelings were easily "stirred" in young children, and these feelings would give children deeper insights into life's experiences.

## Early Professional Projects

Realizing that parents did not have the child development knowledge that teachers had, Hill ran study classes for parents which she hoped would help parents understand their children more fully. She trained teachers and was active in the professional community of early childhood. The International Kindergarten Union (IKU), formed in 1892, had become the kindergarten teacher's professional association, and through this organization Hill worked for a wider interpretation of Froebel's ideas and a more open use of his methods. Hill was president of the IKU in 1908.

*With small changes in wording, these could be topics for lively parent-teacher study groups today; however, such groups are extremely rare. Where are current forums for discussion of issues that affect both teachers and parents? Dewey, Hill and many others found such forums stimulating for all involved.*

The Louisville Kindergarten Club had lively parent-teacher study groups. The 1896 – 97 program listed the following topics:

| | |
|---|---|
| *"October* | *History of child study; the basis of future education* |
| *November* | *Physical defects and influence upon child development* |
| *December* | *Children's appetites and foods* |
| *January* | *Folk-lore among children* |
| *February* | *Sex characteristics in children* |
| *March* | *Causes and manifestations of anger, fun, humor in children* |
| *April* | *Causes, expression and effects of fear in children"* |

**— quoted in Jammer, *Patty Smith Hill and Reform of the American Kindergarten***

In 1903, kindergartens in Louisville became part of the public school system. Although the benefits and increased opportunities excited her, Hill had some serious reservations about the loss of some key values of kindergarten. She feared that the following would happen:

- Standardized system would overwhelm the key components of kindergarten practice.
- Parent education would be lost.
- Readiness push for early reading, writing and computation would compromise the kindergarten programs.

Her fears unfortunately materialized. Key goals of quality early childhood programming in the kindergarten are still sacrificed just as Hill feared.

**The four Hill Sisters. From left to right, Mary Hill, Mildred Hill, Billy Jones (the dog), Jessica Hill and Patty Smith Hill. All the sisters were actively involved in kindergarten and social service work. (Used with permission of the ACEI and the ACEI Archives, Special Collections, University of Maryland.)**

## The Seven "Hills" of Louisville

Hill's sisters also became involved with the kindergarten movement. Mildred helped create music for songs and games and taught music for the Louisville Free Kindergarten. Mary graduated five months after Patty from the Louisville Training School. She taught in the first kindergarten in a Louisville Public School and collaborated with Patty on some of her writing. Her particular interest was in psychology and in social settlement work. She also established a City Federation of Mothers Clubs, which predated the Parent Teacher Association of Louisville. Both Mildred and Mary died in 1916. Jessica taught at Columbia Teachers College in the primary education department.

Patty's brother Archibald was active in humanitarian work as head of Neighborhood House, the first social settlement centre in Louisville.[4] Along with her kindergarten work, Mary assisted her brother in this endeavour. Wallace entered the business world in railroad, bridge and financial institutions. It was said that Louisville was like Rome in that it was built on seven Hills (Martha and her six children). Martha was an active member of the Louisville Free Kindergarten Association. The family remained close, often taking holidays together.

## New York and Debates with Susan Blow

Louisville kindergartens became known through the United States, and Hill had been instrumental in raising them to this national profile. In the Fall and Winter of 1904, Hill was invited to Columbia University to lecture on her work with kindergartens. Susan Blow, who remained the prime advocate of more traditional interpretations of Froebel's ideas, also gave lectures during the series. The following shows the topics of the lectures:

Lectures on Kindergartens Between Susan Blow and Patty Smith Hill – Fall 1904

| | | |
|---|---|---|
| October 26 | Work and Play in the Kindergarten | Miss Hill |
| November 2 | Representative and Experimental Play in the Kindergarten | Miss Hill |
| November 9 | The Place and Limitations of Domestic Work in the Kindergarten | Miss Hill |
| November 13 | Kindergarten Music | Miss Hill |
| November 16 | Rhythm in the Kindergarten | Miss Hill |
| November 20 | The Free Play Program | Miss Blow |
| November 23 | Ideals in the Kindergarten | Miss Hill |
| November 27 | The Herbartian Program | Miss Blow |
| December 4 | The Mixed Program | Miss Blow |
| December 7 | The Relation of Nature Study, Art and Dramatic Expression | Miss Hill |
| December 11 | The Froebelian Program | Miss Blow |
| December 14 | Some Tendencies in Kindergarten Programs | Miss Hill |
| December 18 | A Path-breaking Idea | Miss Blow |
| December 21 | The Educational Value of Humor | Miss Hill |

Fee for the entire course, $6.00. For kindergarten teachers, $3.00.

**— ACEI Archives,<br>University of Maryland**

---

[4] Insights into Archibald Hill's life and work are contained in a manuscript by his wife Mary Anderson Hill, housed in the ACEI Archives at the University of Maryland.

James Russell was Dean at Teachers College and wanted his students to hear both sides of controversial issues:

> *"But it was with some trepidation that I invited this young David from Kentucky to meet the Goliath of Froebelianism at Teachers College. It was a battle royal, but every stone from the sling of the youngster found its mark and the outcome was never in doubt."*
>
> **— quoted in Fine, "Patty Smith Hill: A Great Educator"**

The two women debated about the relative merits of play and work and the value of free versus directed play. Hill believed in some of Froebel's ideas but felt they should not be taken without critical analysis and modification when needed. Hill respected Froebel's method but did not see him as the "sole prophet of truth." Psychological findings of the time were also beginning to counter the formalism and rigidity of Froebel. Hill focused on including the needs and interests of children in more functional ways.

Hill admired Froebel and saw his contributions but found his followers to be dogmatic:

> *"In their hands his incomplete experimentation grew into a cult. The purpose of the kindergarten movement ceased to be a progressive scheme of education and became a system."*
>
> **— from an interview with Hill in Bailey, "Who's Who in The Schools: Patty Smith Hill"**

---

***A Busy Speaker***

January Lecture Series by P. S. Hill from
January 11 – January 24, 1905

The Use of Froebel Gifts and Outside Material

The Proportion of Nature and Symmetry

Kindergarten Occupations, New and Old

Dictation, Imitation and Originality in the Kindergarten Gifts and Occupations

Symbolism in the Kindergarten

Kindergarten Plays and Games

Stories and Rhymes in the Kindergarten

Legitimate Subject-matter of Kindergarten Program

Legitimate Channels of Expression for Subject-matter of Kindergarten Program

The Significance of Progress and Conservatism in the Kindergarten

**— cited in a Teachers College notice housed in the ACEI Archives, University of Maryland**

---

Programs based on people's ideas sometimes do become "systems," rigid in their approach and not reflecting changes and new ideas. Some Montessori programs still demonstrate this strict adherence to ideas developed by one person. Hill was aware of this and commented that Froebel too changed his ideas throughout his life and would expect his followers to adapt and change as well. Hill was a determined leader who confronted Susan Blow and the "establishment" with energy and knowledge. Two early articles, "The Future of the Kindergarten" (1909) and "Second Report" (1913), focused on Hill's emerging new vision of kindergarten. She provided a thorough analysis of the origin and development of Froebel kindergartens, seeing a need for changes to reflect urban environments in North America. Hill was convinced that Froebel would have responded to current advances in knowledge and adjusted his program:

> *"... its [kindergarten] complete realization demands the open-minded study of the contributions of those illuminating sciences which Froebel would have been the first to welcome, had he lived to our day."*
>
> — ***The Future of Kindergarten***

She called for a reconstruction of his theory and practice.

Hill eloquently described the kindergarten leaders who broke with tradition:

> *"Fortunately there are in every generation leavening elements that refuse to bend the knee to the god of custom or tradition."*
>
> — **"Kindergartens of Yesterday and Tomorrow"**

## Teacher Education

**Patty Smith Hill in about 1908. (Used with permission of The Filson Club Historical Society, Louisville, Kentucky.)**

In 1906 Hill moved to New York to teach at Teachers College at Columbia University, where she stayed for the next 30 years. Two laboratory schools were run by Teachers College. The Horace Mann School followed strict Froebelian ideas and primarily had children of high-income families. The Speyer School[5] in Harlem (P.S. 500) was attended by children from poor and immigrant families, reflecting many ethnic groups. The approaches to education were much more open at the Speyer School, and Hill chose to do her school research and study in this freer environment. The school promoted ethnic, cultural and racial awareness to enhance self esteem, expand children's experiences and contacts, support tolerance and, above all, to form a common base among people. Children retained the same teacher for five years to build relationships and improve learning. The school was much like a settlement house with programs for mothers and an afterschool program for older children. Children's decision making was supported, and teachers functioned as guides and mentors.

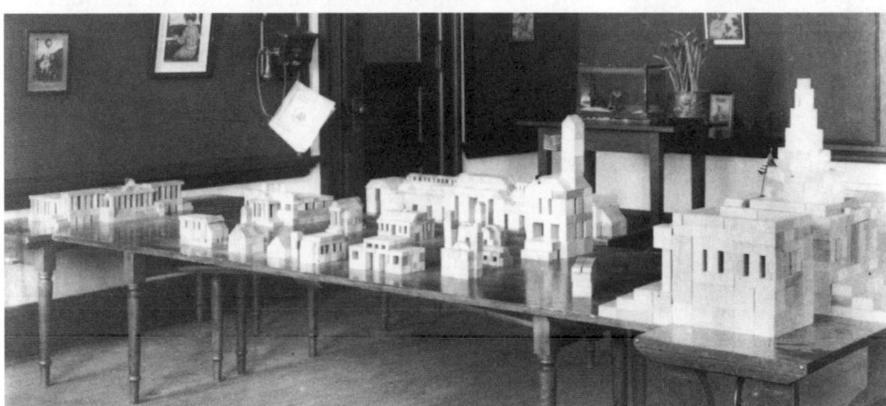

**This city constructed of blocks was made in 1915 when Hill had moved to New York. You can see the Froebel blocks used in a much more elaborate and developed manner. (Used with permission of the ACEI and the ACEI Archives, Special Collections, University of Maryland.)**

A key part of the teacher training that Hill emphasized was learning to observe and to study children. She wrote an article called "The Speyer School Experimental Play Room" reporting on her approach to teacher education. Students gained a fresh insight into children by observing their play life. The students kept detailed

[5] This school is highlighted in chapter 9 of *Celebrating Diverse Voices: Progressive Education and Equity* edited by Frank Pignatelli and Susarina Pflaum. The article by Joseph Kleinman "P.S. 500 Speyer School: An Early Experiment in Urban Alternative Public Education" has excellent background information about the innovative program at this school and its relevance for current work. *Teachers College Record* also contains articles by A. I. Gates and G. Bond (1936) and L. S. Hollingsworth (1936 and 1938) describing the work of the school.

**Patty Smith Hill chose the open environment of the Speyer School in Harlem to do her child-study work. The school was based on activity projects and had a mixed racial and ethnic group of children. Her goal was for teachers to grow in their ability to study children. (Used with permission of Special Collections, Milbank Memorial Library, Teachers College, Columbia University.)**

records and discussed their findings to develop and refine their personal observation and research skills. Teachers would need to be researchers in their own classrooms, not relying solely on authority and tradition. Her goal was for teachers to *grow* in their ability to see and study children.

Hill's choice of the Speyer School was also motivated by her concern for the poor and marginalized people in society. She had a much larger social view, seeing kindergarten as one means to improve society as a whole.

Her conviction that young children were capable of self-government, creativity and initiative grew. Tremendous opposition emerged against her ideas but decreased when John Dewey added his support for her approach; Dewey's clout and influence on others was obvious in this situation:

> *"When I first wanted to experiment with giving children freedom in choice and use of materials, we dared to call the departure neither a kindergarten or a school. To avoid controversy we described it as a 'playroom'. We kept records of every child in the group, and we proved gradually that freedom did not mean disorder."*

Even though the school's reputation was helped by the support of Dewey and William Kilpatrick, Hill maintained that

> *"there was a hard fight for every inch gained."*
>
> **— from an interview with Hill in Bailey, "Who's Who in The Schools: Patty Smith Hill"**

**This cooking class was held at the Speyer School, one of the programs where Hill did her child-study work. (Used with permission of Special Collections, Milbank Memorial Library, Teachers College, Columbia University.)**

In 1910 Hill became Head of the Department of Kindergarten Education. She respected Dean Russell but also challenged him on a number of occasions. She was not afraid to stand up for what she believed. In 1913 she argued for subject matter specialists in the department:

> *"the teaching of young children demands such skillful adaptation of subject matter to their immaturity that only specialists who are at home with the kindergarten age can solve it with success."*
>
> **— letter from P. S. Hill to Dean Russell, March 15, 1913. Housed in Special Collections, Milbank Memorial Library, Teachers College, Columbia University.**

She rapidly advanced to full professor in 1922, only the third woman promoted to this level at Teachers College.[6] This was particularly rare for a woman without a formal college degree. In 1929 she received an honorary doctorate and became Dr. Patty Smith Hill, one of those "schoolteaching sisters" the *New York Times* referred to in its article. The president of Columbia, Dr. Nicholas Butler, gave a tribute acclaiming her unending search for the answer to the question "What constitutes the child?" She in turn acknowledged the learning she received from her colleagues in Louisville who supported her experimental endeavours. We continue to question why her contributions have been so undervalued. Few current histories of early childhood or education acknowledge all that Patty Smith Hill added to the field. Yet she *was* listed in such high profile publications as *Who's Who in America* (1920 – 1921), *Leaders in Education* (1932), *American Women* (1937 – 38), and *Women of Achievement* (1940).

Hill structured her courses to promote democratic and creative classroom methods — leadership respecting people rather than allegiance to a particular system. She stressed that supervision of teachers could not be autocratic, as teachers would likely repeat the same methods of instruction they themselves had experienced.

Observation and record keeping were both central to her work. There is a story of a teacher who was teaching kindergarten and would have the same children the next year in grade one. She asked Patty Smith Hill what she should study over the summer to prepare her more for teaching grade one. Hill replied that any extra study was unnecessary. The key thing was to observe the children and follow their lead.

Hill was particularly interested in cultural differences and in celebrations and included these in her teaching:

> *"Our teacher-training schools should see to it that no prospective teacher goes out from such institutions without a wide cultural background for interpreting the festal days of the year."*
>
> **— "Some Uses and Abuses of Christmas Festivities"**

---

[6] The Department later became the Department of Nursery School, Kindergarten, and First Grade Education. Staff of the Department included leaders such as Charlotte Garrison, Agnes Burke, Annie Moore, E. Mae Raymond, Alice Dalgliesh, Alice Thorn, Mary Reed, Edith Conrad, Edna Hughes and Mary Rankin.

**Patty Smith Hill in Front of Teachers College. Hill advanced to full professor at Columbia Teachers College in 1922. She worked in what became the Department of Nursery School, Kindergarten and First Grade along with others like Alice Dalgliesh, Mary Reed, Edna Hughes, and Charlotte Garrison. (Used with permission of Special Collections, Milbank Memorial Library, Teachers College, Columbia University.)**

Hill supported broad liberal arts education for teachers as an integral part of professional competency. The arts, humanities, sciences and social sciences would build reflective teaching practice, responsive to changing realities. To teach effectively, teachers had to be constantly aware of the forces at work in a society. They also needed to be with others who offered intellectual challenge and needed to be interested and involved in activities outside teaching. These were high hopes and standards because Hill believed teaching young children played a vital role in a democracy.

The value of liberal arts education is still an issue today amidst increased pressures for job-oriented college and university education. One hundred years after Patty Smith Hill voiced her plea for the arts, Patricia Clements, the Dean of Arts of the University of Alberta, Canada, eloquently spoke in favour of the values of liberal arts education:

> *"The Faculty of Arts is not a business school; it is an environment in which fires are lit and lives transformed. It is a place where intellectual passion and pure mathematics and philosophy and poetry are valued in themselves. But the fires lit here by those things have enormous impact on all of our lives."*

She went on to elaborate on the key results of a liberal arts education, which include "critical, creative and analytic thinking," a "sensitivity to individuals and tolerance of cultural differences in groups," "the ability to conduct original research and to organize complex information," and "the desire to co-operate with others in team projects," among many other skills (quoted in *The Edmonton Journal*, Monday, March 15, 1999).

Though articulated as goals for a liberal arts education, these could equally be seen as goals for children and teachers, and all relate to how we see children growing into adults in our society.

## Nursery School Education

Hill went to Russia in 1929 to look at nursery programs there. She observed new child care arrangements for children of working mothers that included creative care facilities in train stations and on specially designed railroad cars. The trip resulted in the publication of Vera Fediaevksy's book *Nursery School and Parent Education in Soviet Russia* in

**Illustration from a Soviet Nursery Book contained in 1936 book by Hill and Fediaevksy, *Nursery School and Parent Education in Soviet Russia.***

1936. Hill was the collaborator and wrote the introduction. The book is a wealth of surprisingly contemporary ideas of play, equipment, use of observation and real-life learning experiences. Despite political or economic differences, Hill maintained that

*"it cannot be denied that in Soviet Russia babies and little children are considered worthy of the best the State can bestow upon them at any cost."*

We can look today to see if children are considered worthy of the best that can be provided in our city, province, state, or country.

Hill had studied the work in nurseries for munitions workers' children during World War I as well as other nursery programs in England. Interest in nursery schools gained momentum after World War I. As programs increased, Hill saw the chance for Teachers College to be a leader in the emerging field of educating nursery school teachers, so she introduced nursery school education to Teachers College in 1922. Hill brought Grace Owen, an English pioneer in nursery education, to Columbia as a lecturer and wrote of the benefits to the family of nursery school. She wrote of the special needs of nursery school teachers and conducted research to find what made successful teachers at this level[7]:

> *"It [the nursery school] has grown up in a changing world that needed a new, flexible institution to help solve the family problem, to help meet the needs of the mother, the father, and the older children as well as the baby."*
> — **"The Nursery School and the Present Social Order"**

## An Unforgettable Teacher

Hill was always wonderfully playful and comfortable with children. This quotation by one of her colleagues, Charlotte Garrison, describes the planned visit of the Queen of Romania to the Horace Mann Kindergarten:

> *"Queen Marie had requested especially to visit the kindergarten to see the work being done with young children. The children were back for a special afternoon session for the purpose. A big fire blazed in the fireplace — the red carpet was out — but no queen. She had stayed to visit with a nurse at St. Luke's Hospital who had been in Romania during the war and was a close friend. As time went on and no queen came something had to be done — so we asked Miss Hill to come in and shake hands with the children whose little noses were being worn out pressed to the windows waiting for the queen. Remember, we never thought of fooling the children but just thought to give them some consolation. Miss Hill came in wearing a wonderful foreign embroidered dress and looked the part of a queen. The children*

[7] See Hill's "The Education of the Nursery School Teacher" in *Childhood Education*, October, 1926.

> *probably thought that anyone so dressed up must be a queen, that Miss Hill was the 'real thing' and they were delighted to meet her. Some asked her where her crown was, but even explanations did not disillusion them. We did not know what a hit Miss Hill had made until she told us that all the rest of the year when she met the children in the halls or around the neighborhood she was greeted with, 'How are you, Queen?'"*
>
> **— quoted in Snyder, *Dauntless Women in Childhood Education***

In addition to her playfulness, Hill was known for her generosity, sincerity and devotion to students. She always had time for students. Students flocked from across the country to study with her. One former student stated that students expected to learn something "big" in Hill's classes, and they were not disappointed. She was self-effacing and always acknowledged the contributions of others to her work. Hill was a mentor to countless teachers, encouraging and supporting others to solve problems, rather than giving them answers or pre-set solutions.

Hill's inclination to nurture extended to all living things; she rescued rose bushes thrown into trashcans after Easter, reviving them at her country home in Croton, New York. She called the revitalized roses her "garbage roses." Her country home was well known for its exterior paint of red, orange, yellow, green, blue and violet.

## To Rome To See Maria Montessori

Hill was interested in other perspectives on early childhood. She had visited England in 1924 to see the developing nursery school programs. In 1929 – 1930 she went to Italy to study Montessori's methods, travelling with a contingent of teachers from Teachers College along with William Kilpatrick. Hill agreed with some of Montessori's approaches such as auto-education, experimental base, use of materials related to life and emphasis on continued child study. Seeing the materials and how children developed independence stimulated Hill's thinking for her own practice.

However, she fundamentally disagreed with the undervaluing of play, the lack of honouring children's motives and purposes, and the neglect of social learning.

Hill believed there should be more to a program than beautiful handwriting, cleanliness, order or sounding out written symbols. In addition, Hill found that Montessori overlooked children's learning to adapt and live with others:

> *"Montessori's principle [of freedom] would lead to independence at the cost of interdependence. In life outside school, is human freedom based upon dependence upon material or dependence upon other people? Which creates the true freedom?"*
>
> **— quoted in Jammer, *Patty Smith Hill and Reform of the American Kindergarten***

To Hill, Montessori's concept of freedom was pseudo-freedom and disturbing.

She also criticized Montessori followers for their indiscriminate acceptance of a "new" method just as they had blindly accepted Froebel's methods. Hill also saw both approaches as "foreign" to the American experience and environment.

## Writings

Hill wrote extensively[8] though not with the distribution, recognition or profile achieved by John Dewey. She also produced no major works on her educational theories or beliefs. Hill relied primarily on personal demonstration and her skills as a speaker to convey her ideas. She preferred lecturing rather than writing for some unseen audience, and she was eager to discuss her ideas on lecture tours. Some of these speeches (e.g. "Relation of Work and Play in Modern Education") were published in professional journals like the *Kindergarten Review.*

Hill did write articles and introductions to curriculum guides in which she advocated a balance between an open-ended approach to children and the increased emphasis in psychology on setting goals first and then developing means to these ends.

These Introductions include gems of still current wisdom about children and programming.

### The Beginnings of Art in the Public Schools (1924)

> *"Art ceases to be art if any form or technique, no matter how good, is imposed from without."*

### Permanent Play Materials For Young Children (1926)

> *"Toys are the tools of play. As the adult cannot practice the highest type of work without the right materials and tools, in like manner the child must be provided with play materials and tools if he is to secure productive play."*

### Language and Literature in the Kindergarten and Primary Grades (1927)

> *"...think of the ban placed upon thinking by the premium placed upon silence and inactivity in many of our schools. How can little children grow; either in ability to think or to express thought, in schoolrooms where the social organization is so rigid that both of these important mental activities tend to die of inanition?"*

### The Development of Character Traits in Young Children (1931)

> *"If children express their genuine convictions, beliefs and attitudes only when they suppose authority is absent, we have a fairly just index of what is wrong in the relationship set up by grown people."*

[8] The extensive nature of her writing can be seen in the long list of publications in the reference section at the end of the chapter.

### The School Festival (1931)

*"...the most universal holidays came into being because of their organic relation to the seasons and the human activities and events which each season stimulated."*

### First Experiences with Literature (1932)

*"...continued appeals should be made to the world's best artists to illustrate the texts of children's books, not only with the skill of the artist but with some insight into the effects of pictures upon the children themselves."*

### The Beginnings of the Social Sciences (1932)

*"Unfortunately educators tend to pin little children down to the printed page as early in life as possible. When we realize that the printed page is second-hand experience, and that we are offering this at a period in children's lives when they are tingling with eagerness for opportunities to investigate at first hand the interesting environment in which they live, we can but wonder at our own failure in seeing what little children are trying to discover for themselves."*

### Science Experiences for Little Children (1939)

*"[Children] seem to want literally to 'wallow' in nature — rub nature into themselves, or on themselves. Nine times out of ten when a child astounds adult society with the 'dirt' which he as managed to accumulate on face, hands and attire, he is apt to be smeared with nature. Not satisfied with the adult's studious and analytical approach, or the mature aesthetic thrill stirred by the beauty of a landscape, children must taste, touch, or handle everything for themselves — roll down the hill, tumble in the snow, run against the wind, wade in the stream."*

*"Why must we expect the child to be interested in counting the petals of the flowers before he has planted, nurtured, and gathered or arranged them?"*

### The Behavior of Young Children (1929)

*"They [the parents] are partners in a common business, and success or failure depends upon intelligent co-operation in understanding their own and each other's duties and responsibilities in this partnership."*

In 1923 Hill edited a guidebook for teachers called *A Conduct Curriculum for the Kindergarten and First Grade*. The book was a clear substitute for Froebel's system of kindergarten education. The book's ideas were also strongly influenced by Hall, Dewey and E. L. Thorndike, another colleague of Hill's at Columbia. Hill attempted to balance Dewey's social goals with Thorndike's learning objectives.[9]

---

[9] In *Kindergarten-Primary Activities Based on Community Life* by Lucy Clouser and Chloe Millikan, you can see curriculum based on both Hill's conduct curriculum and Dewey's and Kilpatrick's ideas on project based programming. The book demonstrates the extensive involvement of children in the planning process and long term projects with embedded academic curriculum.

Hill also wrote an article called "Kindergarten" which was part of *The American Educator Encyclopedia*. The Association for Childhood Education International republished her article as a separate booklet in 1942 to commemorate the 50th Anniversary of the Association for Childhood Education. It was reprinted for the 75th (1967) and 100th (1992) anniversaries as well.

In 1930 Hill edited a series of children's readers that were based on children's real life experiences. She tried to represent a variety of racial groups in her books, but no publishing house would consider her portrayals of children!

Graduates of the Teachers College kindergarten program disseminated her ideas as they took leadership roles across the United States and internationally.

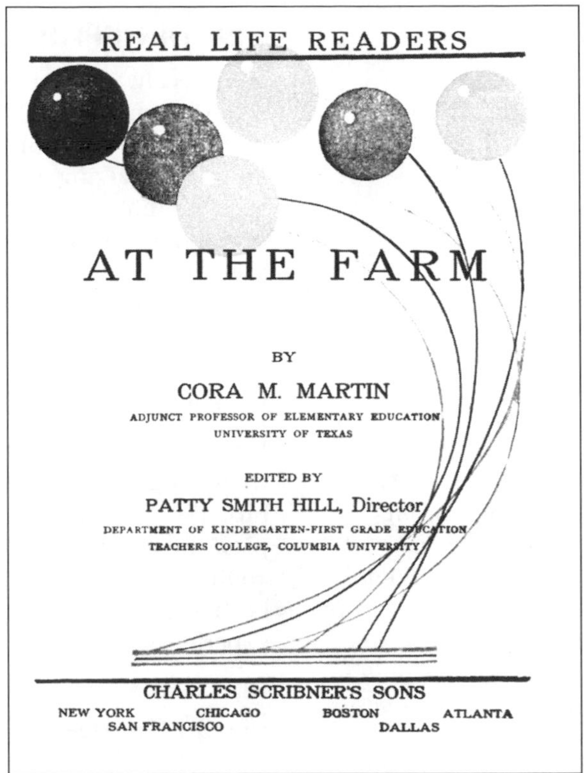

REAL LIFE READERS

AT THE FARM

BY

CORA M. MARTIN

ADJUNCT PROFESSOR OF ELEMENTARY EDUCATION
UNIVERSITY OF TEXAS

EDITED BY

PATTY SMITH HILL, Director

DEPARTMENT OF KINDERGARTEN-FIRST GRADE EDUCATION
TEACHERS COLLEGE, COLUMBIA UNIVERSITY

CHARLES SCRIBNER'S SONS

NEW YORK CHICAGO BOSTON ATLANTA
SAN FRANCISCO DALLAS

Bob and Nancy fed
their ponies.
Nancy fed Dick.
Bob fed Paint.

Paint was hungry.
Dick was hungry, too.
Two hungry little ponies!
Bob and Nancy fed
their hungry ponies.

47

Dinner Time for Ponies

Father said,
"Come, Bob, feed your pony.
Come and feed Paint.

"Come, Nancy, feed your pony.
Come and feed Dick.
Paint and Dick want their dinner."

46

**At The Farm. Hill edited many books including a series of readers (*Real Life Readers*) based on experiences of children. The illustrations were photos of people. (From C. Martin's *At The Farm* published in 1930 by Charles Scribner's Sons of New York. Edited by P.S. Hill.)**

## Learning From Children

Hill was always open to learning from children. She described a time when she was leading "circle time"; suddenly a child asked her *who* she was talking to anyhow. She then disbanded the circle as a program element and began talking with individual children and small groups on topics of genuine interest to them. Another time a child wanted to name a classroom canary. Instead of naming it himself, he organized a "town meeting" to discuss the problem. As an educator Hill learned that the small spontaneous group was the principal working unit for children. She discovered that children had "purpose," concentration, and perseverance when they worked on projects that they initiated and planned, such as a week-long construction of a Fifth Avenue New York bus.

*Hill's writings encourage us to think about contemporary views of play in programming. What has happened to play in programs today? Is the play program a "fill-in" when "real learning" is not the focus? Is it a reward for completing the real work? Is the trend to increased formal teacher-planned experiences to accelerate skill acquisition? Or is the trend to in-depth project learning utilizing children's and adults' planning skills together?*

Hill was clear in her assessment that play was the medium of learning for the young child. Play had purpose and meaning for each child and brought each child into contact with others. Because of the naturalness of play, the teacher could observe children and discover needs, interests, and abilities — all providing information for future planning. She felt that both a child's self-image and role within a group were integral to play experiences.

Hill saw the need for a new engaging curriculum for children that mirrored Dewey's concepts of interest and absorption:

> *"We need a new curriculum of stories, songs, games, materials, etc. etc, which hold the child at the kindergarten period with the minimum of coercion and persuasion from the teacher. The test of worth in these should be their actual holding power under conditions of freedom. The test will not be the teacher's ability to hold the child to the material, the story, the game, the problem in hand, but do these presented appeal to the child as his own, whether the teacher is present or absent? Can the teacher leave the individual or the group, with any assurance that activities will continue to hold when she withdraws her authority, her influence, and her personality?"*
>
> — **"Kindergartens of Yesterday and To-Morrow"**

**An ad for the Hill Floor Blocks in *Appleton Review*, April 29, 1932. The Appleton Wood Products Company in Appleton, Wisconsin manufactured these blocks. (Used with permission of the Outagamie County Historical Society, Appleton, Wisconsin.)**

## Blocks

Hill also designed and developed large construction blocks that became known as the **Patty Smith Hill Floor Blocks** (or simply Hill Floor Blocks). One of the school carpenters, Mr. Driscoll, assisted her in the beginning stages. The Hill Floor Blocks were long maple and basswood boards that slid into deep grooves in upright corner blocks. These unstructured materials allowed older kindergarten children to build sturdy and large structures of even two and three stories.

Her childhood once again provided inspiration and guidance as she remembered when she and her siblings had tried to make houses big enough to get inside but there were no available materials:

*"We tried placing boards on top of barrels but the construction was so shaky that we were compelled to lie down after creeping 'upstairs'. In 1898 I studied with Dr. Luther Gulick who had the first school of play in America, and I took for my problem a new set of building blocks on a scale sufficiently large to enable children to play in the houses, stores, and barns they built. We worked on this scheme twelve or thirteen years before we devised our present set of blocks which schools all over the world are using."*

**— from an interview with Hill in Amidon, "Forty Years in Kindergarten"**

Hill wanted larger materials and explained her rationale to the manufacturer in 1936:

*"In 1895 when these experiments were initiated under my supervision in the kindergartens of Louisville, Ky., I had just returned from a summer's study under G. Stanley Hall and his colleagues where psychologists, physicians and hygienists criticized severely the traditional kindergartens of the day, for their use of small blocks and handwork which threw strain upon the young child's small undeveloped muscles of eye and hand. In 1898 there was another conference of psychologists and physicians under the direction of Luther Halsey Gulick, where my first experiments along these lines were exhibited and reported. The encouragement given then and in later studies under Dr. John Dewey, made me more and more determined to devise building blocks and other materials sufficiently large to demand the use of the large fundamental muscles of little children."*

**— quoted in Carlton, *Caroline Pratt: A Biography***

*Blocks like the Hill Floor Blocks do not exist now. How could you re-design or modify them to be safe but meet the play needs that Hill articulated?*

Children could "enter" into the structures and create houses, stores, railroad stations and other buildings, increasing possibilities for socio-dramatic play. Roofs and floorboards could be added. Heavy wire rods and pegs and holes secured the long blocks for added stability. Cotter pins and wooden wheels allowed children to create wheels for their wooden vehicles and pulleys for cranes and elevators. Children needed to work together on the large structures; thus, the blocks fostered group work and cooperation. Despite all their positive aspects, the weight of the blocks and the reliance on wires, pegs and holes for stability proved to be potential safety hazards and eventually resulted in a discontinuation of these blocks.[10]

**This photo was taken in 1934 at the Lincoln School of Teachers College in the summer demonstration school. The children are using Hill Floor Blocks to create a sailboat in a project on boats. (Used with permission of Special Collections, Milbank Memorial Library, Teachers College, Columbia University.)**

**Taken in 1910 at the Lincoln School Kindergarten in Lakewood, Ohio, this photo shows the Hill Floor Blocks used as a large ticket office. (Used with permission of Special Collections, Milbank Memorial Library, Teachers College, Columbia University.)**

## Toys

Hill was concerned with the nature of toys provided for children and the dangers of mechanical toys:

> *"The tendency of the mechanical toy is toward 'you touch the button and I do the rest.'*
>
> *What can the child do with it? Does it stimulate the child's imagination, invention, originality and industry, or does the toy do for the child what the child should do for himself?"*
>
> **— from 1911 handwritten notes of Patty Smith Hill, obtained from the archives of The Filson Club, Louisville, Kentucky. The notes were for an address called "Toys and Books" given at a toy exhibit.**

[10] A detailed description of the blocks and their multiple usages is contained in Chapter 3 of *Permanent Play Materials for Young Children* written by Charlotte Garrison in 1926.

## Origins of ACEI and NAEYC

Hill was also concerned with the rapid growth of nursery schools staffed by people who had little or no knowledge of how children grow and learn. She organized the National Committee on Nursery Schools in 1926 to address these issues and to effect improvements by

- establishing and promoting standards,
- providing an opportunity for knowledgeable people in the field to exchange knowledge about child development and education,
- spreading information about children and about what preschool programs should offer.

In establishing the National Committee on Nursery Schools in 1926, Hill and others had three goals in mind. Compare these to the current goals of the National Association for the Education of Young Children.

Other early organizers were Harriet Johnson and Lois Meek Stolz. The Committee's first project was to write a bulletin on minimum standards for nursery schools. This Committee then became the National Association for Nursery Education (NANE) which in turn became the National Association for the Education of Young Children (NAEYC), which remains a leading early childhood professional association. Hill was the first honorary member of the NANE, an organization that actively encouraged membership from all socio-economic levels as well as ethnic and racial backgrounds.

Hill also continued her work with the International Kindergarten Union (founded in 1892) which became the Association for Childhood Education (founded in 1930) and later the Association for Childhood Education International (ACEI). She was president of the Association, sat on many committees and edited its journal, *Childhood Education.* She was vice president of the first Child Welfare Association, working along with G. Stanley Hall who was president.

Hill promoted the continued nurturing of new leaders in the field:

> *"We need leaders of the highest intellectual caliber, leaders who will dedicate their abilities to this...inspiring call...Where one is ready a dozen is needed."*
> — **"Safety First vs. Adventure in the Profession of Teaching"**

So the "schoolteacher from Louisville" was a key founder and leader in the two key international professional associations of early childhood that are still active and growing today.

An active member of numerous other professional groups, Hill belonged to 16 organizations, as listed on her 1935 biographical resume.[11]

[11] This biographical information is housed in the ACEI Archives at the University of Maryland.

*What other local, national or international early childhood organizations are you familiar with? What journals do they publish? What are the benefits to belonging to professional associations?*

**Association for Childhood Education International (ACEI)**
17904 Georgia Ave. Suite 215
Olney, Maryland 20832
U.S.A.

Website: http://www.udel.edu/bateman/acei

**National Association for the Education of Young Children (NAEYC)**
1509 16th Street, NW
Washington, D.C. 20036-1426
U.S.A.

Website: http://www.naeyc.org

## Kindergarten Goals

*Hill was concerned with the over-measurement of objectives and goals for children. What do you think is lost with this approach? Why has there been a resurgence of testing children's abilities?*

In all her thinking and work, Patty Smith Hill continued to walk the tightrope between open programming and pre-established, goal-oriented programming. For goals to be operational, they needed to be behavioural and broken down into measurable specific objectives. She was deeply concerned that this specificity would lose the essence of the more overall goals:

> *"We must, however, endeavor to make them [goals] a means of wider freedom; otherwise we may clip the wings of the child, robbing these early years of their naïve and carefree spontaneity."*
>
> **— quoted in Snyder, *Dauntless Women in Childhood Education***

Hill's goals for kindergarten could apply equally to older children and adults. These goals also reflect her sense of balance and respect for the child's initiative and purposes. Her goals were that the child would develop the ability to do the following:

- initiate purposes and plans,
- persevere or "stick to one's job" or project despite difficulties,
- lead and follow intelligently,
- work alone or in a group,
- know when one needs help and where to get the help,
- give fair criticism to self and others and finally to benefit from such criticism.

Patty Smith Hill believed in goals but had grave concerns about the over-emphasis on measurement that would miss essential aspects of an early childhood program:

> *"I often say to our students, 'Measure everything you can, but don't give up a thing simply because you can't measure it.' We are only fumbling with new tools. There are values that still escape our formulas."*
>
> **— from an interview with Hill in Bailey, "Who's Who in the Schools: Patty Smith Hill"**

Hill continued to develop her concepts of projects for children. In a 1921 session with the IKU she described four sources of projects, explaining that projects could be

- self-initiated and developed,
- borrowed from other children and self directed,
- suggested by the group,
- suggested by the teacher (in some circumstances).

The projects should also have some social components, allowing children to think, act, and plan independently if needed and to plan with and for other people.

---

The debate on "basic skills" rages today, and it seems appropriate to review Hill's articulation of what is really basic for young children.

Recently, Herb Kohl (in *Basic Skills*) articulated a redefinition and new conceptualization of what it means to focus on basic skills for children. He lists the following skills as basic for children in any school or child care program:

1. "The ability to use language well and thoughtfully.
2. The ability to think through a problem and experiment with solutions.
3. The ability to understand scientific and technological ideas and to use tools.
4. The ability to use the imagination and participate in and appreciate different forms of personal and group expression.
5. The ability to understand how people function in groups and to apply that knowledge to group problems in one's own life.
6. The ability to know how to learn something yourself and to have the skills and confidence to be a learner all your life."

Alice Keliher has also written an article entitled "BACK to Basics or FORWARD to Fundamentals?" (from *Young Children*, September 1986, Volume 41, Number 6). She challenges the ideas of returning to old conceptions of the basics. Instead she lists key program components for the 21st century to equip children to live in their ever-changing milieu. Each child must be seen as an individual with a range of individual differences. Learning must be embedded in meaningful experiences. Good teachers are intrigued by children, listen to children and plan learning experiences based on their knowledge of children. Finally a partnership with parents is pivotal to education's goals.

It is fascinating to review these three sets of goals/skills and to compare them to what is now seen as "basic" in many early intervention programs. It is easy to lose track of more important skills children need when small easily measurable objectives are overemphasized.

---

## Continuity of Early Childhood

Hill saw a need to unify kindergarten and primary practice and programs. Children's nature and development was a continuous process with no sharp distinctions or separation:

> *"The period from four to eight is practically one, and our school systems should unite the corresponding grades by training teachers for kindergarten and primary together, so that a teacher may be prepared to teach the child anywhere from his fourth to his seventh or eight year. The results of such a unification would be equally beneficial."*
>
> — **"Some Hopes and Fears for the Kindergarten of the Future"**

Hill was concerned with the boredom and indifference she saw in some grade one children. Where had interest and imagination gone? She believed that a dialogue between kindergarten and primary teachers would allow children to experience more continuity in their learning.

She worked with Grace Langdon, also of Teachers College, to research common practices in nursery schools, kindergarten and first grade. Questionnaires were sent out with questions such as,

- "Do you visit in the homes of children?
- Do you have frequent informal interviews with the parents?
- Do you urge the parents to observe in the school frequently?
- Do you keep progress reports of each child?
- Do your children have outdoor play at school daily?"

If respondents answered "no," they were then asked to explain why they did not do these things.

These responses were tabulated and further research questions raised:

- "How can cooperation between parents and teachers best be brought about?
- How can the desirable continuity in the child's home and school living be brought about?
- By what means can the desirable continuity from level to level be made possible?"

**— Langdon and Hill, "An Informal Comparative Study of Teaching Procedure"**

## Child Guidance

Hill always saw children's behaviour in the contextual framework of the school and its environment. Behaviour only had meaning within the situation.

In 1933 she wrote an article entitled "Educational Guidance in the Nursery School, the Kindergarten and Elementary Grades," in which she discussed studies that had compared teacher and psychologist/psychiatrist views of standards of child behaviour:

> *"The conception of behavior held by mental hygienists leads them to rate highly those personality traits which promote the child's future happiness and usefulness in society, whereas teachers tend to rate highly the more submissive traits which make it possible for them to drive the child in his progress in school subjects with least interruption."*

She warns against blaming the teacher, for

> *"Her success as an educator is judged not by the development of her pupils in character and personality but by their progress in school subjects. The mental hygienist. . . . is looking forward to the child's ability to survive in life situations with the highest degree of satisfaction to himself and service to the public."*

In the same article, Hill encouraged teachers to work with parents and mental health experts to ensure a new and better social order.

Hill condemned the practice of failing students, requiring them to repeat grades:

> *"The economic waste of 'repeaters' is the smallest end of this tragedy. The heavy end of the tragedy falls upon the child himself— building up a sense on inferiority and failure at the very onset of life. After repeated failure such children become 'problem children', a sad name to apply to a… child who may have failed as much or more through our stupidity than his own. No wonder that truancy sets in."*
>
> — **"Educational Guidance in the Nursery School, the Kindergarten, and the Elementary Grades"**

Hill favoured a balance between individual freedom and the needs of others and was also aware of the difficulty of achieving this balance. Teachers needed to model consideration for others if children were to learn this. Hill saw "discipline" on an evolving continuum:

> *"The ideal situation is one in which the home and school can cooperate in the guidance of the child so that all his experiences are enriching ones and tomorrow is always learning from yesterday. Genuine guidance should help the child grow in wisdom — in knowledge of the reasons or principles involved, in technique with which to control a like experience when it arises in the future, in his attitude toward the act itself in order to induce readiness to repeat the desirable conduct in the future. Like all arts, guidance is difficult to acquire."*
>
> — **"School Discipline — a Continuing Evolution"**

## Later Life Projects

Hill remained active her entire professional career and maintained a ceaseless pace in her work. Between July and September of 1931, for example, she was asked to speak at eight different places, from Memphis to Toledo to Washington, D.C. This was along with her work at Teachers College and all her other projects!

---

In 1927 there was a dinner at the Hotel Aster in New York City honoring Patty Smith Hill's 40 years in teaching. The written program included these 12 questions:

I. "Who started to teach in September 1887 and is still going strong?

II. Who wrote Good Morning to You?

III. What famous educator has a pirate ancestry?

IV. Which member of the faculty of Teachers College has a country home the exterior of which is painted red, orange, yellow, green, blue and violet?

V. In whose class room discussions does the following sentence frequently occur — "Class, this is not for publication, but....."

VI. Whose favorite illustrative material is "Cora, a member of my household?"

VII. Whose building blocks have pleased children by the thousands?

VIII. Who is today the "outstanding representative of kindergarten education"?

IX. Who makes appointments for "six weeks from next Tuesday"?

X. Who is suggested by the following adjectives: human, sympathetic, humorous, progressive, inspiring?

XI. Name a prominent professor who has been known to rescue discarded rose bushes from ash cans?

XII. Whose visions of forty years ago have become realities and whose visons of today will keep us busy for another forty years?"

**— program from the ACEI Archives at the University of Maryland**

The answer to all questions was Patty Smith Hill, of course!

---

Hill retired from Columbia in 1935 in the midst of the Depression and became a Professor Emeritus from the University. She continued to reside in New York with a summer house in Clinton, Connecticut.

After retiring from her teaching duties, Hill continued to support the children of the poor and unemployed through the Federal Emergency Nursery Schools, securing additional funds from the New York Foundation. She advocated universal pre-school education. Agnes Snyder summarized Hill's vision:

> *"The establishment of the nursery school was advocated by Professor Hill merely as an opening wedge into a far more comprehensive project: the development of a school which would bring together all the resources of the*

*university — art, architecture, engineering, medicine, drama, education — in a concentrated effort on the improvement of a urban community and which would at the same time serve as a laboratory school for the training of teachers in a deeper understanding of their responsibilities toward the community."*

**— from "Plans for the Further Development of Hilltop"**

Hill got involved with New College, an experimental, socially oriented part of Teachers College. The organizers felt that teachers needed to be more involved in the community if they were to play such a large part in a child's development. Teachers in training needed to be exposed to different ways of life, and therefore were given opportunities to live on farms, work in social service organizations and live and work abroad. Marks were eliminated and narrative evaluations were based on broader views and records of performance. In the year-round program, students could progress at their own rates and graduate when requirements were met.

The following is a description of New College by Agnes Snyder[12] who worked there with Thomas Alexander, the driving force behind the College:

*"Instead of the usual educational courses, the students were given a broad experience in living. Everyone went into industry and worked with his hands side by side with regular employees. We found a primitive North Carolina farm abandoned, rundown. The students had to raise their own food, make repairs, survive on their own. Students went into the slums and into foreign lands. They had to speak the language, enroll in school and live like other people in that country. There were no grades, but extensive records on each student which they helped keep. They conferred with advisors and prescribed their own future plans. The seminars began in the freshman year and the students went out, studied their communities and school and raised question to which they sought answers. There was no time limit and no one graduated until he had proven his efficiency as a teacher."*

**— quoted in ACEI Later Leaders Committee,**
***Profiles in Childhood Education***

The College was "successful" in terms of teacher training but was closed in 1939, citing financial problems as the reason for closing. A dedicated and committed group worked to maintain its existence, but the academic world was not ready for such an experiment. Is it today?

All of her work had an equal focus on the family and the community. Hill forged on with new ideas and established a 100-acre family camp outside New York City near Monticello called the Patty Smith Hill Farm to provide a rural experience for urban families. She contributed furniture, paintings and a piano as well as money from a fund created by former students. The idea developed out of a community centre in New York that wanted a rural centre to further its experiment in co-operative living. Hill's dedication of

[12] Agner Snyder had a long and active career in early childhood education. There is a short biography of her in ACEI Later Leaders Committee's *Profiles in Childhood Education*. She was also the author of *Dauntless Women in Early Childhood Education, 1856 – 1931.*

the farm provides insight into her commitment and goals for the future. She believed democracy could only be achieved through the process of cooperative living:

> *"The farm must be a place for all of us to work out our dreams. This is not to be a place with those things provided by others for us. No, we must work out for ourselves a community embodying our ideals of justice and good will for all — creating one spot in this war-ridden world where life is healthier, happier and more beautiful because of our beliefs in the possibility of a better world."*
>
> **— quoted in "The Patty Smith Hill Farm," a paper presented at the National Education Association in St. Louis in 1940 by Wanda Swieda and Nedra Jones**

The project was an evolving one, and Hill knew creating a democratic society took time and effort. The project also focused on the development of initiative, the growth of tolerance, and a common bond of interest between parents and children.

She also worked with Hilltop Community Centre one block from Columbia University in an urban slum area called Manhattanville. Despite its proximity, the University had previously done nothing to address the problems of the area. Hill saw the centre as a beacon for positive activity for the poor and ethnically diverse population of the neighbourhood. Her article "Hilltop: A Community Experiment" chronicles the inner-city early childhood programs for poor and immigrant families. Home visits were an integral part, and community shops were involved with the project. Parent education[13] involved demonstrations of child home care, shopping and food preparation, and refurbishing old furniture. She wrote an article — "Is There Danger in Your Home?" — for *McCalls Magazine* looking at how parents could make their homes more conducive to happiness and development for children and for parents. Her look at play-spaces in this article harkens back to her own child-friendly childhood.

Parents also participated in opportunities outside their parenting roles. When visits to arts and cultural events floundered,

> *"we hit upon the idea of creative celebrations of high-days and holidays of all races and faiths.*
>
> *The contributions of all nations to the richness of our national culture was stressed, together with ways and means to plan our part in preserving these, thus broadening our own sympathies and understanding of other peoples."*
>
> **— "Hilltop: A Community Experiment"**

The United States had a "melting pot" image of immigrant settlement where racial and cultural backgrounds would be assimilated, but Hill strove to strengthen and celebrate children's ethnic and religious backgrounds. She provided "inclusive programming," supporting and respecting the cultural backgrounds of families long before it was fashionable or written

---

[13] Patty Smith Hill had been awarded a distinguished service medal for her work with parents in the New York schools in 1928 from the United Parents Association of Greater New York and *Parents Magazine*. She was the first person ever to receive this award.

up in the literature. Often there were discussions of how to celebrate the ethnic backgrounds of the families in the program. Hill recounted some amusing moments in a St. Valentine's Day discussion with mothers when the discussion moved from the children's celebration to issues of sweethearts and personal sex problems of the parents.

Hilltop Community Centre programs grew to include programs for school-aged children and high school and adult education classes in the evening. She saw the school programs as the coordinating and directive agent for community regeneration. Hill had a belief that community work should be a required and integral part of the training for teachers as well as for architects, artists, preachers, rabbis and others.

## A Lifelong Advocate

Hill believed there was an important connection between early childhood and society and that proper education in the home and at school could have profound implications. Hill's recommendations in the following powerful statement on war and peace written in the late 1930's continue to lie unheeded:

> *"I am more and more convinced that the conception of 'might makes right' and war, as the only means of settling differences of conviction, arise first in the home, the school and community life in which those institutions have their being. This left me with the belief that false conceptions of war and peace must be traced back to their beginnings in these institutions, and newer conceptions of human relationships established there before international relations can be altered and democracy survive. If children can grow up in democratic family life, where superiority of strength refuses to exploit weakness and immaturity, where ideals of autocratic authority are supplanted by those of protection, nurture and development, then children have the right start toward creating a better society than ours today. If children are educated in schools where they learn tolerance and respect for differences in race, creed, and age levels of maturity, settling difficulties through discussion and arbitration rather than through fists, the ability to arbitrate will take care of itself in international affairs. If the communities in which the families live and have their being set the standard of community welfare for all, irrespective of differences in race and creed, war will be wiped out in time to come."*
>
> **— quoted in Swieda, "Cooperative Education Through A Community Association"**

Though Hill's health deteriorated, she remained active professionally.

She wrote a compelling letter to the editor of the *New York Times* in 1939 reacting to the proposal to abandon kindergartens due to budget constraints of the state of New York.

She died at her home in New York on May 25, 1946 at the age of 78. She was buried in Louisville's Cave Hill Cemetery.

To The Editor of the New *York Times*:
July 12, 1939

# Sacrificing Kindergartens

## Proposal to Abandon Them in New York Is Viewed With Amazement

I have followed with amazement the long continued threats to the New York public kindergartens unless the curtailed State budget is restored.

Responsibility for this short-sighted, wasteful proposition is difficult to trace, as no group will willingly face the universal criticisms voiced by noted educators, welfare workers and parents now pouring in not only from New York City but from the nation at large.

What seems to shock all intelligent and humane citizens, irrespective of the persons responsible for the decisions, is the apparent readiness or willingness to seize upon the youngest and most helpless members of society as the first to be sacrificed upon the altar of political warfare or possible economic necessity. Why political parties or educational administrators should rob first those whose very immaturity makes it impossible to cry out for that justice and mercy which any civilized society owes them is difficult to fathom. Have these little ones no right to their just proportion of the school tax, even with a cut budget?

It is said that one of the first laws of high-grade sportsmanship is the demand for the strong to protect the helpless. For this reason one cannot understand, even with an enforced cut budget, the apparent willingness to "take it out" on the youngest in the educational family when there seems to be not enough to provide amply for all age levels. If mercy makes no appeal to either politicians or educational administrators, mere justice might suggest an equal cut all along the line, starting with our various city-supported colleges and so on down the line to the kindergarten, each in turn accepting a proportionate curtailment.

As one reads the educational news in the daily press and discovers new appointees on the faculties of these various institutions of higher learning in Greater New York, side by side in the columns threatening the kindergartens, righteous indignation rises to protest. Why not merge some of these highly expensive institutions and turn over the savings for the little ones now to be turned out of our public schools? Again, the enormous appropriations for bridges, parkways and roads make one wonder if such as these are more important to the future of society than the education of the human beings who are later supposed to benefit by them.

Historically, it is a well-accepted fact that the tendency to sacrifice first those who are too weak to protect themselves or the tribe is a survival of savagery, when war or famine set up cannibalism or other protective measures, when those too weak or too feeble to bear arms must go first.

We must maintain kindergartens for little children, whose birthright is a fair start in life, in the one institution consecrated to the physical, emotional, social and educational health and well-being of early childhood.

Will the citizens of this, the richest and supposedly one of the most enlightened cities in the world, accept this unjust, if not illegal, procedure? It will not only humiliate us in the eyes of other cities striving to keep their kindergartens open at any cost, but may lower our national standard of child care over the whole country, especially in cities of less wealth and fewer educational opportunities.

If this step is an evidence of political manoeuvres in our school system, we should remember this at the polls, in selecting our candidates for Albany, looking into their views on the education of all the children of all the people.

Patty Smith Hill,
Professor Emeritus of Education,
Columbia University.
New York, July 8, 1939.

In 1963 the University of Louisville set up a lecture series honoring Patty Smith Hill. William Kilpatrick suggested the idea, and the series was established by the Louisville ACE, the Louisville Kindergarten Alumni Association and the Louisville Children Under Six. Early speakers included James Hymes, Walter Waetjen and Alice Keliher.

William Kilpatrick wrote a letter to Hill's sister right after her death expressing his sense of loss and grief. He acknowledged the tremendous influence Patty Smith Hill had on his own developing educational ideas and on the kindergarten movement:

> *"she almost single handedly deserves the credit for the kind of kindergarten we now have. All future historians must so recognize it."*
> **— from letter by William Heard Kilpatrick, June 3, 1946, housed in the ACEI Archives, Special Collections, University of Maryland**

Hill received accolades from around the world. The Louisville Kindergarten Alumnae Club wrote that she had a "vision beyond her time," "deep respect for others," a "regard for their rights," and a "magnetic personality" (from an undated letter to the editor of the *Times* by Elizabeth Hannan). Winifred Bain paid tribute to Hill in the September 1946 issue of *Childhood Education*, saying she was "one of that unusual group of women in American education, all of strong humanitarian purpose and high intellectual caliber" and that she "translated the thoughts of such educational leaders as G. Stanley Hall, John Dewey, and E.L. Thorndike into the practice of teaching young children."

## Her Words Speak Today

A talk Hill gave in 1926 was slightly reworded and reprinted in 1987 in *Young Children*. Only at the end of the article "The Function of the Kindergarten" do readers realize when it was written and who the author was. The words and issues remain stunningly current.

Her words of advocacy also provide a beacon today to support us as we move to the future:

> *"Don't put all your strength into fighting your opponents and ideas of the past. Put all your faith and effort into the present and future."*
> ***— from an interview by Bailey, "Who's Who in the Schools: Patty Smith Hill"***

Hill focused on many issues in her career that remain challenges and trends for us today. She was concerned with

- the over-focus of teacher education on curriculum and educational guidance, ignoring key principles of child development,
- the relative isolation of young children from their family life and from the community,
- the lack of cross-discipline collaboration for the provision of services to young children and their families.

In 1916, she spoke of the need for "best practice" irrespective of model of education:

> *"These experimental kindergartens have one aim — namely, to discover what is best for the child at this period, be it kindergarten, Montessori, or what not. They are eagerly endeavoring to discover the native tendencies of the child at this period and the most developing materials for these instincts and impulses to feed upon. It is the period, not the system, we are striving to protect and enrich."*
>
> **— "Kindergartens of Yesterday and To-Morrow"**

*In elections of today, the deficit and the debt are often main topics. Children and families are rarely mentioned. At the same time, we have increasingly strong research to demonstrate the cost saving to society of quality early childhood programs. It appears that knowing that programs save money, and more important, improve educational progress and reduce social problems is not enough to put early childhood and child care on the top of the agenda. Why?*

In a radio broadcast in 1932, she decried the lack of funding for programs for young children:

> *"our boards of education in many communities are largely drawn from business and financial circles. Trained, as they frequently are, to think first in terms of dollars and cents, 'balancing the budget' at any cost, appears to be the primary duty."*
>
> **— "The Kindergarten Child in the New Deal"**

A year later she wrote an article elaborating her concerns and the shortsighted view of poorly funded early childhood programs:

> *"Why must the youngest children suffer first and the most disastrously?"*
>
> **— "Shall The Youngest Suffer Most?"**

## Hill's Own Retrospective Thoughts

After she retired, Hill reflected on her work with comments that continue to be thought provoking for early childhood educators. All the following quotations are from an article "Patty Smith Hill and Progressive Education by B. Fine in 1936.

> *"We were considered dangerous radicals down in Louisville and later at Teachers College. We were something of a curiosity simply because of our break with tradition."*
>
> *"Criticisms were continued when we attempted to abolish all formal games and to give opportunities to children to create their own dramatizations, drawings, paintings and modeling."*

*Why do you think people initially thought Hill to be a "dangerous radical"?*

Dangerous radicals? Is change so threatening? Early childhood continues to struggle to promote and support programming and approaches that meet children's needs. Why are professionals in this field not heard?

> *"We not only stood for children's ability to learn to depend upon themselves in creating their own forms of expression, but we emphasized the tremendous importance of first hand contacts with nature, through excursions to parks, the zoo, the river, the railroad station. We insisted that creative expression must grow out of experiences in real life situations and that prescribed adult forms preceding these first hand experiences were blind, unintelligent and empty."*

Real life programming! First-hand experiences! Meaningful and engaging programs for young children. These are still dreams as the pressures for early formal learning increase:

> *"We also endeavored to help teachers to see that creative play when analyzed into its constituent elements revealed the beginnings of all later subject matter of the school in its content. This paved the way for unifying the kindergarten and the primary grades, making it possible for the child to pass from one into the other without experiencing the sense of shock which the formality of the primary grades often forced upon him."*

Learning is a continuum. Academic learning embedded in children's play and projects is integral to sound early childhood programming. Play with blocks can support children's learning of equivalence, topology, classification, seriation, conservation of number and many other areas of math and other academic subjects. It takes a skilled and knowledgeable teacher with expertise in subjects to make all this happen. It takes clear articulation of the potential learning to help others see beyond the seemingly simple play with blocks:

> *"The need for punishment and discipline rapidly disappeared as we learned to work with instead of against the nature of the child."*

We have learned a lot about child guidance and its connection to problem solving, programming and child development. Punishment should not be a part of programs for young children, and yet it remains in methods such as "time out." What has happened? Have we forgotten the words of Hill and others? We need to refocus on the nature of the child.

William Heard Kilpatrick credited Patty Smith Hill for the transformation of kindergarten practice:

> *"The modern kindergarten has children playing at things that actually interest them. They have big blocks, big enough to build houses for children to play in [he is referring to the Patty Smith Hill Floor Blocks]. They have dolls to play with and apparatus that challenges and interests children. The children genuinely play and teachers encourage genuine creative work on the part of the children. And for this change, they are indebted to Miss Patty Hill, more so than to any other person."*
>
> **— quoted in Tenenbaum, *William Heard Kilpatrick***

G. Stanley Hall wrote to her in 1913:

> *"If I am worthy of a place with people who have influenced the kindergarten, it is because I have been rather your man Friday, and rehearsed and repeated your kindergarten ideas."*
>
> **— quoted in Gwinn, "Patty Smith Hill: Louisville's Contribution to Education"**

*Why do you think the* New York Times *referred to P.S. Hill as a "schoolteacher from Louisville" rather than as a full professor at Columbia Teachers College, founder of the NAEYC, creator of Hill Floor Blocks, etc?*

She was a "schoolteacher from Louisville" but also an internationally known scholar and educator who dramatically changed early childhood practice within a family and community context. Hill's absorbing interest was in the growth of children, not in creating a static educational system.

> *"Let us see the child in his family and community setting and realize the necessity for us to play our part in legislation, that those laws which directly and indirectly affect child welfare may be passed, respected, and obeyed."*
> **— from "The Right of the Young Child to Security in An Insecure World," 1938**

*The Filson Club Historical Society in Louisville, Kentucky was established in 1884 to collect and preserve historical materials related to Kentucky. It has a special collection of Patty Smith Hill papers and the contents can be viewed at its website: http://www.filsonclub.org/*

*Filson Club*
*1310 South Third Street*
*Louisville, Kentucky 40208*
*U.S.A.*

*The University of Maryland, McKeldin Library, also houses the ACEI archives with a collection of Patty Smith Hill materials.*

*McKeldin Library*
*University of Maryland*
*College Park, Maryland 20742*
*U.S.A.*

*Website: http://www.lib.umd.edu/mck/mckeldin.html*

## Patty Smith Hill — References for Further Study


ACEI Later Leaders Committee. (1992). *Profiles in Childhood Education 1931 – 1960.* Wheaton, MD: Association for Education International.

Amidon, B. (1927). Forty years in kindergarten: An interview with Patty Smith Hill. *Survey Graphic, 2* (6), 506 – 9, 523.

Bailey, C. (1931). Who's who in the schools: Patty Smith Hill. *American Childhood, 17* (1), 5 – 6, 55 – 56.

Barnes, E. (1914). *The psychology of childhood and youth: Outlines of thirty lectures.* New York: Huebsch.

Burton, F., & Graves, G. (1895, April). Patty Smith Hill. *The Kindergarten News, 5* (4), 109 – 111.

Burton, F., & Hill, P. S. (1901, April). The work of Anna E. Bryan in Louisville, Ky. *Kindergarten Magazine, 13* (8), 436 – 439.

Carlton, P. (1986). *Caroline Pratt: A biography.* Unpublished doctoral dissertation, Teachers College, Columbia University, New York.

Clouser, L., & Millikan, C. (1932). *Kindergarten-Primary activities based on community life.* New York: The Macmillan Company.

Committee of Nineteen. (1924). *Pioneers of the kindergarten in America.* New York: The Century Co.

Cremin, L., Shannon, D., & Townsend, M. (1954). *A history of Teachers College, Columbia University.* New York: Columbia University Press.

Cross, E. (1898, April). The work of the Chicago Free Kindergarten Association. *Kindergarten Magazine, 10,* 509 – 515.

Curwen, A. (1899). Connectedness and continuity in musical education. *Child Life, 1* (3), 121 – 124.

Davis, M. D. (1964, November). How NANE began. *Young Children,* 106 – 109.

Edwards, K. (1922). Pre-kindergarten education. *Kindergarten and first grade, 7,* 316 – 318.

Fediaevsky, V. (1936). In collaboration with P. S. Hill. *Nursery school and parent education in Soviet Russia.* New York: E. P. Dutton.

Fine, B. (1936, May). Patty Smith Hill: A great educator. *American Childhood,* 17 – 18.

Fine, B. (1936, June). Patty Smith Hill and progressive education. *American Childhood,* 10 – 12.

Foulkes, M. A. (1984). Gifts from childhood's grandmother — Patty Smith Hill. *Childhood Education, 6* (1), 44 – 49.

Garrison, C. (1926). Permanent play materials for young children. (Patty Smith Hill, Ed.). New York: Charles Scribner & Sons.

Gates, A. T., & Bond, G. (1936). Some outcomes of instruction in the Speyer Experimental School (P.S. 500). *Teachers College Record, 38 (3), 206 – 217.*

Gulick, L. H. (1920). *A philosophy of play.* New York: Charles Scribner's Sons.

Gulick, L. H. (1920). *The principles of psychology.* New York: Holt.

Gwinn, F. F. (1954). *Patty Smith Hill in Louisville.* Master of Arts Thesis for the University of Louisville, Louisville, KY.

Gwinn, F. F. (1957). Patty Smith Hill: Louisville's contribution to education. *The Filson Club History Quarterly, 31* (3), 203 – 226.

Hannan, E. (no date). Letter to the *Times*. Housed in the ACEI Archives, University of Maryland.

Happy Returns of "Happy Birthday." (1989, December 26). *New York Times.*

Heffron, I. C. (1934). *Francis Wayland Parker: An Interpretive Biography.* Los Angeles: Ivan Deach, Jr.

Hewes, D. (1976). Patty Smith Hill: Pioneer for young children. *Young Children,* 297 – 306.

Hewes, D. (1996). *NAEYC's first half century: 1926 – 1996.* Washington, DC: NAEYC.

Hill, P. S. (1890, September). Typical lessons for mothers and kindergartners "By their fruits ye shall know them." *Kindergarten Magazine, 3*(1), 31 – 35.

Hill, P. S. (1890, October). Typical lessons for mothers and kindergartners "By their fruits ye shall know them." *Kindergarten Magazine, 3* (2), 62 – 66.

Hill, P. S. (1890, November). Typical lessons for mothers and kindergartners "By their fruits ye shall know them." *Kindergarten Magazine, 3* (3), 119 – 123.

Hill, P. S. (1902, June). What shall be the standard of requirements and experience for training teachers? *Kindergarten Magazine, XIV* (10), 636 – 639.

Hill, P. S. (1902, June). What shall be the standard of requirements and experience for training teachers? *Kindergarten Review, 12,* 624 – 627.

Hill, P. S. (1902, September). Punishment. *Kindergarten Review, 13,*11 – 17.

Hill, P. S. (1906). The relation of play and work in modern education. *Kindergarten Review, 17* (1), 7 – 14.

Hill, P. S. (1906). The Speyer School experimental play room. *Kindergarten Review, 17* (1), 137 – 140.

Hill, P. S. (1907). Some conservative and progressive phases of kindergarten education. In M. Holmes (Ed.), *The sixth yearbook of the National Society for the Scientific Study of the Child Part II.* Bloomington, IL: Public School Publishing.

Hill, P. S. (1907, April). Some friendly suggestions to I.K.U. visitors in New York. *Kindergarten Review, XVII* (8), 453 – 457.

Hill, P. S. (1909). The future of the kindergarten. *Teachers College Record, 10,* 371 – 398.

Hill, P. S. (1910). The history of the kindergarten song in America. *Kindergarten Review, XXI* (4), 193 – 206.

Hill, P.S. (1910, October). The liberal and conservative movement in kindergarten education. *Atlantic Educational Journal,* 14, 29.

Hill, P. S. (1911). Toys and books. [Handwritten notes of P.S. Hill for a lecture]. Address given in 1911 at a Toy Exhibit. Notes housed in the Patty Smith Hill Collection, The Filson Club Historical Society, Louisville, KY.

Hill, P. S. (1913). Second report. In Th*e kindergarten reports of the committee of nineteen on the theory and practice of the kindergarten.* Boston: Houghton Mifflin.

Hill, P. S. (1913). Some hopes and fears for the kindergarten of the future. *Proceedings of the twentieth annual meeting of the International Kindergarten Union.* Washington, DC: International Kindergarten Union.

Hill, P. S. (1913, March 15). Letter to Dean Russell, Teachers College, Columbia University. Reference Number RG 6: James Earl Russell Papers Folder 240. Housed in Special Collections, Milbank Memorial Library, Teachers College, Columbia University.

Hill, P. S. (Ed. and Introduction). (1914). Experimental studies in kindergarten theory and practice. *Teachers College Record, XV* (1), 1 – 70.

Hill, P. S. (Ed.). (1915). *Experimental studies in kindergarten theory and practice.* New York: Teachers College, Columbia Universities.

Hill, P. S. (1916). Kindergartens of yesterday and to-morrow. *The kindergarten and first grade, 1,* 331 – 333.

Hill, P. S. (1924). Introduction to *The beginnings of art in the public schools* by M. Mathias. New York: Scribner & Sons.

Hill, P. S. (1925). Changes in curriculum and method in kindergarten education. *Childhood Education, 2* (3), 99 – 106.

Hill, P. S. (1926). Introduction to *Permanent play materials for young children* by C. Garrison. New York: Charles Scribner & Sons.

Hill, P. S. (1926). The nursery school and the present social order. *Intelligent Parenthood.* Chicago: University of Chicago Press.

Hill, P. S. (1926, October). The education of the nursery school teacher. *Childhood Education, 3,* 72 – 80.

Hill, P. S. (1927). First steps in character education. *Childhood Education, 3,* 355 – 359.

Hill, P. S. (1927). Introduction to *Language and literature in the kindergarten and primary grades* by E. Troxell. New York: Charles Scribner's Sons.

Hill, P. S. (1927). Safety first vs. adventure in the profession of teaching. *Childhood Education, III* (7), 297 – 298.

Hill, P. S. (1927, October). Preschool education as a career. *NEA Journal, 16,* 209 – 210.

Hill, P. S. (1928, August – September). The home and the school as centers of child life. *Progressive Education, 5,* 211 – 216.

Hill, P. S. (1929). Introduction to *Music for young children* by A. Thorn. New York: Charles Scribners's Sons.

Hill, P. S. (1929). Introduction to *The behaviour of young children* by E. Waring & M. Wilker. New York: Charles Scribner's Sons.

Hill, P. S. (1929). The strategic position of the kindergarten in American education. *Childhood Education, 6* (4), 147 – 152.

Hill, P. S. (1931). Can education in art appreciation be continuous? Pre-kindergarten training. *American Magazine of Art, 23* (4), 296 – 300.

Hill, P. S. (1931). Future possibilities for continuity without standardization in curricula for nursery school, kindergarten and first grade. *Childhood Education, VII* (10), 530 – 531.

Hill, P. S. (1931). Introduction to *The development of character traits in young children* by A. McLester. New York: Charles Scribner & Sons.

Hill, P. S. (1931). Introduction to *The School Festival* by A. Linnell. New York: Charles Scribner & Sons.

Hill, P. S. (1932). Introduction to *First experiences with literature* by A. Dalgliesh. New York: Charles Scribner & Sons.

Hill, P. S. (1932). Introduction to *The beginnings of the social sciences* by M. Reed & L. Wright. New York: Charles Scribner & Sons.

Hill, P. S. (1932). Introduction to *The golden flute: An anthology of poetry for young children* by A. Hubbard & A. Babbitt, New York: The John Day Company.

Hill, P. S. (1933). Shall the youngest suffer most? *California Journal of Elementary Education, 2,* 62 – 65.

Hill, P. S. (1933, October). School discipline — a continuing evolution. *Child Study, 11,* 12 – 15.

Hill, P. S. (1933, October). The kindergarten child in the New Deal. *American Childhood, 19,* 5 – 6.

Hill, P. S. (1933, November). Educational guidance in the nursery school, the kindergarten, and the elementary grades. *Understanding the Child, 3,* 3 – 5, 31.

Hill, P. S. (1934). Some uses and abuses of Christmas festivities. *Childhood Education, XI* (3), 99 – 103.

Hill, P. S. (Ed). (1934). *The practical value of early childhood education.* Washington, DC: Association for Childhood Education.

Hill, P. S. (1934, July). Is there danger ahead? *Parents Magazine, 9,* 15 & 73.

Hill, P. S. (1937). Hilltop: A community experiment. *Childhood Education, 13* (5), 201 – 205.

Hill, P. S. (1937). Introduction to *The Horace Mann Kindergarten for five-year-old children,* by C. Garrison, E. Sheehy, E. Dalgliesh, & A. Dalgliesh. New York: Teachers College.

Hill, P. S. (1938). The right of the young child to security in an insecure world [abstract]. *Proceedings of the Seventy-Sixth Annual Meeting of the National Education Association of the United States, New York City, June 26 – 30.* Volume 76, 467. Housed in the Archives of the ACEI at the University of Maryland.

Hill, P. S. (1939). Introduction to *Science experiences for little children* by C. Garrison. New York: Charles Scribner's Sons.

Hill, P. S. (1939, July 8). Sacrificing kindergartens [letter to the editor]. *New York Times,* July 12,1939.

Hill, P. S. (1942, reprinted in 1967 and 1992). *Kindergarten.* Washington, DC: ACEI. (Original published in *The American Educator Encyclopedia*)

Hill, P. S. (1987). The function of the kindergarten. *Young Children, 42,* 5, 12 – 19, 56. (Original work published 1926)

Hill, P. S. (July 13, no year). *The young child and the New Deal.* [transcript]. Broadcast over W.N.Y.C. July 13 for the United Parents Association of New York, Housed in the Archives of the ACEI at the University of Maryland.

Hill, P. S. (no date). *Shall the youngest suffer the most?* New York: The Parents Magazine. Housed in the Archives of the ACEI at the University of Maryland.

Hill, P. S. (no date). The project: An adaptation of a life method of thought and action. In *Proceedings of the twenty-eight annual meeting of the International Kindergarten Union*, May 2 - 6, 1921, 153 - 155.

Hill, P. S., & Hill, M. (1890, December). Typical lessons for mothers and kindergartners "Behold I bring you good tidings of great joy, which shall be to all people." *Kindergarten Magazine, 3* (4), 199-203.

Hill, P. S., & Hill, M. (1891, January). Typical lessons for mothers and kindergartners. Transportation — Part I. *Kindergarten Magazine, 3* (5), 266 - 270.

Hill, P. S., & Hill, M. (1891, February). Typical lessons for mothers and kindergartners. Transportation — Part II. *Kindergarten Magazine, 3* (6), 310 - 315.

Hill, P. S., & Hill, M. (1891, March). Typical lessons for mothers and kindergartners. "Awake, thou that sleepest." *Kindergarten Magazine, 3* (7), 379 - 385.

Hill, P. S., & Hill, M. (1891, April). Typical lessons for mothers and kindergartners "He hath made everything beautiful in his time." *Kindergarten Magazine, 3* (8), 443 - 447.

Hill, P. S., & Hill, M. (1891, May). Typical lessons for mothers and kindergartners. Rain — Part I. *Kindergarten Magazine, 3* (9), 515 - 520.

Hill, P. S., & Hill, M. (1891, June). Typical lessons for mothers and kindergartners. Water for drinking. *Kindergarten Magazine, 3* (10), 571 - 575.

Hill, P. S., & Hill, M. (1896). *Song stories for the kindergarten.* Chicago: Clayton F. Summy.

Hill, P. S., & Langdon, G. (1930, May). Nursery school procedures at Teachers College. *Revue internationale de l'enfant, IX* (53), 398 - 407.

Hill, P. S., & Barnard, E. F. (1934, May). Do you harbor an unknown enemy in your home? *McCalls Magazine,* 53, 69.

Hollingworth, L. (1936). The founding of Public School 500: Speyer School. *Teachers College Record, 38* (2), 119 - 128.

Hollingworth, L. (1938). An enrichment curriculum for rapid learners at Public School 500: Speyer School. *Teachers College Record, 39* (4), 296 - 306.

James, W. (1891). *The principles of psychology*. London: Macmillan.

James, W. (1918). *The principles of psychology. Volume One.* New York: Dover Publications, Inc. (Original work published 1892)

James, W. (1918). *The principles of psychology. Volume Two.* New York: Dover Publications, Inc. (Original work published 1892)

Jammer, M. C. (1960). *Patty Smith Hill and reform of the American kindergarten.* Unpublished doctoral dissertation, Teachers College, Columbia University.

Keliher, A. (1986, September). Back to basics or FORWARD to fundamentals? *Young Children, 41* (6), 42 - 44.

*Kindergarten Problems.* (1912). Includes The materials of the kindergarten by MacVannell, J.A. and The future of the kindergarten by Hill, P.S. New York: Teachers College, Columbia University.

Kohl, H. (1982). *Basic skills.* Boston: Little, Brown & Co.

Langdon, G., & Hill, P. S. (1931, June). An informal comparative study of teaching procedure. *Childhood Education, 7*, 531 - 540.

Martin, C. (1930). *At the farm.* New York: Charles Scribner's Sons.

Miss Bryan returns to her Kentucky home to instruct poor children. (1887, August 11). *Louisville Courier-Journal.*

Mitchell, A., & David, J. (1992). *Explorations with Young Children.* Mt. Rainier, MD: Goyphon House.

Moore, A., & Hill, M. (1898). *Songs of nature and childlife.* Chicago: Clayton F. Summy Co.

Moore, A. (1916). Miss Mildred J. Hill — Miss Mary D. Hill. *The Kindergarten and First Grade, 1* (9), 406 - 407.

New York Kindergarten Association. *Annual Reports, 1890 - 1903.* New York: The De Vinne Press.

Odland, J. (1996). The gift of music. *Childhood Education, 73* (1), 32 B - C.

Peltzman, B. R. (1998). *Pioneers of early childhood education: A bio-bibliographical guide.* Westport, CT: Greenwood Press.

Pignatelli, F., & Pflaum, S. (Eds.). (1993). *Celebrating diverse voices: Progressive education and equity.* Newbury Park, CA: Corwin Press.

Rasmussen, M. (1961). Over the editor's desk. *Childhood Education, 37* (7), 352 - 353.

*Report on Hilltop Nursery School up to 1935. Part I.* [Report]. Housed in the Patty Smith Hill Collection, The Filson Club Historical Society, Louisville, KY.

Rudnitski, R. (1995). Patty Smith Hill: Gifted early childhood educator of the progressive era. *Roeper Review, 18* (1), 19 - 25.

Russell, J. (1902). Purpose of the Speyer School. *Teachers College Record, III* (5), 261 - 265.

Shapiro, M. S. (1983). *Child's Garden: The kindergarten movement from Froebel to Dewey.* University Park, PA: The Pennsylvania State University Press.

Shy woman teachers who wrote child's ditty figure in plagiarism suit over Broadway hit (1934, August 15). *New York Times*, 19, column 6.

Swieda, W. (1939, November). Cooperative education through a community association. *Progressive Education,* 16, *480 - 492.*

Swieda, W., & Jones, N. (1940). *The Patty Smith Hill farm (An experiment in cooperative living).* Paper presented before the supervisors of practice teaching at the National Education Association meeting in 1940 in St. Louis, MI.

Snyder, A. (1936, January 21). *Plans for the further development of Hilltop.* Letter from Agnes Snyder of New College, Teachers College, Columbia University, New York, New York. Housed in The Filson Club Historical Society, Louisville, KY.

Snyder, A. (1936, October). *Hilltop under way.* [Report]. Housed in the Patty Smith Hill Collection, The Filson Club Historical Society, Louisville, KY.

Snyder, A. (1972). *Dauntless women in childhood education 1856 – 1931.* Washington, DC: ACEI.

Tenenbaum, S. (1951). *William Heard Kilpatrick: Trail blazer in education.* Introduction by J. Dewey. New York: Harper.

Weber, E. (1969). *The kindergarten: Its encounter with educational thought in America.* New York: Teachers College Press.

# Chapter 10 — *Caroline Pratt*

**1867 – 1954**

*"The assumption of the schools that children can only understand their own environment by approaching it from environments far apart from their own experience is putting all the carts in the world before all the horses and, furthermore, confusing the horse and cart relationship beyond redemption."*

— **Pratt and Stanton, *Before Books***

*"The world seems to be full of people who can talk but who have little ability to put information to work."*

— **"Recording Mental Health and Treatment"**

*"[Children] belong to the animal kingdom, not to the vegetable. One can confirm children to a program of physical inactivity in school, and they will seek activity outside the school where they are free to choose."*

— **"Animal or Vegetable?"**

Caroline Pratt always thought she wanted to work with children, but her focus changed as she constantly learned from observing and interacting with them. She truly "learned from children."

She was born in Fayetteville, a village east of Syracuse in upper New York State, on May 13, 1867, two years after the end of the American Civil War. The Pratt family was active in the early days of the town, and Caroline had two brothers (John and Henry) and one sister (Elizabeth). She spent her early years participating in the varied tasks required of village and farm life, often self-directed and embedded with responsibility.

Her life spanned huge technological changes. Pratt's father, Henry, was a Civil War veteran who engaged in various business ventures. Her family used their first phone in a local store, yet she would live to see television dominate the airwaves, plastics take over manufacturing, and farming become industrialized.

**Caroline Pratt was born in Fayetteville, New York, in 1867. This photo was taken of the town when she was about 13 years old and shows the village with its shops, houses and buggies. (Used with permission of Barbara S. Rivette, Manlius Town Historian, Chittenango, New York.)**

Caroline spent summers on relations' farms and was known as Carrie to friends and family. Early in her life, her great uncle Homer had declared that "Carrie was always good with children." Her great aunt Cynthia used to say she could "turn a team of horses and a wagon in less space than a grown man needed to do it."

Caroline remembered school as relatively unimportant for her meaningful learning, which lay outside the school door in the real world. School was a place focusing on "things far away and long ago" though she did enjoy the company of other children:

> *"The things that I remember as a child are the long rovings in the woods on Saturdays, the farm where I spent a brief period every summer, the village 'baby hole' where the boys learned to swim and which I was allowed to visit properly guarded when it wasn't in use, the times when some child broke the school monotony by crawling under the desks, the yielding to the earnest pleading of a companion to play hooky, the dramatic play we carried on in the 'back yard.' These were the times I lived during my childhood."*
>
> — **Pratt and Stanton, *Before Books***

**Caroline Pratt taught in the Fayetteville Union Free School. This picture was taken in 1888, a year before the school was built. Classes met in various buildings around the village at this time, and Caroline's class of The Little School was held in the Grange Hall. Pratt was 21 and is standing at the right of the photo. Colleague Meary Dowd is on the left, and Clara Arms is in the centre. (Used with permission of Fayetteville Free Library, New York.)**

Carrie enjoyed a happy, active childhood among a large family; she learned to read at four, sitting on her grandmother's knee. Her childhood, however, was shadowed by her father's ill health as he became an invalid, more and more dependent on his wife and children.

By age 17, Carrie was teaching a ten-week summer session in a one-room school near Pratt's Falls:

> *"I was seventeen when I taught my first class — a one-room school in the country — and I had none of the benefits of normal school, teacher training, not even possibly, had ever heard the word pedagogy. What I did have was a deep conviction ... that a desire to learn was natural and inevitable in children."*
>
> — ***I Learn From Children***

Even at this early stage of her career, Pratt knew that symbols needed a base in reality, and she used small coloured cubes to help children learn numbers.

After finishing high school in 1886, she taught for five years in the village school, Fayetteville Union Free School.

The family suffered a tragedy just before Caroline turned 22 when her ill and severely depressed father committed suicide.

## College Life

Academically gifted, Pratt attended Columbia Teachers College, Columbia University, in 1892 on a scholarship. While enrolled in the two-year kindergarten teacher education program, she found the teaching repressive and questioned the practices of the prevalent Froebel curriculum. She later reflected that she disagreed with children being asked to sit in quiet morning circles and "[dance] like a butterfly when they would rather roar like a lion." Pratt felt the "kindergarten got them ready to be bamboozled by the first grade." Summing up her disdain for her kindergarten training and her rebellion, she described the prevalent Froebel teachings as nonsensical "mystical fol-de-rol." She grew increasingly uncertain about the validity of the concept of universal truths. She later commented that

> *"the kindergarten was founded on the play idea, but the kindergarten is a system of teaching the children how to play. The kindergarten acknowledges the play activities of children in general, but is not recognizing their desire to experiment."*
>
> **— "Experimental Schools"**

*Questioning the teachers? Questioning the system and current theory? Questioning the college? Challenging the status quo is often essential for significant changes and progress in our society. What role has questioning the prevailing beliefs played in your college or university life? Should we encourage children to question?*

Her challenging questions meant that she was not a "shining" student. Unable to continue, Pratt approached the Dean and asked to withdraw. He suggested that she switch to Manual Training (arts and crafts) since she came from a farm upbringing and the program would be more utilitarian. Her challenges did not stop in this Program, and she questioned why they were learning to use tools but *never* made a real project — no useful application of the skills. She remembered that they only reluctantly gave her the diploma.

Pratt learned two useful things from her program. The first was an appreciation of the potential for block play after seeing kindergarten children use the Patty Smith Hill Blocks:

> *"She had designed the blocks herself, for the children in her classes to use during their free periods. They were not a part of her teaching program, but I had watched what the children had done with them during those short play periods when they could do what they liked. To me those play periods seemed the most important part of the school day.*
>
> *Of all the materials which I had seen. . . these blocks of Patty Hill's seemed to me best suited to children's purposes. A simple geometrical shape could become any number of things to a child. It could be a truck or a boat or a car or a train. He could build buildings with it, from barns to skyscrapers. I could see the children of my as yet unborn school constructing a complete community with blocks."*
>
> ***— I Learn from Children***

In the Manual Training Program, she also learned to work with wood, and she later used these skills to design and build blocks and other play equipment. Her experiences were the foundation for the school that would later became a reality.

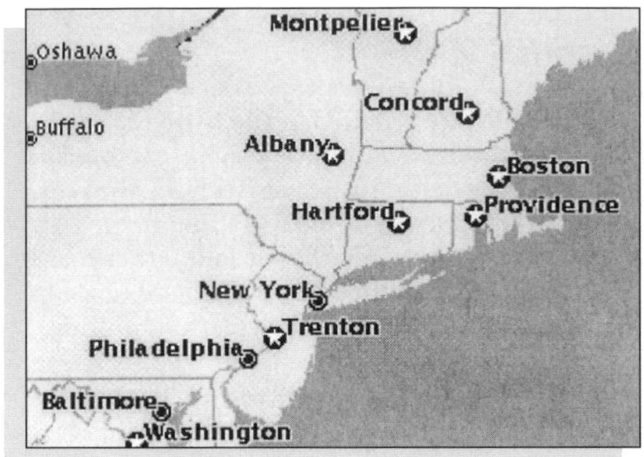


## Philadelphia

Pratt started teaching in the manual training shop in the Normal School for Girls in Philadelphia in 1894. Pratt taught a total of seven years in the Normal School.

She immediately began reflecting on her own work and felt she was

> *"helping to perpetuate a system which held no real educational value."*
>
> — ***I Learn From Children***

Even though she was not satisfied with her teaching, students appreciated her.

This was written by Olive Hart when *I Learn From Children* was published:

> *"You were a bit of light in a rather dark educational pattern. Thank you for writing your book, but more especially for being what you were to us in our years of searching for a bit of understanding."*
>
> — **Carlton, *Caroline Pratt: A Biography***

In the summer she travelled to Naas, Sweden to look at their industrial arts program (the sloyd or Slojd method) that used models rather than isolated exercises.[1] Children made common useful articles such as penholders or wooden mixing bowls. But she was still dissatisfied by the methods she saw. These models would not satisfy the children's desires and interests, and she found the work routine, as only the teachers planned projects. The essence of industry was missing. Pratt also described the children working on identical models as being like violin bows in a symphony orchestra, all moving in exact unison.

Pratt had also seen Montessori materials and felt

> *"Madam Montessori's didactic material is purposeful only from the adult point of view. When the stair is finished, the teacher's purpose is fulfilled. [If children made other uses], the teacher would have stopped them because Madam Montessori considered this a desecration of the material."*
>
> — ***Experimental Practice in the City and Country School***

[1] Two detailed accounts of the Slojd system are by Evelyn Chapman and Madeline Ward, both in the *Journal of Education*. "Sloyd" actually means "sleight of hand" or "skill."

During this period, Pratt was also influenced by the poverty she saw around her and the problems of industrialization and child labour. Pratt became a close friend of Helen Marot[2], a Quaker activist in Philadelphia. Marot strongly influenced Pratt's ideas and perspective on the social problems she was seeing. Marot at one time edited a magazine called the *Dial*. The magazine had contributions from John Dewey and from Thorstein Veblen, an economist and social critic who coined the phrase "conspicuous consumption."

THE DIAL

ROBERT MORSS LOVETT, *Editor*

GEORGE DONLIN — CLARENCE BRITTEN — HAROLD STEARNS

*In Charge of the Reconstruction Program:*

JOHN DEWEY — THORSTEIN VEBLEN — HELEN MAROT

***The Dial* was edited at one point by Helen Marot with John Dewey and Thorstein Veblen as frequent contributors. (From *The Dial*, 1919, Volume 66, Number 781.)**

Marot was also a librarian; she co-founded a library of economics and political science and held lively discussion groups on social and political issues.

Pratt was drawn into Marot's investigation of living conditions in the slums of Philadelphia. They toured homes where women were doing piecework/custom tailoring for the garment industry:

> *"It was for me a bitter eye-opener, that experience. The work was done in the home, with no limit to the hours the people worked, and no check on the working conditions. Helen and I often discussed the futility of trying to reform the school system, if after leaving school human beings had to earn their living under such conditions as these.... It seemed to me that a school's greatest value must be to turn out human beings who could think effectively and work constructively, who could in time make a better world than this for living in."*
>
> — ***I Learn From Children***

This quotation comes from Pratt's major writing, *I Learn From Children,* which was dedicated to her mentor and life-long companion, Helen Marot. In her dedication, Pratt wrote of Marot that she was one "whose spirit lives on." They shared ideas and a social dream until Marot died in 1940.

---

[2] See "Helen Marot" in *Notable American Women 1607 – 1950: A Biographical Dictionary,* edited by E.T. James.

Marot was equally stimulated by Pratt's ideas and dedicated *Creative Impulse in Industry* (1918) to Pratt:

> *To Caroline Pratt*
>
> *Whose Appreciation of educational factors in the play of children, intensified for the author the significance of the growth processes in industrial and adult life.*

*Creative Impulses in Industry* was based on a survey sponsored by the Bureau of Educational Experiments of Lucy Sprague Mitchell (see chapter 11). Marot studied the potential for creativity and intellectual pursuit in industrial production and enterprise and proposed an experiment for young people to produce wooden toys that would test out her ideas. Her choice of this area again shows Pratt's influence. Marot also rebuked the toy manufacturers of the day for making toys that did not meet the needs of children's play. This remains a concern of early childhood educators:

> *"The market does not supply the children with the sort of material and the sort of tools they require in their play schemes."*
>
> — **Marot, *Creative Impulse in Industry***

During this period Pratt took courses by correspondence from the University of Chicago and at the University of Pennsylvania where she was influenced by the ideas of Charles Hanford Henderson. Henderson was the former headmaster of New York City's Pratt Institute in Brooklyn and advocated treating each child as a complete organism, balancing all areas of development. Henderson wrote a book in 1902 entitled *Education and the Larger Life,* and it contained his ideas on organic education and ensuring all areas of development were addressed. He decried social injustices and cherished the sacred nature of children's interests.

Pratt was convinced that education could provide children with the skills and the attitudes to help them in future life. She believed that education was a way that society could be transformed, that if children experienced a different life in the classroom, they would be able to make changes outside. A better world was always her vision. In this way, she reiterated the concerns and dreams of both Pestalozzi and Owen.

---

The ideas of Pratt are echoed in the words of J. W. Grant MacEwan, an environmentalist, author, politician, agricultural leader, and former lieutenant-governor of Alberta, Canada. His creed emphasizes the need to respect the environment and to make a better world:

> *"I believe I am an integral part of the environment, and, as a good subject, I must establish an enduring relationship with my surroundings.*

**Grant MacEwan (1902 – 2000), Canadian environmentalist, politician, author and agricultural leader. Grant MacEwan's creed parallels Caroline Pratt's aim to develop individuals who would make a difference in the world around them. (Photo used with permission and taken by Doran Clark, Edmonton, Alberta.)**

> *I believe the biggest challenge is being a helper rather than a destroyer of the treasures in nature's storehouse, a conserver, a husbandman, and a partner in caring for the Vineyard.*
>
> *I am prepared to stand before my Maker, the Ruler of the entire universe, with no other plea than that I have tried to leave things in His Vineyard better than I found them."*
>
> **— quoted in Von Hauff, *Everyone's Grandfather***

What role does education have? Pratt and MacEwan had the same vision of creating thinking human beings who would make a difference in the world. Pratt dedicated the rest of her life to improving the Vineyard around her. Her own college education had been bereft of a social vision or focus on social injustice, but such a vision was at the core of her educational work throughout her career.

---

## New York

In 1901 Pratt and Marot went to New York, looking for a better place to implement their ideas on social change. Pratt worked in several settlement schools, which had been set up to improve social conditions in the slum areas. While in New York, Pratt also taught in some private schools and worked part time for the Women's Trade Union League. In these early programs, she began experimenting with children's planning their own manual arts projects.

She was a keen observer of children and learned from watching them. One day she watched a son of a friend play with blocks, toys and boxes to create a railroad town; the boy was

> *"setting down his understanding of the way things worked, the relationships of facts to each other.... This was the way a young child, if freed to do so, would go about educating himself on the subject which was of most immediate, intense interest to him — the world in which he lived."*
>
> ***— I Learn from Children***

Today we do not question these three basic ideas: respecting childhood, valuing the purposes and goals of children and observing children. These are not new ideas, but Pratt began to build on her immense realization that these ideas needed to be built into programs that would allow children to take their learning into their lives:

> *"If we could keep this desire alive through childhood and into adult life... we would release a precious powerful force. The child would learn in such a way that his knowledge would actually go with him from the schoolhouse into the world."*
>
> ***— I Learn from Children***

She made an observant comment about adult disapproval of children keeping materials to themselves and not sharing:

> *"It is interesting to note that what is regarded as a 'vice' in a child is a 'virtue' in the business world of today."*
>
> — **"As To Indoctrination"**

She felt that children's drives for learning would be lost if teachers did not relate learning to the children's immediate lives:

> *" I dreamed of a child world in which the railroads and city streets, farms and factories, the stuff of which the real world is made, could be brought down to children's scale so that they might grasp it. I had envisioned a community of children who could, in their own way, through the child activity which we misguidedly call play, reproduce this world and its functioning. Such a community of little individuals, equals in size and strength and understanding as adults are equals in their own adult communities, would learn not only physical truths about the world, but social truths as well, the all-important truths of people with many individual differences who must live and work with each other."*
>
> — ***I Learn from Children***

## Hartley House

**Hartley House, in New York City, was the site of Caroline Pratt's early work with open-ended carpentry with children as well as her first play group. (Used with courtesy of Social Welfare History Archives, University of Minnesota, Minneapolis.)**

Pratt switched her attention to young children but with a renewed focus on learning through play. She began this work at Hartley House, a west-end New York settlement house. Her early teaching there was running an after school carpentry program, which focused on developing observation and thinking through projects. At Hartley House, she had the freedom to develop her program in ways that were unheard of in the school system. She described working with boys making sleds during a snowy winter. Instead of keeping them until the end of term to exhibit, Pratt allowed the children to take them outside right away and try them out. The boys also made snow shovels and iron scrapers to use:

> *"There were no drawings given out for these. Each boy solved his own problems, explaining to the teacher his next step. There were no measurements dictated. Thus the work kept the salient characteristics of industry — the motive, immediate usefulness of the object made; the opportunity to grow mentally through solving problems and inventing."*
>
> — **"Tools vs. Rules"**

Pratt described a boy whom teachers saw as deficient mentally because he could not point to the middle of a piece of wood. Pratt saw that the child had a "school attitude" that did not make him think and described him as "school stupid." She asked him instead if he were going to break the wood in half for a friend, how would he do it? He pointed to the middle. The problem was made more difficult by asking for the exact middle of seven inches. Pratt asked him how he would divide seven apples between two people, and he was able to say each would get three and the last would be divided in half. He then could solve the problem with the seven inches of wood.

Pratt wrote an article called "Carpentry Classes" about her work with the children at Hartley House for their Annual Report of 1901 – 1902. She describes the then-radical idea of letting children choose their own models that could be used for real purposes in their lives. Pratt saw innumerable values in this process, from assuming responsibility to training judgment to thinking through plans. She saw the idea of projects as

> *"Something which retained the play element but which was really work in the best sense of the term"*

and thought projects had the

> *"great advantage of spontaneous effort towards a desired end."*
>
> — **"Carpentry Classes"**

| | | |
|---|---|---|
| May Mathews, 3d Assistant | @ 25.00 | 300.00 |
| Harriet M. Johnson, Trained Nurse, | @ 40.00 | 480.00 |
| —— —— Substitute " | @ 40.00, 2 mo. | 80.00 |
| —— —— Cooking teacher, | @ { 40.00, 2 mo. / 5.00, 8 mo. | 120.00 |
| Stephen Lindenfelser, Boy's Club Director, | @ 60.00, 8½ mo. | 510.00 |
| Joseph Helm, Gymnastic Instructor, | @ 60.00, 8⅓ mo. | 500.00 |
| John Davis, " " | @ 3.00, 68 lessons, | 204.00 |
| —— —— Girls' " " | 2.00, 75 " | 150.00 |
| Caroline L. Pratt, Carpentry teacher, | @ 3.00, 250 " | 750.00 |
| Albert Reigert, Printing " | @ 22.00, 8 mo. | 176.00 |
| —— —— Millinery " | @ 2.00, 40 lessons, | 80.00 |

**The Board minutes of Hartley House, of March 1,1905 show Caroline Pratt's salary for teaching 250 carpentry lessons. (Used with courtesy of Social Welfare History Archives, University of Minnesota, Minneapolis, Minnesota.)**

The Board minutes show that in 1905 Caroline Pratt was paid $3.00 per lesson for 250 classes for a total of $750.00. It is interesting to see in the same minutes the name of Harriet Johnson as nurse and cooking teacher. She was a visiting nurse with the Henry Street Service and later head of a visiting teacher program with the Public Education Association. She had also worked with Patty Smith Hill in the early days of the National Association for Nursery Education (see chapter 9) and later became a key person in the programs of Lucy Sprague Mitchell (see chapter 11).

As she got more interested in play, Pratt gave talks at Hartley House on ways parents could encourage children's play.

While at Hartley House, Pratt became acquainted with Archibald Hill, brother of Patty Smith Hill. He had studied settlement work at the University of Chicago and devoted his life to the movement.

In 1913, Pratt had the opportunity to set up a program for young children at Hartley House. She had just two months to run a children's program and was given floor space in the assembly room and the opportunity to plan the program. She sought five year olds to attend her experiment and supplied the room with her hand-made blocks and toys, clay, crayons and paper. The two months and the children themselves taught her about the merits of learning through play. Pratt realized

- the importance of first hand experiences and self-directed plans, the value of field trips and socio-dramatic play,
- the significance of letting children find answers to their own questions,
- play's relationship to development intelligence,
- imagination's base in real things,
- the need to nurture the play impulse.

---

Archives of Hartley House

Social Welfare History Archives

University of Minnesota

University of Minnesota Libraries
320 Elmer L. Andersen Library
222 21st Avenue South
Minneapolis, Minnesota 55455
U.S.A.
Website: http://special.lib.umn.edu/swha/holdings-serv.html

---

**This undated photo is likely of Caroline Pratt (on right) with her play group at Hartley House. Identification of Pratt done with the assistance of City & Country School staff. (Used with permission of Social Welfare History Archives, University of Minnesota, Minneapolis.)**

## The Play School

Two months later, in 1914, Pratt founded The Play School in a three-room apartment. From the beginning, she did not focus on accumulating facts:

> *"But to know something and to be able to relate and use that knowledge is the beginning of learning to think."*
>
> — ***I Learn From Children***

The name of the school was a "telegraphic way of saying that in our way of teaching, the children learned by playing."

Pratt felt that children had given her the best definition of play:

> *"Play is what you do because you want to, and work is what you do because it has to be done."*
>
> *"A good many people have tried to define work and play with less success. To make it a bit more palatable to the adult, I might translate it into these terms: Play centers in the process and work centers in the result. Neither definition should be construed to exclude pleasure in work or interest in the results of play."*
>
> — **"Two Basic Principles of Education"**

Pratt also saw the school as experimental, but she emphasized that the experiments were **by** the children and not **with** children.

The Play School was located in Greenwich Village, a low-rent area in lower Manhattan. Greenwich Village was renowned as a section of New York where artists, writers and free thinkers lived and worked. It was a place of cultural and intellectual stimulation with a rich mix of immigrant groups. Many of the children attending her school came from these more "bohemian" families as well as families of tradesmen and laborers. She began again with six four year olds from the local community, often going into the streets and approaching parents of young children, asking if the children would like to attend her school.

The first year she had a class of six children. The second year had children from four through six years of age. In the early years, there was free tuition, and the school depended on private donations. Pratt often said both the environment for children and the tuition were free! She did get some financial support from a trade union activist Edna Smith and later from Lucy Sprague Mitchell. Parents could choose to contribute funds if they were able. Later, tuition fees were charged, though scholarships were maintained to ensure the diversity of children and families.

In the early years, critics expressed concerns about the lack of emphasis on early learning of the three R's, but the artists and writers were more open to her new ideas and believed creativity and problem solving were important. Pratt did believe that the children would be "ready" as they engaged in play and in-depth projects. The definition of "readiness" and what this entails in programming is an ongoing issue that emerges with each of the historical figures.

As the program grew, the school moved to a rented house on Thirteenth Street, and Pratt, Marot, and Smith lived in an upstairs section:

> *"Now the school could stretch its muscles more; the children could spill over into our living space when occasion demanded."*
>
> — ***I Learn From Children***

In 1915 Helen Marot highlighted the school in an article in *The New Republic*:

> *"As a result of leaving use and time of use of materials to children, the most striking thing of the school is concentration."*
>
> — **"The Play School: An Experiment"**

## Children and Creativity

> *"In its physical terms the plan was simplicity itself: a goodly floor space, basic materials for play, and many children using them together."*
>
> ***— I Learn From Children***

Simplicity, yes! But normal for the day, no!

The prevailing view was that children became creative through literature, art, music and dance. Pratt had a significantly different perspective:

> *"Instead of literature being the spur to children's imagination, we have found that it is quite the other way round — it is their imagination which stimulates the creation of literature! A child who has been read a story about a fairy in a flower is far less likely to turn up with a story of his own than a child who has seen a tugboat on the river. The more closely he has observed the tugboat, the more deeply he has been stirred by it, and the more eagerly and vividly he will strive to re-create it, in building, in drawing, in words."*
>
> ***— I Learn from Children***

Pratt involved artists in the program. William Zorach, an American sculptor from Lithuania, became the first art teacher in the school in 1918. He worked in stone and wood and was one of the foremost sculptors in the United States; his work still stands in the Whitney Museum and Radio City Music Hall in New York:

> *"When I was in Yosemite Valley I met Caroline Pratt.... She saw [my daughter] riding on a burro and said to me, 'I wish you'd bring her to our school. I'd love to have her.' In exchange for tuition I went to the school for a few hours twice a week to watch and guide the children in art work.*
>
> *I was the first person in this country, to my knowledge, to give children large sheets of paper and showcard colors.*
>
> *I feel much of the art work in schools is due to my pioneering — to letting children express themselves and develop, without superimposing grown up ideas upon them. I don't mean by freedom that I just let them muddle around. It was rather a method of subtle and intelligent guidance. I would look at their work as I would look at an artist's work and we would discuss things as if we were all artists."*
>
> **— Zorach, *Art is My Life: The Autobiography of William Zorach***

Charles Pollack, another artist, also taught at the school, and folklorist Margaret Bradford taught music. Charles (brother of Jackson Pollack, who also did some work for the school) described the integration of the arts with the curriculum:

> *"It is difficult to isolate for discussion the art program of an experimental school since art plays so integral and important a part in the entire school program. The painting, clay, or shop teacher may discuss intelligently his particular function and purpose in the program, but he cannot do so unless he relates the multiplicity of the children's experiences to their group activities and to their individual and social experiences.*

> *Beginning with block building and excursions into their immediate city environment — activities which are rich in possibilities for young and eager minds — children are led to explore and gather knowledge with which to picture their world. Block building gives the first opportunity for objectifying these early impressions. Here develops, along with muscle co-ordination, constructive group activity; the first creative expression of ideas; the first struggle with recalcitrant material and technique."*
>
> — **"Art in an Experimental School"**

The Play School (and City and Country School later, when it changed its name) kept a permanent collection of children's art work as part of its record keeping and a reflection of children's growth.

The Reggio Emilia Approach today reflects a similar use of resident artists in schools.[3]

## The Arts Community

The people around her in Greenwich Village — the working people, the artists, and the immigrants — influenced Pratt. All brought a richness of life to the school program.

She was also influenced by the artistic debate of the day between impressionism and expressionism. Monet, Renoir, Cezanne and Degas were impressionists, seeking visual reality, conveying what they saw without analysis. Expressionists transformed nature as they communicated their inner vision and unique meanings. Some of Gaugin's and Van Gogh's work is expressionistic as is work by Soutine, Rouault, Kokoschka, Schiele and Ensor.

Was children's art a mirror of what was out in the world? Or was their art a way of making personal meaning out of what they saw and did? Was it a way to interpret experiences? Pratt felt that each child had an artistic life and that free play was art. Children's creations with paint, clay, blocks, and dramatics were art productions. Art was the expression of their lives and feelings as well as a re-creation of what they had experienced. She felt both expressionism and impressionism worked together in children.

Children were creative artists, thinking about problems:

> *"He starts out with an idea to be sure but it is an idea which he needs to clarify through his method of dealing with it .... Such a method is a method of thinking. It is in opposition to the logical method in so far as the latter claims to be able to set up the whole proposition before work begins."*
>
> — ***Before Books***

[3] See reference to *The Hundred Languages of Children* by Edwards, C.P., Gandini, L. and Staley, L. for more information on the Reggio Emilia Approach. Note too that the Reggio Emilia Approach is a unique model that finds its roots from many sources. An informative website for the approach is: http://ericps.ed.uiuc.edu/eece/reggio/reglink.html#at

She saw the development of intelligence and other mental processes linked with the development of imagination:

> *"Imagination and intellect must do fine team work with the material with which they are concerned. It is like the building of a wall of uneven stones — a dry stone wall. While the stone wall — the actual material — grows under the hands of a skillful intelligence, the evaluation of the next stone to be placed also is going on. The fringe of the intellect (the imagination) plays with successive possibilities. The evaluation of the next stone primarily is a study of relationships. It may be that imagination is the ability to see new and varied relationships."*
>
> — **"Imagination and Literature"**

Pratt acknowledged her indebtedness to the arts community of New York:

> *"Later I came to know many artists and writers and to be eternally in their debt, for they were my first applicants, the first parents who voluntarily brought their children to my school. Creative people, doing battle in their own lives against the set ways of the past, they were quick to recognize and value an approach to children which would cherish the child's innate creativeness instead of stifling it. Militant fighters for their own individuality, many of whom had sacrificed home and security to follow the call of their own talents in freedom, they had a ready sympathy for the precious individuality of the child. And they were not afraid of anything new merely because it was new."*
>
> — ***I Learn from Children***

In 1952, a cookbook of Greenwich Village artists, authors, etc. was published with an apple pie recipe of Caroline Pratt. The descriptor of Pratt is particularly noteworthy. Her rural youth had taught her where milk came from and how butter was made. The apple pie could easily be at the centre of a project on apples and baking. You can just imagine the field trip to an apple orchard, picking apples, and later making the pie.

116 GREENWICH VILLAGE GOURMET

DEEP DISH APPLE PIE

CAROLINE PRATT
writer

8–10 tart apples, to fill your baking dish
1 cup sugar
3 Tbs. minute tapioca
$\frac{1}{4}$ cup water
handful of raisins
juice of $\frac{1}{2}$ lemon
jigger of brandy (optional)
1 tsp. nutmeg
pie dough

Peel and slice apples into a pan of water. Mix tapioca, sugar, and water, and let stand while you prepare and roll out pie crust.

Butter a 2–3" deep baking dish. Drain apples thoroughly, mix in raisins, and fill the dish. Over all, sprinkle the nutmeg, lemon juice, and if you have it, a good jigger of brandy. Pour the sugar and tapioca mixture over the top. Lay the crust over the apples, and press down around the edge. Cut a number of gashes to allow steam to escape.

Bake in a hot oven about 40 minutes––until apples are tender and the crust has a brown edge.

Serves 6––best with brandied hard sauce.

Caroline Pratt

A pioneer in progressive education, Miss Pratt recently reported her experiences in a volume unusually well received: "I Learn From Children".

Greenwich Village Pioneer. Caroline Pratt lived and worked in Greenwich Village, New York. This is her apple pie recipe. (From C. Wheeler's *Greenwich Village Gourmet* published in 1949 by Bryan Publications of New York.)

## Dramatics

Pratt saw play as dramatization in many forms, according to different ages, and as a key growing-up process. Children learned to search for new information — materials and facts — for their dramatic play:

> *"Facts in use are facts related. If a child dramatizes with a doll as a center, she relates her facts until a whole domestic situation is set up."*
>
> *"The value of drama seems to lie in getting ready for it. Through this getting ready, children broaden their knowledge, their sympathies; they are growing up."*
>
> *"Perhaps the greatest value of dramatics in elementary schools lies in the opportunity it offers to children to produce an organized picture of which they themselves are the media. Though children are pretending, they are learning to live together harmoniously, and this alone is an invaluable experience for them."*
>
> **— "Growing Up and Dramatics"**

Pratt's own childhood experiences as well as observations of children provided the background research for these beliefs.

## Field Trips

Pratt felt children needed extensive experiences with their immediate environment through what she called "absorbing trips."

Field trips in the neighbourhood and in the city were a large part of the program, ensuring first-hand experiences that would be the basis for more elaborate play later on. Trips also trained children's observational skills. Pratt felt skilled teachers could anticipate a child's readiness for a particular experience and could ask leading questions. She also cautioned against teachers asking too many questions that would stifle curiosity or expecting immediate response from children as to their impressions of the trips.

*How do you utilize field trips as a central element in curriculum for young children?*

Field trip experiences would lead to investigations and activities to increase understanding:

> *"We went to the blacksmith's as the children have begun to play horse without much information. Two horses were in the shop and the children saw the making and measuring of the shoes by one smith, while another hammered on the finished products.*
>
> *Mrs. Mitchell and I took ten children to Staten Island on the ferry. They noticed the light and the big bell on the end of the ferry pier. They were delighted by the number of boats they saw; barges carrying coal and sand, train barges carrying coal cars, freighters and schooners at anchor."*
>
> ***— Before Books***

She described another trip to a paper store that led into a whole set of other experiences:

> *"After visiting a retail paper store where vast quantities were stored, the children wished to find out something about the making of paper. One of the teachers discovered a paper mill within the confines of the city and took them there. They saw step after step in the process of making paper, from wood pulp until it was turned out of the factory ready for the printing press. The discovery of the wood pulp also took the children to our own lumber camps. The chance to study earth conditions which make lumbering possible as well as the life of the lumber jack may be fruitful."*
>
> **— "Children in Their Neighborhoods"**

**Brooklyn Bridge**

A record of the six-year-old group's weekly trips in 1920 – 21 (November through May) included:

Gansevoort Market
Christopher St. Ferry
Gansevoort Market to buy pigeons
Jefferson Market and a stable
Steamer Guiana at Quebec Co. docks
Return to Docks to see Guiana sail for West Indies
Visit to new school under construction
East River at 10th Street
Back to revisit Guiana on return trip
Ferry to Hoboken, home by Elevated
Grand Central Station
Battery Park and ferry to Staten Island, back by Elevated
Pennsylvania Station
Fire Engine House on W. 10th St. and to docks to revisit Guiana
Brooklyn Bridge
Docks at Hudson River
Visit to White Star Liner Cretic
Visit new school building.

**— Stott, *Record of Group VI***
**[See end of chapter for a more complete Record of Group VI.]**

**Pennsylvania Station**

**Battery Park**

**Gansevoort Market**

**Children in the Play School, and later City and Country School, took extensive field trips around New York City. A list from 1920 – 1921 for the six year olds included Battery Park, Pennsylvania Station, Gansevoort Market and Brooklyn Bridge. (All photos used with permission of the Collection of the New York Historical Society.)**

## The Library

The library was a central focus of the school and complemented all the first-hand learning. Children were encouraged to be independent researchers of primary sources, as textbooks were not used.

Margot Adler[4], writer and radio journalist, was a "graduate" of City and Country School; she described her memories in her autobiographical book *Heretic's Heart*:

> *"Of all the rooms, it was the library that was truly our paradise. It was a fairly small room with an old wooden floor painted black. Sunlight poured through two very tall windows. At the center was a long table. Small wicker chairs with frayed red pillows created the outer circle.*
>
> *We entered this hushed sanctuary as if under a spell. There we sat, legs crossed, or knees up to our chest, or one leg splayed out, occasionally chewing on bookmarks or pencils, drinking in page after page."*
>
> **— Adler, *Heretic's Heart***

## Program Elements at the Play School

Evelyn Dewey, John Dewey's daughter, visited the school in 1915, and a positive discussion of it was included in the Deweys' joint publication, *Schools of Tomorrow*. Pratt felt that this was the first recognition of the school in the educational world.

Pratt believed in "readiness" but not resulting from the pressures of schools or society. She was convinced that children would learn reading, writing and arithmetic if *the outcomes were significant to the child.* Learning would then be natural, and children would become ready. Information

[4] Margot Adler is the granddaughter of Alfred Adler, Freud's collaborator.

and knowledge were not seen as ends in themselves, but as a process of getting the information that formed the core of an education. Children needed the power to educate themselves.

Pratt summarized the key components of The Play School in 1917 in a bulletin from the Bureau of Educational Experiments:

> *"First, that the children already live and have developed, and will continue to live and develop, in surroundings with which the school has had nothing to do. Second, that children have always had a tendency to carry out in play the processes which they have seen going on about them. Third, that the complexity of modern life makes it necessary to interpret it for the children if they are to understand and use and adapt themselves to it. Fourth, that to carry out these processes they must have tools and materials suited to their childish purpose. Fifth, that any social enterprise, such as a school, creates its own problems which have to be met, and that these problems may be met naturally in a school by the children themselves."*
>
> **— Charlotte Winsor (Ed.), "The Play School," *Experimental Schools Revisited***

**Caroline Pratt titled her one book *I Learn From Children*, and this title reflects the essence of her life's work. "What is a school? To answer that a school is a place of learning is no answer at all, but only another way of stating the question. A place of learning what? A place of learning, how?" (Used with permission of City & Country School, New York.)**

A typical morning program for four year olds was

- indoor play (about an hour),
- outdoor play (about an hour),
- midmorning snack of crackers and milk,
- stories or sensory play,
- indoor play.

Leila Stott, the teacher of the six year olds, recorded the program for an entire school year . These records commented on specific activities and approaches in four categories: play experiences, practical experiences, special training and organization of information.

*Considering the excerpts (end of chapter) from Stott's* Record of Group VI, City and Country School 1920 – 1921, *how do you see teachers as classroom researchers?*

Another section illustrates the ways in which curriculum subject areas were covered through play and activities. **[See end of chapter for *Record of Group VI*].** Here is one entry about the activities and experiences in the academic area of geography:

> ***Geography***
> ***New York City and Harbor:***
>
> *Orientation by points of compass. Construction with blocks of sections of city and harbor for play schemes. Tracing on floor of routes taken on trips. Tracing the same on picture map of Manhattan. Tracing steamer routes on map and globe. Elevated railroads, surface cars, subways and Hudson tubes. Connection with mainland by ferries, bridges, railroads and tubes.*

## City and Country School

Pratt worked closely with Lucy Sprague Mitchell, another educator of the time (see chapter 11). Sprague Mitchell taught in the school starting in 1916 and added her unique expertise with the play value of language. She developed songs and stories that reflected the children's experiences. The Play School became one of the research sites when Lucy Sprague Mitchell set up the Bureau of Educational Experiments (B.E.E.), and Pratt was a founding member of the Working Council of the B.E.E. In 1916 Mitchell offered Pratt rent-free space for her school in a set of six converted brownstones with interconnected backyards in MacDougal Alley in the Village.

*What is in a name? Does "play" mean it is not a* ***real*** *school? Is a play school different than a nursery school? Does the word make a difference? Does a Head Start Program have more learning that a day care? Words do make a difference in how people perceive a school or program for children, and Pratt struggled with this issue.*

But the two had some disagreements. When The Play School expanded into the elementary grades, Sprague Mitchell convinced Pratt that it needed a more "academic" title, and it was re-named The City and Country School. Another account of the name change, in *Before Books,* indicates it was the older children who protested against the use of the word "play," wanting a different image for their school. In any case, Pratt always preferred the name Play School as there could be no better definition of her goals and intentions for a school.

The name change to City and Country School in 1921 was significant in the emphasis on extensive trips to the country. Farm life would later be discussed and recreated in part in the classroom. Field trips were a central part of the program from the beginning, and the school maintained a school vacation farm in Hopewell Junction, New York, where children could milk cows, cultivate gardens, make structures using cement, and so on. The camp was eventually abandoned after 13 years when more and more families took their children on family holidays to other places outside the city.

Pratt stated the main thesis of City and Country School in a 1927 article entitled "Making Environment Meaningful":

> *"To study the interests and abilities of the growing child as they are manifested, to supply an environment that, step by step, must meet the needs of his development, stimulate his activities, and orient him to his enlarging world, and that shall at the same time afford him effective experiences in social living — this in brief has been the thesis of the City and Country School."*

She continued to stress the experimental and changing practices of the school. It was never static.

## Reflective Practice

Pratt saw The City and Country School as constantly evolving, with the children being instrumental in what happened at the school:

> *"A school, like a home, is where you find it, and to the traditional school, it makes little difference what the surroundings are: the curriculum is fixed, though the children differ vastly, and the burden on the teacher is to fit the children to the school but the school as I envisioned it had no fixed limits, no walls. It would take shape under the children's own hands. It would be as wide and high as their own world, would grow as their horizons stretched. And as children make use of whatever they can find around them for their learning, so would the school."*
>
> — ***I Learn from Children***

Her reflection on practice with children is evident as a key element throughout the history of her work at Hartley House, The Play School and City and Country School. Pratt was a researcher with children, a practitioner who studied children. Even in her early writing (1902) about her experiences at Hartley House, she knew that teachers would be learners *with* children:

> *"[The teacher] feels that, after all, there is a chance for her to grow through her teaching, and not become the traditional, dictatorial school teacher of the past. Her attitude becomes one of humility."*
>
> — **"Carpentry at Hartley House"**

Methods and materials were discussed, evaluated and modified as the staff "percolated like coffee pots constantly on the boil with new ideas."

Harriet Cuffaro, a former teacher at City and Country School, remembers the impact of this reflective atmosphere on her teaching:

> *"[The children] questioned what I took for granted and saw what I had not thought about or imagined.*
>
> *While child development was still an essential factor in my planning, I thought less in terms of stages and characteristics. Constructs about children began to give way to named children who were alive and present in the room.*
>
> *All the thinking and rethinking, the questioning and self-evaluation, made me feel vulnerable because teaching is so public."*
>
> — **Cuffaro, *Experimenting with the World***

## Genesis of Pratt's Ideas

The school and its ideas were the result primarily of Caroline Pratt, her colleagues and the children. She proposed methods, not theories. Unlike some of the other historical figures, her ideas did not primarily stem from eminent educational theorists or other progressive schools, though similarities can be seen. She did indicate that Charles Hanford Henderson[5] (a proponent of organic education) and Marietta Pierce Johnson[6] (a teacher in Fairhope, Alabama) influenced her. Elements of project-based work, focus on the whole child and relying on children's initiative can be seen in the work of both these people.

Marietta Johnson had a particular focus on the "play spirit" and education's role in change:

> *"Play is essential to the child's life and growth, and essential also for the adult. It should begin at the beginning and last throughout life, changing form but growing stronger with the years. Play develops the sense of humor and establishes… a power to meet the difficulties of life."*
>
> *"If education is to become the conscious agent of building a better world, it must emphasize the all-round life of the learner."*
>
> — ***Youth in a World of Men***

Pratt maintained an anti-theoretical stance. She did read Dewey and Piaget but refused to discuss their theories. She did not want to be hamstrung by formulas or the need to articulate her own theory.

She was openly critical of Montessori:

*Imagine a conversation between Pratt and Montessori. On what would they agree? Disagree?*

> *"The Montessori schools were not interested in the development of the whole child, but in the main, the goal was a quick and easy way to open up the world of books to children."*
>
> — **"As To Indoctrination"**

---

[5] See *Education and the Larger Life* and *What is it to be Educated* by Charles Hanford Henderson.

[6] Chapter 7 has an extensive section on Marietta Johnson's Organic School. See also a chapter in John and Evelyn Dewey's *Schools of Tomorrow,* Johnson's own book *Youth in a World of Men,* two articles by Joseph Newman in *The Harbinger* (see References in Chapter 3), or "The Organic School" by Newman in *"Schools of Tomorrow," Schools of Today.*

> *"The Montessori, distinguished from the kindergarten method, is a system of training. It gives the children more freedom to move about in their environment and to choose what they will do, but the material from which they have to choose is designed to train … teaching is transferred from the teacher to blocks, to bits of fabric, to weights, to sandpaper letters, and to figures. The children may not use this material to carry out purposes of their own, but only for the purpose for which it was originally designed. As the children's use of material is limited, so is their development. In the Montessori schools the children's activities do not function from their own point of view. The children build a stair but they cannot put it to use."*
>
> — **"Experimental Schools"**

Aware of Freud, Jung and other psychoanalysts, Pratt did not pursue their approaches or orientations. She did refer children to professional help if deep-seated emotional problems arose. She believed that teachers were not to function as amateur psychiatrists.

She did not want children to be introduced prematurely to books and literature, foregoing real experiences.

Pratt opposed the concept of habit formation as developed by Hill, Earl Barnes and others. She did not feel that it fully recognized the creative art of the teacher:

> *"Habit formation or the training of special abilities sets aside this seeking quality and substitutes mechanical forms through which individuals tend to become standardized."*
>
> — ***Before Books***

Pratt was influenced by Patty Smith Hill and her work with play, curriculum and blocks. In *I Learn from Children,* she recounts a story that Hill told of a friend's child who was playing with blocks. Hill had arrived for supper and the mother briskly asked the child to pick up the blocks and get washed for supper. The child kicked the block structure, angry at the insensitive interruption of his elaborate project. Pratt implored teachers and parents to be more responsive to a child's world and help with necessary transitions.

## Resistence to New Ideas

Despite the fame and influence of supporter John Dewey, progressive schools like City and Country School were still not readily accepted. A *New Yorker* magazine cartoon showed a child looking up at a teacher and asking, "Do I have to do what I want to do *all* the time?" Another derogatory cartoon showed children running around the teacher who sat with a dunce cap on her head. Some schools did allow unfettered "freedom," but this was not the case with Pratt's program.

Charlotte Winsor, a Bank Street College professor and former City and Country School teacher, said,

> *"When anyone heard that you taught at City and Country School, for example, you were the butt of dinner table jokes and conversations, and almost all the time had to defend your position in the world."*
>
> — **Dropkin and Tobier (Eds.), *Roots of Open Education in America***

During the Depression, parents could not always afford to send their children to the school. Teachers worked for little or no pay, though the school later paid their salaries back.

Pratt believed that the school should fit the nature of the child and not the other way around. Today we continue with questions about the "fit" between children, child-development knowledge and the functioning of the schools.

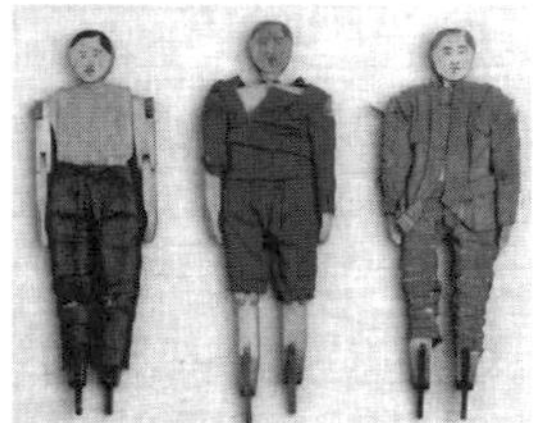

**Do-With Dolls. Photo taken by Pamela Telford, parent of City & Country School, 2000. (Used courtesy of City & Country School, New York.)**

## Blocks and Other Materials

Pratt saw blocks and other adaptable play materials as providing ways children could organize their experiences, raise new inquiries and offer opportunities for new relationships. Adaptable materials allowed children to carry out their own purposes and plans in reconstructing the world and its functioning. Children in urban areas did not have the natural materials Pratt had when she was a child, so she created similar materials that did not have pre-determined representations. Basic materials of clay, wood, and paper were also always available.

She designed **Do-Withs** as the toys that could be used to recreate the children's experiences. These flexible, wooden jointed dolls and toys often revolved around farm and home schemes — people, sheep, pigs, horses, hay wagons, horse with cart, and others. They were made simply, so older children could actually construct them in the carpentry shop.

She demonstrated these at the 1922 Child Welfare Exhibit in both Chicago and New York, giving talks as to their usage. A play space was provided for the children at the exhibit:

> *"In this exhibit we have selected toys with which the children can do things. There are no toys at which the children merely look. We are here to advise you to select such toys as are here shown and also to keep in mind a scheme. You could have made the horse answer in your childhood because you knew that the meaning of horses was all mixed up with harnesses and wagons and stables and feedboxes. But now the toys themselves must teach the process and must be more suggestive of the play to be carried out with them."*
>
> — **"Toys: A Usurped Educational Field"**

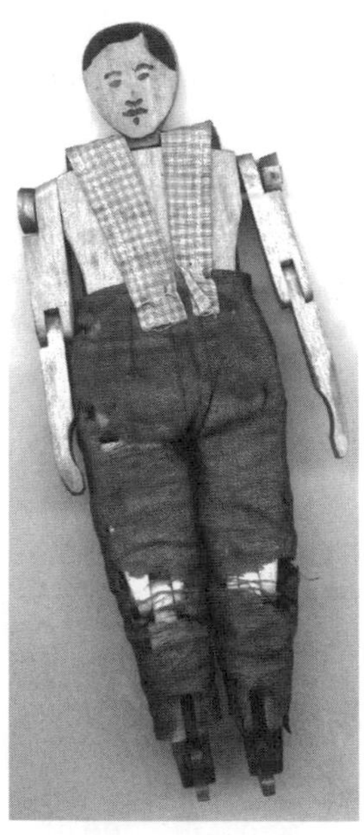

**Caroline Pratt created Do-Withs like this to use in dramatic play and help children reproduce their experiences of their own environment such as house, street or barn schemes. (Used with permission of City & Country School, New York.)**

She worked with a Mr. Castleman to manufacture the Do-Withs. This failed as a commercial endeavour, due perhaps to the lack of an advertising and promotional campaign or to the abstract and opened-ended nature of the materials. But Pratt took the problem in stride and saw it as an opportunity to take stock and look for new directions.

She condemned the nature of most toys for children as "you push, we do the rest":

> *"the toy shops [are] in fierce competition to get the latest thing to tempt the unwary, and the briefly delighted children passing through and making an occasional selection, only to find when they reach home that it contains little for them."*
>
> — **"Toys: A Usurped Educational Field"**

*What are the advantages of unit blocks for math? Science? Social studies?*

Toys, instead, should be a way for children to connect the roles of people to social structures in society.

Pratt later designed **unit blocks**. She used her woodworking skills to design and build these blocks after seeing the Patty Smith Hill blocks used by older children. She wanted blocks that would be better for younger children but also useful for older children. She wanted blocks that were more flexible and allowed children to recreate their experiences and express their thoughts of the world around them. Pratt's were hardwood, non-coloured, in many shapes and mathematically precise in their unit relationships, based on a 1:2:4 proportion. The basic unit was 1 3/8" x 2 3/4" x 5 1/2" and remains the same today. Rounded shapes like pillars and curves interfaced with the basic rectangular solids and triangles. Both stability and precision were critical for their usage. In 1943 the Pratt Project Play Blocks were illustrated in *Play Centers for School Children* by Adele Franklin and Agnes Benedict and manufactured by Educational Equipment Company (Edco). It was owned and operated by Murray Shapiro at 69 Bank Street. Current catalogues and manufacturers still guarantee the blocks for 50 years!

**Pratt designed and developed unit blocks but never patented them as she believed they were only pieces of wood until children created structures from them. Their design and flexible uses have withstood the test of time, and the blocks are in every early childhood equipment catalogue. (From the personal collection of Jennifer Wolfe. Photo taken by Kitty Ng.)**

Pratt never patented these blocks, even when City and Country School was in dire financial difficulties. She never gained any monetary compensation for these very successful blocks. It is interesting that their future manufacture by a variety of companies retained the proportions and sizes of the original Pratt blocks. Her lack of concern for control over their production is in dramatic contrast to the control that Montessori enacted on her materials and equipment.

For Pratt, the blocks were mere pieces of wood until they gained meaning from the children. She called them "free materials" to distinguish them from the blocks in a Froebel kindergarten or a Montessori program:

> *"In calling these materials free materials I can best distinguish them from the materials of the kindergarten and the Montessori schools. Their uses are various. They are not designed for some specific educational purpose of an adult, but are incidental to child life and child purpose."*
>
> — ***The Play School: An Experiment in Education***

Pratt knew that children could learn about shape, size, and scale from these blocks. They could create objects — a truck, plane, boat, barn or high rise building — and represent experiences from their environment. The blocks would lend themselves to solitary, parallel, and co-operative play. This multi-usage was very important to her planning. Unit blocks were first popularized by Harriet Johnson in her book *The Art of Blockbuilding* in 1933.

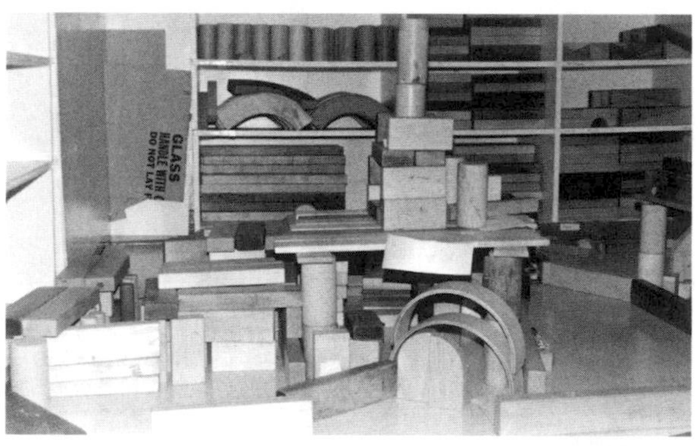

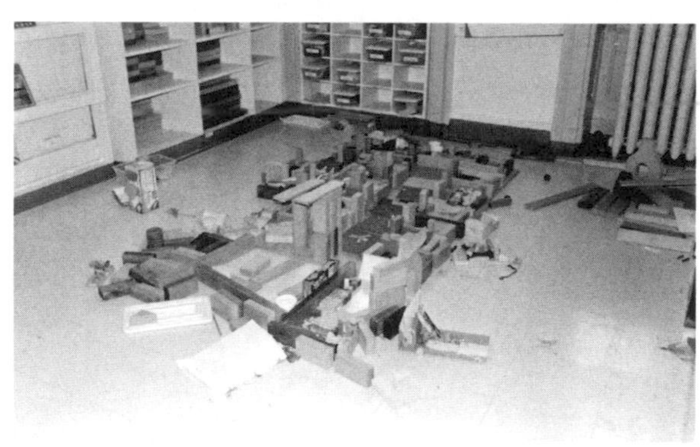

**Caroline Pratt invented unit blocks, and these have been at the centre of children's programming at City & Country School. These photos were taken at different times in the school's history. (Used with permission of City & Country School, New York.)**

*Why don't most primary grades include unit blocks in their program?*

More recently, numerous books and articles have been written documenting the use of unit blocks in areas of study including mathematics, science and social studies. *The Block Book*, edited by Elisabeth Hirsch; *Exploring Learning*, edited by Pat Gura; and *The Complete Block Book* by Eugene Provenzo, Jr. and Arlene Brett are some examples.

Robert Louis Stevenson's poem "Block City" (in *A Child's Garden of Verses*) is a poetic expression of the versatility and uniqueness of block play for children:

*What are you able to build with your blocks?*
*Castles and palaces, temples and docks.*
*Rain may keep raining, and others go roam.*
*But I can be happy and building at home.*

*Let the sofa be mountains, the carpet be sea,*
*There I'll establish a city for me:*
*A kirk and a mill and a palace beside,*
*And a harbour as well where my vessels may ride.*

*Great is the palace with pillar and wall,*
*A sort of a tower on top of it all.*
*And steps coming down in an orderly way*
*To where my toy vessels lie safe in the bay.*

*This one is sailing and that one is moored:*
*Hark to the song of the sailors on board!*
*And see on the steps of my palace, the kings*
*Coming and going with presents and things!*

*Now I have done with it, down let it go!*
*All in a moment the town is laid low*
*Block upon block lying scattered and free.*
*What is there left of my town by the sea?*

*Yet as I saw it, I see it again.*
*The kirk and the palace, the ships and the men.*
*And as long as I live and where'er I may be,*
*I'll always remember my town by the sea.*

Pratt also created six-inch-high wood cutouts of people (**Wedgie People**), which represented everyday community workers and family members. Wide at the bottom and thin at the top, they stood easily and were used as accessories to the block play.

**WEDGIE WOOD PLAY PEOPLE AND ANIMALS**
***Attractive wood figures, screened on both sides and wedge shaped so that they can stand easily without toppling.***

**BA 10 Community Workers:** 7 figures (fireman, policeman, milkman, doctor, nurse, mailman, worker) .......... **$3.95**

**BA 11 Family Group:** 6 figures (father, mother, boy, girl, grandmother, grandfather) .......... **3.50**

**BA 12 Farm Animals:** 10 animals (horse, cow, pig, hen, rooster, goose, lamb, 2 chickens, duck) .......... **3[illegible]0**

**BA 13 Zoo Animals:** 6 animals (elephant, zebra, tiger, lion, giraffe, polar bear).......... **2.95**

**Wedgie People. This description is from a 1952 toy catalogue of Young Playways in Washington D.C., owned by George Wolfe. (From the personal collection of Jennifer Wolfe.)**

Block accessories — wood, clay, paints, string, hose, clock springs — were *basic* materials that children could use to create needed objects for their play.

**Pratt's hollow blocks allowed children to build large structures. (From the personal collection of Jennifer Wolfe. Photo taken by Kitty Ng.)**

Pratt also designed large **hollow blocks** to encourage large muscle play and experiences that used more physical energy. They were light and could be easily lifted, carried and stacked. These blocks allowed children to climb over and climb in while developing balance, strength, coordination and social skills. In some of her earlier writings, these are also referred to as yard blocks and were also in units (10" x 10" and 10" x 20"). Sizes vary somewhat today by different manufacturers.

Charlotte Winsor remembers the key role of blocks in the program:

> *"As I look back, my experience with these children up to the age of six and seven — the amount of creative life that they were able to express in their blockbuilding — was almost reverent."*
>
> **— quoted in R. Dropkin and A. Tobier (Eds.), *Roots of Open Education in America***

All these blocks and materials were adaptable for varying uses and ages.

Recognizing the need children have to manage "danger," Pratt took off the guard rails on climbers, slides and platforms. As the children got older, they would have additional risks/dangers but always within their developmental ability. She was always concerned with safety. Today we still discuss how high block structures should be built, how high the playhouse should be and other issues concerning balancing safety with children's inclination to explore.

## Role of the Teacher

What was the teacher's role? Certainly it was not passive in Pratt's viewpoint. Teachers needed to be sensitive to children, extending their learning to assist children's own search for answers and knowledge. If a child saw a truck, the teacher might ask,

- What's inside the truck?
- Where is it going?
- Where did it come from?
- What makes the truck go?
- What will happen to the materials inside the truck?
- Who is driving the truck? What does he do?

Pratt's description of the teacher shows the tremendous responsibility that sensitive, responsive teachers have. Their role does not resemble the mechanical use of a curriculum guide, teacher's manual, or packaged methodology:

> *"It is she who must make the day-by-day, even the moment-by-moment decisions which added up to a teaching method. She who must learn about her subjects — the children — by working with them; she who must frame her curriculum around their changing needs as they developed, both individually and in the group. She who must know how to act quickly in a specific situation. She who must deal each day with such questions as how far we shall push our ideas of order on the children; just when they are ready for short cuts in learning, like correct shop practices, or the multiplication tables; what kind of information they need, and when and how it should be offered to them. And she it was who met the deeper problems of the child, the problems of emotion and behavior."*
>
> **— *I Learn From Children***

Pratt saw the teacher as a guide for children, observing their behaviour and helping them get what they needed.

If adults lose the experimental method,

> *"They fail to take the child's pioneering method into account, to respect it, to give it elbow room."*
>
> **— "Learning By Experience"**

She also believed that one great teacher could always make a difference in a child's life.

## Curriculum

*If Jean Piaget had visited Caroline Pratt's Play School or City and Country School, would he have found the ideas consistent with his ideas on child development? What would be different?*

There were four main curriculum components developed in the school:

- **play experiences** — dramatic play, blocks, art, etc.;
- **practical experiences** — cooking, care of materials, shop work, etc.;
- **organization of information** — trips, discussions, use of books and stories, etc.; this area was originally called enrichment of experience;
- **skills or techniques (special training)** — sense training, number work, music techniques, and language arts.

Behavioural records of each child were kept from year to year in these four areas:

> *"Records in which the teacher's opinion is not backed up by the child's behavior are thrown into the discard."*
>
> — **"Recording Mental Health and Treatment"**

An 11-year record of "Michael" from age three through fourteen was published in *Progressive Education* to help teachers study and support the process of healthy growth.

> *"The children and teacher made the curriculum."*
>
> — **Introduction to Stott, *City and Country School: Record of Group VI 1921***

Abstractions needed concrete realities for children, or symbols would become empty and meaningless. Pratt used the example of the symbol **5**:

> *"It is a curlicue, a scribble on a piece of paper. He can make a hundred of them and they won't mean a thing. They mean no more to him than the words an adult pours into his ear in answer to a question, the verbal information which he cannot absorb."*
>
> ***— I Learn From Children***

Children would not be taught to count but were helped to learn that number has a relationship — purchasing school supplies, setting the table, estimating quantities, using numbers in their block work.

Pratt eloquently describes the nature of real learning:

*Pratt believed in basic open-ended materials in a play-based program. How valid is this approach today?*

> *"Compare the actual making of a toy steam boiler and experimenting with forms for findings its cubical contents on the spot as an introduction to 'cubic measure,' with having a teacher present cubic measure as a worked-out form. Such handling of mathematics as the former secures a confidence and regard in the individual as a creator of new forms and processes. He learns to think of himself as an inventor, a discoverer in an unlimited field. He learns to open his arms and eyes to opportunity, to seek it and recognize it."*
>
> ***— Before Books***

Isolated facts have no meaning in life and take on meaning only when they relate to each other. Children became first-hand investigators of subject matter, and knowledge became what the children got out of the subject matter. Pratt pleaded that children's inquiries should be encouraged and prized, not stifled or diverted. She chided schools that created a "paper curriculum" instead of working with children.

The younger children's program was dominated by play and by the community. The real world became their classroom. Blocks and other creative media were the tools they used to explore their world:

> *"We are not willing to have the children dominated by subject-matter. We want them to form strong habits of first-hand research and to use what they find; we want them to discover relationships in concrete matter, so that they will know they exist when they deal with abstract forms, and will have habits of putting them to use."*
>
> — **"Making Environment Meaningful"**

The Play City

**Children recreated in play the city they explored in field trips. (From C. Pratt's *Experimental Practice in the City and Country School* published in 1924 by E. P. Dutton & Co. of New York.)**

Interesting education issues arose. Should children go to zoos? Pratt initially supported these field trips to see exotic animals; however, she soon came to reject them as the animals were too far from their natural habitat. Instead, children were encouraged to focus on animals they were familiar with in their own environment.

Fairy tales? Plato asked this question thousands of years before. Pratt said fairy tales should not be used until the child could distinguish fantasy and reality:

> *"Fairies and witches, magic carpets and wishing rings can do worse than confuse him; they provide such easy excitement that he is discouraged from examining more closely the real world, so tame and familiar on the surface, to find the exciting revelations it too contains. Since it is the real world he must learn to live in, it seems to me we are thus giving him at the start a greater handicap than progressive educators are accused of doing when they appear to neglect the three R's."*
>
> — ***I Learn From Children***

There was no taboo on fairy tales, but they were not to substitute for the "here and now" and direct experience. Fantasy was also only one part of imagination, which was encouraged in many other ways.

*Experimental Practice in the City and Country School* is primarily an extended record of the seven-year-old group with detailed accounts of the program and investigations by the children.

Traditional academic subjects were not ends in themselves but tools to help children with their own learning:

> *"Instead of putting teacher and children into a straitjacket at the outset, with a rigid set of requirements for the year's work, we allowed the job, the group's interests, the events that were the talk of the dinner table at night or the headlines of the morning paper to guide them. Each group teacher kept in mind the needs of the next year's job in skills, and found ways to prepare children for them. Staff discussions laid down in broad outline the direction each year's work would follow and the subject matter it was likely to cover, but each group, as it went through the school, took its own way also through the many fields of learning spread before it. And they acquired, not only habits of learning that would see them through a lifetime... but also an amazing quantity of sheer information — absorbed it, understood it, held it ready for use where they needed it."*
>
> ***— I Learn From Children***

## Motivation

Pratt rejected rewards just has she had rejected the "big stick" in work with children. Children's motivation would develop as they devised purposes and persevered to work through them:

> *"This principle of motivation is, to me, what the new education stands or falls by. It stands us in good stead that the children seem to have entered the world with a certain physical set-up which demands opportunity for play and work — and that they accept the opportunity. Our opponents characterize the opportunity as one 'to do as one pleases,' but we think it is an opportunity to produce; to produce not because one merely remembers, not because one is told to, but because all one's faculties are primed for work. What one produces under such circumstances is to a degree creative; . . . its essential characteristic is a motivation from within."*
>
> ***— Experimental Practice in the City and Country School***

## "Jobs" Program

The spirit of Pratt's childhood village life was re-created in the approach of jobs, with the older children doing community school work projects. Planning, execution and accomplishment would be part of experiencing whole jobs. The first **job** developed was the school store, and it provided an integral service to the school's functioning. The eight-year-old children planned and built the store and then opened it for business. The children learned through the whole process about carpentry, money, ordering, organization, arithmetic, and reading — all in the context of real life. A committee of children ran the store each day. The books were balanced at the end of each week, and buying supplies was an ongoing task:

> *"I know only that children cannot escape practical arithmetic if it is taught in connection with a job."*
>
> ***— I Learn From Children***

**Block Printing. (Used with permission of City & Country School, New York.)**

**One of the "jobs" that gave children a sense of real work was operating a printing press. The press would be used to print the children's stories, magazines, woodcuts and other school materials. Printing also led to the study of the history of printing. (Used with permission of City & Country School, New York.)**

The job of store also led the children into studies of the origin of paper (visiting paper mills in the process), a study of stores in the past, a visit to a cargo ship loaded with raw rubber from the Amazon, and a study of the first settlers and their relationship with native Americans.

The store job's success led to other ideas for jobs throughout the school. The ideas came from the children but also had obvious origins in Pratt's early experiences growing up in Fayetteville:

- a school post office,
- printing press,
- lunchroom,
- school newspaper (*The Yardbird*),
- school journal (*The Bookworm's Digest*),
- photographic records for the school/ photography studio,
- toy making (the "Never Bust Toy Company")

Pratt felt that these were relevant and meaningful to the children at City and Country School. A rural school might have very different **jobs** related to the children's environment and needs — chicken industry or cooperative store, for example.

Each of the jobs involved extensive academic learning embedded in the needs of the real work and many extensions of learning through associated interests and questions. The children were absorbed in learning curriculum:

> *"Jobs as the core of an elementary school curriculum have proved themselves to our satisfaction over and over again, and from every point of view. The absorption of children in their jobs, the way in which, like healthy plants, they throw roots out in every direction from the job to draw in ever more educational nourishment — in the practical skills, in geography and history, in literature and music and the arts — to us this is the surest confirmation that we have enlisted that potent and precious force, the child's urge to learn, in his education."*
>
> ***— I Learn from Children***

Pratt tells the story of a teacher who went on to another school and adopted the idea of activities but not jobs. Returning for a visit, she complained that her children did not have the responsibility of the children in City and Country School. Pratt looked her in the eye and responded with only one word: **Jobs!**

Jobs also unified all levels of the school as children interacted in the school store or post office:

> *"One does not have to talk about social studies in such a school — social studies are replaced by social experiences."*
>
> **— "Social Experiences — Not Social Studies"**

*What "jobs" would you think appropriate for your current group of children? How would you initiate such a "jobs" program?*

Pratt felt that children gained resourcefulness, a sense of competence, achievement, initiative, creativity, and respect for others in the work process. This in turn would help children develop a sense of self and of others — lifelong strengths. She saw the school functioning as a self-sufficient democratic community and part of her vision for the future.

Margot Adler (in *Heretic's Heart*) gives her perspective on the "real magic" behind the program:

> *"City and Country took as an axiom an idea that has been echoed by a host of philosophers and writers from Marx to Muir to Einstein — that when you try to pick out something by itself, you find it connected to everything else in the universe. And in school that meant that every historical period we studied was reflected in the poems and paintings we created, the plays we presented, even in the math and science we were taught, and most certainly in the books we read. We dipped into each period and claimed it as our own."*

## Rhythms and Music

Established by Ruth Doing in the 1920's, **Rhythms** was a unique movement program that included live piano accompaniment. Children re-created experiences and expressed themselves with the additional use of scarves, ropes, mats, hoops, balls and rings. Margot Adler in *Heretic's Heart* describes the axial function of "rhythms":

**The rhythms room involves piano accompaniment to children's pantomimes and movement experiences. Materials such as scarves and hoops aid in interpretation. (Used with permission of City & Country School, New York.)**

> *"The gym was on the top floor, a simple room with a polished wood floor and one wall covered with Swedish bars. The pianist would play an assortment of classical selections, and not only would we dance and skip and leap, but often we would hear a piece of music and be told, 'You are now under the sea,' and we would pretend to be anything from sea creatures to submarines. Sometimes in this 'rhythms' class we would act out scenes from periods of history, with only large colored silk scarves for props: a market scene in ancient Egypt, perhaps, or an alchemist's shop in the Middle Ages. Usually these scenes were taken from the historical periods we were studying in the classroom and often these were later expanded into plays or musicals.* ***The rarest and most precious aspect of this curriculum was that everything was connected."***

Music and singing were integral parts of the program, and children learned an eclectic assortment of songs from many traditions, often connected to the topic or era they were studying. Margot Adler (in *Heretic's Heart*) describes music as ***"the binder and healer"***:

> *"song was a doorway into an entirely new world. It was a group creation, a way into a shared state of ecstatic harmony."*

## Teacher Education

Pratt knew that she would need to find progressive teachers to work in her school:

> *"I was for my part very deeply involved in the search for teachers for the age groups as we added them. There was then no source for such teachers as I envisioned, no training school which could supply me with this most precious kind of material."*
>
> **— *I Learn From Children***

She wanted teachers of high calibre as described by Mary Card, a former teacher:

> *"She was more concerned with the personality of the individual and his or her relationship with the children. Her early teachers were dynamic, for the most part well read, full of social concerns, and interested in children having meaningful experiences in relation to their studies."*
>
> **— quoted in Hirsch, *Caroline Pratt and the City and Country School***

Caroline Pratt believed strongly in her role in teacher education and always had student teachers as part of the program. All student teachers gained the knowledge that play was serious business for children. Frank and Theresa Caplan were two of her students who went on to write about and study play.[7] Frank Caplan was the first male nursery school student teacher with City and Country School, joining the school in 1932. Frank and Theresa Caplan also went on to establish Creative Playthings to produce educational learning materials for children. In the early days of the business, Frank cut and sanded Caroline Pratt unit blocks in the back of the shop while customers waited in the front.

What was Pratt like as a supervisor and teacher educator? The following are all quotations from former teachers:

> *"I think she rarely missed a day coming to my classroom that first year. She didn't always stay long — but she was always there. She loved the little children — and as old as she was by that time — she could relate easily and well to three year olds." [Pat Clark]*
>
> *"We had a few battles about play equipment I remember. She felt — and I agreed and still do agree with her (within limits) — that to develop the imagination and an ability to think the fewer props and the more raw materials a child is given the better he will develop his own powers of thinking. However I felt Caroline went a bit far sometimes. She was horrified because I wanted to introduce a few rubber dolls .... It wasn't until the last day of the school year that she grudgingly, as always, admitted I'd done a good job and hoped I'd come back the next year. I did — for four years — and enjoyed every minute of it." [Pat Clark]*
>
> *"In my first year she left me to do things in my own way. It was a hard year for me as I had had a spinal fusion in the summer and I was not allowed by my M.D. to start work before November. I had planned to work in the print room with the Elevens but with my unfamiliarity with printing (which I had planned to learn that summer) I took the Nines instead. There were several disturbed children in the group, difficult to control and exhausting for one in limited health — Caroline was most considerate, would give me advice only when I asked for it and was never critical." [Mary Card]*
>
> **— quoted in Hirsch, *Caroline Pratt and the City and Country School***

[7] See *The Power of Play* by Frank and Theresa Caplan.

**Pete Seeger, American folksinger, with his grandson Tao Rodriguez Seeger. Seeger created many songs for both children and adults. He helped with a fundraiser for City and Country School when it was financially struggling. Years later, his grandson helped with a school field trip on the Hudson. (Photo courtesy of Pete Seeger. Taken by Andrew de Lory.)**

## A Teacher Cooperative

As the school grew from Pratt as the sole teacher, the administration reflected her desire for a cooperative venture. An executive committee was formed to review and set salaries for all staff (including Pratt) and to provide a governance body.

However, she found that teachers did not want to be involved with the fiscal, educational and daily administrative details of the school. The school incorporated as a teacher organization with a principal, secretary, treasurer and an elected board of directors.

The school had a condition that stipulated that no one should receive financial profit from the school.

In 1929 after the fall of the stock market and the gradual withdrawal of funds from Lucy Sprague Mitchell, City and Country School experienced a severe fiscal crisis. A supporter, journalist and humorist Franklin P. Adams called it "the little schoolhouse in the red." Teachers' salaries were cut, and some paid money back to the school. The goal always remained to provide tuition for students in need.

Additional money was raised from the parents, and benefits helped the school weather the crisis. In 1936 a Spring Tonic was held with Franklin Adams (columnist and author), George Gershwin (composer), Dorothy Parker (short story and verse writer), George Kaufman (dramatist and journalist) and Gypsy Rose Lee (entertainer). A country fair *in the city* featuring singers Leadbelly and Pete Seeger, raised other needed funds for the school.

## Other School Ventures

An after-school program began in the 1930's to serve the needs of children living in apartments who had limited possibilities for physical activity. Time was spent outside as well as in the shop, clay room and kitchen — activities selected by the children.

In 1936, there was a joint project with the Chelsea School, in the public system, to assist it in developing an after-school program using City and Country methods (jobs, trips, play materials). Supported by the Public Education Association and numerous educational advisors, the work was extended to another school in Harlem. This project also involved community liaison personnel.[8]

[8] *Play Centers for School Children* by Adele Franklin and Agnes Benedict describes the project and is dedicated to Caroline Pratt.

## Writings

I Learn from Children *showed Pratt's highly reflective approach to teaching as she developed materials and methods. What have you learned from children or families to assist your practice?*

Pratt was primarily a practitioner with children and teachers and wrote relatively little. Aside from *I Learn from Children,* she wrote a number of short articles and parts of books[9], including

- *Experimental Practice in the City and Country School* with Lula Wright in 1924;
- *Before Books* with Jessie Stanton in 1926;
- a chapter in *Experimental Schools Revisited,* edited by Charlotte Winsor, which is a compilation of bulletins from The Bureau of Educational Experiments;
- "Two Basic Principles of Education," an article in the *New Republic* in 1930.

Although she did not emphasize the need to write the ideas down, Pratt hoped others would build on the ideas developed at The City and Country School:

*Caroline Pratt was primarily a practitioner and wrote relatively little. Describe an early childhood professional you know who exemplifies the experimental approach that Pratt had — learning from children.*

> *"But my plea that I was too busy learning about children to make speeches about them was perfectly sincere. To spend my time talking when there was so much work to be done seemed to me wasteful.*
>
> *And dangerous too. All my life I have fought against formula. Once you have set down a formula, you are imprisoned by it.*
>
> *I would not be talked into marking out any blueprints for education, outside the school or within it."*
>
> ***— I Learn from Children***

Pratt rarely gave interviews, though she relented on the 25th anniversary of the start of the Play School. She insisted that the reporter from the *New York Herald Tribune* follow her around the school as she talked. As they walked around the school seeing children make soap, play violins and build boats, she had the following retrospective comments about her work:

> *"I think the most important thing we have found is the block building program for children up to eight years of age, and jobs for the older groups. I mean responsible jobs. Through these responsibilities they learn many co-ordinated academic topics, such as arithmetic, spelling and geography. These jobs also lead to new avenues of study. In the printing shop, for example, the older pupils are stimulated to learn about earlier forms of recording-manuscripts, hieroglyphics, also about the development of printing, its effect on modern education and the economic system.*
>
> *The way it works out is that the school activity — say dramatics — initiates the need of calculating the cost of material and labor. That brings in mathematics problems.*

[9] Complete list is at end of chapter in reference section.

*She believed children should look at things that make them think, not simply 'stuffed birds':*

*He should go to the grocery store, and inquire where the cabbages come from, and how they reached the city, and how they were preserved from decay, and why they cost so much more in the city than on the farm. He should establish a habit of looking for relationships in the adult world. If he sees a coal cart, he should begin to ask questions about coal, and he should then be taken to the river to see the scows unloading and so forth."*

**— quoted in Bugbee, "Miss Pratt Says Find Child a Job He Likes and He'll Teach Himself"**

**Caroline Pratt in 1939. (Used with permission of Fayetteville Free Library, New York.)**

## Personal Life Events

Early in 1910 Pratt owned a farmhouse in the Berkshire Mountains in Massachusetts and spent her summers there with Helen Marot and other friends. Winters were spent living on 12th Street close to City and Country School.

In 1924 Pratt built a cottage on Memensha Pond on Martha's Vineyard, an island off the southeast coast of Massachusetts. It quickly became a mecca for other City and Country supporters and the arts community.

When Helen Marot died of a sudden heart attack in 1940, Pratt experienced a deep sense of loss of a kindred spirit who had shared her life and provided constant intellectual dialogue. Caroline Pratt became ill the following year and began to slow down. She retired in 1945. The school's leadership was unstable for a few years until Jean Murray became principal and stayed for the next 30 years.

When Pratt retired in 1945, she was confident that the teachers would continue to learn from children and carry on the experimental spirit:

> *"They cannot, as I cannot, look upon our school as a static achievement merely to be preserved. As I saw it in its earliest formative days, they continue to see it as a living organism, with a vitality of its own, putting forth new growth to meet the needs of children in their own time."*
>
> **— quoted in Hirsch, *Caroline Pratt and the City and Country School***

Pratt remained active as principal emeritus of City and Country School. As principal, Jean Murray carried on the traditions and philosophy of Caroline Pratt.

---

Ruth Goode, a writer, shaped Caroline Pratt's words into her combined autobiography and treatise. *I Learn from Children* was published by Simon and Schuster when Pratt was 81 years old. Ruth Goode's and Richard Simon's children had attended City and Country School. The book describes in detail how Pratt developed her practice and theory while working directly with children. It received rave reviews and has been published in languages as diverse as Swedish, Hindi, Chinese and Urdu.

---

After a winter of failing health, Pratt died in June of 1954. The *New York Times* obituary (June 7, 1954) stated,

> *"Children convinced Miss Pratt many decades ago that they were 'alert, persistent, self-respecting little personalities' to whom school should offer more than the Three R-s and discipline. Upon this discovery, Miss Pratt based a lifetime of teaching devoted to the proposition that a school ought to fit children and not the children to the school."*

Two days later, a letter to the editor by Charles A. Reich, a lawyer and graduate of City and Country gave the following acclaim:

> *"Our schools owe a great deal to Caroline Pratt, whose long and creative life ended this week. She knew that learning can be an exciting adventure. She was able to sharpen, not blunt, the natural intellectual curiosity of children. They went eagerly to her City and Country School. Many of the methods of teaching she pioneered came to be accepted within her lifetime and, wherever they were, school days are happier and more rewarding."*
>
> **— *New York Times*, June 9, 1954**

**Caroline Pratt was buried in her hometown of Fayetteville, New York. The inscription on the stone reads: DAUGHTER, CAROLINE PRATT, MAY 13,1867, JUNE 6, 1954 "I LEARN FROM CHILDREN." (Used with permission of Barbara S. Rivette, Manlius Town Historian, Chittenango, New York. Taken by Barbara Rivette.)**

Her brother Henry was the only immediate survivor, and Pratt was buried in the family plot in Fayetteville.

City & Country School is currently located at 146 West 13th Street. (Used with permission of City & Country School, New York, New York.)

## City & Country School Today

The City & Country School is open today in the New York City neighbourhood where Pratt began her experiment. The school address is:

**The City & Country School**
**146 West 13th Street**
**New York, New York 10011**
**U.S.A.**

website: http://www.cityandcountry.org

The school for children from 2 – 13 years of age remains with much of the original focus and intent of Caroline Pratt.

Blocks are still a central part of the program for the younger children, as with them children learn to work cooperatively and to plan projects. Older children still use blocks but with increasing complexity. Language arts, social studies, math, reading, writing and other curriculum areas are intertwined in their projects, field trips and investigations.

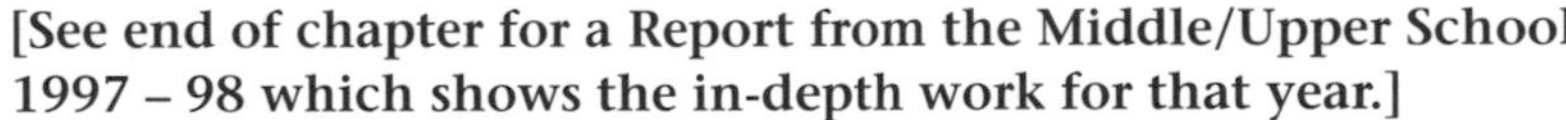

**[See end of chapter for a Report from the Middle/Upper School 1997 – 98 which shows the in-depth work for that year.]**

Classes remain very small (around 18 per class) to accommodate individual differences. Primary sources, instead of textbooks, are used for projects, and research is a foundation of the school program. Other program elements still include music, shop (woodworking), art, outdoor play, rhythms and science.

Some changes have occurred to reflect the world today. These include

- a more diverse group of children from outside the Greenwich Village neighbourhood,
- enrollment of well over 200 children,
- different "jobs,"
- technology (e.g. computers) integrated into the curriculum.

The school is still a teacher cooperative with teachers on the Board of Trustees, and the school continues to grow with the times. Many of the teachers are Bank Street Teachers College–trained. Head teachers normally have a Masters in Education. Assistant teachers return to be head teachers at City and Country when they attain the appropriate degrees.

A Parents Association is a communication link between families and the School. After-school programs, a summer day camp and a "behind the sciences" camp combine to provide full-year programming.

City and Country has produced a video called *Learning From Children* that provides an overview of the City and Country program and its philosophy. The video can be obtained from the school.

Emily Alford taught in City & Country School and described her perception of the order and discipline:

> *"The order in the school seems to emerge from a trust in the children themselves, their capacity and their worth as human beings. The discipline is not an imposition by teachers and administrators, but the consequence of a certain curriculum evolved over the years."*
>
> **— Emily Alford, "A Personal Narrative"**

Jean Murray, who was a friend and colleague of Pratt, describes the continuity of practice from Pratt's time into the present:

> *"As the curriculum at City and Country evolved, Caroline Pratt kept her eye on the things that gave children the deepest satisfactions, and by trial and error she and her staff gradually evolved the basic curricular structure which the school still practices today: give the children experiences that will fit their stage of development and that have inherent in them unlimited opportunities for learning — learning as all children do learn best, by involvement, by really needing new information, or a new skill, by using it and then going to further exploration."*
>
> **— City & Country School (1997, Nov. 15),**
> **"Caroline Pratt's Story" [Online].**
> Website http://projects.ilt.columbia.edu/

Lewis Mumford, a social philosopher who was critical of the dehumanizing nature of modern technology, praised City & Country School for creating Plato's vision of education:

> *"… if I were writing for posterity, I would record our country's pride that you, in the twentieth century America, had made real Plato's ancient dream, of a school in which all the arts and skills and sciences that men need would be taught to children through play; because you had made the child feel at home in his larger environment, had become playful."*
>
> **— Carlton, *Caroline Pratt: A Biography***

*It's Rude To Interrupt* is a video about an innovative school in Vancouver, British Columbia, Canada. The teacher acknowledges Caroline Pratt as one of her key mentors. The video can be purchased from its producer:

*Randy Rotheisler*
*Templeton Secondary School*
*727 Templeton Drive*
*Vancouver, British Columbia V5L 4N8*
*Canada*
*Website: http://templeton.vsb.bc.ca*

*Teachers in the Vancouver area can borrow the video by contacting:*
*Vancouver School Board Media and Library Services*
*VSB Education Centre*
*1580 W. Broadway*
*Vancouver, British Columbia V6J 5X8*
*Canada*
*Website: http://vsb.bc.ca*

## Record of Group VI
### *The City and Country School 1920 – 1921*
### *Leila Stott*

## Play Experiences

"**Store** — Playing store was definitely initiated by me, with Miss Pratt's help, and made the regular program for Friday mornings. It was the first indoor activity that seemed to start a real play spirit among the whole group, and new features have been added spontaneously each week. C.C. was the first one to catch on to the idea of making a store, and he became the first store-keeper. The others all built houses and shopped. When their money was gone, they made clay objects to sell to reimburse themselves. A.W. was a janitor, and earned extra money by going out for a day's cleaning in the store. The next week she remembered that Friday was the day for playing store, and all went at it with zest, making different kinds of stores, so that they could buy and sell to each other. Besides grocery stores and china stores, there was a restaurant, an art store."

"**Outdoors** — In the yard nearly all worked together, building a boat. They showed splendid co-operation in handling heavy roof pieces, which had to be carried by at least 5 or 6 children together and raised or lowered by all at the same moment to be put in place. S.S. has been riding a stick the whole yard period in spite of constant efforts on my part to divert him. He would abandon it for awhile but go right back to it. He played it was a train. It seemed the same type of obsession he has about pulling the wagon and both are definitely associated with train play. He objected to leaving the stick, when we went in, and wanted, at least, to hide it, so no one else could get it, but I insisted that all the material is for all the children, so it must be left for the next class. The following week, for the first time, he successfully joined the group play. He was pulling the cart around alone, as usual, playing train, while 2 or 3 others were building a train of the big blocks. I took the cart away from him and told him the block construction was a train and to go help finish it. He did, with help from me at first in making connections, and his knowledge of train travel was so great that the others gladly accepted his contributions. The cart later was used again for drawing blocks for the main construction, but his interest never failed, and he had no social difficulty. He called out to me once to say, 'This is more fun than the cart.'"

## Practical Experiences

"**Cooking** — Six children at a time have cooked on Monday, Tuesday and Thursday, and, for the first time M. L. and Ct. C. and S.S. were eager to join this group. No one was required to cook but first choice was given each day to alternate groups, and vacancies caused by voluntary withdrawals were filled by those from the other group who were eager to go. J. M. and A. W. seem most keen in this interest. After their cakes are in the oven, two children are chosen by Miss H. each day to wash up and the rest return to the class room (about 10:30 usually) and watch the time, with my assistance, to go back and get their cakes out of the oven and bring them up to the class to be sampled. On Thursday, for the first time, this group provided refreshments for the Teachers' Meeting, and made very successful gingerbread for this event. A.W. and J. M. served the tea, and were most delighted to do so. Both were very serious."

"**Shop** — Some of the children have seemed so little interested in shop work and have brought back such poor projects, even when they started off with a real purpose in view, that I asked Miss Pratt for help. She went herself to the shop and by helping M. L. to attain a higher standard of workmanship in making a caboose to be used in his block play, she aroused in him a real interest, which kept him working hard and gave him a pride in his product, which he did not feel in the cruder type of work. S.S. was fired to do likewise, and, with the help of Mr. R., also produced a caboose that would run on the block tracks. Wheels were left off intentionally, as experience had taught that these do no function satisfactorily on the block tracks. C.C. and E. J. finished their house and have been busy painting it inside and out and making stairs for it."

## Organization of Information

"**Discussions** — The week began with a review of the food seen at Gansevoort Market, and tracing it to its source, both nearby products from New Jersey and Long Island and Eastern or Southern fruit brought by train from distant points. On the picture map of New York the children traced the routes by which the farm wagons came from New Jersey and Long Island by ferries or bridges. Later in the story period, Mrs. Mitchell discussed other products brought into New York by boat and the children mentioned coal, building materials, shoes, milk, meat, stoves, wood and various articles of household use.

The discussion led next day into the question of how and where the river started, and C.C. said the rain started it. A.W. said it met other streams and pointed out on the map instances to illustrate how a river grew in this way."

"**Trips** — On Friday morning it was foggy and the sound of the fog horns turned our thoughts to the river, so we started at 9:30 for the docks, and spent the whole morning there. On the way we met a man with a grindstone, and stopped to watch him sharpen knives. A horse met in the street aroused curiosity as to his bit, and special kind of shoes with sharp points. At the docks interest was first held by the unloading of sand by machinery from a barge, and the loading of rails in small pieces on to a big steamer from a barge. Following the children's lead, we went out on to one of the piers, and found a steamer from the West Indies in dock. We secured permission to go on board. The ship is to be in dock till next Friday, and we planned to come back again and see her leave."

## Special Training

"**Number** — About ten minutes is usually spent just before going to lunch playing 'number games' with small blocks. These games consist in recognizing at sight the number of blocks shown in combinations up to 8. This is never done apart from the concrete objects, and is an individual occupation."

"**Language** — *Pinocchio* was read for nearly an hour on a rainy morning, during the normal yard time. Only M. L. remained out of the group, working on a carpentry job he was interested in finishing, but listening incidentally. Mrs. Mitchell read the first part of 'Meadowland Farm' by request, after the trip, and tied it up to farmers and wagons seen at the Market. Also after the trip on Wednesday, the group composed a story of their experiences with Mrs. Mitchell's help."

## Report from the Middle/Upper School

"**The Clearwater Sail** — The VIIIs and XIs sailed on *The Mystic Whaler* to experience life aboard a schooner on the Hudson River. Students sang songs with Tao Rodriguez, grandson of Pete Seeger, sifted through various kinds of plankton and other sea life, and examined maps of the estuary.

**The VIIIs Longhouse** — Inspired by their study of the Lenape Indians on Manhattan Island long ago, the VIIIs built a longhouse in their classroom. They took great pride in their accomplishment and had group meetings inside their construction. They later gave tours to Lower School Groups.

**The IXs 'Event'** — The IXs retold their history study in the form of a staged reading which was performed alongside a large-scale diorama of pioneers on the Oregon Trail. The costumed children read their 'script,' which was interwoven with songs they had learned in music. The final treat was a concert of original songs written by the IXs and a feast of foods they had prepared.

**The Xs visit a Monastery** — In addition to their usual trips to the Cloisters and to the Cathedral of St. John the Divine, the Xs spent a day at the Holy Cross Monastery in upstate New York where they had lunch with Benedictine monks. Their continuing interest in the monastic life and medieval cathedrals fueled the creation of their play.

**The XIs Renaissance City and Sonnet Reading** — When the XIs finished presenting their independent research on various Renaissance topics, they decided to turn their room into a Renaissance city. Huge murals were painted and hung around the room, and parents were invited in to hear students recite Shakespeare sonnets they had memorized.

**The XIIs see *The Cure at Troy*** — The Cocteau Repertory Company performed the Seamus Heaney version of *Philoctetes* by Sophocles this year. In preparation, the XIIs read and acted out scenes from the original play (in translation) and were later treated to an evening at the theater to see *The Cure at Troy*.

**The XIIIs Trip to Plymouth and Boston** — The XIIIs visited Plymouth and Boston to complement their American history study of colonization and the foundation of U.S. government. The highlight of the trip for the XIIIs was a guided tour of the Underground Railroad.

**A Visit from Margy Burns Knight** — Author Margy Burns Knight met with several groups throughout the School to talk about her writing process. Margy showed us the many beautiful illustrations and copy changes in her books *Talking Walls* and *Welcoming Babies*."

**— City & Country School Annual Report 1997 – 1998**

The events of September 11th had an enormous impact upon all of us. In an effort to support our community, the Parents' Association asked Dr. Bruce Arnold and school psychologist Eileen Fitzgerald to speak with parents about the continuing effects of September 11th and C&C served as a weekly meeting place for teachers from P.S. 89, who had been displaced from their school. Parent Kristin Sands, a professor of Islamic Studies at NYU, spoke to Upper School students. Additionally, the IXs took classroom supplies to displaced students from P.S. 234, parents cooked for emergency workers at our local precinct ... And with bulbs donated by the Netherlands, the XIIs, IVs and Vs planted daffodils on 23th Street in a city-wide program to improve morale.

**—from the 2001–2002 End of Year Highlights City & Country School**

## Caroline Pratt — References for Further Study


Adler, M. (1997). *Heretic's heart.* Boston: Beacon Press.

Alford, E. S. (1964). A personal narrative or, a happy discovery in the deserts of education. *Bennington College Bulletin, 32* (3), 8 – 12.

Antler, J. (1987). *Lucy Sprague Mitchell: The making of a modern woman.* New Haven, CT: Yale University Press.

Beck, R. (1942). *American progressive education 1875 – 1930.* Unpublished doctoral dissertation, Yale University, New Haven, CT.

Beck, R. (1958, December). Progressive education and American progressivism: Caroline Pratt. *Teachers College Record, 50,* 129 – 137.

Bode, B. H. (1925, April 8). Experimenting with education. *The Nation,* 387 – 388.

Bugbee, E. (1939, December 4). Miss Pratt says find child a job he likes and he'll teach himself. *New York Herald Tribune.*

Caplan, F., & Caplan, T. (1973). *The power of play.* Garden City, NY: Anchor Press.

Carlton, P. (1986). *Caroline Pratt: A biography.* Unpublished doctoral dissertation, Teachers College, Columbia University, New York.

Caroline Pratt dies: Headed 'Play School'[obituary]. (1954, June 7). *New York Herald Tribune.*

Caroline Pratt, educator, dead [obituary]. (1954, June 7). *The New York Times.*

Chapman, E. (1887, February). *Slojd Journal of Education, IX,* 71 – 74.

Children, experimenters in Miss Pratt's school. (1954, June 11). *Vineyard Gazette.*

Cremin, L. (1961). *The transformation of the school.* New York: Alfred Knopf.

Cuffaro, H. (1995). *Experimenting with the world: John Dewey and the early childhood classroom.* New York: Teachers College Press.

Dewey, J., & Dewey, E. (1915). *Schools of tomorrow.* New York: E. P. Dutton.

Dewey, J., & Dewey, E. (1962). *Schools of tomorrow.* Toronto, Canada: Clarke, Irwin & Co. (Original work published 1915)

Dropkin, R., & Tobier, A. (Eds.). (1976). *Roots of open education in America.* New York: Workshop Center for Open Education.

Edwards, C. P., Gandini, L., & Forman, G. (Eds.). (1993). *The hundred languages of children: The Reggio Emilia approach to early childhood education.* Norwood, NJ: Ablex.

Franklin, A., & Benedict, A. (1943). *Play centers for school children.* New York: William Morrow and Company.

Gandini, L. (1993). Fundamentals of the Reggio Emilia approach to early childhood education. *Young Children, 49,* 4 – 8.

Goffin, S. (1991). Special book review feature — I learn from children. *Young Children, 47,* 62 – 64.

Gura, P. (Ed.). (1992). *Exploring learning: Young children and blockplay.* London: P. Chapman.

Henderson, C. H. (1902). *Education and the larger life.* Boston: Houghton & Mifflin.

Henderson, C. H. (1914). *What is it to be educated?* Boston: Houghton & Mifflin.

Hirsch, E. (Ed.). (1996). *The block book (3rd ed.).* Washington, DC: NAEYC.

Hirsch, M. (1978). *Caroline Pratt and The City and Country School: 1914 – 1945.* Unpublished doctoral dissertation, Rutgers, The State University of New Jersey, New Brunswick, New Jersey.

I learn from children [The vineyard bookshelf]. (1948, November 5). *Vineyard Gazette.*

James, E. T. (Ed.), James, J. N., & Boyer, P. S. (Associate Eds.). (1971). *Notable American women, 1607 – 1950: A biographical dictionary.* Cambridge, MA: Belknap Press of Harvard University Press.

Johnson, H. (1933). *The art of blockbuilding.* New York: The John Day Co.

Johnson, M. (1929). *Youth in a world of men.* New York: The John Day Co.

Koepke, M. (1989). *Learning by the block.* New York: City and Country School. (Originally in *Teacher Magazine,* 1989).

Lanser, S., & McDonnell, L. (1991). Creating quality curriculum yet not buying out the store. *Young Children, 47,* 4 – 9.

Lascarides, V.C. & Hinitz, B. (2000). *History of Early Childhood Education.* New York: Falmer Press.

Lauderdale, W. B. (1981). The City and Country School. In *Progressive education: Lessons from three schools.* Bloomington, IL: Phi Delta Kappa Educational Foundation.

Marcus, L. (1948). *The founding of American private progressive schools 1912 – 1921.* (Doctoral Dissertation, Harvard University, 1948).

Marot, H. (1915, November 6). The Play School: An experiment. *The New Republic,* 16 – 17.

Marot, H. (1918). *Creative impulse in industry.* New York: E. P. Dutton & Co.

Miss Pratt's island place is left to her school. (1954, June 25). *Vineyard Gazette.*

Miss Pratt's will. (1955, December 9). *Vineyard Gazette.*

Newman, J. (1997, October 7). Experimental school, experimental community: The Marietta Johnson School of Organic Education in Fairhope, Alabama. *The Harbinger,* n.p. Retrieved March 25,1999 from the World Wide Web: http://entropy.me.usouthal.edu/harbinger/xvi/971007/newman.html

Newman, J. (1997, October 28). The Organic School after Marietta Johnson. *The Harbinger,* n.p. Retrieved March 25, 1999 from the World Wide Web: http://entropy.me.usouthal.edu/harbinger/xvi/971028/newman.html

Peltzman, B. R. (1998). *Pioneers of early childhood education: A bio-bibliographical guide.* Westport, CT: Greenwood Press.

Pollack, C. (1935). Art in an experimental school. *Art for today's children.* Washington, DC: Association for Childhood Education.

Pratt, C. (1902). Carpentry classes. *Fifth Annual Report of Hartley House, July 1,1901 – September 30th, 1902, 20 – 27* [housed in Social Welfare History Archives, University of Minnesota Libraries].

Pratt, C. (1902, June). Carpentry at Hartley House. *The Commons, 12*, 11 – 14.

Pratt, C. (1911, September). Toys: A usurped educational field. *The Survey, 26*, 893 – 895.

Pratt, C. (1913, September). Tools vs. rules. *The American Teacher*, 98 – 101.

Pratt, C. (1919, April 19). Experimental schools. *The Dial, 66*, 413 – 415.

Pratt, C. (1921). Introduction to *City and Country School: Record of Group VI* by L. Stott. New York: City and Country School.

Pratt, C. (Ed). (1924). *Experimental practice in the city and country school.* New York: E. P. Dutton & Co.

Pratt, C. (1925). Collective formulations in curriculum. *Progressive Education, 2* (4), 231 – 235.

Pratt, C. (1927, April – June). Making environment meaningful. *Progressive Education, 4* (1), 105 – 108.

Pratt, C. (1929). Children in their neighborhoods. *Child Study, 6* (5), 110 – 112.

Pratt, C. (1930, July 2). Two basic principles of education. *New Republic,* 172 – 76.

Pratt, C. (1931). Growing up and dramatics. *Progressive Education, 8* (1), 7 – 9.

Pratt, C. (1933). Learning by experience. *Child Study, 11* (3), 69 – 71.

Pratt, C. (1934, Jan./Feb.). As to indoctrination. *Progressive Education*, 106 – 109.

Pratt, C. (1935). Social experiences — not social studies. *Educational Method, 15* (2), 101 – 104.

Pratt, C. (1936). Imagination and literature. *Progressive Education, XIII* (8), 617 – 620.

Pratt, C. (1936). Recording mental health and treatment. *Progressive Education, XIII* (1), 27 – 31.

Pratt, C. (1938, May). Animal, or vegetable? *New York Teacher*, 12 – 13.

Pratt, C. (1939). Growing up and dramatics. In G. Hartman & H. Shumaker (Eds.), *Creative expression.* Milwaukee, WI: E. M. Hale & Co.

Pratt, C. (1940, December). Michael. *Progressive Education,* 553 – 557.

Pratt, C. (1948). *I learn from children*. New York: Harper and Row.

Pratt, C. (1973). The play school: An experiment in education. In C. Winsor (Ed.), *Experimental schools revisited.* NY: Agathon Press. (Original work published 1917).

Pratt, C., & Stanton, J. (1926). *Before books*. New York: Adelphi Co.

Provenzo, E., Jr., & Brett, A. (1983). *The complete block book*. Syracuse, NY: Syracuse University Press.

Reich, C. (1954, June 9). Tribute to Caroline Pratt. *New York Times.*

Remembering Miss Pratt. (1955, December 16). *Vineyard Gazette.*

Retires after 32 years in school she founded. (1945, May 25). *Vineyard Gazette.*

Rugg, H., & Shumaker, A. (1928). *The child-centered school.* New York: World Book Co.

Sadovnik, A. & Semel, S. (Eds.). (2002). *Founding mothers and others: Women educational leaders during the progressive era*. New York: Palgrave.

Semel, S., & Sadovnik, A. (1995). Lessons from the past: Individualism and community in three progressive schools. *Peabody Journal of Education, 70* (4), 56 – 85.

Semel, S., & Sadovnik, A. (Eds.). (1999). *"Schools of Tomorrow," Schools of Today: What happened to progressive education.* New York: Peter Lang.

Sochen, J. (1972). *The new woman: Feminism in Greenwich Village 1910 – 1920.* New York: Quadrangle Books.

Staley, L. (1998). Beginning to implement the Reggio Emilia philosophy. *Young Children, 53* (5), 20 – 25.

Stott, L. (1921). *City and Country School: Record of Group VI 1921.* New York: City and Country School.

Vacation for these two, vital in their interest in the world about them, includes work as well as play. (1937, July 30). *Vineyard Gazette.*

Von Hauff, D. (1994). *Everyone's grandfather: The life and times of Grant MacEwan.* Edmonton, Canada: GMCC Foundation.

Ward, M. (1888, December). Slojd at Naas. *Journal of Education, X*, 562 – 563.

Was author and editor [obituary of Helen Marot]. (1940, June 7). *Vineyard Gazette.*

Weber, E. (1969). *The kindergarten: Its encounter with educational thought in America.* New York: Teachers College Press.

What children want to do is to work. (1939, December 29). *Vineyard Gazette.*

Wheeler, C. (1949). *Greenwich Village gourmet.* New York: The Bryan Publications.

Winsor, C. (Ed.). (1973). *Experimental schools revisited: Bulletins of the Bureau of Educational Experiments.* New York: Agathon Press, Inc.

Zorach, W. (1967). *Art is my life: The autobiography of William Zorach.* Cleveland: World Publishing.

# Chapter 11 — *Lucy Sprague Mitchell*

**1878 – 1967**

*"The chief job of a school is to provide strategic situations for discovering significant relationships and for using them."*

— **"Social Studies for Future Teachers"**

*"Children's best chance to be learners, doers, creative, constructive members in the society they live in as adults is to have lived lives which gave these qualities a chance to grow steadily.... A good life for children is, above all, a chance to keep growing as 'whole children.'"*

*"Our very future depends on our children and our schools."*

— ***Our Children and Our Schools***

Childhood indelibly affects later life. Patty Smith Hill gained her sense of play from her excursions into the fields and her mother's sense of the special nature of childhood experiences. A very different childhood affected Lucy Sprague.

## Early Chicago Years

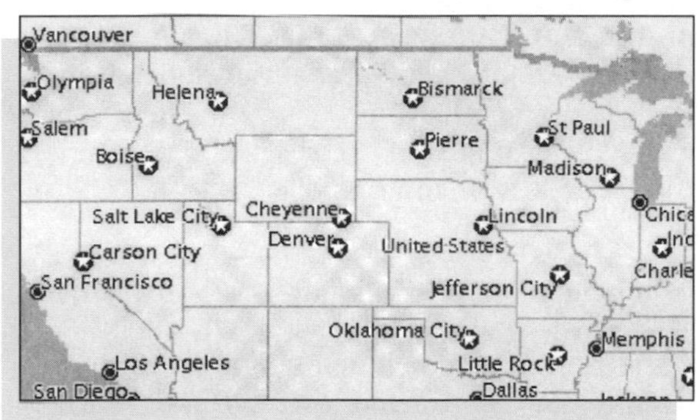


She was born in 1878 in Chicago, Illinois, the fourth of six children (Mary, Albert, Nancy, Lucy, Otho and Arnold). Her father, Otho, began a small grocery chain that grew into a large successful business, Sprague Warner & Company, that later evolved into General Foods. Lucy's father was one of the entrepreneur businessmen[1] who helped turn Chicago into a major urban centre after the Civil War. Her mother, Lucia Atwood, had a strong musical background but was an invalid most of her life. Submissive under the domination of her husband, Lucia faded into the background of the household. She suffered ongoing depression and headaches. Later in life, Lucy would search for a marriage that would not repeat the patriarchal experience in her parents' marriage.

Lucy remembered her childhood as full of fear and guilt. Discipline and order were overwhelming. Sins, as seen by her parents, were recorded each night on a calendar with stickers (gold for no sins, silver for little ones and red for big ones). The Sprague children were put into a dark closet to meditate on their sins, and physical punishment was common. Baths and bedtimes were strictly regulated at 15-minute intervals. She remembered her childhood as emotionally barren and joyless. This is in stark contrast to Hill's happy memories.

[1] Other entrepreneurs included Philip Armour, who ran a meat packing plant; Marshall Field, who owned a dry goods and department store; and Cyrus McCormick, who invented the reaping machine and built a factory for reaping machines and other farming machinery. George Pullman, another businessman of the time, designed the first railroad sleeping car with folding upper berths and seats below that extended into lower berths; he established the Pullman Palace Car Company to manufacture sleeping cars, dining cars and parlour cars.

As a child, Lucy became anxious, frightened and lonely. Introspective and shy, she retreated from others, kept secret notebooks, engaged in dress-up play and learned from the many books she read. Often too stressed to attend school, she and her younger siblings were tutored at home. Her father had an extensive library, and she read through his works of classical literature, mythology, metaphysics and oriental mysticism. Lucy and her family also took many trips around Chicago exploring many aspects of the city.

**Alice Freeman Palmer had been president of Wellesley College and was dean at the University of Chicago when Lucy Sprague first met her. Later Lucy lived with the Palmers while attending Radcliffe College. Alice Freeman Palmer was a strong professional female role model for Lucy in her youth and early adulthood. (Used with permission of the Wellesley College Archives, Margaret Clapp Library, Wellesley College, Wellesley, Massachusetts)**

Otho Sprague had helped fund the opening of the University of Chicago, the Chicago Orchestra and the Chicago World's Fair in 1892. The family thus became acquainted with John Dewey, who was then at the University of Chicago. Lucy got to know John Dewey when he was a dinner guest at the Sprague household. Lucy was inspired to read some of Dewey's works, learned about education and began to question her upbringing even more.

Another influential person Lucy was introduced to was Alice Freeman Palmer[2], former Wellesley College president, who stayed with the Spragues when she came to Chicago as part-time dean at the University of Chicago.

Lucy's father was also a benefactor of Hull House, an inner-city community centre and centre for social reform established by a social worker named Jane Addams. Hull House had previously attracted the interest of John Dewey. In 1884 Otho split with Jane Addams over her support of the Pullman workers' right to strike. Wages had been reduced in the Pullman Palace Car Company, but the rents in the company town remained constant. Lucy agreed with Jane Addams and her support of the workers, and the conflict between Otho and Addams created another rift between Lucy and her father.

Both Alice Palmer and Jane Addams were mentors and role models for Lucy Sprague as a young woman.

---

[2] See biographies of Palmer in *Women Educators in the United States 1820 – 1993,* edited by Maxine Seller, *Alice Freeman Palmer: The Evolution of a New Woman* by Ruth Bordin and *The Life of Alice Freeman Palmer* by George Herbert Palmer.

## California to Radcliffe

In 1893, serious health problems forced the Sprague family to move to Sierra Madre, California, northeast of Los Angeles. Two of Lucy's younger brothers had died, one from the croup and one from typhoid, and a sister had a mental breakdown. Her mother remained depressed, and her father suffered ongoing hemorrhages in his lungs from tuberculosis he had contracted in the Civil War. Lucy nursed the family for a year while she was attending the Marlborough School in Los Angeles as a boarding student during the week. It was a school run by Mary Caswell, a woman who believed strongly in female education, and Lucy learned and enjoyed the educational experience. She was 16, and this was her first regular school attendance; her previous encounters with learning had been primarily out of school, a fact that would affect her later vision of schools.

**Lucy Sprague attended the Marlborough School in Los Angeles from 1894 – 96, when she was 16 and 17 years old. This photo was taken during her time at the school. The school, at the corner of 23rd and Scarff Streets, had been the Marlborough Hotel. (Courtesy of the Marlborough School, Los Angeles, California.)**

**This is a view of the library at the time Lucy Sprague attended the Marlborough School in Los Angeles. The school was founded and directed by Mary Caswell. Lucy gained a renewed sense of herself as a young woman while attending Marlborough. (Courtesy of the Marlborough School, Los Angeles, California.)**

*Mary S. Caswell founded The Marlborough School in 1889. Early in its history (and during Lucy Sprague's time at the school), it operated in the old Marlborough Hotel in Los Angeles. Caswell supported female education and told the students, "the day when it was interesting to be helpless is far in the past" (quoted on website of Marlborough School, http://www.marlborough.la.ca.us/admin/news/heritage.html; retrieved August 20,1999).*

*Lucy Sprague heard these words and developed self confidence and resourcefulness as part of the curriculum.*

*The Marlborough School continues to serve young women in Los Angeles.*

*The Marlborough School*
*250 South Rossmore Ave.*
*Los Angeles, California 90004*
*U.S.A.*

*Website: http://www.marlboroughschool.org*

Lucy was then invited by Alice Freeman Palmer and her husband George Herbert Palmer, Chair of the Harvard Philosophy department, to live in Cambridge, Massachusetts so she could attend Radcliffe College. She entered Radcliffe in 1896 against her father's wishes. She majored in philosophy and studied with William James (a pragmatist who believed truth derives from results and outcomes) and George Santayana (who believed in a psychological approach to the mind). The Palmers lived in the Harvard Yard, next to the president's house, and Lucy Sprague met many of the faculty.

**Lucy Sprague graduated with first class honours from Radcliffe College in Cambridge, Massachusetts with a major in philosophy. (Used with permission of Radcliffe College Archives.)**

Sprague graduated in 1900 *magna cum laude* (with first class honours) in philosophy. She was the only Radcliffe student that year to achieve this distinction. At Radcliffe she had found an experience that allowed her to go beyond her family experience. She found new intellectual interests and gained self-confidence; she was class president and actively participated in sports. Through higher education, her world began to change. The exposure to new ideas and new perspectives allowed her to grow in many directions. She found both intellectual and personal freedom. Her life with the Palmers also involved personal contact with the intellectuals of the day and the opportunity to live with a strong, independent thinking woman.

Her family members were still ill, and Lucy returned to California to nurse them. Her mother died, and her father became chronically ill. She enrolled in a landscape gardening course at Throop Institute, but that did not appeal to her, so she left again to travel with the Palmers in Europe. Alice Palmer died suddenly in Paris, and Lucy remained with George Palmer as a housekeeper in Cambridge. She felt caught in a vise, limited by Palmer's personal expectations and a sense of duty and missing the energy and magnetism of Alice Palmer. Taking courses at Harvard, she also became a secretary/assistant to Radcliffe's dean.

**Lucy Sprague was Dean of Women and English Professor at the University of California, Berkeley. (Used with permission of Archives of Bancroft Library at the University of California, Berkeley, BAN CMSS CD 4047 volume1, facing p.35.)**

## Berkeley Years and "The Heart Culture"

With a recommendation from George Palmer, Sprague was offered a job as an assistant to the dean of first-and second-year students at the University of California at Berkeley. She moved west to assume this position in 1903. Three years later, she became the first female dean of women and one of the first two women professors hired at Berkeley when she attained a position in the English department. There was tremendous resistance to women on faculty, as they were seen as intellectually inferior beings and their involvement in academic life as unwomanly.

The dean's role was supposed to be as a surrogate mother or warden to the 2,000 female students, but Sprague transformed the role and focused on educational and social opportunities for women. She worked to improve housing conditions for women going to college and started sex education courses. Her learning to teach this to adults translated later into a similar approach with young children, answering their questions on sexual issues when they arose. She rose beyond her own childhood where sex was never discussed.

Weekly receptions in her home centred on examinations of social conditions in the San Francisco area and included poetry readings. Sprague introduced what she called a "heart culture" to the young college women she worked with. She organized field trips to see asylums, courts, prisons, orphanages, waterfront docks and schools. Lucy learned along with the students as they explored the community around the university. She supported students' rights to self-government and believed students needed to see the real world beyond the academic ivory tower. During her tenure as Dean of Women, she ensured that women had a strong presence on campus. She spent nine years at the University of California at Berkeley, six as Dean of Women.

## New York

In 1908 Otho Sprague died, and this emotionally freed Lucy from her family obligations. She left California for New York on a leave of absence in 1911 – 1912 to study the possibilities for women in careers outside education. When she had polled women students at Berkeley, 90% planned on a career in teaching as they saw no other options. In New York she created six focused learning apprenticeships for herself in different social service agencies including the Henry Street Settlement (with Lillian Wald), the Salvation Army and the Russell Sage Foundation (with Pauline Goldmark), Consumers League (with Florence Kelley) and the Charity Organization Society (with Mary Richmond).

*Alice Palmer, Julia Richman and Jane Addams were mentors for Lucy Sprague Mitchell. Describe some mentors you have had. Why were they significant in your life and career?*

As part of the study, she visited and worked with Julia Richman[3] who was the district superintendent of education. Despite her initial plan to look for work outside the education field, Lucy Sprague returned to education and reform of schools as her life focus. Through this work, Sprague came to see

- public education as a way to deal with social problems,
- the need to see the whole child in a family context,
- the need for children to learn far beyond their classroom life.

> *"Our early work with children and teachers required small schools, fluid situations, where experimental work could be carried on and full records kept. But such work we always regarded as preliminary laboratory work. Public schools always held our deepest interest, and our ultimate aim was to make our contribution to public school education."*
>
> ***— Our Children and Our Schools***

She returned briefly to California in 1912 and married Wesley Clair Mitchell (nicknamed Robin) who was a world-famous economist. Wesley was 37 and Lucy was 33 when they married. He was committed to her social ideals, and she came to believe that she could continue her professional life goals and also have a marriage. She had found a compassionate husband who accepted her fully in her life endeavours.

---

[3] Information on Julia Richman, Lillian Wald, Florence Kelley and Mary Richmond can be found in *Women Educators in the United States 1820 – 1993*, edited by Maxine Seller.

Many college educated women in the early part of the 20th century remained single (e.g. Patty Smith Hill, Caroline Pratt and others), in part to maintain their professional independence.

**Partheneia — "The Dream of Derdra." Lucy Sprague organized pageants such as this one which showcased women and encompassed many expressive arts. This is the view of the entrance of the Spirits of the Sun. (Used with permission of Archives of Bancroft Library at the University of California, Berkeley, VARC PIC 400:108.)**

Just before moving permanently to New York, she organized a women's pageant at the University of California, modelled on the "Partheneia," an event at eastern colleges demonstrating female ideals, uniting women and showcasing the expressive arts. Over 1,000 women participated in the cooperative endeavour that involved music, drama, poetry, costumes and elaborate sets. Sprague saw this as an opportunity for students to translate their experiences into a creative project.

After a European honeymoon, she and Wesley moved to New York where both found satisfying professional careers. Wesley became a professor of economics at Columbia University and director of the National Bureau of Economic Research. He was also a good friend of Lawrence Frank, another economist who went on to write about children's play. Frank was head of the Lucy Spelman Rockefeller Memorial, funding child study and parent education centres throughout the United States. It is clear that both Lucy and Wesley had a strong influence on him and his views on early childhood and social reform.[4]

The Mitchells were involved with the arts and social reform and were avid readers of all current issues in psychology, sociology, economics, technology and political science.

At this time Lucy Sprague Mitchell began her in-depth study of children. She took courses and taught at Teachers College, Columbia University, along with John Dewey and Edward Thorndike, who was developing tests for children's ability to learn. Lucy continued the personal friendship with Dewey that had started when she was a young person in Chicago.

She worked as a visiting teacher in homes and saw the critical link between home and school and the need to look at the whole child's needs. Her supervisor in the Visiting Teacher Project was Harriet Johnson, who was both a nurse and teacher. Johnson went on to become the first director of the Bank Street Nursery School:

> *"the person who above all others helped me to understand children and to keep a sane balance in all the confusing interests that pressed upon me was Harriet Johnson. I count her as my greatest teacher. . . . She was thoroughly*

[4] Lawrence Frank's ideas can be seen in an article called "Fundamental Needs of the Child."

> *scientific, always pushing for evidence, always open-minded, experimental, always re-examining her own practices in the light of new evidence. Yet she was humanly warm with children, full of delight at their ways, humorous and playful with them, a true companion as well as a profound student of little children."*
>
> — ***Two Lives***

Sprague Mitchell continued with her interest in sex education projects and also did some work on the psychological testing of children with Elisabeth Irwin (who later founded the Little Red School House, another progressive school in New York City). She taught nursery school, kindergarten and at Caroline Pratt's Play School, finding the philosophy similar to her own developing ideas on first-hand experiences and the role of creative expression. Harriet Johnson had first introduced her to Pratt.

Her emerging ideas on education were already in stark contrast to the regimentation boasted by the superintendent of the New York Schools, who was quoted as saying,

> *"I like to pause at 11 o'clock and reflect that all over New York thousands of pupils are reading the same page of the same book."*
>
> **— quoted in obituary of Lucy Sprague Mitchell, *New York Times*, Oct. 17, 1967**

In the midst of her professional career, she had four children, two of whom were adopted — John, Sprague, Marian and Arnold.

Her life, both personally and professionally, had a child focus. She acknowledged the support of her husband in helping her achieve this balance.[5]

## A Gift From Her Cousin That Changed Her Life

At this point Lucy Sprague Mitchell received an unexpected and fortuitous gift from a double first cousin (same sets of grandparents), Elizabeth Sprague Coolidge. She agreed to give Lucy financial support for any educational project of her choosing! Her own interest was in music, as she said to Lucy,

> *"My real interest in life is music. But I don't think music is going to get me into heaven. I have a feeling that my best chance of heaven is to do something for education."*
>
> **— quoted in Antler, *Lucy Sprague Mitchell: The Making of a Modern Woman***

[5] There is an intriguing article by Joyce Antler exploring Mitchell as "mother" in *Women and the Structure of Society* edited by Harris and McNamara. Mitchell continually balanced her roles as mother, wife and professional. In addition, Antler in "Was She a Good Mother" presents Sprague Mitchell's children's perspective on their mother's multiple roles.

Lucy described to her cousin an idea called the Bureau of School Information that many of her friends (John Dewey, Evelyn Dewey, Caroline Pratt, Helen Marot, Harriet Johnson, Elisabeth Irwin and others) had discussed. They had envisioned this bureau as a way to study children. The money from Elisabeth made their vision a reality. Her cousin had some unusual conditions for the bequest. She wanted no reports, and the full $50,000 needed to be spent each year. These were 1916 dollars!

## The Bureau of Educational Experiments

*If you could design your own funded educational project as Mitchell did, what would your dream be?*

The Bureau of Educational Experiments (B.E.E.) was formed to teach and to do research on progressive education. Researchers and practitioners were brought together to work jointly in the study of children. The Bureau collected and disseminated information about existing practice and developed new innovative projects. Initiatives were launched into the areas of school nutrition, educational testing, visiting teachers, school playgrounds, day cares, nursery schools and demonstration programs.

Mitchell wanted to work at the grass roots of educational and social change:

> *"I was tired of working in an academic ivory tower, with golden domes but no firm foundations. I wanted to mix cement and sharp stones and build an educational foundation which would develop people with live thinking and live feelings."*
>
> **— quoted in Biber, *Lucy Sprague Mitchell 1878 – 1967***

The Bureau of Educational Experiments opened in October of 1916 in Greenwich Village with the Play School of Caroline Pratt as its informal laboratory school. Mitchell described the plan of the B.E.E. in an unpublished autobiography:

> *"We were to organize a group of specialists who knew children at first hand but from different angles — doctor, psychologist, social worker, teacher, parent, perhaps anthropologist — and together we were to work out ways of learning more about children, their growth, their interests and drives, their ways of learning, thinking, feeling, in different stages of development. . . . Schools were to be both our laboratories for studying and recording how children behaved under different situations and experimental centers where our findings would be used in planning for their children.*
>
> **— quoted in "Progressive Education and the Scientific Study of the Child: An Analysis of the Bureau of Educational Experiments"**

## The Working Council

*Could a college or university be run without a president and with a form of non-hierarchical administration? Could a day care centre operate without a director? An elementary school without a principal? What other forms of administration can you envision for organizations you have worked with?*

The world is full of hierarchies, organizations with higher and lower ranks. We often assume that is the way systems must function, but a Working Council ran the Bureau of Educational Experiments. Caroline Pratt, Wesley Mitchell, Harriet Johnson, Elisabeth Irwin and Evelyn Dewey were all members, with John Dewey as an honorary member. Policies were formulated and implemented collectively with a democratic structure. Lucy Sprague Mitchell did not want to be "president" of anything and stayed only as the chairperson of the Working Council. She reported to the Council and not vice versa. She saw her role as a guardian of the multidiscipline approach that was the cornerstone of B.E.E. projects. This organizational structure was an example of cooperative governance. She wanted to avoid administrative systems that looked like ladders or feudal hierarchies and that removed responsibility from those not at the "top."

Instead she promoted cooperative decision-making. She saw immense possibilities of collaborative work among people and promoted "joint thinking," "joint planning" and "group focus" as management styles. Peers would work together to develop policy, plan and budget. She referred to it as "consecutive cooperative thinking."

**The Bureau of Educational Experiments opened in 1916, and by the 1920's, Mitchell was actively involved in research, laboratory schools, writing and teaching. (Used with permission of Special Collections, Milbank Memorial Library, Teachers College, Columbia University.)**

## Early Projects

There were initially four divisions, or departments, of the B.E.E.:

- **Teaching Experiments,**
- **Social, Physical and Mental Experiments,**
- **Records and Statistics,**
- **Information** (clearinghouse and publisher of child development findings).

The expanded Laboratory School in 1919 included 3 programs:

1. **Nursery School** — 4 months through 3 years with an emphasis on physical movements and sensory experiences;

   *"Now what can we say about the educational needs for babies under three? We try to design an environment which is designed for babies, designed to give them rich sensory and motor experiences, designed to give them appropriate learning through experimentation, designed to give them adventure without danger to life or limb, designed to give them contact with their peers without demanding inappropriate adjustment. In short, an environment planned with educational needs in mind."*

   **— Harriet Johnson quoted in Dropkin and Tobier (editors), *Roots of Open Education in America***

2. **City and Country School** (formerly Play School) — 3 years through 7 years — concrete experiences and field trips, self expression and play;
3. **7 – 8 year old program** — work experiences with more complex self-expression.

The four main principles of the B.E.E., as expressed in its 1919 statement, were to guide the school for the next period:

i. growth, not learning specific curriculum;
ii. whole child approach to learning and growth;
iii. growth stimulated by experience/activity and expression of experiences;
iv. focus on researching stages through measurement to establish norms.

The latter two were not seen in other progressive schools of the day, but Sprague Mitchell knew that expressions of creativity needed a base of experience. She often referred to this as "first-hand input" and "first-hand output."

The emphasis on scientific measurement was affected by Arnold Gesell's growth studies but even more by the quantitative focus in other social science disciplines. The Bureau embraced the emerging faith in scientific process but was determined that the whole child would not be lost in the testing and quantitative research. Though physicians, psychologists and others were involved, teachers were the primary researchers. They observed and collected daily records of children's activities, projects and use of equipment.

---

Arnold Gesell (1880 – 1961) was an American psychologist who studied with G. Stanley Hall at Clark University. He founded the Clinic of Child Development at Yale University and later the Gesell Institute of Child Development. Gesell observed children to develop normative data on different ages. Gesell felt that these norms (sometimes called "ages and stages") were not rigid and that intensified educational programs could not accelerate children's maturation. Gesell saw the nursery school as a key component in education at a critical time in a child's development. Along with Patty Smith Hill, Gesell was on the advisory board of *Children* magazine, started in 1926. In 1928 the name changed to *Parents'* magazine.

---

The researchers saw their focus as going beyond other child study projects in using the information to plan environments for children's fullest development.

Harriet Johnson articulated this clearly:

> *"...no where do we find studies of behavior which take place in an environment where activities are self-initiated and concerned with materials they can control. This is our special contribution."*
>
> **— quoted in Antler, "Progressive Education and the Scientific Study of the Child: An Analysis of the Bureau of Educational Experiments"**

Later the Bureau focused more on qualitative measurement of the progressive stages in childhood, as statistical findings were not enough to guide educational planning.

Measurement often lost critical elements that were not easily measured but should not be ignored, according to Mitchell and her co-workers. She described an incident when children wiggled, and the researchers could not record that information. The Bureau was interested in both wiggles and emotions of children.

One early project was supposed to be the publication of Alice Dewey's records kept at the Dewey School in Chicago. However the project was never completed, as Sprague Mitchell wanted commentary along with the observations, contrary to Dewey's vision.

The focus of the Bureau of Educational Experiments/Bank Street later became known as the ***developmental interaction approach***. Curriculum was based on individual development of children, and learning occurred through the interaction with people and with the environment.

The interaction was also between the cognitive and social-affective areas of development. The interdependence of the developmental processes is at the core of the *developmental interaction* approach.[6]

---

[6] This approach is described thoroughly by Barbara Biber in *The Preschool in Action* by Mary Day and Ronald Parker and in *Becoming a Teacher of Young Children* by Margaret Lay-Dopyera and John Dopyera.

Sprague Mitchell insisted that the divisions of the B.E.E. reflect the policies of many and resisted naming programs after individuals. The sole exception was made for Harriet Johnson who had run the nursery school for so many years. The nursery school assumed her name after her death in 1934.

COOPERATIVE SCHOOL FOR STUDENT TEACHERS

BUREAU OF EDUCATIONAL EXPERIMENTS

**Offers a progressive education experience to students of progressive education.**

*Seminar Courses and Classroom Participation*

69 BANK STREET NEW YORK CITY

**Cooperative School for Student Teachers. This ad was placed in the Smith Alumnae Quarterly in 1931 to attract college-educated women to the new teacher education program at the Bureau of Educational Experiments. (Courtesy of Smith College Archives.)**

## Teacher Education

Teacher education emerged as another primary focus of the Bureau of Educational Experiments. The Cooperative School for Teachers was established in 1931 and was originally called The Cooperative School for Student Teachers. The Cooperative aggressively recruited students from women's colleges (such as Smith and Bryn Mawr) as well as teachers from nursery schools. A four-year college degree or equivalent was required for admission into the Cooperative School for Teachers.

An enthusiastic report on the Cooperative School was submitted to the *Bryn Mawr Alumnae Bulletin* in May of 1931:

> *"It proposes to stimulate students to both a scientific and an artistic attitude towards their work and towards life. A complex plan, you say — of course it is, but modern life, educational and otherwise, is complex. If more of our teachers could have such attitudes, the quality of education possible for children would be rare and vivifying!"*
>
> **— Seeds, "Alumnae Adventures in Education"**

The following quotation is from the first catalog (course calendar) of the Cooperative School for Teachers:

> *"Our aim is to help students develop a scientific attitude towards their work and towards life. To use this means an attitude of eager, alert observations; a constant questioning of old procedures in the light of new observations; a use of the world as well as of books as source material; an experimental open-mindedness; an effort to keep as reliable records as the situation permits in order to base the future upon actual knowledge of the experience of the past."*
>
> **— quoted in Antler, "Progressive Education and the Scientific Study of the Child"**

At the Cooperative School for Teachers, student teachers combined practical experiences in experimental schools with courses in child development, curriculum and the arts. Courses in pedagogy were excluded. Performing dancers, musicians and artists often taught workshops. Students needed to recapture the essence of childhood experience through re-discovering the arts themselves. The students worked in social service agencies, took field trips throughout the city, and received instruction from artists in the community. All were expected to try writing for children to become more attuned to childhood experience as readers and listeners. Practice teaching was the integrating core of the program.

## Mitchell as College Teacher

Students used to say that Lucy Sprague Mitchell could make any topic fascinating to learn from the "economic history of potatoes" to the "habits of the octopus."

Sprague Mitchell's language classes focused on appreciating children's own use of speech and understanding of the world. She helped students using direct descriptors rather than abstract or interpretive words. Students learned about rhythm, pitch, structure and sound quality of children's language. The following are some quotes by Sprague Mitchell from classes in Language in the fall of 1931:

> *"The reason for writing for children is not to get good stories on the market; it is the thing that it does to you when you make that attempt. You should think of it as a laboratory ... producing things. You don't estimate the products as of world value, but of value to the children. Whether you do good writing or not, from the point of understanding children's language, writing is one of the best things you can do."* ***October 9 class***
>
> *"When a piece of writing makes your legs ache, it comes back to the real experience."* ***October 17 class***

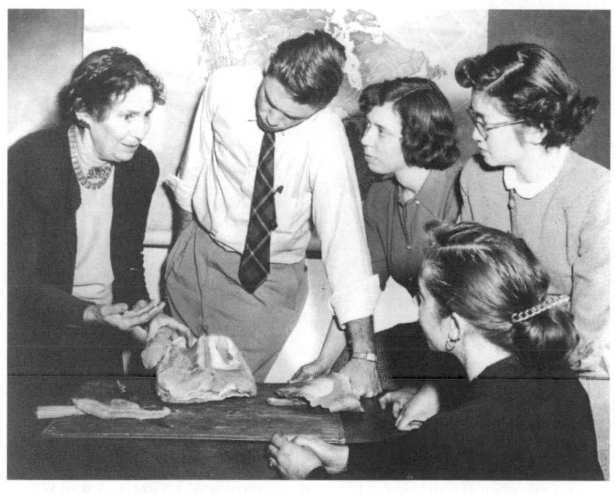

**Lucy Sprague Mitchell. Taken in the 1950's, this photo shows Mitchell with a group of student teachers. (Used with permission of Special Collections, Milbank Memorial Library, Teachers College, Columbia University.)**

Sprague Mitchell was famous for what she called "Five Finger Exercises" in which students stood outside the building and collected data with their five senses for 10 – 15 minutes with their eyes shut for the last 5 minutes. Afterward, the students would see what data they had collected and what interpretations they made. Observing is a key cognitive skill for children, and the data collected in observation becomes the source of other problem solving for children.

Another quotation from the first catalog gives a sense of the wider goals of the teacher training:

> *"We are interested in imbuing students with an experimental, critical, and ardent approach to their work, and to the social problems of the world in which they, as adults, must take an active part. If we accomplish this, we are ready to leave the future to them."*
>
> **— quoted in Raushenbush,**
> ***The Higher Education of Women***

### GROUP TO SEE AREA OF BOOTLEG MINING

**Students at Teachers' School Will Survey Conditions Among Coal Workers**

Formal lectures in human geography and social problems will be put aside this week when the students of the Cooperative School for Teachers at 69 Bank Street start on a visit to the coal mines and steel mills of Eastern Pennsylvania. Under the leadership of Mrs. Lucy Sprague Mitchell and Mrs. Eleanor Bowman of the School's staff, the students will seek answers to their inquiries through first hand observation and experience.

They will spend two and a half days in the mining towns of Mahanoy City and Hazelton, the heart of the bootleg mining industry, where they will visit both the "holes" of the bootleg miners and the large legitimate mines of the Lehigh Valley Coal Company.

Visits to one-room rural schools to see what kind of education is offered to children in an economically depressed region, as well as contacts with local social agencies and an opportunity to accompany public health nurses on their home visits, will be included in the student's experience.

Similarly, students will explore community public opinion on the problems of the coal industry through interviews with coal company officials, local business men and members of the United Mine Workers of America.

A delegation of the Independent Anthracite Miners Association (bootleg miners) will take students on a tour of the entire region. Following the study of the local situation, Joseph Agor, a member of former Governor Earle's Anthracite Coal Industry Commission, will confer with the students on the results of their own explorations and on the problems of the coal industry as viewed from the larger viewpoint of the State and nation.

On subsequent days, students will visit the steel mill of the Alan Wood Steel Company at Norristown, confer with similar local groups, and attend a hearing of the Labor Relations Board, followed by a meeting with the regional director. The trip will conclude with a study of housing developments in Philadelphia and environs.

The trip, which is the fifth annual field investigation of its kind into neighboring States, starts today. Students will travel by private automobiles, returning at the end of the week.

**The Cooperative School for Teachers took extensive field trips including one to the coal mines and steel mills of Eastern Pennsylvania. (Copyright 1939 by the New York Times Co. April 2, 1939. Reprinted by permission of the *New York Times*.)**

Teachers needed to be active and reflective practitioners. How many times would you see this in a university calendar for teacher education? For any post-secondary program?

Careful admissions screening searched for individuals who respected themselves, made independent decisions, and dealt with life's problems:

> *"Our antennae are tuned, we hope, to an awareness of whether or not he feels himself a growing, going-on person rather than an arrived final-product."*
>
> *"The children haven't much chance if the teacher is in constant terror of her director, the children's parents — or of failure."*
>
> *"The growth anticipated for all students is that their interest in children will be based on an affectionate respect for them, increasing curiosity and knowledge about them, and a satisfaction through work with them that makes teaching a strenuous art — not a chore."*
>
> **— Ross, "The Makings of Teachers at the Cooperative School for Student Teachers"**

Students received both a general education and an interdisciplinary education so they would be able to teach in an effective manner. The whole teacher was educated to help the whole child learn:

> *"We had come to believe that the 'learning process' is fundamentally the same in adults and children — intake experiences followed by outgo experiences. On this basis we organized a curriculum, in teacher education of adult intake and adult outgo... we tried in all fields to give firsthand experiences (in studio, laboratory and field work) to supplement 'book learning', to conduct the courses... with full discussions, and tie in all this work with. . . direct experiences with children in the classrooms."*
>
> ***— Two Lives***

## Field Trips

Students at the Cooperative School for Teachers went on field trips throughout New York, sometimes starting at 5 a.m. to see the early morning activity in the meat or fish markets or at the piers. These field trips harkened back to Sprague Mitchell's childhood trips through Chicago and the ones she organized with students in Berkeley.

Students also had extended field trips (called "long trips") to Washington, D.C. and to the Appalachian Mountains to explore the connections between geography, social elements, political structures and economic issues. The experiences and impressions were used as basic materials for student teacher work in the arts and language — the same model that would be used with children.

## Teachers Workshops and the Head Start Connection

Though Sprague Mitchell worked primarily in private schools, her goal was to influence the public school system. The Bureau of Educational Experiments had many collaborative projects with the community and its schools. From 1943 – 1946 Sprague Mitchell worked with P. S. 186 in Harlem and the New York Board of Education.

**[See end of chapter for an excerpt of Mitchell's article "Programming for Growth at P. S. 186."]**

The project was later extended to other schools. The original Head Start Programs in the early 1960's used Bank Streets Programs as their model for children's programming.

## Bank Street College

In 1950, the Bureau of Educational Experiments officially became the Bank Street College of Education, a graduate program in education. It had already informally been called Bank Street as the longer name was "polysyllabic intimidation" according to Wesley Mitchell.

The credo for Bank Street was written by Mitchell and is just as relevant today:

- A zest for living that comes from taking in the world with all five senses alert.
- Lively intellectual curiosities that turn the world into an exciting laboratory and keep one ever a learner.
- Flexibility when confronted with change and ability to relinquish patterns that no longer fit the present.
- The courage to work, unafraid and efficiently, in a world of new needs, new problems, and new ideas.
- Gentleness combined with justice in passing judgments on other human beings.
- Sensitivity, not only to the external formal rights of the "other fellow," but to him as another human being seeking a good life through his own standards.
- A striving to live democratically, in and out of schools, as the best way to advance our concept of democracy.
- Our credo demands ethical standards as well as scientific attitudes. Our work is based on the faith that human beings can improve the society they have created.

**— retrieved March 18, 1999 from**
**http://www.bnkst.edu/html/about/credo.html**

At the age of 75, Sprague Mitchell did become president of the Bank Street College of Education but only under pressure from the Board of Trustees:

> *"The Trustees made me accept the title 'Acting President'."*
>
> **— from a letter to Elizabeth Coolidge, quoted in Bailey, *An Exception To the Rule***

Her belief in cooperative governance continued. She remained Acting President until 1956 when John Niemeyer took over.

For 40 years, Lucy Sprague Mitchell guided the B.E.E. and its work in early childhood and was instrumental in setting its educational philosophy.

## Pratt and Mitchell

Sprague Mitchell's association with Caroline Pratt began with their initial meeting in 1913 at the Play School.

In 1915 Mitchell proposed that Pratt move the Play School to her own house at MacDougall Alley. In the next year, the school did move to a converted stable behind the house, though the school later spread directly into the house. Mitchell was one of the key teachers at the school, focusing on language.

In 1921 the Mitchells moved, as did the Play School with them. The Play School was on West 12th and West 13th Streets. It was at this point that Sprague Mitchell pressured Pratt to change the name of the school to City and Country School. This was one of several professional disagreements between the two women, and City and Country School eventually split off into a separate project. Pratt wanted more autonomy in working out her ideas:

> *"It was the work side that disturbed me. My method of work, the two educational ideas I had originated while in Caroline's school — analysis of children's language and geographic thinking — seemed 'academic' to Caroline, more I think, because she did not put her mind on my work than because my work was inconsistent with hers. I regarded Caroline Pratt as a kind of genius. I still do. But I came to realize that my pattern of work did not fit hers nor hers fit me. She worked best in an atmosphere where her own thinking was not challenged or interrupted by ideas originated by others; I worked best where ideas from many sources were being pooled and evaluated jointly. I found I could neither develop my own growing interests nor make much of a contribution to school thinking."*
>
> ***— Two Lives***

Pratt gave her an "impetus" and a laboratory for her early learning about children and about teaching, but Sprague Mitchell eventually grew beyond what Pratt taught her:

> *"I learned much in the years that I taught at City and Country School [formerly called the Play School] that I think I could not have learned as thoroughly or as rapidly with anyone except Caroline Pratt. But she clipped*

*my wings. I think she could not help it. Caroline's way of thinking and working and my way of thinking and working were too different to make it profitable for us to work together any longer."*

***— Two Lives***

## Work with Children's Language

Sprague Mitchell was a prolific writer of books for children. They reflected the same child-centred approach as her other work with children; she sat still, watched and listened to children. She saw language as another art form and was critical of Jean Piaget for his lack of appreciation of the art qualities of language (rhythm, sound and pattern).

One of her most famous books was the *Here and Now Story Book*. It was first published in 1921 by the B.E.E. and had stories and jingles for children from 2 – 7 years of age. She saw children's language as an art medium, a means of experimentation and a way for human beings to enjoy the world. The language experience was created and savored.

---

"I recall Lucy Sprague Mitchell's Here and Now story books which I read to my children. They were a refreshing taste of reality in the midst of fairy tales, Peter Rabbit, and Winnie the Pooh. In the wake of Here and Now came other books about contemporary life and people. Readers in classrooms became more realistic. Families were no longer lily white, with Mother and Dad and Dick and Jane and Spot all living in some rural idealized never-never land."

**— Gerry Meyrich, reflecting on the impact of the *Here and Now Story Books*, personal communication, March 2000**

---

The stories were written by her and others but were derived from the language of children. A guide told teachers and parents how to use the book, and the content was derived from the here and now world of things and people in children's lives. This guide was the source of one of the disagreements with Pratt. Pratt believed that there was no need for people to have an introduction with theory and analysis; going directly to children to learn was a more effective way than reading someone else's experience. This schism between the two women increased in the 1920's.

**Mitchell at age 83 at the Bank Street College of Education. Lucy Sprague Mitchell had a unique ability to work with both children and adults, appreciating and nurturing individual strengths. (Used with permission of Rare Book and Manuscript Library, Lucy Sprague Mitchell Collection, Butler Library, Columbia University, New York.)**

The focus of the book was on the children's first-hand experiences as starting points. The stories were more likely to have trucks and buses than queens or fairies. Sprague Mitchell, like Plato long ago, was a harsh critic of the violence in children's literature. She was also concerned with the pervasive sex role stereotyping. Both these issues remain with us.

The book also was written to help children make sense of and establish some order in a world that could be unpredictable and unstable. She made extensive use as well of children's invented language and there was almost always a modern urban setting (skyscrapers, airplanes, tugboats and trolleys). Mitchell hoped that teachers and parents would gain a renewed interest in listening to the freshness and beauty of children's own language.

**Lucy Sprague Mitchell was a prolific writer and published the *Here and Now Story Book* in 1921. Using children's natural language, the book focused on the immediate experiences of children rather than myths and fairy tales that were then considered appropriate children's literature. The book received initial condemnation from library reviewers but eventually it became well regarded. (Used with permission of Special Collections, Milbank Memorial Library, Teachers College, Columbia University.)**

For all these reasons, the book elicited great controversy when published. The *New York Times* found it shocking, and the *Horn Book Magazine* felt that the sense of wonder and the beauty of classical myths and folklore would be lost. Librarians denounced the book feeling that childhood was a state of innocence and nurtured by folk tales. Some people even referred to this controversy as the "Fairy Tale War," and Mitchell's approach was disparagingly called the "Beep beep crunch crunch" school of children's literature.

By 1937, when the new edition (*Another Here and Now Story Book)* was published, the public was more accepting. Margaret Wise Brown worked with Sprague Mitchell on this edition. The *Horn Book Magazine* and the *New York Times* gave it positive reviews this time. It included selections about rural and urban life and added more humour.

Remember the
goldfish?
Remember?
Remember the
goldfish?

Goes round and
round!
Umn!
Swims?
Umn!
Sleeps!
Umn!

Remember the
goldfish?
Has no hands.
No.
Has no feet.
No.

Remember the
goldfish?
Has no hands!
Remember the
goldfish?

This poem on the left, which was included in the book, was dictated by a two year old, and shows the play of language.

Sprague Mitchell saw the words as designs in sounds, not unlike designs in block play.

She saw five characteristics of young children's language:

> *"(1) that children talk to themselves without need of response; (2) that they seem to get satisfaction from such use of language; (3) that they talk what they act; (4) that much of their speech is rhythmic, often to the point of genuine patterns; and (5) that they report their observations in direct, concrete, sense or motor terms."*
>
> — **"Children's Experiments in Language"**

As part of her work with six year olds at City and Country School, she recorded her unique approach as well as individual and group children's stories in a book by Leila Stott, *Record of Group VI*. The examples are remarkable in the children's use of language.

The following was created after a trip to the docks:

> *How We Saw the Burnt Guiana*
>
> *Then we went into the dock. Everybody had to hold hands to cross that awful street with freight trains. We went across and got to the dock, and went to the Captain's house to ask him could we go on the boat. He told us it isn't on the left side, it's on the right. We went up the steep stairs and the water was right below them. A man told us that the Guiana got on fire in the West Indies and they had to put it out before they came up and the man said they were repairing the boat. It came up two days late. Blankets were burned brown and fruit was burned.*
>
> *Then we asked him where the crew slept and he showed us an old dirty room and we saw a couple of cats to catch the rats.*
>
> *We saw the engine room and the engine and where the trimmers and stokers work down in the bowels of the ship, and a sky-light for air way down in the engine room. We went up to the Captain's bridge and saw the compass and rang the bell they told time with. They ring it every half hour.*
>
> *A man that we saw before on the ship said he had two cocoanuts in the office for us so he went to the office and the cocoanuts weren't there, so he came back and said he would go up the cargo hold and pick out some cocoanuts for us. He came back and gave us four cocoanuts and then we went home.*

Another account of Sprague Mitchell's work with children and language at City and Country School is recorded in "Five-Year-Old's First Language Work" written in 1926 in *American Childhood.*

A memorable poem, written by Lucy Sprague Mitchell herself, captures the joy of words and the sensitivity to children's lives and language:

**The House of the Mouse**

The house of the mouse
is a wee little house,
a green little house in the grass,
which big clumsy folk
may hunt and may poke
and still never see as they pass
this sweet little, neat little,
wee little, green little,
cuddle-down hide-away
house in the grass.

Though known for her "here and now" approach, she supported imagination,

> *"which makes the young reader more alive to the sensuous and motor world in which they live, imagination which quickens their images, which makes reality realer."*
>
> — **"Imagination in Realism"**

Sprague Mitchell also wrote a series of books to connect ecological and sociological elements for children. Many of these books were unlike any others available at that time.

***Horses Now and Long Ago***

— in 1926; went from known to the unknown; from the horses that children might have seen to those back in history

*Name some children's authors and their books that deal with the "here and now" that Lucy Sprague Mitchell advocated.*

***North America: The Land They Lived in for the Children Who Live There***

— in 1923; immediate environment to more distant ones; showed how people in different regions used the earth's forces in their work

***Manhattan Now and Long Ago***

— in 1934; highlighted work in the borough of Manhattan but as it had been affected by ecological factors; stories, poems, maps, photographs and trips to take

***Young Geographers***

— in 1934; child would make geographic meaning through discovering relationships; 2nd half of the book showed children how to make graphic relief maps and plastic 3-dimensional maps, neither of which was on the market at that point; ecological perspective of humans with the environment.

For Lucy Sprague Mitchell, the essence of thinking involved seeing, understanding and interpreting relationships. These books were intended to help that process.

Active exploration produced real learning:

> *" I want to turn even quite young children into research workers. I want maps which are tools for research, not mere demonstrations. I want diaries by explorers, not mere facts or stories about explorers."*
>
> — **"Geography for Children"**

Sprague Mitchell was concerned with educators oversimplifying the complex situations that surround children to a point of falsification and triteness. She opposed the one-dimensional and simplistic focus on family, community helpers or neighbourhood without appreciating the complexities of children's relationships to their environment.

She also focused her attention on the unique nature of the urban environment and on the way Americans worked together to create a society.[7] "Who Built The Bridge" was originally published by the Council Against Intolerance in America; in this story Sprague Mitchell recounts the many workers who created a new bridge for a town:

> *"New Americans and old Americans; workers in stone, workers in cement, workers in steel, sandhogs,[7] tugboat captains and bridge engineers; nearby townspeople and faraway steel workers, miners and railroad men — workers of many kinds that build that great bridge."*

## The Writers Laboratory

Sprague Mitchell's commitment to literature for children extended into another project called **The Writers Laboratory**, a workshop set up in 1937 to help writers of children's books understand the developmental needs and interests of children. She also wanted to make sure the authors understood children's use of sounds, rhythms, and imagery that was such a part of their spoken word.

Concerned with the lack of racial and ethnic diversity amongst children's writers, she provided scholarships to ensure that a more varied racial and class mix of writers attended the Laboratory.

---

[7] A sandhog is someone who works under air pressure to sink bridge caissons or to build a tunnel.

**Margaret Wise Brown. After enrolling in the Bureau of Educational Experiments, Margaret Wise Brown joined the Writers Laboratory. (Used with permission of Brooklyn Museum of Art. Gift of Wallace Putnam from the Estate of Consuelo Kanaga. Photo by Consuelo Kanaga 1894 – 1978, 82.65.1824.)**

Margaret Wise Brown[8] was one of the earliest and the best known of the writers who attended the workshop. She had enrolled at the B.E.E. and combined her talent for writing with her emerging knowledge of children and their world. Known as "Brownie,"[9] she had extraordinary talents as an emerging writer.

When Brown was looking for an illustrator, a young artist named Clement Hurd came, and Brown insisted he subject his illustrations to the "child test" in the nursery school. This was a new experience for Hurd who was only used to the scrutiny of art critics and teachers. Brown had given him lines like "Once upon a time, there was a great bumble bug and a tiny little bubble bug." Uneasily he put out his paintings but was relieved when the nursery school teacher congratulated him on holding the children's attention for five minutes. These illustrations (child tested in the nursery school) became part of *Bumble Bugs and Elephants*, his first collaboration with Margaret Wise Brown. The book was printed on durable cardboard with a spiral binding to withstand heavy toddler usage.

Hurd went on to illustrate *The Runaway Bunny, The Diggers, Goodnight Moon* and other Brown books.

**Margaret Wise Brown wrote children's books that remain classics today such as *Runaway Bunny, Goodnight Moon* and *The Diggers*. (From the personal collection of Jennifer Wolfe. Photo by Kitty Ng.)**

[8] See *Margaret Wise Brown: Awakened by the Moon*, a biography by Leonard Marcus; "Margaret Wise Brown: Awakened by You Know Who" by Angela Estes in *Children's Literature* edited by Butler, Dillard and Keyser; and "Child's Best Seller" by Bruce Bliven, Jr. in Dec. 2, 1946 *Life*.

[9] It was a Bank Street tradition to adopt such pet names.

When Brown died in 1952 at the age of 42, she had added over a hundred children's books emphasizing the "here and now." She was the editor of an experimental children's publishing house, William R. Scott & Company. Brown contributed the additional dimension of seeing dreams and fantasies as part of the immediate lives of children, as much as the train or skyscraper. In this quotation from the 1951 *Book of Knowledge*, the goal of the Writers Laboratory can be seen:

> *"We speak naturally, but spend all our lives trying to write naturally."*

Other members of the Writers Laboratory included Madeline Dixon, Ruth Krauss, Louise Woodcock, Leone Adelson, Cathleen Schurr, Marguerite Rudolph, Eve Merriam, Helen Kay, Edith Thacher Hurd, William Hooks, Irma Simonton Black, Elizabeth Helfman and Jane Siepmann.

Many of these authors' books are still in print and show the sensitivity to children and their lives. **[See end of chapter for fuller list of authors and books].**

In the Writers Laboratory, a dozen or so people met each Wednesday afternoon (and sometimes into the evening) to discuss their work, sip tea or sherry and eat pastries. The room was at the top of 69 Bank Street, and Mitchell usually sat on a worn green sofa. She smoked a cigarette and spread out her papers that usually overfilled her briefcase. Mitchell had a sense of humour that encouraged young writers to greater efforts.

*From your reading of books produced by members of the Writers Laboratory, how did the authors reflect an understanding of children and their lives?*

Mitchell would provide information on children and child development. The earliest members always had direct experience with children so there were fresh ideas from children's language. Pearl Buck (writer), Alice Keliher (educator and psychologist)[10], Max Lerner (poet) and others came as guests to stimulate discussions. Margaret Wise Brown brought her Kerry Blue terrier, Smoke, who curled up at her feet. Mitchell never took charge but did propose certain exercises to help authors with their writing. One task was writing the same story for different age groups, which challenged their assumptions about children. Children's interests and spontaneous language were at the core of the writing tasks.

## Songs For Children

*In your program, what kinds of songs have you created about children's unique experiences? Think of some recent field trips with children and how you might develop some songs related to the field trips.*

Sprague Mitchell worked also on songs for children that would reflect their lives. *Songs for the Nursery School* by Laura Pendleton MacCarteney contains many of these songs.

Lucy Sprague Mitchell wrote "Moon, Moon" and "Resting Time" in this collection.

---

[10] A biography of Keliher is included in the ACEI Later Leaders *Profiles in Childhood Education* 1931-1960 and in Bardwell and Spicola's *Early Childhood Education: Personalities.* Keliher worked with Arnold Gesell at the Yale Clinic of Child Development, taught university, lectured, wrote extensively, worked on government committees, and consulted. Keliher was always an optimist despite the challenges in the field.

*Describe some children's songs that relate to everyday experiences of young children. Do you know who wrote these? Why do we tend to be more familiar with authors of children's than writers of children's songs?*

Real-life events and experiences continue to captivate children and make the current songs of Woodie Guthrie, Pete Seeger, Ella Jenkins, Raffi, Paul Hann, Sharon, Lois and Bram, Charlotte Diamond and Fred Penner come alive.[11]

**Lucy Sprague Mitchell was fascinated by language and wrote extensively for children, both stories and musical verses. (From Laura Pendleton MacCarteney's *Songs for the Nursery School* published in 1937 by The Willis Music Company of Cincinnati, Ohio.)**

[11] The Smithsonian Collection of Folkways Recordings has an invaluable database and collection of children's recordings. Their website is: *http://www.si.edu/folkways/*

To order a recording, mail to:
Smithsonian Folkways Mail Order
Dept. 607
Washington, D.C. 20073-0607
U.S.A.

*All the historical figures (except Montessori) supported the value of play in children's learning. Why is it still undervalued in society today?*

## Ideas and Their Impact

What were Sprague Mitchell's enduring beliefs about education?

- Learning should be an active and dynamic process of discovery.
- Theory should never be separate from practice.
- Teachers must study children's development to adapt schools at every stage of growth.
- Teachers should foster a continuing connection between educational theory and practice and research in child development.
- Teachers must be self-reflective.
- The more teachers know about the world around them, the more enriched the program will be for children.
- Schools must be connected to the community at all levels.
- The whole teacher must be educated to teach the whole child.
- Multidimensional maturity levels should override any chronological age norms.

The following description of children's experiences with blocks reflects her belief in the whole child and active investigation as the process of learning:

> *"Grown-ups are still prone to organize a curriculum for one area of learning and then another, and to work out equipment that they think will develop one patch of a child and then another. But children just refuse to respond in this piecemeal fashion. They remain consistently whole people, reacting to situations with all their lively interests mixed together. They are small scientists eagerly investigating the world that they can lay their hands on; small human beings interested in other human beings; dramatists playing out their experiences, modifying them to give themselves a strategic position in the world of grown-ups; workmen exulting in their techniques; artists enjoying design and pattern-form, balance in size and color, repetition."*
>
> **— 1945 introduction to Johnson, *The Art of Blockbuilding* (1966 reprint)**

## Curriculum Design

Sprague Mitchell had a clear vision of the learning process with three integrated elements:

1. intake — contact with the real world through observations, interactions, trips, source materials, investigations; discovery
2. digestion/absorption — processing the intake
3. outgo — doing something, expressing new ideas, planning a course of action, testing out ideas; using relationships; play, art, scientific findings, expressive organized thought

All three must be part of the process and would be the same throughout a person's life, though the nature of the elements would change and develop. An adult might see a documentary or read a book and change her view of the situation, emerging with a new way of thinking or seeing. An event, an encounter with a person, or travel might have equal learning potential.

The Cooperative School for Teachers focused on the same three elements for its emerging teachers. They too had "intake" and "outgo" experiences with social understanding at the core:

> *"the present day teacher must deal with the psychology of his students and with the culture or human geography or whatever we wish to call the world medium in which we all live; and, above, all, with the relationship between the two."*
>
> — **"Social Studies for Future Teachers"**

Sprague Mitchell described a walk she took with a four-year-old child and her later attempt to evoke visual images for the child and describe her own memories of the walk. The child looked at her and asked if she was talking about that certain point in time in the walk when her *legs ached.* Same walk, different perspective. The child's recall depended on her own experience and memory of the aching muscles.

Connections needed to be made with the real world so children could understand the social and physical environments. She learned that meaningful experiences exist when children connect the **new** to what is already known:

> *"A city child has never experienced a barn with a horse's stall and horse's food. My New York five-year-olds who had never been out of the city, put their horses to bed under covers and went to the A. & P. store built of blocks to buy them milk and steak! When we took our first group of five- and six-year-olds … to the country, they interpreted everything from their life on Greenwich Avenue. When Rosalind saw the minnows in the pond she cried, 'Look at the live sardines!' And when these city children saw a hen sitting on her eggs, they asked the farmer if he bought these eggs for her at the A. & P."*
>
> — **"Ages and Stages"**

Curriculum emerged from the children and their lives, which acted as a springboard for study; schools helped the children investigate ideas more deeply.

Feeling and thinking were both integral parts of learning. Instead of pre-ordained curriculum plans for schools, teachers based their programming on understanding how children learn and then began planning around their immediate environment. Particular facts were only important as children fit them into a scheme of thinking. At the same time teachers needed to be constantly aware of subject matter in guiding the children's learning.

## Colleagues

Where did she get her ideas? From children and from the thinkers of the day. But she also put the ideas into practice with ongoing "experimentation." There was much theory in child development at this point from many theorists including Piaget, but his works were not translated into English until the early 1920's, and it would be another few decades before his ideas reached the classrooms for children. Meanwhile many people benefitted from Sprague Mitchell's ideas that were put into immediate practice. Although she admired both Piaget and Dewey, Mitchell was critical of the fact their works were written in language that was not accessible or understandable to most people.

She had other disagreements with Piaget. In a 1927 book review of Piaget's The *Language and Thought of the Child*, Sprague Mitchell said his work was of "outstanding interest" but she also saw limitations:

*Why do you think there is a Montessori Method but not a Dewey, Hill, Pratt or Sprague Mitchell method?*

> *"We could wish he had studied what situations brought speech and what kinds of speech.*
>
> *Nowhere in all his analysis is there a hint that he thinks of the play with words as a permanent and precious part of human language.*
>
> *One could wish Piaget had experimented with the understanding and recall of patterned language as well as with logical.*
>
> *I believe not one of his major conclusions is new to teachers who have been observing children's behavior objectively in their successive growth stages and who regard their work as the establishment of an environment suited to meet these needs of growth."*
>
> **— Review of Piaget's *Language and Thought of the Child***

Sprague Mitchell felt that she understood and was describing the learning process as a teacher and not a philosopher. She saw herself as someone who did the spade work, not just the planning.

Sprague Mitchell's tribute to Dewey is contained in an early manuscript of *Young Geographers:*

> *"Dewey's great contribution to the education of children was, in my thinking, turning the attention of teachers of children to children, themselves, and how they learn as well as to the content they were taught. Some schools actually said 'they taught children, not subject matter' — a grotesque misinterpretation of Dewey if not an impossibility."*
>
> **— quoted in Matthews, *Lucy Sprague Mitchell: A Deweyan Educator***

*Lucy Sprague Mitchell depended on interaction and learning from colleagues. Describe how your career or education has benefitted from the input of colleagues.*

Lucy Sprague Mitchell also developed her ideas from her diverse group of friends and colleagues. The importance of colleagues is shown not just in the life of Sprague Mitchell but also with Caroline Pratt and Patty Smith Hill. Sprague Mitchell certainly knew famous people like Dewey, G. Stanley Hall and Thorndike. But she also had a circle of colleagues who were **practitioners** in the field of early education. They provided her with ideas, criticism, reflection and support. Among these were:

- Harriet Johnson (nurse, visiting teacher and nursery school teacher[12]),
- Margaret Wise Brown (children's author; see *Margaret Wise Brown: Awakened by the Moon),*
- Caroline Pratt (see chapter 10),
- Elisabeth Irwin (organizer of the Little Red School House),
- Evelyn Dewey (daughter of John Dewey),
- Jessie Stanton (director of Bank Street Nursery School after Harriet Johnson died; author),
- Barbara Biber[14] (psychologist/educator),
- Agnes Snyder[15] (educator, poet, philosopher, music composer),
- Charlotte Winsor (teacher of children and adults).

## Later Life

In 1948 Wesley Clair Mitchell died. Her emotional support vanished, and Lucy again felt lonely and inadequate, as she had when she was a child and young adult. Sprague Mitchell wrote an autobiography/biography of herself and her husband entitled *Two Lives: The Story of Wesley Clair Mitchell and Myself.* Published in 1953, it was one of the first 20th century books to look at female issues of combining marriage, children and career.

A book review of *Two Lives* said the work

> *"offers a better look at changing human and sex relationships than Simone de Beauvoir. The world it shows us gleams of what may happen when we learn to say, not Men and women — and — children but Men and Women and Children."*
>
> — **Ernestine Evans, "A Happy Family Album"**

---

[12] Harriet Johnson's writings include *School Begins at Two, The Visiting Teacher in New York City, The Art of Blockbuilding,* and *Children in the Nursery School* and "A Nursery School Experiment" in *Experimental Schools Revisited* (edited by Charlotte Winsor).

[13] See article on Barbara Biber Bodansky by Sullivan, cited in References at the end of this chapter.

[14] There is an insightful article on Agnes Snyder in *Profiles in Childhood Education 1931 – 1960* published by the ACEI; her credo involved knowing the issues facing humankind and participating in their solutions.

**This photo was taken in the 1950's at the end of her active career with Bank Street College. During this period she wrote an autobiography/biography of herself and her husband entitled *Two Lives.* In 1956 she moved to Palo Alto, California to write poetry and essays, and she lived to the age of 89. (Used with permission of Special Collections, Milbank Memorial Library, Teachers College, Columbia University.)**

Mitchell retired from Bank Street College in 1956 and moved to Palo Alto, California. She lived in a small house under an oak tree with a view toward the mountains. She spent her time writing poetry and short essays and continuing to understand herself. In 1966 at the 50th anniversary of Bank Street College, Lucy Sprague Mitchell flew to New York at the age of 88 years. She spent time interacting with children and commented to the Board that she was glad the place was still "alive and moving."

Her writing renewed some of her self-confidence and creativity as it had in her early years. She died in October 1967 at the age of 89 at her Palo Alta, California home. At the time of her death Sprague Mitchell was writing a book entitled *Every Stage of Life Has Its Song: My Song has Been a Woman's Song.*

In a remembrance celebration for her in December of 1967 at Bank Street, she received the following tributes:

> *"[she] was tonic to me."* ***[John Niemeyer, President of Bank Street]***
>
> *"The bombshell [in reference to the here and now curriculum] broke and the pieces are still flying."* ***[Edith Thacher Hurd, children's author]***
>
> *"Curtains were opened on worlds waiting to be discovered, and Lucy charted the way. Often I have heard her say that a person lives best who puts the largest number of tentacles out into his world, and then tries to catch something on each of them."* ***[Charlotte Winsor, former student and colleague]***
>
> **— quoted in Biber,**
> ***Lucy Sprague Mitchell, 1878 – 1967***

## Bank Street Today

Bank Street College of Education remains an active leader in early childhood and teacher education. It confers only graduate degrees and is independent of any university — a unique model. Programs of study range from early childhood and elementary education to leadership in museum education to early intervention. There is a School for Children (pre-kindergarten through grade 8) and a Family Centre (birth through 3 years of age), a Division of Continuing Education and a Publications and Media Group.

*Social Studies — A way to Integrate Curriculum for four-and-five-year-olds* is a video available from Bank Street that demonstrates the Bank Street program for children.

*Mitchell was part of a group of people who worked to make the world a better place with education as the central focus. Teaching was more than a job, more than a career. It was the opportunity to change lives (of children and of teachers) and to create a new social reality. Education was also seen within the contextual framework of social conditions of the day.*

*Why has each of us chosen early childhood? Is it a job? Is it a way to help children realize their potential? Are questioning and inquiry pivotal to our practice? Is reflective thinking a central component of our work? Is education a tool to improve society?*

Their web site is: http://www.bnkst.edu/html/about/index.html

Address:
610 West 112th Street
New York, N.Y. 10025-1898
U.S.A.

## Lessons For The Future

Sprague Mitchell looked at goals in a way that speaks to us as if she were writing today:

> *"What, then, is a good life for children? An active, a full, a rich life of meaningful experiences at each stage of their development. It is a sound humanitarian impulse to give children such lives. But it is more than that. A good life is a life in which one keeps growing in interests, in breadth of emotions and powers of expression, in depth and extent of human relations. Growth in all one's powers. . . leads on to an adulthood which is not static, completed, but still retains the capacity and the eagerness to grow. Adults, for good or bad, retain in their very fiber the results of their childhood experiences. Children's best chance to be learners, doers, creative, constructive members in the society they live in as adults is to have lived lives which gave these qualities a chance to grow steadily. . . . A good life for children is, above all, a chance to keep growing as 'whole children.'"*
>
> ***— Our Children and our Schools***

The field of early childhood has always been in a state of change. It represents the issues addressing all of society. What guides do we have when we don't know what path to take? Lucy Sprague Mitchell had wise ideas on advocacy that speak to us now:

> *"Critical times are questioning times. We feel confused and without direction when our old ways do not work. We feel something has gone wrong somewhere in our basic cultural patterns and attitudes that we were not able to prevent a new crisis or are not better able to handle it when it comes. And we wonder what we should do about it. It is so today in these critical worrying times. One of the questions many people are asking is, 'How can our schools be improved — how can they develop people equal to the problems that their own lives and the times bring to them?' This question is asked. . . in the hope that if we find an answer, we may get nearer to the solution of some of our basic social problems."*
>
> ***— Our Children and Our Schools***

*After reading the Epilogue that follows this chapter, what are your thoughts on the need to reclaim the wisdom of relatively unknown women educators and practitioners?*

The final element in the credo of Bank Street speaks clearly of Mitchell's answer:

> *"Our credo demands ethical standards as well as scientific attitudes. Our work is based on the faith that human beings can improve the society they have created."*

The future *is* in our work.

*Lucy Sprague Mitchell Collection*
*Rare Book and Manuscript Library*
*535 West 114th Street*
*Butler Library, 6th Floor*
*Columbia University*
*New York, New York 10027*
*U.S.A.*

# Programming for Growth at P. S. 186

**— from "Programming For Growth at P. S. 186" by Mitchell**

"How could these curriculum ingredients — formal subject matter to be covered in each year and the familiar neighborhood sights and sounds — be welded into programs for growth? What kinds of growth did we want for our children? What did these children need at various stages of their development in order to go forward to the next stage? What more must we add to the curriculum to meet the needs of these children and to give them a good life in school? These were the questions which teachers and Bank Street staff at P.S. 186 asked themselves.

No two teachers worked out identical programs. The teachers themselves were different in their backgrounds, their interests, their facility in various teaching techniques. The children were different in age and background, and these differences led to different kinds of programs.

The children in each class differed from the children in other classes. But all had bodies that craved action, all had minds that responded with lively interest to some aspects of the world around them, all lived with other human beings — families, classmates, teacher — in relationships which were satisfying or disturbing. Whatever the program, it must give adequate and healthful exercise for bodies, minds and emotions. Healthy growth depends upon exercise. How could bodies be given enough exercise with little play space and classrooms with screwed-down desks? How could intellectual curiosities be sustained or awakened with prescribed subject matter not necessarily fitted to the interests of these children? How could children be given satisfying experiences? How develop independence and a group sense with forty or so in a class?

From the many programs worked out by various teachers, I have chosen three to illustrate the methods of work by which the above questions were answered.

## More Progress in Reading When it Grows Out of Experience

A teacher of a first grade class faced the problem of teaching reading. Early in her program she took her children on a trip — not a long trip for the children were numerous and young and not yet accustomed to trips. Before the trip she found out from the custodian when coal was to be delivered to the school. When the truck arrived, she and the children gathered on the sidewalk. They all watched. The teacher did not talk much. Even the children spoke little. Their eyes and ears were too busy for much talk. They watched the driver grind the crank that raised the body of his truck, take the cover off the hole in the sidewalk, put up the chute. Then the coal began to slide. Subdued noises from the children — not words, just noises like the coal. They watched the driver put the cover over the hole. Now they knew what that round thing was for. They watched the driver climb up into his seat. "Goodbye!" they yelled. Now they knew a driver of a coal truck. He is a strong worker. He is their friend.

Back in the room the teacher did not at once ask the children about the trip. She knows that six-year-olds take a period for digestion before an experience becomes a part of themselves. The next day the children gather for a discussion time. On the board she writes, "We heard the coal." She asks what the coal sounded like when it slid down the chute. A chorus of sounds follows. One by one, she writes on the board what various children say. With excitement the children read the sounds. They have made up a story! They can read it!

We heard the coal.
The coal said,

> "Bang, bang, bang, bang,
> Sh, Sh, Sh, Sh,
> Bump, bump, bump,"

and so on down the list. That was the first of many charts about the coal.

There were charts about what the children saw in the school cellar — the big pile of coal, the big furnace, the hot glow as the custodian's helper opened the furnace door, the way he shovelled in the coal, the big pipes from the furnace, the little pipe connected with the radiator in their room. Now they knew how their room was kept warm. They could read it over and over.

More charts about what they saw and heard on the East River — little tug boats, barges heaped with coal, big derricks unloading it. Machines and men doing work. More strong workers.

The children dramatized almost everything they saw. They were drivers of coal trucks; custodian helpers; men unloading barges, derricks, tooting boats. Gravel was coal. Blocks were furnaces, trucks, barges — anything.

This series of trips, discussions and dramatic play might be called a unit on coal. It was not, however, an isolated episode. Rather it was a part of a study of home, school and neighborhood on a six-year-old play level. Other workers, other city work entered the curriculum — the scissors grinder who sharpened the butcher's knife and the tailor's scissors, the neighborhood butcher using his sharp knife, the tailor using his scissors, the bake shop, the garage, the milk truck bringing the little bottles of milk which the big children brought to their room. Trips, discussions, dramatic play, and a whole series of stories about themselves which the children could read. More stories about things the children could not go to see. Some stories out of printed books; some written by the teacher.

In what ways were these first grade children growing as they took the early steps in the difficult techniques of learning to read?

They were growing as *thinkers*. Thinking is seeing relationships. They were seeing the relationships in the world they lived in — their homes, their school, their neighborhoods, their city. They were learning about work and workers.

They were growing as *scientists*. They were making observations and recording them. They were growing by the scientific method of research.

They were growing as *artists*. Their experiences turned into paintings, dramatic play, dancing, stories. They were learning not only by taking in information but by giving it out in their own terms.

They were growing as *social beings*, learning social techniques. A trip is a big social experience. So is dramatic play. So is a discussion. So is creating stories. All these shared experiences helped to build a sense of groupness as well as to develop independence.

All of these growths were a part of the children's total school life. They were not scheduled — one period for bodily growth, one for mental, another for social growth. A child is an organism, and an organism reacts as a whole to a situation. It is only for convenience in our talk that we split these growths into separate compartments. A happy child learns better than an unhappy child, an active child better than a passive child. Reading was a part of a total experience, a part of living, a skill which helped the children to do something they wanted to do, namely, to record and read a pleasant experience."

## Bank Street Writer's Laboratory

### Leone Adelson

All Ready for School
All Ready for Winter
Dandelions Don't Bite
Mr. Twitmeyer and the Poodle
Please Pass The Grass
The Terrible Mr. Twitmeyer

### William Hooks

A Dozen Dizzy Dogs
A Flight of Dazzle Angels
Circle of Fire
Crossing the Line
Doug Meets the Nutcracker
Feed Me!: An Aesop Fable
Freedom's Fruit
How do You Make A Bubble?
Lion and Lamb
Little Poss and Horrible Hound
Lo-Jack and the Pirates
Maria's Cave
Mean Jake and the Devils
Moss Gown
Mr. Baseball
Mr. Big Brother
Mr. Bubble Gum
Mr. Dinosaur
Mr. Garbage
Mr. Monster
Mystery on Liberty Street
No Way, Slippery Slick
Peach Boy
Pioneer Cat
Read-A-Rebus: Tales and Rhymes in Words and Pictures
Rough Tough Rowdy (A Carrotville Adventure)
Snowbear Whittington: An Appalachian Beauty and the Beast
The 17 Gerbils of Class 4A
The Ballad of Belle Dorcas
The Girl Who Could Fly
The Gruff Brothers
The Legend of the Christmas Rose
The Legend of the White Dove
The Mighty Santa Fe
The Monster from the Sea
The Mystery of the Missing Tooth
The Mystery on Bleeker Street
The Mystery on Liberty Street
The New Extended Family: Day Care That Works
The Rainbow Ribbon
The Three Little Pigs and the Fox: An Appalachian Tale
Three Rounds with Rabbit
Ups and Downs with Lion and Lamb
When Small is Tall and Other Read-Together Tales
Where's Lulu?

### Edith Thacher Hurd

Christmas Eve
Come and Have Fun
Come with Me to Nursery School
Dinosaur, My Darling
I Dance in my Red Pajamas
Johny Lion's Bad Day
Johnny Lion's Book
Johnny Lion's Rubber Boots
Last One Home is a Green Pig
Look for a Bird
No Funny Business
Rain and The Valley
Sailers, Whalers and Steamers
Song of the Sea Otter
Starfish
Stop Stop
The Black Dog Who Went into the Woods
The Faraway Christmas: A Story of the Farallon Islands
The Mother Beaver
The Mother Chimpanzee
The Mother Deer
The Mother Kangaroo
The Mother Owl
The Mother Whale
The So-So Cat
This is the Forest
Wilson's World

### Helen Kay

A Day in the Life of a Baby Gibbon
A Lion for a Sitter
A Name for Little-No-Name
An Egg is for Wishing
Apes
Apron On, Apron Off
City Springtime

One Mitten Lewis
Picasso's World of Children
Pony for the Winter
Snow Birthday
The First Teddy Bear

## Ruth Krauss

A Hole is to Dig: A First Book of Definitions
A Very Special House
The Backward Day
Bears
Big and Little
Bouquet of Littles
The Bundle Book
Charlotte and the White Horse
Everything Under a Mushroom
A Good Man and His Good Wife
I Can Fly
I'll Be You and You Be Me
I Want to Paint My Bathroom Blue
I Write It
Is This You
Little Boat Lighter Than a Cork
Minestrone: A Ruth Krauss Collection
Monkey Day
My Little Library: Jamberry, the Carrot Seed, Leo the Late Bloomer
Open House for Butterflies
Somebody Else's Nut Tree and Other Tales from Children
Somebody Spilled the Sky
The Birthday Party
The Carrot Seed
The Growing Story
The Happy Day
The Happy Egg
The Cantilever Rainbow
The Big World and the Little House
This Beast Gothic
Very Special House
What a Fine Day for
You're Just What I Need

## Eve Merriam

12 Ways to Get 11
A Gaggle of Geese
A Poem For a Pickle
A Sky Full of Poems
A Word or Two With You
Blackberry Ink
Boys & Girls, Girls & Boys
Catch a Little Rhyme
Chortles
Daddies at Work
Family Circle (a book of poetry)
Fighting Words
Finding a Poem
Fresh Pain
Goodnight to Annie
Goodnight to Annie: An Alphabet Lullaby
Halloween ABC
Higgle Wiggle
Independent Voices
Inner City Mother Goose
Mommies at Work
Out Loud
Quiet Please
Rainbow Writing
The Birthday Door
The Christmas Box
The Hole Story
The Singing Green
The Story of Ben Franklin
The Wise Woman and Her Secret
Train Leaves The Station
Unhurry Harry
Where is Everybody?
You Be Good and I'll Be Night

## Margaret Wise Brown

A Pussycat's Christmas
Animals in the Snow
Another Important Book
A Child's Good Morning Book
A Child's Good Night Book
A Pussycat's Christmas: Christmas Cards
Christmas in the Barn
Baby Animals
Big Red Barn
Brer Rabbit: Stories from Uncle Remus
Christmas in the Barn
Country Noisy Book
David's Little Indian
Don't Frighten the Lion!
Duck
Four Fur Feet

Fox Eyes
Goodnight Moon
Goodnight Moon Bedtime Box
Goodnight Moon — Reading Chest
Goodnight Moon With Other
Home for a Bunny
I Like Bugs (Road to Reading. Mile 1)
I Like Stars (Road to Reading...Mile 1)
Important Book
Little Brass Band
Little Chicken
Little Donkey, Close Your Eyes
Little Fireman
Little Fur Family
Little Lamb PB; Vienna
Little Lost Lamb
Margaret Wise Brown's A child's Good Night Book
Margaret Wise Brown's Pussy Willow
Margaret Wise Brown's the Color Kittens (Golden Storybook)
Margaret Wise Brown's Wonderful Storybook
My World
Nibble Nibble: Poems for Children
Noisy Book
On Christmas Eve
Once Upon a time in the Pigpen and Three Other Stories
Pussy Willow (Little Golden Readers)
Read Together Poems, Book 4
Read Together Poems, Book 7
Red Light, Green Light
Red Light, Green Light (A Blue Ribbon Book)
Runaway Bunny (Board Book)
Shhhhhh Bang: A Whispering Book
Sleepy ABC
Sleepy Little Lion
Sneakers: Seven Stories About a Cat
The Best Loved Tales by Margaret Wise Brown: Mister Dog/the Color Kittens/Seven Little Postmen
The Country Noisy Book
The Day Before Now
The Dead Bird
The Diggers
The Dream Book
The Fish With the Deep Sea Smile
The Friendly Book (Little Golden Readers)
The Golden Birthday Book
The Golden Bunny (Golden Look-Look Books)
The Golden Egg Book
The Goodnight Moon Room (Pop-Up Book)
The Indoor Noisy Book
The Little Fir Tree
The Little Fireman
The Little Scarecrow Boy
The Noisy Book
The Quiet Noisy Book
The Runaway Bunny
The Runaway Bunny With Doll
The Sailor Dog
The Seashore Noisy Book
The Sleepy Book (Little Golden Readers)
The Sleepy Men
The Steamroller: A Fantasy
The Summer Noisy Book
The Train to Timbuctoo (Family Storytime, No. 4)
The Whispering Rabbit (Little Golden Book)
The Winter Noisy Book
The Wonderful House (The Little Golden Treasures Series)
Three Little Animals
Three Orphan Kittens
Two Little Trains
Under the Sun and the Moon and Other Poems
Wait Till the Moon is Full
Walt Disney's the Grasshopper and the Ants
Walt Disney's The Old Mill
Walt Disney's the Ugly Duckling
Wheel on the Chimney
When the Wind Blew
Where Have You Been?
Willie's Adventures: Three Stories
Young Kangaroo

## Elizabeth Helfman

Celebrating Nature
Maypoles and Wood Demons
On Being Sarah
Signs and Symbols of the Sun
Strings on Your Fingers (with Harry Helfman)
Water for the World

## Lucy Sprague Mitchell — References for Further Study


ACEI Later Leaders Committee. (1992). *Profiles in childhood education 1931 – 1960.* Wheaton, MD: Association for Education International.

Antler, J. (1981, Spring). Feminism as life-process: The life and career of Lucy Sprague Mitchell. *Feminist Studies, 7,* 134-155.

Antler, J. (1982, Summer). Progressive education and the scientific study of the child: An analysis of the Bureau of Educational Experiments, 1916 – 1940. *Teacher's College Record, 83* (4), 559-591.

Antler, J. (1984). Was she a good mother? Some thoughts on a new issue for feminist biography. In B. Harris & J. McNamara (Eds.), *Women and The Structure of Society* (pp. 53-66). Durham, NC: Duke University Press.

Antler, J. (1987). *Lucy Sprague Mitchell: The making of a modern woman.* New Haven, CT: Yale University Press.

Antler, J. (1988). The educational biography of Lucy Sprague Mitchell: A case study in the history of women's higher education. In J. Faragher & F. Howe (Eds.), *Women and Higher Education in American History* (pp. 43-63). New York: W.W. Norton.

Antler, J. (1992). Having it all, almost: Confronting the legacy of Lucy Sprague Mitchell. In S. Alpern, J. Antler, E. Perry, & I. Scobie (Eds.), *The challenge of feminist biography*. Chicago: University of Illinois Press.

Ayers, W. (1988). A teacher's life more fully lived. *Teacher's College Record, 89* (4), 579-586.

Bailey, J. (1991). *An exception to the rule: Bank Street College of Education as an independent professional school (1916 – 1990).* Unpublished doctoral dissertation, The College of William and Mary in Virginia.

Biber, B. (1967). *Lucy Sprague Mitchell, 1878 – 1967.* New York: Bank Street College of Education.

Bliven, B., Jr. (1946, December 2). Child's best seller. *Life.*

Bordin, R. (1993). *Alice Freeman Palmer: The evolution of a new woman.* Ann Arbor, MI: The University of Michigan Press.

Cenedella, J. (1996/1997). *The Bureau of Educational Experiments: A study in progressive education* (Doctoral dissertation, Teachers College, Columbia University, 1996). UM1 9713871.

Davidson, J. (1982, July 23). Bank Street and children's writers. *Publisher's Weekly*, 80-81.

Day, M., & Parker, R. (1977). *The preschool in action.* Boston: Allyn & Bacon.

Dropkin, R., & Tobier, A. (Eds.). (1976). *Roots of open education in America.* New York: Workshop Centre for Open Education.

Estes, A. (1994). Margaret Wise Brown: Awakened by you know who. *Children's Literature 22,* 162-170

Evans, E. (1953, June 14). A happy family album. *New York Herald Tribune Book Review.*

Frank, L. (1937). Fundamental needs of the child. *Mental Hygiene, 22,* 353-379.

Gordon, E. (1988). *Educating the whole child: Progressive education and Bank Street College of Education, 1916 – 1966.* Unpublished doctoral dissertation, State University of New York at Stony Brook.

Gordon, L. (1990). *Gender and higher education in the progressive era.* New Haven, CT: Yale University Press.

Greenberg, P. (1987). Lucy Sprague Mitchell: A major missing link between early childhood education in the 1980s and progressive education in the 1890s – 1930s. *Young Children, 42* (3), 70-84.

Group to see area of bootleg mining. (1939, April 2). *New York Times*, Sec 03, p. 2.

Healy, E. (1931, August). A new educational venture. *Practical Home Economics*, 237-238.

Johnson, H. (1916). *The visiting teacher in New York City.* New York: Public Education Association of the City of New York.

Johnson, H. (1933). *The art of blockbuilding.* New York: The John Day Co.

Johnson, H. (1936). *School begins at two: A book for teachers and parents.* New York: New Republic, Inc.

Johnson, H. (1972). *Children in "the nursery school."* New York: Agathon Press. (Original work published 1928)

Johnson, H. M. (1966). *The art of blockbuilding.* New York: Bank Street College of Publications. (Original work published 1933)

Lascarides, V.C. & Hinitz, B. (2000). *History of Early Childhood Education.* New York: Falmer Press.

Lay-Dopyera, M., & Dopyera, J. E. (1993). *Becoming a teacher of young children* (5th ed.). New York: McGraw Hill.

Lucy Sprague Mitchell is dead: Founder of Bank Street College [obituary]. (1967, October 17). *New York Times,* p. 44.

MacCarteney, L P. (1937). *Songs for the nursery school.* Cincinnati, OH: The Willis Music Company.

Marcus, L. (1991). Awakened by the moon. *Publishers Weekly 238,* (33), 16-20.

Marcus, L. (1992). *Margaret Wise Brown: Awakened by the moon.* Boston: Beacon Press.

Matthews, E. (1979). *Lucy Sprague Mitchell: A Deweyan educator.* Unpublished doctoral dissertation, Rutgers, The State University of New Jersey, New Brunswick, New Jersey.

Mitchell, A., & David, J. (1992). *Explorations with young children.* Mt. Rainier, MD: Goyphon House.

Mitchell, L. S. (1908, December). The forms and results of student social activities. *Publications of the Association of Collegiate Alumnae Magazine, 3* (18), 50-53.

Mitchell, L. S. (1914, June 20). School children and sex idealism. *Survey, 32,* 327-28.

Mitchell, L. S. (1921). Language work from October to January. In Stott, L., *City and Country School: Record of group VI.* New York: City and Country School.

Mitchell, L. S. (1921/revised 1948). *The here and now story book.* New York: E. P. Dutton.

Mitchell, L. S. (1924). *The here and now primer: Home from the country.* New York: E. P. Dutton.

Mitchell, L. S. (1926). *Horses now and long ago.* New York: Harcourt-Brace.

Mitchell, L. S. (1926, April). Five-year-old's first language work. *American Childhood, 2.*

Mitchell, L. S. (1926, April – June). Maps as art expression. *Progressive Education, 3,* 150-53.

Mitchell, L. S. (1927). Review of Piaget's *The language and thought of the child. Progressive Education, 4,* 136-139.

Mitchell, L. S. (1927, November 16). Geography for children. *New Republic, 52,* 355-57.

Mitchell, L. S. (1928, January – March). Children's experiments in language. *Progressive Education, 5* (1), 21-27. Also published (1932) in G. Hartman & A. Shumaker (Eds.), *Creative expression: The development of children in art, music, literature and dramatics.* For the Progressive Education Association. New York: John Day Co.

Mitchell, L. S. (1928, July – September). Making young geographers instead of teaching geography. *Progressive Education, 5,* 217-23.

Mitchell, L. S. (1928, November 24). Geography for children. *Saturday Review of Literature, 5,* 414.

Mitchell, L. S. (1929, November). Map making in the schools. *American Childhood, 15,* 5-8.

Mitchell, L. S. (1929, September – November). Geography with five-year-olds. *Progressive Education, 6,* 232-37.

Mitchell, L. S. (1931). *North America: The land they live in for the children who live there.* New York: Macmillan.

Mitchell, L. S. (1931, March). A cooperative school for student teachers. *Progressive Education, 8* (3), 251-255.

Mitchell, L. S. (1931, July). Geographic thinking. *New Era, 12,* 245-48.

Mitchell, L. S. (1931, November). Imagination in realism. *Childhood Education, 8,* 129-31.

Mitchell, L. S. (1932, April). Children as geographers. *Education, 52,* 446-50.

Mitchell, L. S. (1933). *Skyscraper* (with E. H. Naumburg & C. Lambert). New York: John Day.

Mitchell, L. S. (1933). *Stories for children under seven.* New York: John Day. [Titles in the series: *Streets, Trains, Boats and Bridges.*]

Mitchell, L. S. (1934). *Manhattan now and long ago* (with C. Lambert). New York: Macmillan.

Mitchell, L. S. (1934, January). Social Studies and geography. *Progressive Education, 11,* 97-105.

Mitchell, L. S. (1934, November). Harriet M. Johnson: Pioneer, 1867 – 1934. *Progressive Education, 11,* 427-29.

Mitchell, L. S. (1935, May). Social Studies for future teachers. *Social Studies, 26,* 289-98.

Mitchell, L. S. (1937). *Another here and now story book.* New York: E.P. Dutton.

Mitchell, L. S. (1938, February). Ages and stages. *Child Study, 15,* 144-47.

Mitchell, L. S. (1938, March). Natural regions of the United States: Their work patterns and their psychologies. *Progressive Education, 15,* 187-209.

Mitchell, L. S. (1938, November). Ages and stages. *Child Study, 15,* 144-147.

Mitchell, L. S. (1939). Children's experiments in language. In G. Hartman & A. Shumaker (Eds.), *Creative Expression.* Milwaukee, WI: E. M. Hales & Co.

Mitchell, L. S. (1939). Maps as art expression. In G. Hartman & A. Shumaker (Eds.), *Creative Expression.* Milwaukee, WI: E. M. Hales & Co.

Mitchell, L. S. (1940). *My country 'tis of thee: The use and abuse of natural resources* (with E. Bowman & M. Phelps). New York: Macmillan.

Mitchell, L. S. (1942). The people of the U.S.A.: Their place in the school curriculum (with J. Boetz and others). New York: *Progressive Education Association.*

Mitchell, L. S. (1943, February). Tribute to a pioneer [Elisabeth Irwin]. *Progressive Education, 20* (2), 65.

Mitchell, L. S. (1944). *Red, white and blue auto.* New York: William R. Scott.

Mitchell, L. S. (1944). Research on the child's level: Possibilities, limitations, and techniques. *31st Annual Schoolmen's week proceedings, University of Pennsylvania Bulletin,* pp. 111-19.

Mitchell, L. S. (1945). *Guess what's in the grass.* New York: William R. Scott.

Mitchell, L. S. (1945). Play based on neighborhood work: Harriet Johnson nursery school and little red school house. *Nursery Education Digest, 3,* 2-5.

Mitchell, L. S. (1945, December). Programming for growth at P.S. 186. *Childhood Education, 22,* 173-78.

Mitchell, L. S. (1945/revised 1954). *Our growing world.* New York: D.C. Heath. [Titles in the series: *Farm and City, Animals, Plants and Machines, Our Country.*]

Mitchell, L. S. (1946, January). Making real teachers. *Education Outlook, 20,* 52-63.

Mitchell, L. S. (1946 – 48). *Golden books (Bank Street Series).* New York. [Titles in the series: *The Taxi That Hurried* (with Irma Black and Jessie Stanton), *New House in the Forest, A Year on the Farm, A Year in the City, Fix it, Please.*]

Mitchell, L. S. (1950). *Our children and our schools.* New York: Simon and Schuster.

Mitchell, L. S. (1951). Who built the bridge. In *Told under the stars and stripes: Stories selected by the Literature committee of the Association for Childhood Education. New York: Macmillan.*

Mitchell, L. S. (1953). Margaret Wise Brown: 1910 – 1952. *Children Here and Now, 1,* 18-20.

Mitchell, L. S. (1953). *Two lives: The story of Wesley Clair Mitchell and myself.* New York: Simon and Schuster.

Mitchell, L. S. (1954). Jimmy wonders how things work. *Children Here and Now, 2,* 13-15.

Mitchell, L. S. (1955). *Becoming more so: Children here and now, 3,* 2-5.

Mitchell, L. S. (1956). *Believe and make-believe.* New York: E.P. Dutton.

Mitchell, L. S. (1957). Everychild: The miracle of growth. *Children Here and Now, 40th Anniversary Issue,* chap. 5, 2-8.

Mitchell, L. S. (1963). *Young geographers: How they explore the world and how they map the world.* New York: Basic Books. (Original work published 1934)

Mitchell, L. S., Lewis, C., Schonborg, V., Sonneborn, R., & Stall, D. (1954). *Know your children in school.* New York: Macmillan Co.

Palmer, G. H. (1908). *The life of Alice Freeman Palmer.* Boston: Houghton Mifflin Company.

Peltzman, B. R. (1998). *Pioneers of early childhood education: A bio-bibliographical guide.* Westport, CT: Greenwood Press.

Phelps, M., & Brown, M. W. (1937, May – June). Lucy Sprague Mitchell. *The horn book,* 158-163.

Pignatelli, F., & Pflaum, S. (1993). *Celebrating diverse voices: Progressive education and equity.* Newbury Park, CA: Corwin Press.

Raushenbush, E. (1978). Three women: Creators of change. In H. Astin & W. Hirsch (Eds.), *The Higher Education of Women: Essays in honor of Rosemary Park* (pp. 29-52). New York: Praeger.

Rivinus, T. M., & Audet, L. (1992). The psychological genius of Margaret Wise Brown. *Children's Literature in Education, 23* (1), 1-14.

Ross, E. H. (1937, November). The makings of teachers at the Cooperative School for Student Teachers. *Progressive Education, 14,* 502-509.

Seeds, N. (1931, May). Alumnae adventures in education. *Bryn Mawr Alumnae Bulletin,* 17-18.

Seefeldt, C. (1997). *Social studies for the pre-school-primary child.* Upper Saddle River, NJ: Prentice-Hall.

Seller, M. (1994). *Women educators in the United States, 1820 – 1993.* Westport, CT: Greenwood Press.

Smith, M. (2000). Who was Lucy Sprague Mitchell...and why should you know? *Childhood Education* 77 (1), 33-36.

Solomon, B. M. (1987, May 23). A heart culture. *The Nation,* 690-692.

Stanton, J. (1990). The ideal teacher — and how she grows. *Young Children, 45* (4), 19. (Original work published 1954).

Sullivan, R. (1993, September 16). Dr. Barbara Biber Bodansky, 89, child development expert, dies. *New York Times, 142,* 49456, B10.

Wellhousen, K. (1994). Using the 1930's 'here and now' curriculum to teach cultural diversity in the '90s.' *Social studies and the young learner, 6* (3), 9-11.

Wilde, S. (Ed.). (1996). *Notes from a kidwatcher: Selected writings of Yetta M. Goodman.* Portsmouth, NH: Heinemann.

Winsor, C. (Ed.). (1973). *Experimental schools revisited.* New York: Agathan Press.

ROOTS

# Epilogue — Missing and Found: The Voices of Early Childhood

*"I think it is important not to leave behind everything we already know about children as we go on learning new things . . . carefully observing children as they play and building curriculum that's appropriate for each child from what we see and hear. That should be the core. . . . I think we made a mistake when we moved so far away from child study and got so focused on memorizing what theoreticians and researchers say, covering a curriculum, and teaching techniques."*

**— Millie Almy quoted in Greenberg, "What Wisdom Should We Take with Us as We Enter the New Century"**

*"Many times I have asked myself why so little biographic material existed in educational literature comparable to other professions — particularly so little about women."*

**— Agnes Snyder quoted in Rasmussen, "Agnes Snyder: Dauntless Woman in Education"**

History is comprised of stories, but the word seems to emphasize the predominance of male figures in these stories. This emphasis on male participants is true in the recording of the history of early childhood as well; Montessori is the only woman to have achieved the notoriety of the males investigated in this book.

Most people who would know of Piaget, Erikson, Dewey and Freud would not be familiar with their female contemporaries such as P.S. Hill, Caroline Pratt or Lucy Sprague Mitchell. These women, and countless others, did not get the fame of the men of the day. For example, even in the classic book on progressive education by Lawrence Cremin in 1961, *The Transformation of the School*, scant or no mention is made of these pioneer women. The tenor of the times did not see women as theorists or researchers, though it was acceptable for them to be teachers. The "famous" men did not reference the work of these women, though the women often referenced Dewey and others. There are politics related to referencing that are described by Yetta Goodman in a book called *Notes from a Kidwatcher* (edited by Sandra Wilde). Most current histories of education or even early childhood education don't even mention these women.

Today many teachers (women and men) are doing active research in their own classrooms; early childhood teachers observe, reflect and critique their practice. However, the information is rarely disseminated or recognized, largely because work with young children in kindergarten or day care or playschool is often not considered important.

There have been some articles written about why the ideas of Lucy Sprague Mitchell and others have not been widely distributed or written about in the literature. The following quotation from an article on Lucy Sprague Mitchell provides some insight:

> *How is it that few in our field know of Lucy, one of ECE's founders, and not of ancient vintage? How is it that early childhood book and article references lavish attention on far lesser and more recent writers, but seldom if ever mention our profession's numerous heroines? How is it that a teacher educator can submit a manuscript to a prestigious professional journal with a cover letter stating, "Until now, no one has looked at cooperative behaviors in young children"? How is it that we often read that ECE research began in the 1960s? Are we forgetting to pass on our professional heritage?*
>
> *Why are we denying these early educators' contributions by ignoring them? Have we accepted the traditional cultural assumption that child care is "women's work," and is therefore low status, so what's so great about those old nursery school teachers anyway? Are we saying that our field, because a woman's field regardless of the many warm and wonderful men in it, did not count until the male psychologists entered it in the 60s?*

**Lucy Sprague**

*How is it that within the confines of our world, at least, Lucy Sprague Mitchell isn't famous? One reason doubtless is that if one prefers to work by consensus, collectively, collaboratively, collegially, or cooperatively, as many women and some men do, as Lucy did, fame is likely to go the other way. Society prefers the autonomous leader and the hierarchy. (It is concluded that the person who has outpaced and outmaneuvered all others is the survivor, that others have surrendered their power, that they are weak and unimportant.)*

*To progressive educators, harsh discipline was anathema, interpersonal interaction was of prime importance, and emotional expressiveness through play and the arts were highly prized. Lack of discipline is soft. Love and friendship are soft. The arts (unlike the sciences) are soft. Emotional expressiveness is soft. Children are soft. Little children are softer still. And women are softest of all, as are the areas of work historically allocated to them (caring for the ill, the poor, the children — health services, social services, education — and within education, in increasing degrees of softness: education of* young *elementary children, nursery school education, and child care.)*

*Our cultural ideal, on the other hand, is tough, hard, and masculine. "Hard" science, for example, is far more highly esteemed that a "soft" field such as "domestic science." Is it coincidental that when, in the 60s, the leadership of our field for the first time became suddenly male, psychosocial went out of fashion and cognitive, learning objectives, scientific terminology, and statistical research swooped in? We have managed to overlook the progressives' extensive scientific research not because it wasn't done primarily by males, but because, far worse, it wasn't even done in the male mode — distanced, termed "objective," wreathed in statistics. The progressives "just" observed, recorded, hypothesized, experimented, and did the other things scientists do.*

**Alice Chipman Dewey**

*And a word about "objective": Though masculinists have traditionally led us to believe that there is such a thing as objective research and scholarship — and that the males of our species are more objective than the females, whose area of expertise is the subjective — feminist scholars in history, sociology, science, and so on have in recent years shown that objectivity is impossible for one and all. All of us look at our subject through our personality and values (including gender), our politics, historical era, socioeconomic and racial background, level of education, and so forth. In large part, the scientific research of the progressives and their contributions to the arts of education, have been ignored because of the gender-warped thinking which has skewed much of what we are (or are not) taught of history.*

*Besides, the progressives were promoting radically different childrearing and educational practices. Different equals deviant equals loony — the train of thought is easy to see.*

**Marietta Johnson**

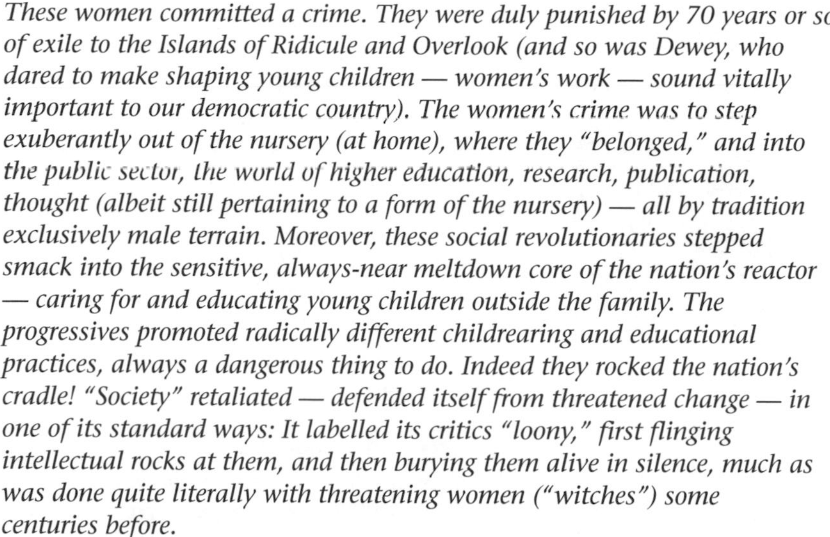

*These women committed a crime. They were duly punished by 70 years or so of exile to the Islands of Ridicule and Overlook (and so was Dewey, who dared to make shaping young children — women's work — sound vitally important to our democratic country). The women's crime was to step exuberantly out of the nursery (at home), where they "belonged," and into the public sector, the world of higher education, research, publication, thought (albeit still pertaining to a form of the nursery) — all by tradition exclusively male terrain. Moreover, these social revolutionaries stepped smack into the sensitive, always-near meltdown core of the nation's reactor — caring for and educating young children outside the family. The progressives promoted radically different childrearing and educational practices, always a dangerous thing to do. Indeed they rocked the nation's cradle! "Society" retaliated — defended itself from threatened change — in one of its standard ways: It labelled its critics "loony," first flinging intellectual rocks at them, and then burying them alive in silence, much as was done quite literally with threatening women ("witches") some centuries before.*

**— Polly Greenberg, "Lucy Sprague Mitchell: A Major Missing Link Between Early Childhood Education in the 1980's and Progressive Education in the 1890's - 1930s," *Young Children*, July 1987**

It is time to reclaim the learnings and wisdom of Patty Smith Hill, Caroline Pratt, Lucy Sprague Mitchell, Marietta Johnson, Alice Chipman Dewey, Julia Weber Gordon, Mary Hammett Lewis, Agnes Snyder, Ella Flagg Young and other women who have been overlooked in the mainstream accounts and texts of early childhood. Students of early childhood should be as familiar with them as they are with Jean Piaget or Erik Erikson. These were women full of passion, energy and determination, deeply involved with educational reform. They continue to influence our practice with young children and their families in a community context.

**Caroline Pratt**

It is encouraging to see more articles and books highlighting the contributions of these women to the education of children and future teachers. *Founding Mothers and Others: Women Educational Leaders During the Progressive Era* edited by Sadovnik and Semel and *Intersections: Feminisms/ Early Childhoods* edited by Hauser and Jipson are two additions.

These women were experimenters who constantly reflected on their practice as it evolved. In a reference to the Cooperative School for Student Teachers in 1913, Elizabeth Healy speaks of this process:

*"Experimental methods need not be viewed as guinea-pig-and-laboratory exercises, because sound education, like life, is experimental — and dynamic. Progressive methods need not be interpreted as a cover for license and aimless freedom, because our future depends on conscious efforts toward progress. Modern methods have been clouded with prejudice, because modern has been interpreted as the isolated present rather than the product of the past."*

**— Elizabeth Healy, "A 'New' Educational Venture," *Practical Home Economics*, August 1931**

Ella Flagg Young

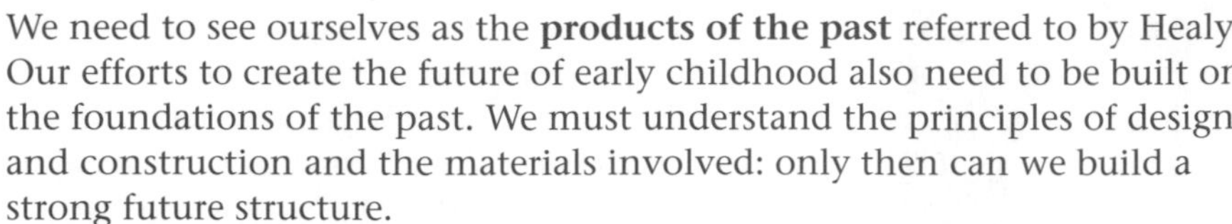

We need to see ourselves as the **products of the past** referred to by Healy! Our efforts to create the future of early childhood also need to be built on the foundations of the past. We must understand the principles of design and construction and the materials involved: only then can we build a strong future structure.

## Dedication

In 1924, the Committee of Nineteen of the International Kindergarten Union wrote *Pioneers of the Kindergarten in America* to improve standards, extend knowledge and " **. . . advocate the right of childhood to the best that educational guidance can supply.**" Its dedication, in a book that highlights leaders in the field, looks to the future that we still strive for:

> *"To the new generation of teachers who are to carry on the work so nobly begun by the pioneers, this book is affectionately dedicated. The men and women whose lives are recorded here labored in the hope that a better day was to dawn through a better type of education. To the cause of childhood they gave the last full measure of devotion. To it they consecrated their lives. To those who are to follow on in their footstep, they leave the rich heritage of faith that the best is yet to be in the kindergarten and in the world."*

It is individuals who make a difference in early childhood — women and men working with children and families, teaching, writing, speaking out, and participating in professional organizations.

Patty Smith Hill

Agnes Snyder once had the students in a history of education class create a production entitled "Weavers of the Unbroken Thread." The history of early childhood is a tapestry created by voices that have been famous and many more that have worked unheralded in communities throughout the world with children and families. We are all weavers of the unbroken thread; we are the voices of early childhood.

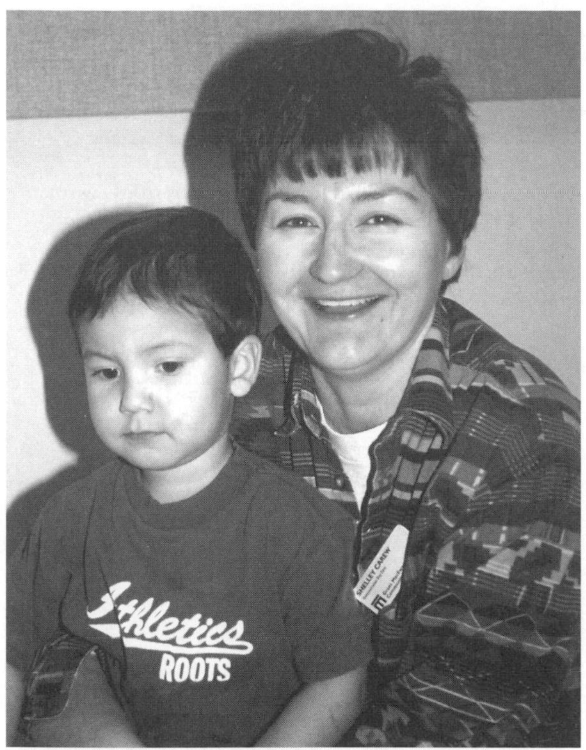

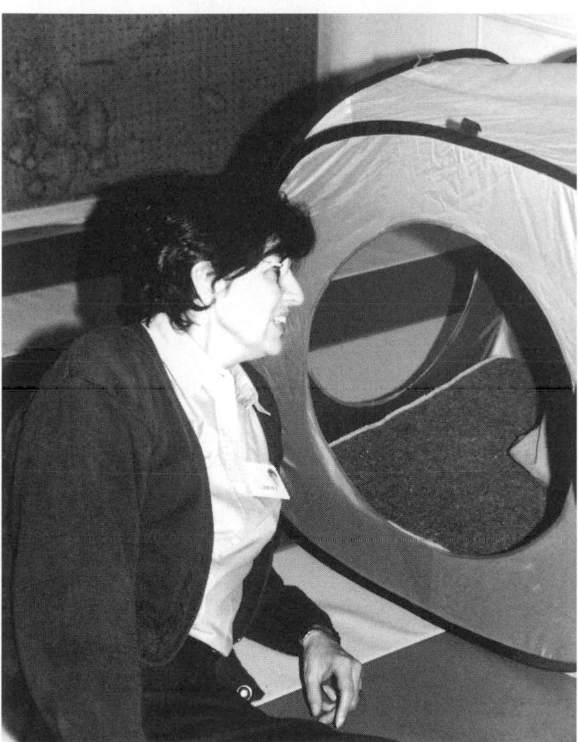

**Child Care Workers — Reflective Practitioners. Individuals like Shelley Carew, Colleen Friendship, Luz Maria Miranda, and Darla Maurer work directly with children and families. They learn from their reflective practice, showing new leadership and wisdom for the future. (Used courtesy of Grant MacEwan Day Care, Grant MacEwan College, Edmonton, Alberta. Photos taken by Jennifer Wolfe, 2000.)**

## Epilogue — References for Further Study

Committee of Nineteen. (1924). *Pioneers of the kindergarten in America.* New York: The Century Co.

Cremin, L. (1961). *The transformation of the school: Progressivism in American education.* New York: Alfred Knopf.

Greenberg, P. (1987). Lucy Sprague Mitchell: A major missing link between early childhood education in the 1980's and progressive education in the 1890s - 1930s. *Young Children, 43,* 70 – 84.

Greenberg, P. (2000). What wisdom should we take with us as we enter the new century? An interview with Millie Almy. *Young Children, 53* (1), 6 – 10.

Hauser, M & Jipson, J.(Eds.).(1998). *Intersections: Feminisms/early childhoods.* New York: Peter Lang Publishing, Inc.

Healy, E. (1931, August). A new educational venture. *Practical home economics,* 237-238.

Lascarides, V.C. & Hinitz, B. (2000). *History of Early Childhood Education.* New York: Falmer Press.

Rasmussen, M. (1990). Agnes Snyder: Dauntless woman in education 1885-1973. *Childhood Education, 67* (1), 34 – 39.

Sadovnik, A. & Semel, S. (Eds.). (2002). *Founding mothers and others: Women educational leaders during the progressive era.* New York: Palgrave.

Wilde, S. (Ed.). (1996). *Notes from a kidwatcher: Selected writings of Yetta M. Goodman.* Portsmouth, NH: Heinemann.

## Historical Figures — General References for Further Study

ACEI Later Leaders Committee. (1992). *Profiles in Childhood Education 1931 – 1960*. Wheaton, MD: Association for Education International.

Aries, P. (1962). *Centuries of childhood: A social history of family life*. New York: Alfred A. Knopf.

Bardwell, W., & Spicola, R. (1975). *Early childhood education: Personalities*. Denton, TX: Texas Women's University.

Beatty, B. (1995). *Preschool education in America*. New Haven, CT: Yale University Press.

Braun, S., & Edwards, E. (1972). *History and theory of early childhood education*. Belmont, CA: Wadsworth.

Caplan, F., & Caplan, T. (1973). *The power of play*. Garden City, NJ: Anchor Books.

Cohen, B. (1969). *Educational thought*. London: Macmillan.

Cole, L. (1966). *A history of education*. Toronto, Canada: Holt, Rinehart & Winston.

Corsini, R. (Ed.). (1984). *Encyclopedia of psychology*. New York: J. Wiley.

Corsini, R. (Ed.). (1994). *Encyclopedia of psychology* (2nd ed.). New York: J. Wiley.

*Current Biography*. (1998). New York: H.W. Wilson.

Curtis, S. J., & Boultwood, M. E. A. (1965). *A short history of educational ideas*. London: University Tutorial Press.

Deasey, D. (1978). *Education under six*. London: Croom Helm.

DeVries, R., & Kohlber, L. (1987). *Programs of early education*. New York: Longman.

Doxey, I. (1990). *Child care and education: Canadian dimensions*. Scarborough, Canada: Nelson Canada.

Dudek, M. (1996). *Kindergarten architecture: Space for the imagination*. London: E & FN Spon.

Duggan, S. (1948). *A student's textbook in the history of education*. New York: Appleton-Century-Crofts, Inc.

*Encyclopedia of world biography: An international reference work*. New York: McGraw Hill.

Forest, I. (1927). *Preschool education: A historical and critical study*. New York: The Macmillan Company.

Forest, I. (1949). *Early years at school*. New York: McGraw-Hill Book Company.

Good, H. G. (1947). *A history of western education*. New York: The Macmillan Company.

Gordon, I. (Ed.). (1972). *Early childhood education: The seventy-first yearbook of the national society for the study of education Part II*. Chicago: The University of Chicago Press.

Hailman, W. N. (1874). *Twelve lectures on the history of pedagogy*. New York: American Book Company.

Isenberg, J., & Jalongo, M. (1997). *Major trends and issues in early childhood education: Challenges, controversies, and insights*. New York: Teachers College Press.

James, E. T. (Ed.). James, J. W., & Boyer, P. S. (Associate Eds.). (1971). *Notable American women, 1607 – 1950: A biographical dictionary*. Cambridge, MA: Belknap Press of Harvard University Press.

Lascarides, V.C. & Hinitz, B. (2000). *History of Early Childhood Education*. New York: Falmer Press.

Lawrence, E. (1972). *The origins and growth of modern education*. Baltimore: Penguin.

Lazerson, M. (1972). The historical antecedents of early childhood education. In I. Gordon (Ed.), *Early childhood education: The seventy-first yearbook of the national society for the study of education Part II* (pp. 33-53). Chicago: University of Chicago Press.

Meyer, A. (1975). *Grandmasters of educational thought*. New York: McGraw-Hill Book Company.

Monighan-Nourot, P. (1990). The legacy of play in American early childhood education. In E. Klugman & S. Smilansky (Eds.), *Children's Play and Learning* (pp. 59-85). New York: Teacher's College Press.

Morrison, G. (1995). *Early childhood education today*. Upper Saddle River, NJ: Merrill Publishing.

Osborn, D. K. (1991). *Early childhood education in historical perspective*. Athens, GA: Daye Press.

Peltzman, B. R. (1998). *Pioneers of early childhood education: A bio-bibliographical guide*. Westport, CT: Greenwood Press.

Prochner, L & Howe, N. (2000). *Early childhood education and care in Canada*. Vancouver: UBC Press.

Roopnarine, J., & Johnson, J. (1987). *Approaches to early childhood education*. Columbus, OH: Merrill.

Sadovnik, A. & Semel, S. (Eds.). (2002). *Founding mothers and others: Women educational leaders during the progressive era*. New York: Palgrave.

Saettler, P. (1968). *A history of instructional technology*. New York: McGraw-Hill.

Seefeldt, C. (Ed.). (1990). *Continuing issues in early childhood education*. Columbus, OH: Merrill Publishing Company.

Seller, M. (1994). *Women Educators in the United States 1820 – 1993*. Westport, CT: Greenwood Press.

Shapiro, M. S. (1983). *Child's Garden: The kindergarten movement from Froebel to Dewey*. University Park, PA: The Pennsylvania State University Press.

Shimoni, R. (1990). *A historical overview of the development of early childhood services*. (ERIC Document Reproduction Service No. ED. 334 000)

Sicherman, B., & Green, C. (Eds.). (1980). *Notable American women: The modern period*. Cambridge, MA: Belknap Press of Harvard University Press.

Snyder, A. (1972). *Dauntless women in childhood education, 1856 – 1931*. Washington, DC: ACEI.

Spodek, B., & Saracho, O. (Eds.). (1990). *Early childhood teacher preparation*. New York: Teachers College Press.

Tanner, D., & Tanner, L. (1990). *History of the school curriculum*. New York: Macmillan & Publishing Co.

Ulrich, R. (1954, 1982 revised). *Three thousand years of educational wisdom*. Cambridge, MA: Harvard University Press.

Ulrich, R. (1968). *History of educational thought*. New York: American Book Co.

Weber, E. (1969). *The kindergarten: Its encounter with educational thought in America*. New York: Teachers College Press.

Weber, E. (1984). *Ideas influencing early childhood education: A theoretical analysis*. New York: Teachers College Press.

White, S., & Buka, S. (1987). Early education: programs, traditions and policies. *Review of Research in Education, 14,* 43-92.

Williams, L., & Fromberg, D. (Eds.). (1992). *Encyclopedia of early childhood education*. New York: Gorland Publishing.

*Website: http://www.socsci.kun.nl/ped/whp/histeduc/*

# Index